FINANCING SPORT

by
Dennis R. Howard, Ph.D.
The Ohio State University
and
John L. Crompton, Ph.D.
Texas A&M University

FITNESS INFORMATION TECHNOLOGY, INC.
P.O. BOX 4425, UNIVERSITY AVE.
MORGANTOWN, WV 26504

Library of Congress Card Catalog Number: 94-61287

ISBN 1-885693-00-1

Cover Design: James M. Williams/Micheal Smyth
Copyeditor: Sandra R. Woods
Printed by: BookCrafters

Printed in the United States of America
10 9 8 7 6 5 4 3 2 1

Fitness Information Technology, Inc.
P. O. Box 4425, University Ave.
Morgantown, WV 26504 USA
(800) 477-4348
(304) 599-3482 (Phone/Fax)

SPORT MANAGEMENT LIBRARY

The **SPORT MANAGEMENT LIBRARY** is an integrative textbook series targeted toward undergraduate students. The titles included in the Library are reflective of the content areas prescribed by the NASPE/NASSM curriculum standards for undergraduate sport management programs.

FORTHCOMING TITLES IN THE SPORT MANAGEMENT LIBRARY

Case Studies in Sport Marketing
Communication in Sport Organizations
Ethics in Sport Management
Fundamentals of Sport Marketing
Legal Aspects of Sport Entrepreneurship
Management Essentials in Sport Organizations
Sport Facility Planning and Management
Sport Governance in the Global Community
Sport Management Field Experiences (**NOW AVAILABLE**)

About the Authors

Dennis R. Howard, Ph.D., is Head of the Graduate Program in Sport Management at The Ohio State University. Prior to coming to Ohio State in 1992, he served on the faculty at the University of Oregon for 13 years. Dr. Howard has authored or co-authored 3 books and numerous articles in sport and leisure management publications. His research focuses on the financing and marketing of sport. He has served as a featured speaker at numerous professional conferences and consults with a variety of sport and leisure organizations. He is a Fellow in the American Academy of Leisure Sciences and serves on the editorial boards of the *Journal of Sport Management* and *Leisure Sciences*. A native of the San Francisco Bay Area, Dr. Howard earned degrees from the University of Oregon, University of Illinois and Oregon State University.

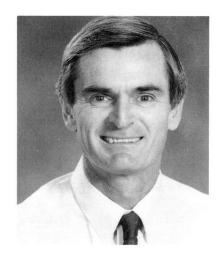

John L. Crompton, Ph.D., is a Professor in the Department of Recreation, Park, and Tourism Sciences at Texas A&M University. He received his basic education at Loughborough College and Loughborough University in England and at the University of Illinois. Subsequently, he was a principal in the largest sport and recreation consulting organization in the United Kingdom. He came to Texas A&M in 1974. For some years he taught graduate and undergraduate courses in both the Department of Marketing and the Department of Recreation, Park and Tourism Sciences, but now teaches exclusively in the latter Department. Dr. Crompton's primary interests are in the areas of marketing and financing recreation, sport and tourism services. He is author or co-author of 5 books and a substantial number of articles and monographs in the recreation, sport, tourism and marketing literatures. He has received a variety of national awards recognizing his work from professional associations and has delivered keynote addresses at national conferences in a number of countries.

TABLE OF CONTENTS

ACKNOWLEDGMENTS

We are particularly conscious of the debt we owe to the many colleagues and students whose encouragement, enthusiasm, and contributions have been critical to our completing this 3-year project. Dr. Janet Parks, Editor of the Sport Management Library Series deserves special mention. She provided the initial stimulus for the text by inviting us to write it. Her unflagging support, timely and insightful reviews, and constant encouragement were crucial to keeping us on task.

Our work has been influenced by many students who have participated in our classes since this project began. Their constructive criticism stimulated us to revise and clarify many of our ideas. Former graduate students Allen Brooks, Pam Gill, Bruce Javitz and Dan Mahony were particularly helpful in gathering reference materials.

Special thanks to Trevor Slack at the University of Edmonton and Scott Branvold at Robert Morris College for their review of our original manuscript. We are also particularly grateful to Denny Hoobler, Director of Development in the Athletic Department at Ohio State University, Mark Jennings, Director of Men's Athletic Fund Raising at the University of Iowa, Pat Ogle, Executive Director of Fresno State's Bulldog Foundation and Laura Clontz, Director of Development in the Department of Athletics at the University of Nevada, Las Vegas, all of whom shared their expertise and information with us in the preparation of Chapter 13 on Fund Raising. The contributions of Paul Krebs, Associate Director of Athletics and Ann Chasser, Director of Trademark and Licensing at Ohio State University to Chapters 1 and 6, respectively, are also greatly appreciated.

Throughout this book we have relied on a number of journalists who provide insightful commentary on the business of sport. While we reference their work throughout the text, we would like to give special recognition to Murray Chass, Michael Ozanian, Murray Sperber, Stephen Taub and Andrew Zimbalist. Their thoughtful analysis on the problems and issues confronting the managed sport industry provided important context for this text.

Finally, our sincerest thanks go to our wives Lin and Liz and our sons, Tim and Dan, and daughters, Christine and Joanne. It was only through their support that this book was written.

PREFACE

Managers of the managed sport industry are confronted with the certain reality of doing more with less. The declining availablity of many traditional revenue sources, coupled with rapidly escalating costs, has placed sport managers under intense pressure to obtain the financial resources necessary to sustain their organizations. It is our view that, now more than ever, managers must assume a proactive rather than a reactive role in confronting the fiscal challenges facing them. Organizations that will flourish will have managers who adopt an entrepreneurial approach, relentlessly seeking out new resources as well as aggressively exploiting existing sources to ensure that their constituents, clients, and/or fans receive the most effective service or experience possible.

This book is intended to provide students in professional sport curricula and professional practitioners with the first comprehensive coverage of the many traditional and innovative revenue acquisition methods available to sport organizations. Along with conventional income sources, such as tax support, ticket sales, concessions and fund raising, readers will receive in-depth exposure to more recent innovations related to licensing sport products, media sales, and corporate sponsorships. The book does not include material on budgeting procedures or financial analysis techniques. The focus of this text is on resource acquisition; thus, financial management and budgeting are outside its scope--they are operational tools used to manage the resources rather than acquire them. We believe the material in this text to be very different from what has appeared in both other general finance texts and in the existing sport management literature.

It is our hope that through the "nuts and bolts" treatment of each revenue acquisition method, augmented by numerous examples of their application, readers will feel confident in their ability to transfer the techniques to actual practice. Although the preponderance of examples used is drawn from the context of intercollegiate and professional sport, because to date that is where they are most commonly found, it is hoped that the reader will also be able to see how the concept or technique being illustrated could be adapted to other segments of the managed sport industry.

The creation of this text has been a collaborative effort. Every aspect of the organization, research, and writing of the book has been a joint endeavor between the two senior co-authors. John Crompton's academic training and personal experience in the areas of economics and general finance led to his assuming primary responsibility for writing the chapters dealing with public investment issues (chapter 2), economic impacts (chapter 3), and sources of public sector funding (chapter 4), as well as the section on corporate sport sponsorship (chapters 9-12). Drawing on his long-time association with the managed sport industry and his teaching and research interests in sport finance, Dennis Howard took the lead in developing the introductory chapter (chapter 1) and chapters dealing with various applied aspects of revenue acquisition, including joint venture partnerships (chapter 5), ticket operations (chapter 6) and fund raising (chapter 13). He also provided overall coordination of the text. However, throughout the development of the text, each of us has made significant contributions to the work of the other.

In those areas where neither co-author felt he possessed the necessary expertise to handle a topic in sufficient depth, an effort was made to identify the most knowledgeable expert on the subject. We were very fortunate to persuade two eminent authorities in their respective specializations to contribute chapters to our text. Dickie Van Meter, who is currently the president of the fastest growing sport licensing firm in North America, Licensing Resource Group, Inc., agreed to provide a chapter (7) on licensing sport products, a relatively new and potentially substantial source of income for sport organizations.

Chris Bigelow, the president of The Bigelow Companies, a leading foodservice and merchandise consultant to stadiums, arenas, and sports teams across the country, contributed a chapter (8) dealing with the many critical issues managers face in developing and operating a concessions and souvenir sales program. Their contributions substantially enhance the final product . From no other source will students and sport managers obtain such crucial "trade secrets" and insights into how to maximize the potential of licensing, media, and concession sales for their organizations.

This text is aimed at upper division and graduate students in professional preparation curricula in sport management. Much of the material has been tested in our own classes and has been revised in response to feedback. Because of the mounting fiscal pressures facing many sports organizations, we believe that many practicing professionals also will find the book a valuable resource. At every opportunity we have shared the content of the book with interested practitioners, whose enthusiastic reactions have given us confidence that the book can truly assist and advance the practice of professional sport managers.

Dennis R. Howard
The Ohio State University
Columbus, Ohio

John L. Crompton
Texas A&M University
College Station, Texas

CHAPTER 1

THE FINANCIAL CHALLENGE

Learning Objectives

After completing this chapter, the reader should be able to:

1. recognize the social and economic factors confronting sport managers compelling them to "do more with less."
2. understand that the current operation of sport organizations is shaped largely by income generation and cost containment strategies.
3. understand the impact of Title IX on the financing of collegiate sports.
4. explain the current income and cost structure of professional sport in North America.
5. discuss the role of a sport manager as an *entrepreneur*, searching out and exploiting opportunities which will enhance the service capabilities of the organization.

CHAPTER 1

THE
FINANCIAL
CHALLENGE

Never before have sport managers faced as many complex challenges as confront them today. An increasing number of managers face the daunting challenge of coping with a situation in which traditional revenue sources are declining at the same time that costs are rapidly escalating. This "double whammy" is placing great pressure on administrators of sport programs. In recent years, traditional sources of revenue--tax support, media revenues, and in many cases, gate receipts--have all declined. Many sport organizations are sustaining substantial budget cuts, forcing changes in their traditional patterns of operation. Maintaining programs even at current levels requires that sport managers learn to do "more with less."

It is this new reality that has caused managers to look beyond the traditional financing concepts and strategies that have been used and to supplement them with new imaginative approaches. It is the basic theme of this text that managers of sport organizations are required to seek out scarce resources from a wide range of possible sources and to use their marketing and financing skills to ensure that the scarce resources acquired are allocated in such a way that they yield optimum social and economic benefits. These are exactly the requirements of an entrepreneur. Indeed, we view the contemporary sport manager as an entrepreneur. Increasingly, effectiveness in collegiate and professional sports will be achieved by managers who aggressively seek out resources for their organizations. Once these resources have been identified, the effective manager will understand how best to exploit them to ensure that the organization's consumers (e.g., fans, participants, members) receive maximum satisfaction.

Although the focus of the book is on the two largest segments of the sport industry, intercollegiate and professional, the methods and strategies of revenue acquisition discussed in the following chapters can be adapted to a wide range of public and private club sport organizations. Throughout the book numerous references and examples are drawn from a variety of sport settings.

THE FINANCIAL STATUS OF
INTERCOLLEGIATE ATHLETICS

Because they have a social and educational mission, intercollegiate programs may receive tax support and donations from external sources. In the United States, institutions of higher education traditionally have been classified as either public (tax supported, state controlled) or private (independent of government). However, though they operate in different political and environmental contexts, athletic departments in private and public institutions are often indistinguishable in terms of organizational design and programs. Most athletic departments, particularly the 300 "big-school" programs in Division I of the National Collegiate Athletic Association (NCAA), are structured as self-supporting auxiliary enterprises. An increasing number of athletic departments in state colleges and universities are losing their traditional direct tax support, so even within public universities many athletic departments operate essentially as private enterprises largely independent of the academic governance process of the institution.

Symptomatic of a national trend, the Illinois Board of Higher Education in November, 1992 proposed total elimination of state taxes used for sport programs at universities in the state. At stake was approximately $100 million of support for intercollegiate athletics at the state's twelve colleges and universities ("Athletic Notes," 1993). Similarly, in 1993 nearly $10 million in state support for intercollegiate athletics in the state of Washington was at risk as the legislature struggled to close a $1.8-billion budget shortfall. Elimination of the state subsidy could result in Washington State University's losing an annual subsidy of almost $1.8 million in support of its women's sport programs. Like their counterparts in private institutions, athletic programs in public colleges and universities increasingly must pay their own way, balancing their budgets through student tuition and fee contributions and revenue generated from gate receipts, donations, sponsorships, other fund raising, and in the case of larger institutions, media rights (television and radio) sales. The following scenario is becoming increasingly common:

Students at the University of California at Davis have approved a fee increase that will keep as many as ten sports off the chopping block--at least for now. The University's sports program faced a cut of at least $600,000 next year, which would have forced the elimination of up to half of its 20 sports teams. But, thanks to an aggressive lobbying campaign by a new booster group called Students Supporting Athletics, nearly two-thirds of the students who voted agreed to pay $34 more each quarter to help the sports program, the Student Health Center, and other programs that faced cuts. The increase will remain in effect for three years, after which students will vote on continuing it. The euphoria over the referendum may be short-lived, however, given California's continuing budget crisis. The University now faces a $35 million shortfall for next year, and the plan to reduce the deficit calls for the university to phase out all money that the athletics department gets from state general funds, including most of the coaches' salaries. ("Athletic Notes," 1993, p. A30)

A great majority of the approximately 800 active members of the NCAA and 520 affiliates of the National Association of Intercollegiate Colleges (NAIA), mostly smaller colleges, are heavily subsidized, generating only modest levels of income. Even among the most prominent athletic departments, only one or two sports, generally men's football and basketball, can be considered commercial or "profit-driven" enterprises. The ability of either of these sports to generate substantial net income often is crucial to maintenance of all the other nonrevenue-producing men's and women's sports (swimming, tennis, track and field, etc.). As a result, all but a handful of institutions are struggling to break even in the operation of their total multisport programs.

Annual expenditures for intercollegiate athletics now exceed $1 billion (Raiborn, 1990). The average total annual budget for institutions with major football and basketball programs amounted to $10.75 million in 1990. The high degree of commercialization in collegiate sport is evident in the high salaries of coaches, the emphasis on television contracts, the prominence of corporate sponsorships, and the emergence of licensing agreements. For the modern sport manager, charged with maintaining the financial solvency of a college sport program, the adage "It's no longer a game, it's a business" is more true than ever. It has been noted that "the imperative to become more businesslike" is a dominant characteristic of big-time college athletics. (Hart-Nibbrig & Cottingham, 1986, p. 55).

The indisputable reality of modern collegiate sports is that its day-to-day governance is shaped largely by financial considerations, such as cost containment and income generation. This emphasis is not just a preoccupation of the recognized "big powers" of collegiate athletics. In the 1990s higher education in general is under intense financial pressure from the ravages of inflation and eroding support, which has led to athletic programs at small colleges being scrutinized more closely than ever before. Although they were never intended to be fully self-supporting, athletic departments at NCAA Division II and III and NAIA levels are being required to earn a greater share of their costs. Although programs at this level offer fewer or no athletic scholarships and have significantly lower budgetary expenditures related to recruiting and staffing than do Division I programs, financial self-sufficiency is virtually impossible, particularly for those programs offering football. With gate receipts contributing typically less than 20% of the total cost of intercollegiate athletics, small colleges (particularly NCAA Division III and NAIA) must rely on student tuition and/or fees for approximately half of their budgetary support (Raiborn, 1990). As many small colleges grapple with declining enrollments and rising educational costs, the pressure to reduce subsidy support levels for athletics has intensified.

The unassailable reality of collegiate sport programs at all levels today is that they are no longer able to pay their own way. According to the NCAA, almost three-fourths of the largest collegiate athletic programs are losing money (Raiborn, 1990). Even football, the "cash cow," is suffering, with 89% of all college football teams (and 75% at Division I) spending more than they make (Sperber, 1990). Evidence suggests that smaller college programs at the Division III and NAIA levels are experiencing even greater financial pressure, with from 75-90% reporting deficits (Raiborn, 1990).

The former Executive Director of the NCAA, Dick Schultz, commented that "You can probably count on your two hands the number of athletic departments that actually have a surplus annually" (Sperber, 1990, p. ix). The following data were provided by the Raiborn Report (1990):

1. Among the big-time football programs in Division IA, 45% are running deficits averaging $638,000 annually.
2. Of the Division IAA football programs, 94% are running deficits averaging $535,000 per year.
3. Of Division III football programs, 99% are incurring annual deficits on average of about $69,000.

Two factors in particular have intensified the financial pressures confronting intercollegiate athletics: escalating tuition costs and gender equity. According to the U. S. Department of Education, tuition at the average public university will rise 70-80% between 1988 and 2000 (Krupa & Dunnavant, 1989, p. 34). The same source indicates that scholarship costs at a school like the University of Alabama, for example, will increase from $3 million in 1988 to about $6 million annually in 2000. Federal (Title IX) and state legislation mandates gender equity in the provision of men's and women's intercollegiate sports, but makes no funds available to implement this worthy goal. The NCAA prescribes investment in women's sports proportionate to the number of females in the student body. Yet, due to years of neglect, women's sports at most institutions currently contribute no more than 5% to 10% of the total revenues generated by average collegiate athletic programs (Raiborn, 1990).

In a generic sense, the response options to these pressures are limited. According to Homer Rice, Athletic Director at Georgia Tech, " 'You can either create ways to add revenue, or cut costs' " (cited in Krupa & Dunnavant, 1989, p. 33). However, some are dubious that much, if any, progress will be made toward the second alternative. Deloss Dodds, Athletic Director at the University of Texas, claimed, " 'It's clear that we're not going to be able to limit spending' " for college athletics (cited in Krupa & Dunnavant, 1989, p. 33). Carrying the point further, he asserted that "There's a tendency in college athletics, like Congress, to spend if you have it" And spend they have. According to figures released by the NCAA in 1990, from 1982 to 1989, athletic department expenses for almost all NCAA affiliate athletic departments nearly doubled (Raiborn, 1990). It will be difficult to reduce the current level of costs because higher tuition costs and gender equity compliance requirements will place continued financial demands on athletic department budgets.

Certain requirements currently in place constrain cost reduction options available to many college administrators. As Sperber (1990) points out, the NCAA now requires even the smallest Division IA schools to sponsor a minimum of 13 teams (men's and women's) in 7 sports and to spend a minimum of $500,000 on athletic scholarships in nonrevenue sports. The dilemma facing the average Division I institution is that "nonrevenue" men's and women's sports generate only 8% of the athletic department's revenues, but account for 28% of its costs (Thalman, 1992). Budget cuts and deficits have caused a growing number of universities to make difficult and painful decisions:

- In 1992, California State University, Long Beach made the decision it could no longer afford to play football. According to Athletic Director David O'Brien, " 'The NCAA requirements went up to the point where to compete in Division I-A, you had to have a 30,000 seat stadium and average 17,000 attendance. The fact that we didn't have an on-campus stadium and that we were only averaging 3,200 fans a game would not allow us to do that' " (cited in Foster, 1992, p. 36). Rather than opting to drop a level to Division I-AA, Long Beach State decided to cancel the program altogether. " 'We just felt like we would be better off dropping the sport, and hopefully, when things get better, we can bring it back' " (cited in Foster, 1992, p. 36).

- Other schools at the brink have made compromises to save football. Towson State University and Western Kentucky University have dramatically scaled down their programs by moving toward a nonscholarship emphasis. The change could result in savings of as much as $400,000 to $1,000,000 a year for each institution, respectively. (Foster, 1992).

- Even schools rich in football tradition face crossroads decisions regarding the future of their football programs. Southern Methodist University, struggling to recover from the NCAA "death penalty" that prevented the Mustangs from playing football in 1987 and 1988, suffered a reported $4.8 million loss in 1991. The NCAA's harshest sanction was handed down in 1987 for player payouts. Although the decisions are painful, in the face of a growing budget deficit, SMU officials are seriously considering options ranging from reducing or eliminating scholarship athletics to dropping to a lower NCAA division of competition. (Foster, 1992).

The situation confronting the University of Oregon Athletic Department is illustrative of the wide difference between revenue and nonrevenue sports. In 1992, football and men's basketball generated $6.8 million in gross revenues against $4.9 million in expenditures. The other 12 nonrevenue sports earned a total of $270,000, while their aggregate costs amounted to $2.3 million. According to Sandy Walton, Senior Associate Athletic Director, " 'football and basketball can't continue to carry them (nonrevenue sports) at levels that are being mandated. If it weren't for institutional support [State Board of Higher Education appropriation] we wouldn't be making it.' " (cited in "Rich Brooks," 1992, p. 8G). The mounting insolvency of most college athletic departments has focused attention on the need to rein in escalating expenses. The NCAA established a special committee to identify various ways athletic programs could realize cost savings. One option given serious consideration was to replace the traditional practice of awarding athletic scholarships to cover the complete cost of tuition and room and board with a substantially less costly aid package based on the financial capability of each athlete's family. Serious challenges face the radical shift from "full ride" to "need-based" athletic scholarships. Dick Schultz, the NCAA Executive Director from 1988 through 1993, expressed concern about the equity of a financial aid package based on need, commenting that " 'Some athletes would receive no aid. So then you get into a fairness question. Just because this individual's parents saved their money, it will cost them as opposed to somebody else that hasn't been so frugal' " (cited in Moran, 1992b, p. B5). In spite of this concern, it is clear that college presidents are likely to view this proposal as a viable approach to controlling the single greatest expense of college athletic programs.

NCAA Attempts to Cut Costs

After a nine-month study of the financial crunch confronting collegiate athletic programs, the NCAA's Special Committee to Review Financial Conditions in Intercollegiate Athletics proposed a series of cost-cutting recommendations. According to Big Ten Commissioner and Committee Chair Jim Delany, if these recommendations are adopted, Division IA athletic programs could save between $200,000-400,000 a year. Under the proposal, maximum roster sizes for Division IA and IAA football programs would be reduced about 10%, limited to 105 and 90 players, respectively by 1994. Division IA schools offering the maximum 85 scholarships in 1995 (down from 92 in 1993) would be restricted to 20 walk-on players. Division IAA football programs would be limited to granting 63 scholarships and a maximum number of 27 walk-ons. Other Committee recommendations include ("Update," July 21, 1993, USA Today, p. E2).:
1. Cutbacks in the number of visits by recruits and the number of coaches who recruit off campus, and elimination of the specialized football recruiting coordinator.
2. An end to off-campus scouting of football and basketball opponents, leaving coaches to rely on film.
3. An end to team getaways in local hotels the night before home games and the elimination of off-season training-table meals for athletes.

In what may become a trend, particularly among Division IAA schools, university presidents of the eight Big Sky Conference institutions imposed dramatic cost containment requirements on their league's football programs. Faced with declining state funding and demands for gender equity, the presidents mandated a reduction of six football scholarships a year per school, beginning in 1994. League schools will be limited to 45 scholarships each by the 1996-97 season.

The Impact of Title IX

In an environment of rising costs, athletic administrators are now also being required to confront the enormous financial implications of finally complying with Title IX. A series of dramatic events in the early 1990s required colleges to make a serious commitment to addressing the gender equity issue. For almost two decades after the passage of Title IX of the Education Amendments Act in 1972, many college athletic programs paid only lip service to the notion of equal treatment of sexes. Then, beginning in 1991, in quick succession, three developments gave Title IX great momentum (Moran, 1992a, p. B26):

1. A Supreme Court ruling in the Georgia case, Franklin v. Gwinett Public Schools, permitted for the first time stiff monetary penalties for Title IX violations.
2. The Office of Civil Rights identified "discrimination on the basis of sex in athletic programs" as a priority in its overall enforcement strategy.
3. The Big Ten Council of Presidents adopted a resolution requiring conference schools to achieve a ratio of at least 40% female athletes to 60% male athletes by August, 1997.

The situation facing the Big Ten illustrates the substantial financial challenges confronting schools working toward bringing about greater gender equality in college sports. Overall, a 10% shift in gender representation would be required to meet the conference's 40% minimum female participation goal. When the 40-60 proposal was adopted in 1992, 6,650 athletes represented conference schools in varsity competition. Approximately 2,000 (or 30%) of them were women. If the overall number of athletes remained unchanged, attainment of 40-60 would necessitate the addition of 660 women or the reduction of an equivalent number of men. Given the severe financial constraints facing most institutions, the added strain of dramatically increasing women's participation means that either substantially more revenues will have to be raised, or the elimination of some sport teams is inevitable. For athletic departments like the Big Ten's University of Iowa, which has adopted a more ambitious goal of 50-50, achieving gender equity could cost as much as $500,000 more a year (Finn, 1992). The department has declared that no men's sports will be cut.

In the summer of 1993, the Gender-Equity Task Force appointed by the NCAA called for member institutions to achieve sports participation ratios that matched the proportion of men and women in the student populations: If women make up 50% of a college's student body, they should account for 50% of its intercollegiate athletes (Lorenz, 1993). The proportional representation goal has become the most commonly accepted standard for defining equal opportunity in collegiate sports. Recent court rulings have supported women who have contended that their disproportionately low share of athletic department resources constituted noncompliance with Title IX. In these cases, the "institutions have been told to even out the numbers or demonstrate that the athletic interests of the less-represented group--women--are adequately served" (Lorenz, 1993, p. B2).

Faced with a class-action suit claiming that women were being unfairly denied access to varsity-level sports, the University of Texas at Austin agreed to more than double the number of females participating on varsity teams. A court-ordered settlement required women to represent 44% of all varsity athletes at Texas by the end of the 1995-96 academic year. In order to comply with its participation-rate goal, the athletic department agreed to add not only two new women's teams--softball and soccer--but also to increase the number of female "walk-ons" (varsity athletes who do not receive scholarships) while decreasing the number of male walk-ons (Blum, 1993).

Although the courts have provided the legal authority for advancing the interests of women athletes, the managers of college athletics in the 1990s have to assume greater moral responsibility for ensuring an equitable balance between men's and women's sports opportunities on college campuses. For a growing number of advocates, that

```
╔══════════════════════════════════════════════════════════╗
║                      Figure 1-1                          ║
║   Current Status of Major League Professional Sports     ║
╚══════════════════════════════════════════════════════════╝
```

	■ Major League Baseball
	Founded: National League in 1876, American League in 1901. *Teams*: 28. *Commissioner*: Bud Selig heads owners' executive council. *Net worth*: $3.02 billion.
	■ National Hockey League
	Founded: 1917. *Teams*: 24 (Does not include new expansion teams in Miami and Anaheim, Calif.). *Commissioner*: Gary Bettman. *Net worth*: $1.05 billion.
	■ National Football League
	Founded: 1920. *Teams*: 28. *Commissioner*: Paul Tagliabue. *Net worth*: $3.49 billion.
	■ National Basketball Association
	Founded: 1946. *Teams*: 27. *Commissioner*: David Stern. *Net worth*: $1.99 billion.

Note: Net worth includes gate receipts, media revenues, stadium revenues, operating income, player salaries, and other expenses.
Sources: Financial World magazine, Daily Herald news services.

responsibility extends even beyond the campus. According to Christine Hoyle, Assistant Commissioner of the Pac-10 Conference, " 'Colleges have an obligation to help change attitudes that don't favor women in sports. ... College recruiters, for example, should work more closely with coaches of girls' high school teams to encourage athletes to consider continuing their sports careers in college'" (cited in Blum, 1993, p. A29). Hoyle also believes colleges should promote or sponsor more, and more diverse, summer sports programs and junior leagues for girls.

Finding new revenues and implementing tough cost-containment strategies to achieve the goal of gender equity are major fiscal challenges facing collegiate sport administrators in the 1990s. However, these are challenges that must be aggressively met. The courts have finally decreed there will be no compromise on the issue of gender equity. Whether through compliance or enlightened initiative, college athletics must follow the paths of such institutions as the University of Iowa and the University of Texas at Austin in assuring equal opportunity for women athletes.

The current reality of college athletics is far from its popular perception as a "cash cow" for higher education. In fact, spiraling costs, increased competition, and flat or declining revenues have all combined to place intercollegiate sports programs under severe financial pressure. A large majority are operating at a deficit. Grappling with budget issues--revenue generation and cost containment--will be key issues confronting collegiate sport managers through the end of this century.

THE FINANCIAL STATUS OF PROFESSIONAL SPORTS

In the milieu of professional sport enterprises the common denominator is that their survival is dependent on their ability to generate a satisfactory return on invested capital. This is an ongoing challenge. Recent reports, for example, indicate that one of every three professional teams (36 of 103) in the four major leagues in North America lost money in 1993 (Ozanian, 1994). The reality for many organizations is that traditional sources of revenue—membership fees, gate receipts, concession sales, media sales–are no longer sufficient to cover rising operational costs. There is a greater need than ever before for managers to discover and cultivate new sources of income.

By the early 1990s, the total market value of the four major professional sport leagues in North America had grown to about $10 billion. The relative economic value of each league is shown in Figure 1-1.

Professional sports during the 1970s and 1980s enjoyed unprecedented prosperity. Fan attendance grew to an all-time high, and television networks paid lavish fees for the right to broadcast games. However, early in the 1990s, a different, somewhat bleaker, economic picture of professional sport emerged.

In late 1992, a long-awaited study of the economic status of baseball, which included an accounting audit of each team's financial figures for the 1991 season, reported that industry-wide profits from baseball operations fell 31% from 1990 (Chass, 1992). Baseball's economic struggle is not confined to the major league level. Despite the Professional Baseball Agreement governing major-minor league relations under which parent major league clubs pay the salaries of their minor league players, many of the 170 minor league teams in the United States and Canada are hard-pressed to make a profit. According to one prominent minor-league franchise owner, " 'Minor league baseball is not a terribly profitable business' " (cited in "Minors," 1993, p. 5D). Without the estimated $150 to $200 million annual salary subsidy provided by major league clubs, many minor league executives report they could not continue to operate. Revenue from advertising, ticket sales, and concessions would not be sufficient to sustain a free-standing minor league team. Commenting on the economic state of minor league baseball, Art Silber, owner of a Class A New York Yankee affiliate, stated: " 'It [minor league baseball] certainly pays for itself, but if the fan support were fractionalized, it would be almost impossible to maintain this business. We sure don't make anywhere close to the money the Yankees spend on this team ($30,000 to $35,000 monthly on team salaries)' " (cited in "Minors," 1993, p. 5D).

Despite unprecedented popularity, one-fourth of all National Basketball Association (NBA) teams lost money in 1993. The Indiana Pacers suffered the greatest, with losses estimated at $5.9 million (Ozanian 1994). According to Quirk and Fort (1992), badly managed teams in the National Football League (NFL) can lose more than $5 million or more a year, as seven teams demonstrated in 1992.

Many teams claim to consistently lose money. According to a prominent major league baseball owner, " 'things have gotten very bad in this industry. We're at a point now where over half the teams are losing money' " (cited in Bodley, 1992, p. 2C). The extent and magnitude of the owners' claims are difficult to substantiate. Very few professional sport teams are publicly held corporations. Ownership in most cases is largely in the hands of private individuals, families, or closely held corporations, all of which are under no legal obligation to disclose detailed financial information about their operations. Financial experts and players have repeatedly challenged the authenticity of the owners' claims of financial distress. In the recent court case *McNeil v. NFL*, analysts testifying on behalf of NFL players claimed that "creative accounting procedures" used by owners made the teams' financial positions look much worse than they really were. Paul Beeston, President of the Toronto Blue Jays, reputedly stated, " 'Under generally accepted accounting principles, I can turn a $4 million profit into a $2 million loss, and I can get every national accounting firm to agree with me' " (cited in Zimbalist, 1992, p. 62).

Although the precise magnitude of economic problems facing professional sport is difficult to determine, it is apparent that team owners in the 1990s face financial pressure. A prominent financial publication, examining the economic condition of professional sport, proclaimed, "These are not joyous times in Mudville" (Ozanian & Taub, 1992, p. 34). The report noted that nearly half of the major league baseball teams were losing money; the National Football League had been successfully challenged in court by its players in an effort to liberalize free agency rules, which has driven up costs; and the National Basketball Association's players were demanding that salary cap rules be restructured, threatening almost a decade of labor peace.

Magnitude of Costs and Revenues

Like collegiate athletic programs, professional sports' financial difficulties are the result of costs growing more rapidly than revenues. Rising payroll costs have increasingly eroded the profitability of many teams. While revenues increased 14.6% to $5.1 billion in 1993, during the same period, player costs rose 19.4% to $2.85 billion. As a consequence, operating incomes fell almost 20% (Ozanian, 1994).

An annual survey conducted by a prominent financial publication provides the most comprehensive and realistic estimates of the financial health and condition of professional sport franchises. Since 1987, *Financial World* (Ozanian & Taub, 1994) has compiled an annual valuation survey of professional sport teams constituting the four largest sport leagues in North America: the National Football League (NFL), major league baseball (MLB), the National Basketball Association (NBA), and the National Hockey League (NHL). In determining the economic value of various franchises, *Financial World* calculates each team's operating income (revenue less operating expenses). In doing so, it furnishes an important glimpse into the income and cost structure of professional sport. Revenues are broken down into four categories: (a) gate receipts--home and away game ticket sale revenues; (b) media revenues--national, local and cable TV and radio broadcasting fees; (c) stadium revenues--luxury suites, concessions, parking and souvenir sales; and (d) miscellaneous--licensing and merchandising sales. On the cost side, operating expenses are separated into two major categories: (a) player costs--salaries, bonuses, insurance and pensions, excluding depreciation; and (b) operating expenses--general administrative expenses, rent and stadium upkeep. Table 1-1 combines the data provided for each of the 103 franchises evaluated by *Financial World* in 1994 into an overall summary of revenues and expenses for each of the four professional sport leagues. It facilitates a comparative analysis of the relative importance of each of the revenue sources for each league and illustrates the varying effect of player costs across each of the sports.

The prominent role of media broadcasting fees is very evident. In 1993, national and local television, cable and radio broadcasting garnered $2.46 billion in revenues for all four leagues. The growth in broadcast revenues has been exponential. In 1980, each NFL team received $5.9 million from national television; by 1993 each club's share had grown to $32.5 million. MLB income more than quadrupled over the same period, from $3.3 million per team in 1980 to $15 million in 1992. Even hockey, which relies least upon media revenues, saw a dramatic increase from slightly over $1 million per team in 1985 to $3 million in 1992 as a result of a new agreement with ESPN. The dominant contribution of media fees is most apparent for NFL franchises. The $32.5 million provided by national television contracts to each NFL team in 1993 amounted to over half of the annual earnings of every NFL franchise. For teams in small markets, like the Green Bay Packers, or teams that have struggled at the gate, like the Tampa Bay Buccaneers, national television and radio fees are the team's lifeblood, accounting for as much as two-thirds of their yearly income.

Although baseball and basketball are not in general as dependent as the NFL on media fees, broadcast revenues still furnish the largest source of income for all but two MLB franchises (The Toronto Blue Jays and the Chicago White Sox are the exceptions) and for 19 of 27 NBA teams. Overall, for each league, about 43 cents on every

TABLE 1-1
The Economic Structure of Professional Sport

	MLB	NFL	NBA	NHL
Revenues				
Gate Receipts	34.3% (23.0-60.0)	22.8% (18.0-26.0)	41.0% (35.0-65.0)	59.3% (47.0-71.0)
Media Rights	43.0% (36.0-63.0)	64.9% (55.0-71.0)	40.5% (30.0-55.0)	15.8% (11.0-29.0)
Stadium	14.8% (6.0-25.0)	6.2% (0.0-19.0)	10.4% (2.0-22.0)	10.9% (0.0-23.0)
Misc.	7.9% (4.0-16.0)	6.1% (-4.0-14.0)	8.1% (3.0-17.0)	14.0% (4.0-37.0)
Expenses				
Player Costs	49.4% (30.0-62.5)	54.1% (45.5-62.6)	48.2% (40.0-52.7)	39.2% (20.6-55.5)
Gen. Operating	50.6% (37.5-70.0)	45.9% (37.4-54.5)	45.9% (47.3-60.0)	51.8% (44.8-73.4)

Note: from Ozanian, M. (1994, May 10). The $11 billion pastime. *Financial World*, pp. 50-59.

dollar earned comes from local and national broadcast fees. The great disparity in media earnings is most serious in major league baseball. Unlike national television rights revenues, which are shared equally among all 28 teams, local television revenues are not shared. This provides a substantial advantage to big-market teams like the New York Yankees, which realized more than $45 million in 1993 from local media rights alone. In contrast, Pittsburgh, which is in a much smaller market, earned $3 million. Some analysts predict the situation is moving baseball inexorably toward a two-tier "have and have-nots" system in which financially less endowed smaller market teams will have an increasingly difficult time fielding competitive teams against the wealthy large-market franchises. Traditionally, the practice of revenue sharing was confined to a division of game receipts, whereby the home team would share some portion of the gross gate revenues with the visiting team. More recently, revenue sharing has been extended to include media broadcast revenues. The intent of revenue sharing was to account for market area differences so that a competitive balance could be maintained between clubs in strong and weak markets. The objective of pooling resources for collective benefit has been most extensively pursued in the NFL, where as much as 77% of the total revenues generated by the league is shared among its 28 teams. Visiting teams in professional football receive 40% of the gate receipts; 60% goes to the home team. National TV contracts are negotiated on behalf of the league by the NFL league office; then, revenues are dispersed equally to each of the franchises. Ticket-sale revenue sharing is practiced on a more limited basis by major league baseball, where the visiting team in the American League receives only 20% of the gate receipts and 43 cents/ticket, or less than 5% in the National League. In 1992, MLB teams shared only 36% of the league's total revenues. Neither the NBA nor the NHL shared ticket revenues. The importance of ticket sale revenue varies substantially from one league to another. Both football and baseball depend less on the live gate than do the other leagues. Ticket sales constitute between 23% and 34% of the total income for media-rich football and baseball. In contrast, gate receipts represent the most significant share of overall revenue for some NBA and all NHL teams. The prominence of admissions is particularly evident for hockey, where over half the franchises rely on ticket sales for more than two-thirds of their annual earnings.

It's difficult to assess just how much more revenue big-league franchises can realize from ticket sales. In terms of capacity, basketball, football, and hockey teams already sell more than 90% of their available seats. Only baseball, with half of its seating capacity unused, has significant potential for realizing greater earnings from increased volume of ticket sales. Ticket prices may also have just about reached a peak. Although teams have raised prices by an average of 5-10% per year, it is conceivable that franchise operators have already stretched most consumers' ticket price tolerance levels to the limit. This concern takes on greater meaning when the total or "real" costs of game attendance are considered. A Chicago newsletter, *Team Marketing Report* ("On the Rise," 1994) has developed a "Fan Cost Index" (FCI), which includes all the peripheral costs of going to a game, including concessions, souvenirs, and parking. The 1993 FCI increased at an even faster rate than ticket prices, and the average cost to a family of four to attend a major league baseball game in 1993 was $90.87. The direct effect of ticket prices on attendance, however, is difficult to predict. As Gorman and Calhoun (1994) point out, "The most expensive regular-season baseball experience--that's the $112.83 paid by a family of four, complete with tickets and all the normal extras at a Toronto Blue Jays game-- was also the most popular (p. 99)." The Toronto franchise sold more tickets, over 4 million, than any professional sports team in North America. The impact of ticket prices on fans' willingness to pay for sporting events is discussed at length in Chapter 6 (See Psychology of Pricing).

Facing the Future: Media Revenues and Escalating Salaries
Media Revenues

As Table 1-1 indicates, the prosperity of professional sport is closely linked to the sale of national broadcasting rights fees. This is particularly true for the NFL, where television rights fees constitute the principal source of revenue for all of the league's 28 teams, on an average of almost two-thirds (65.9%) of their total income. By 1993, national broadcasting fees for MBL and the NFL were at an all-time high, with each baseball and football team receiving $15.3 million and $32.5 million, respectively. However, at the end of the 1993 season, the media fortunes of these two leagues moved in opposite directions. Major league baseball faced a precipitous decline in national media revenues. Sliding television ratings (average network broadcast ratings fell 27% from 1989 to 1992), coupled with a sluggish national economy, persuaded major sport advertisers such as Anheuser-Busch, to no longer pay the rates television networks were seeking for prime time sports programming. In the space of 4 years, professional baseball plummeted from a deal with CBS, which guaranteed each franchise around $15 million per year,to a risky "no money up front" joint venture with ABC and NBC. Beginning in 1994, major league baseball, NBC, and ABC formed a 6-year partnership to jointly produce and sell national baseball broadcasts to advertisers. Under the new arrangement, MLB is directly responsible for selling all of the advertising time on its game telecasts. The league receives 85% of the first $140 million worth of commercial air time sold, splits the next $30 million with ABC and NBC, and keeps 80% of all additional revenues. Gone is the annual cash guarantee-- about $365 million per year--that baseball received from CBS under the previous contract. According to the Philadelphia Phillies President Bill Giles, national broadcast revenues may drop as much as 50% to something between $6 to $8 million, particularly during the first 2 years of the new joint-venture agreement (Brown, 1993).

Although television fortunes of MLB have diminished, those of the NFL continue to prosper. In late 1993, Fox Network outbid CBS for the right to broadcast National Football Conference games through 1997. Fox's 4-year bid of $1.58 billion--$395 million per season--represented a 49% increase over what CBS had paid ($265 million average) the NFL in its previous contract. With the additional television rights it sold to ABC, ESPN, and TNT, the NFL's total broadcast revenues for the 4-year period of 1994-1997 amount to a record $4.4 billion. The agreement guarantees each NFL team $38.3 million per year.

A brighter future regarding broadcast rights is evident for both professional basketball and hockey. The popularity of America's "dream team" at the 1992 Olympics propelled the NBA's national television ratings to higher-than-expected levels. In early 1993, Commissioner Stern and NBC agreed to extend the NBA's contract with the network through the 1997-98 season. The rights fee was increased 25% from the current annual payment of $601 million to $750 million. Combined with the $275 million it received annually from its existing contract with TNT, the NBA achieved new levels of prosperity. In 1992, the NHL signed a 3-year agreement with ESPN. The contract raised annual broadcast fees to about $2 million per team.

Escalating Salaries

Table 1-2 illustrates that salary increases over the last decade in every major sports league have been extraordinary. Salary escalation in MLB has led the way. By 1992, one out of every three MLB players earned $1 million or more a year, and almost 100 players earned in excess of $3 million. The average salary of slightly more than $1 million earned by a major league player represented a 67% increase over the $597,537 in 1990 and a quantum leap from the $46,000 paid in 1975. In basketball, with salaries at an average of $1.2 million, the increase during the 1982-92 decade was 275%. In the NFL, average salaries tripled in the 1990s, jumping from $488,300 to $645,000 in 1993 alone.

Table 1-2
Salary Escalation in Professional
Sport Over the Past Decade

	MLB	NFL	NBA	NHL
1993	$1,064,149	$645,000	$1,350,000	$430,000
1992	1,012,424	496,345	1,208,333	400,000
1990	597,537	351,800	990,000	320,000
1988	447,121	226,000	600,000	230,000
1986	406,000	205,000	440,000	198,000
1984	337,000	126,000	340,000	195,000
1982	241,500	104,000	246,000	190,000

Note: Compiled from a variety of publications including *USA Today* (July 29, 1994 p. 2C), *Columbus Dispatch*, (November 12, 1993 p. 5E), Hubbard, S., Moore, D., & Fishler, S. (April, 1994). Sport salaries: Rocketing out of control. *Inside Sports*, pp. 58-69.

The extraordinary increase in MLB salaries is attributable to a collective-bargaining agreement with the Major League Baseball Players Union, which allowed players with 6 years of experience in major big leagues to become free agents. When their contracts expired, these players were free to offer their services to the highest bidder. Compounding the problem further from a cost-control perspective was that owners did not have the ability to control payroll expenses when negotiating with players who had 3-6 years of experience. Players in this category, while not eligible for free agency, are allowed by a clause in the bargaining agreement to go to binding arbitration in the event of a salary dispute with the team. Final resolution of the dispute is made by an independent arbitrator who is required to choose between the salary demand made by the player and the salary offer made by the team. In this process, the player and management each submit a figure, and the arbitrator selects one or the other; no compromise is allowed. Through 1991, of the 317 arbitration cases heard, the owners won slightly more than half (54.6%). However, owners would suggest that most of their victories have been pyrrhic in that even when they win, players are still rewarded with considerably higher salaries than they received the previous season. For example, in 1990, the 10 players who lost their cases received salary increases on an average of 100% (Chass, 1990a). As Zimbalist (1992) points out, there is very "little downside risk" for players because the salary figure owners present in arbitration is invariably higher than their current level of compensation. His assertion is supported by the fact that in the first 18 years of arbitration only 20 players emerged with pay cuts (Chass, 1990b).

Professional football's bargaining agreement between owners and players in 1993 brought an end to a 5-year labor conflict. Its terms are summarized in Figure 1-2. For the first time, NFL players with 5 (reverted to 4 years in 1994) years' experience whose contracts had expired were allowed the right as free agents to move to a team willing to make them the best offer. During the first year of the NFL's free agency system, 118 players changed teams, resulting in an all-time high average NFL player salary of $645,000 in 1993. The NBA has enjoyed relative tranquility since the players' union agreed to a revenue-sharing plan in 1983, which capped salaries at 53% of the NBA's total revenues. However, the situation was projected to disappear as payrolls continued to grow much faster than revenues. Some analysts predicted the situation would cause serious problems when the league's collective bargaining agreement with players expires.

Confronting the Financial Challenge

Like collegiate sport administrators, the managers of professional sport teams have responded to the financial challenge by simultaneously attempting to contain expenses, particularly the rising costs of player salaries, and by searching for new sources of revenue.

Given the highly labor-intensive nature of professional sports, managers recognize the key to containing costs hinges on controlling payrolls. In the face of rapidly rising

---

Figure 1-2
Terms of the 1993 NFL Bargaining Agreement

Agreement at a glance

• **Free agency:** Starting this year, players who have been in the league at least five years and whose contracts have expired will be unrestricted free agents.

• **Salary cap:** If player costs reach 67 percent of designated NFL gross revenue, a salary cap will be triggered and unrestricted free agency will begin for players after four years.

• **Salary guarantee:** Players will receive a minimum of 58 percent of the league's designated gross revenues during each year of the agreement that includes a salary cap.

• **Draft:** It will be reduced from 12 to 7 rounds, plus one round for teams that lose restricted free agents.

• **Damages:** The NFL has agreed to pay $195 million in damages and attorney's fees to settle all outstanding litigation.

• **Rookies:** Total salaries of drafted rookies will be capped at current levels, about $2 million per club. Those levels will increase with the growth of designated revenues.

• **Free-agency exceptions:** Each team will be able to exempt one "franchise" player from free agency for the duration of his career if he is offered a contract at the average of at least the top five players at his position. In 1993, each team will be able to use the right of first refusal on two of its free agents if they are offered a contract at the average of at least the top 10 players at that position. In 1994, every club will have one right of first refusal under the same conditions as 1993.

Source: *Columbus Dispatch*, 1/7/93, E1. Reprinted by permission.

---

player costs, many NFL, NHL, and MLB owners and front-office executives view the salary cap structure currently in place in the NBA as a key feature to embrace if their franchises are to be viable. In 1983, when many teams were experiencing financial difficulty, the NBA players agreed with owners to cap their salaries at 53% of the league's gross revenues. The owners' share of the gross income, including gate receipts and local, network, and cable revenues, was set at 47%. The intent of the "profit sharing" plan was to guarantee players a substantial share of the league's proceeds while, at the same time, creating a built-in safety net for the owners by capping or holding player costs to a fixed percentage of revenues. The landmark labor-management agreement has been hailed as the cornerstone of the NBA's financial success (Swift, 1991).

Although NBA players in the more prosperous 1990s have challenged certain provisions of the salary cap, the agreement ended more than a decade of acrimonious relations between NBA owners and players by making the two parties partners. The revenue-sharing concept has been viewed by many as an appropriate model for all professional sports.

In fact, a crucial element of the 1993 NFL labor agreement that allows veteran players free agency is the imposition of a salary cap. In exchange for limited free agency, the players and owners agreed to a salary cap under which teams were limited to spending not more than 64% of the teams' combined gate receipts and national broadcasting revenues on player salaries. For 1994 the salary cap or maximum player payroll was at $34.6 million per team. Faced with the threat of a more liberal federal court-imposed form of free agency, owners finally agreed to allow players who have been in the NFL for 4 or 5 years and who are in the final season of their contracts to negotiate with any other team. In 1994, about 300 players were eligible free agents under these conditions. These players were able to offer their services to the highest bidder unless their current team exercised one of several options. The new contract allows each team to designate one so-called "franchise" player an untouchable who must be offered a contract at the average of at least the top 5 players at his position. In addition, each team is allowed to apply the right of first refusal to one other player eligible for free agency. In order to keep this player on its roster, however, the club must offer a contract at the average of the top 10 players at that player's position. With the salary cap, NFL owners, like their counterparts in the NBA, received some measure of cost control and predictability. Over the next few years the challenge for NFL front-office personnel will be learning how to manage under the new rules and demands of free agency and the salary cap.

By 1994, the prospects for Major League Baseball and the National Hockey League to implement similar salary cap arrangements with their players were very problematic. In the spring of 1994, baseball owners presented the Major League Baseball Players Association (MLBPA)--the players' union--with a salary cap proposal which would split baseball revenues 50-50, guaranteeing a minimum of $1 billion annually for player salaries. The owners' intent was to create a salary structure in which player compensation was tied to a fixed percentage of team revenues. Similar to the NFL agreement, baseball's proposal would allow veteran players to become free agents after 4 years. A key provision of the owners' proposal was the elimination of salary arbitration. The powerful MLBPA rejected the implementation of a salary cap, insisting that the players' union would resist any effort to place a ceiling on salaries. The players argue that, unlike the NBA with several teams near collapse in 1983, Major League Baseball enjoyed unprecedented prosperity in 1994. Skeptical of owners' claims that as many as 13 teams were in serious financial trouble, the players demanded to be shown the current system isn't working before thay would consider a new system. Most observers believe that the establishment of a salary cap in baseball will be a very difficult sell, particularly given the acrimonious bargaining history between players and owners. At the time of this writing, some analysts predicted that owners' intransigence on the issue of a salary cap would lead to the eighth work stoppage or strike in baseball's history (Chass, 1994).

A similar situation exists in the NHL. Skyrocketing player costs have had a devastating impact on the financial stability of the league. A prominent NHL official claims that " 'we have a situation where teams are spending dollars they do not have and are not likely to have' " (cited in Hubbard, Moore & Fishler, 1994, p. 67). The league owners are pushing hard for a salary cap. While from the owners' point of view, an agreement patterned after the NBA's salary cap is seen as the most likely solution, to date NHL players have balked at such an arrangement.

Buzzwords like "additional revenue streams" and "extending the arena" are now part of the lexicon of professional sport as owners and managers scramble to find new sources of revenue. It is evident that teams have run close to the limit of what they can derive from traditional sources of income, such as ticket and media sales. Although gate and television revenues will continue to be important, increasingly, profit margins will be determined by relatively recent innovations like skyboxes, licensing agreements, and sponsorship. Interestingly, the revenues derived from these new alternatives are only indirectly tied to the game itself. While it was not until 1986 that the NFL made a serious effort to make a profit on their trademarks, each team now makes $1.7 million in national licensing revenues alone (Ozanian & Taub, 1992). Licensing fees from the sale of team merchandise now provide owners in all four major sport leagues with their fastest growing source of new revenue. According to *Financial World* (Ozanian & Taub, 1994), each league should expect incremental gains from licensing royalties of at least 15% for the next several years.

For many teams, skyboxes have become the "cash cows" of the 1990s. Although owners cannot expect individual fans to pay $75 for a ticket, they can ask corporations to pay as much as $225,000 a year to lease a skybox. While the amenities vary, these luxury suites, as they are sometimes called, usually contain such components as carpeting, restrooms, a bar facility, television monitors, and other furnishings conducive to entertaining corporate clients. The inclusion of skyboxes in the new Comiskey Park resulted in an additional $6 million a year to the Chicago White Sox baseball team. The Palace, home to the NBA's Detroit Pistons, was financed entirely from revenues realized from the sale of preferred seating and luxury suites.

ORGANIZATION OF THE TEXT

Many challenges confront the managers of intercollegiate and professional sport organizations. The golden era of unparalleled growth that characterized the 1980s has given way to a future that is less certain. Successful managers will have to find ways to deal with diminishing media revenues, contentious player-management relations over distribution of revenues, attendance, and ticket prices, which for many teams cannot go much higher. Helping managers to cope effectively with the reality of plateauing revenues and rising costs is the essential focus of this book.

Professional sport acquires financial resources from four generic sources which are shown in Figure 1-3: investors' resources, the public sector, the sport enterprise, and external sources. The latter three sources of resources also constitute the financial reservoir from which intercollegiate sport managers have to draw. Discussion of investors' resources is not included in the text.

Earlier in the chapter it was noted that public higher education institutions traditionally received public tax funding to support their educational and social missions, but that this was now declining. Although it may appear incongruous and inappropriate to suggest that public tax dollars should be used to support privately owned professional sport organizations whose mission is to maximize profit, it is estimated that these organizations receive approximately $500 million annually in tax support (Quick and Fort, 1992).

Given the large public investment in intercollegiate and professional sport, the first section of the text focuses on acquiring and using resources from the public sector. Chapter 2 explores justifications used to support the large public investment in professional sport enterprises. The primary argument used tends to focus on economic benefits that accrue to residents of a community from the presence of the professional sport entity. Invariably, economic impact analyses are undertaken to measure magnitude of these economic benefits, and these are central to debates on the public subsidy issue. For this reason, chapter 3 presents the principles of economic impact analysis and highlights common errors that are made by sport organizations that use the technique.

If sport managers are to seek public-sector funding, it is important that they have some understanding of the alternative ways in which public entities can acquire these tax dollars. Thus, chapter 4 provides an overview of tax sources and of the procedures

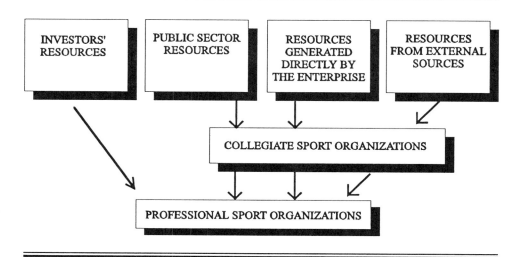

FIGURE 1-3
Sources of Resources for Intercollegiate and Professional Sport

INVESTORS' RESOURCES

PUBLIC SECTOR RESOURCES

RESOURCES GENERATED DIRECTLY BY THE ENTERPRISE

RESOURCES FROM EXTERNAL SOURCES

COLLEGIATE SPORT ORGANIZATIONS

PROFESSIONAL SPORT ORGANIZATIONS

that public agencies have to follow in order to acquire them. Chapter 5 concludes the first section of the text by describing the principles which underlie funding partnerships between sport organizations and public sector authorities. The chapter provides examples of partnership joint venture models that have been implemented effectively.

The focus of Section 2 is the financial resources that accrue to intercollegiate and professional sport organizations directly from the sport enterprise. These are discussed in chapters 6 through 8, which respectively address, revenues from admissions, sale of licensed products, and concessions and merchandising.

Both intercollegiate and professional sport organizations acquire external funds from sponsorship. The first four chapters, 9 through 12, of Section 3 discuss the principles of sponsorship; ethical issues associated with accepting external funds from tobacco and alcohol companies; and marketing, implementation, and evaluation procedures that lead to successful sponsorship partnerships.

For many intercollegiate programs, alumni donations are an integral part of their budget. Hence, chapter 13 describes how to effectively solicit donations. It concludes with a discussion of cause-related marketing, which has emerged as a resource acquisition tool in the past 10 years, and appears to have the potential to develop exponentially in the sport management field in the coming years.

SUMMARY

Successful intercollegiate and professional sport managers in the future are likely to be entrepreneurial. Their task is to imaginatively seek new resources that can be used to help their organizations achieve desired goals.

Although intercollegiate athletic programs have an educational and social mission, the last decade has seen major shifts towards a more commercial approach to obtaining the financial resources necessary to meet those goals. Most athletic departments do not cover their operating costs from revenues accruing from admissions. Increasingly, they have to expand their efforts to generate revenue from merchandising, licensing, and the media, and from external sources.

The two factors that have intensified financial pressures confronting intercollegiate athletics are escalating tuition costs and gender equity. The situation is likely to be exacerbated because costs associated with both these factors are likely to accelerate in the future. The extent to which programs will have to be cut to accommodate these factors will depend upon how successful sport managers are in finding additional resources to match the extra costs.

Professional sports enjoyed unprecedented prosperity in the 1970s and 1980s, but in the 1990s profitable operation is much more difficult to achieve. Income from traditional sources such as ticket and media sales have not kept pace with escalating costs largely due to extraordinary increases in player salaries. Increasingly, profit margins will be the result of innovations such as skyboxes, licensing, and sponsorship.

Questions for Study and Discussion

1. The reality of intercollegiate athletics is that only a very few programs are financially self-sufficient. Identify and explain the conditions which have led to the general economic insolvency of most collegiate athletic programs.

2. Discuss some of the measures recommended by the NCAA to reduce the costs of collegiate sport programs. Are these measures sufficient? What other cost containment strategies would you recommend?

3. Explain the proportional representation goal of Title IX and its implications for the allocation of athletic department financial resources for achieving gender equity. How has the University of Texas responded to this compliance standard?

4. Compare and contrast the current economic condition of each of the four major professional sport leagues in North America.

5. Define the terms revenue sharing and salary cap. Describe the manner in which these concepts have been applied in the four major sport leagues in the U.S. and Canada.

REFERENCES

Athletic Notes. (1993, June 9). *The Chronicle of Higher Education*, p. A30.

Blum, D. (1993, July 14) Walk-ons. *The Chronicle of Higher Education*, pp. A28-29.

Bodley, H. (1992, September 3). Vincent atop hot seat as owners meet. *USA Today*, p. 2C.

Brown, B. (1993, May 11). Supply and demand sets ticket prices. *USA Today*, p. 8C.

Chass, M. (1994, June 7). Owners pull so hard on cap, they're blind to a strike. *New York Times*, p. A22.

Chass, M. (1992, December 12). Owners get a fiscal blueprint for the future. *New York Times*, p. B10.

Chass, M. (1990a, February 22). Players big winners as arbitration ends. *New York Times*, p. A21.

Chass, M. (1990b, March 11). Pay cut is now seldom used tool. *New York Times*, p. A26.

Finn, M. (1992, June). Gender equity: Ready or not? *Voice of the Hawkeyes*, pp. 3, 14.

Foster, D. (1992, September). Football on the brink. *U. The National College Maga-*

zine, pp. 22,36.

Gorman, J. & Calhoun, K. (1994). *The name of the game: The business of sports.* New York: John Wiley & Sons, Inc.

Hart-Nibbrig, N. & Cottingham, C. (1986). *The political economy of college sports.* Lexington, MA: Lexington Books.

Hubbard, S., Moore, D. & Fischler, S. (1994, April). Sports salaries: Rocketing out of control? *Inside Sports,* pp. 58-69.

Krupa, G. & Dunnavant, K. (1989, January 2). The struggle with the downside. *Sports inc.,* pp. 33-38.

Lorenz, M. (1994, March 2). A reality-based plan for achieving gender equity in college sports. *The Chronicle of Higher Education,* pp. B1-2.

Minors might lose their umbilical cord. (1993, July 13). *Columbus Dispatch,* p. 50.

Moran, M. (1992a, June 21). Title IX is now an irresistible force. *New York Times,* B26-27.

Moran, M. (1992b, June 22). Campus changes coming, like it or not. *New York Times,* p. B5.

On the rise. (1994, April). *Team Marketing Report,* p. 6.

Ozanian, M. (1994, May 10). The $11 billion pastime. *Financial World,* pp. 50-59.

Ozanian, M. & Taub, S. (1992, July 7). Big leagues, bad business. *Financial World,* pp. 34-42.

Quirk, J. & Fort, R. (1992). *Pay dirt: The business of professional team sports.* Princeton, NJ: Princeton University Press.

Rich Brooks. (1992, August, 16). *The Register-Guard,* p. 8G.

Raiborn, M. H. (1990). *Revenues and expenses of intercollegiate athletic programs: Analysis of financial trends and relationship 1985-1989.* Overland Park, KS: National Collegiate Athletic Association.

Sperber, M. (1990). *College sports inc.: The athletic department vs the university.* New York: Henry Holt and Company, Inc.

Swift, E. M. (1991, June 3). From corned beef to caviar. *Sports Illustrated,* pp. 74-84.

Thalman, J. (1992, Summer). Sports on the line. *Old Oregon,* pp. 12-17.

Wieberg, S. (1992). State of college football. *Athlon Football 1992,* pp. 92-95.

Zimbalist, A. (1992). *Baseball and billions: A probing look inside the big business of our national pastime.* New York: Basic Books.

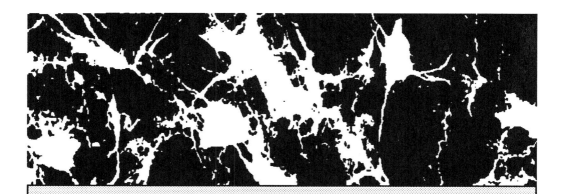

SECTION 1

RESOURCES FROM THE PUBLIC SECTOR

JUSTIFICATION FOR INVESTING PUBLIC RESOURCES IN PRIVATE SPORT FACILITIES AND EVENTS

Learning Objectives

After completing this chapter, the readers should be able to:

1. Discuss the extent to which cities have subsidized the development and operation of major and minor league professional sport teams.

2. Identify and discuss the four basic argumetns used to justify the public subsidization of privately owned sport franchises: increased community visibility, enhanced community image, stimulation of other development, and psychic income.

JUSTIFICATION FOR INVESTING PUBLIC RESOURCES IN PRIVATE SPORT FACILITIES AND EVENTS

Many North American cities are in a state of acute financial crisis. Their tax base is declining at a time when they are confronted with substantial requirements and expectations to meet growing social and infrastructure needs. Remarkably in this environment, they are prepared to subsidize private sports franchises with hundreds of millions of dollars. At the beginning of this chapter we examine the sources of momentum that create this extraordinary largesse. The magnitude of public subsidization of privately owned sports franchises and privately promoted sports events is then described. The primary arguments used by advocates to justify subsidies invariably revolve around economics. Commissioning an economic impact study to demonstrate that economic returns to a community will exceed its investment is now *de rigueur*. Because of the crucial role of these studies in public debate over the issue, the whole of chapter 3 has been allocated to discuss them in detail. That discussion points out the fraudulent procedures that are frequently incorporated in those analyses in order to generate high numbers and recognizes the increasing skepticism towards them of community residents and decision makers.

Justifying public subsidy of minor league teams on the basis of their economic impact is particularly tenuous, since their impact is likely to be analogous only to that of a small local business. For example, a minor league baseball team's gross operating budget, with few exceptions, ranges from approximately $250,000 to $2 million, depending on the level of the league in which the team plays. This compares to the $7 million in gross sales reported by the average grocery store which also employs more people on a year-round basis (Johnson, 1991). The lack of economic impact is apparent from the following data, which were derived from an analysis of minor league baseball teams (Johnson, 1991):

A team employs 5 to 20 individuals beyond its 21 to 26 players and coaches. Some of these employees, if not most, will be employed on a seasonal basis and paid on a commission basis. Players receive a minimum salary of $700 a month during the playing season only (April to August). Workers behind the concession stands and vendors may be volunteers or work on a part-time basis. The profits of a team with no local owners likely will be invested elsewhere.

Visiting teams stay at a hotel in the community, thus increasing that establishment's revenue, but not necessarily increasing employment there. the low per diem given to players (from $5.50 to $14.00) makes it unlikely they have a major impact on the restaurant and bar business. There are two to three umpires per game, a small number of fans occasionally may follow the visiting team to town and stay one night (in many cases they can return home the same night) and scouts and personnel from the parent club visit the community on an irregular basis. (p. 317)

Thus, if economic impact analyses are done correctly, they are likely to conclude in many cases involving major league teams and in virtually all cases concerning minor league team teams, that the economic gains are insufficient to justify the public investment. More prominent attention then is likely to be given to other reasons that may justify the investment, which constitute the major thrust of this chapter. Hence, after an overview of the extent of subsidization, there is a discussion of reasons for it beyond the direct economic impact. These are grouped under four headings: increased community visibility, enhanced community image, stimulation of other development, and psychic income. The first three of these justifications are sequential. That is, image cannot be changed or more strongly defined without exposure, so increased visibility is a prerequisite for enhanced community image. Similarly, stimulation of additional development created by increased tourism visitation or business relocations is likely to be influenced by the image of a community held by individual and corporate decision-makers.

SOURCES OF MOMENTUM FOR PUBLIC SUBSIDIZATION

The willingness of public entities to subsidize private sports franchises is remarkable given the conditions of financial crisis and infrastructure deterioration that prevail in major cities. The conundrum was graphically stated by a letter writer to the *Baltimore Sun* who observed:

The city is full of ruined houses, the jails are overcrowded, the dome is falling off City Hall, there are potholes in the streets, crippled children can't get to school, taxes are up and services are going down — but we're going to have a sports complex. (cited in Richmond 1993, p. 50)

Given the immense fiscal crises confronting city governments and the numerous social and infrastructure needs requiring additional funds, from where does the momentum come to invest hundreds of millions of dollars in what ostensibly appears to be the relatively frivolous project of a sports franchise?

The momentum stems from two sources: the unique legal status of professional leagues, which enables them to collaborate to restrict the supply of teams and the power structure of cities. The role of each of these is discussed in the following paragraphs.

The Legal Status of Professional Leagues

The baseball, football, basketball, and hockey leagues within which franchises play are unique in that they are exempt from normal antitrust rules that prohibit barriers to competition. Thus, the leagues are cartels that have effectively been endowed with the status of a legal monopoly. The leagues operate as cartels in three major ways (Ingham, Howell & Schilperoort, 1987):

> (a) by attempting to restrict interteam competition for players, thereby reducing competitive bidding between teams for player services; (b) by controlling the location and relocation of teams; and (c) by controlling the rights to the national over-the-air broadcast of games and by creating rules that enable teams to exercise control over their over-the-air local broadcast territories (i.e., the sale of home games not included on the national broadcast package and the right to protect the local listener/viewer market from infringement by broadcasts from other teams in the league). (p. 455)

The leagues have used their monopoly power to limit expansion. Major sports appear to be a culturally unique experience for an influential segment of the U.S. population, in that they cannot be replaced by other forms of entertainment. Hence, there are a large number of cities seeking professional sports franchises, and they far outnumber the available supply of teams. The imbalance of supply and demand creates a competitive environment that leads cities to escalate their offers of publicly funded inducements in an attempt to outbid one another for franchises. It has been noted that "teams manipulate cities by selling them against each other in a scramble for the limited number of major league teams. While the cities fight each other, the teams sit back and wait for the best conditions and terms" (Euchner, 1993, p. 179). If major league baseball, for example, had 40 or 50 teams rather than 28, then much of the leverage used to garner public subsidies would be removed.

Franchise owners have demonstrated they are prepared to take advantage of this leverage potential. Thus, in the 1980s there were moves in the NFL of the Raiders from Oakland to Los Angeles, the Colts from Baltimore to Indianapolis, and the Cardinals from St. Louis to Phoenix. The moves of the Raiders and Colts occurred despite long histories of sellouts and financial and playing success (Quirk & Fort, 1992). Between 1970 and 1985 there were 22 franchise moves in the established major leagues (Baade & Dye, 1988). The moves were invariably motivated by big financial inducements from new cities.

In many more instances, the threat of such a move has been sufficient for cities to offer increased public subsidy to keep their franchises from leaving for elsewhere. A primary victim of this tactic has been the city of St. Petersburg, which for many years tried to secure a baseball franchise. The city invested $130 million in the Florida Dome. Instead of attracting a team, St. Petersburg was cynically used by other teams to leverage more public funds from their existing communities. A local official observed, " 'We've been used as a nuclear threat to other communities to make them give their teams whatever they want' " (cited in Corliss 1992, p. 52).

The legal ability to act as a cartel and limit supply gives the leagues extraordinary power with which to intimidate cities. An example of this occurred when the owners of the San Francisco Giants committed to selling the team to a group in St. Petersburg in 1992. The owners subsequently withdrew from this commitment, and the first reaction of St. Petersburg officials was to seek substantial damages through the courts for breach of contract. However, they did not follow through with a suit because they realized that such an action would likely have led to an informal blackballing of the city, which would have negated any future chance of St. Petersburg's ever obtaining a franchise. By collective action, baseball owners would have been able to enforce this informal sanction against St. Petersburg, and they could afford to do it because of the great demand for teams from other cities.

Owner leverage also extends to the movement of franchises in the minor leagues, where parent clubs are continually pressuring their minor league affiliates to relocate if another community will provide improved playing facilities, better player accommodations, or more fans in front of whom to play (Johnson, 1993):

> For example, in 1990, the New York Mets gave Norfolk, Virginia officials an ultimatum to build a $15 million stadium or lose their AAA team, despite a twenty-one year association between the community, its minor league team, and the Mets; and a year later, the Mets announced plans to move their Williamsport (AA) franchise to a new stadium in Binghamton, New York in 1992. (p. 31)

Ironically , when teams perform poorly on the playing field, the tendency for them to use their leverage for enhanced public subsidy is probably at its greatest. Poor performance translates into low income, and under those conditions the only source for increasing it is the public purse. In such periods, teams are likely to claim that their stadiums prevent them from attracting crowds or from maximizing the revenue from those who do attend. Meanwhile, because of a shortage of teams, other cities are willing to bid for the franchise. This strategy was used effectively by the White Sox in the late 1980s to pressure Chicago for a better stadium, using the threat to move to St. Petersburg if this was not forthcoming:

> The White Sox used their momentary poor standing to gain higher profits and a more favorable lease with the Chicago government, and, eventually, a new stadium. By stripping the team of top players, the owners in three years (1985-88) reduced its payroll from $9.1 to $5.8 million, barely half of the major league average of $11 million. With revenues of about $30 million annually, the team increased its short-term profits substantially. And, of course, the club's management used short-term failure not only to initiate cost-cutting measures but to press for a more lucrative long-term relationship with the city.

The White Sox were in a good position to make demands on public authorities because of their lack of success on the playing field. The franchise could claim that it could not build a competitive team because an inadequate stadium and a burdensome lease restricted its resources. As is often the case in negotiations over sports facilities, nothing succeeded like failure. (Euchner, 1993, p. 137)

The leverage exerted by franchises stems not only from the fiscal packages offered by other cities, but also from the sunk costs incurred by their current host cities. Quirk and Fort (1992) explain it in these terms:

The fundamental fact of life concerning stadiums and arenas is that once they are built, they are fixed in place, while the teams that use them are potentially mobile. This puts an enormous bargaining advantage in the hands of teams playing in publicly owned stadiums. Teams can exploit their threat of leaving a city to wring out of the manager of the stadium rental agreements that leave the city pretty much holding the bag. (p. 172)

The Power Structure of Cities

Franchises, and the construction of stadia that accompany them, tend to be enthusiastically recruited by powerful vested interests in communities, such as banks, real estate developers, elements of the tourism industry like restaurants and hotels, insurance companies, and construction firms (Euchner, 1993). These interests are able to influence decision-makers because of their prominent role in political campaigns. At the same time, elected decision makers may see the acquisition of a sports franchise as a highly visible means of demonstrating their leadership capabilities. The local media are likely to be supportive because of the added news and sports interest a franchise brings. These groups are likely to work enthusiastically in support, and they control "the system," that is, the financial, knowledge and legal resources to bring a project to fruition.

Efforts to oppose subsidies to franchises are often perceived to be futile, given the political and economic power of supporters, the difficulty of forming and sustaining any organized opposition without resources, and the pressures and constraints of everyday life. Further, while those supporting investment of public funds in a franchise base their arguments on *particular* benefits that they believe will emerge, those opposed are often able to base their case only on the less convincing grounds that *general* benefits will accrue to the city if these resources are allocated elsewhere. Thus, the opposition's case often lacks the focus and conviction that supporters are able to inject into the debate:

Citizens can make the argument that sports and stadiums are poor development tools and that $200 million can be better spent on education, police, or housing programs; but such arguments often carry little weight, because the results of such spending are undramatic and recipients of the services are unorganized and sometimes even hostile. There is no guarantee that spending the money on education, for example, would markedly improve schools; the money, after all, would not transform the system but would go to the same bureaucracy and neighborhoods, without alleviating the problems of poverty and alienation they are experiencing. Why, then, bother to shift the $200 million from the stadium project to the education system? (Euchner, 1993, p. 60)

When opposition does emerge, it can frequently be undermined by offering benefits to appease opponents. For example, in Baltimore the Waverly Improvement Association agreed to drop opposition to a new stadium, in return for increased funds for rehabilitation of their neighborhood and enforcement of housing codes to drive out slumlords.

THE PERVASIVENESS OF PUBLIC SUBSIDIZATION

The most egregious example of public subsidy of a private organization's sports event is probably the Montreal Olympic Games of 1976. The popular mayor who sought the Games saw them as a way for Montreal to become recognized as a world-class city, and he assured his residents it would not require a substantial subsidy. " 'The Olympics can no more have a deficit than a man can have a baby' " (cited in Roughton, 1990, p. R3). The final public subsidy exceeded $1 billion! A member of the Montreal city council stated, "It was an unqualified disaster. We're going to pay every day of our lives for a two-week party most of us couldn't attend." In 1990, 14 years after the Games, Montreal and the Province of Quebec still had $450 million of the debt outstanding.

The forms in which a public subsidy can be packaged vary widely, but the following examples are illustrative of some of the more common components included in these packages:

1. Using municipal bonds that can be issued at interest rates below those paid by private businesses to pay for stadiums and arenas.
2. Charging a lease fee below what would be paid to a private owner operating the facility. If a commercial market rate of return on a city's invested capital were sought, then the lease fee would not only cover operating expenses but also depreciation and amortization of buildings and equipment, and a desired margin of profits.
3. Foregoing property taxes that should be paid on a facility if it was privately owned.
4. Investing in infrastructure associated with a facility.
5. Using in-kind public services, for example, police services, without charging the market rate for them.

Quirk and Fort (1992) considered the magnitude of these kinds of subsidies in selected stadiums/arenas for which data were available and reported:

There are six facilities—Riverfront Stadium, Superdome, Kingdome, Byrne Meadowlands Arena, Astrodome, and Pontiac Silverdome—showing subsidies of over $10 million per year, with the Superdome showing a horrendous $43 million annual subsidy. The point that has to be kept in mind is that these figures *underestimate* the amounts of subsidies provided by the stadiums and arenas, because data were not available for all investments in the facilities subsequent to original construction. (p. 171)

When the data were extrapolated from their sample to all facilities that hosted major league franchises, Quirk and Fort (1992) estimated the size of the annual subsidy provided by cities and states to the franchises to be approximately $500 million.

The number of facilities in each of the major leagues that are publicly and privately owned is shown in the first two columns of Table 2-1. The table shows that, as of 1991, 65 of the 84 stadiums and arenas (77%) used by major league sports teams were publicly owned (Quirk & Fort, 1992). The remaining five columns of Table 2-1 show the shift that has taken place towards public ownership . In the era after World War II, most major league teams in all sports played in privately owned facilities. Since 1960 all 29 new stadiums constructed have been publicly owned, with the exception of Dodger Stadium, Joe Robbie Stadium, the Rangers' Arlington Stadium (which was bought by the Rangers from the city for the bargain price of $17.8 million), and the Patriots' Foxboro Stadium. Similarly, most new arenas are publicly owned. The exceptions of those built in the 1980s were ARCO arena in Sacramento, the Pistons' Palace of Auburn Hills, and the Timberwolves' Target Center. Quirk and Fort (1992) concluded that approximately $3.0 billion was invested between 1960 and 1990 by cities and states in stadiums and arenas used by major league sports teams.

Quirk (1987) points out the economic momentum which has been created to perpetuate this trend towards using subsidized public facilities:

This pattern suggests a kind of "Gresham's law" ("bad money drives good money out of circulation") for stadiums, with publicly owned stadiums operating at a loss acting to drive privately owned stadiums out of business.

The notion behind the Gresham's law for stadiums is this. Any team that owns its own stadium or that rents from another team has to compete in the market for players with all other teams in its sport, including those that play in publicly owned stadiums.

Table 2-1
Stadium and Arena Characteristics at the Beginning of Each Decade by Professional Sports Leagues 1950-1991

	No.	Public	Private	Percentage Public				
				1950	1960	1970	1980	1991
AL	14	12	2	12	37	75	86	86
NL	12	9	3	0	50	67	83	75
NFL	28	26	2	46	62	71	76	65
NBA	26	17	9	0	0	42	52	65
NHL	20	13	7	36	60	81	96	93

Note: From *Pay Dirt: The Business of Professional Team Sports* (p. 133) by J.P. Quick and R.D. Fort, 1992, Princeton, NJ: Princeton University Press. Reprinted by permission.

Teams that play in publicly owned stadiums are subsidized. They are charged lower rental rates than are teams playing in privately owned facilities, because the rents charged by privately owned facilities have to cover the operating costs for these facilities, if they want to stay in business. This puts the teams playing in publicly owned stadiums at an economic advantage—their costs are lower. And this provides a powerful incentive for teams playing in privately owned stadiums to lobby for the construction of publicly owned facilities or to move to cities that provide such subsidized stadiums. (p. SR8)

The trend towards increased public subsidization of franchises in the major leagues is also apparent in the minor leagues. For example, professional baseball at the minor league level is played in nearly 200 communities in the United States, Canada and Mexico. Over 90% of these teams play in stadiums that are publicly owned and operated. There also has been a boom in new and substantially renovated stadiums at the minor league level, similar to that which has occurred in the major leagues (Johnson 1989). A survey of communities which host minor league baseball teams concluded:

It has become local government policy to enter into a relationship with baseball team owners that generally includes a publicly-owned facility leased by the team to produce between 30 and 75 baseball games for residents and visitors. The communities and teams have devised a variety of financial arrangements to govern this relationship, but as a general rule, an operating surplus is rarely achieved by local government.

Results of referenda proposals in the late 1980s and early 1990s, offer some evidence that residents' willingness to support construction of major league stadiums with public tax dollars may be waning. For example, such referenda failed in Miami (1988), New Jersey (1987), San Francisco (1987 and 1989), Phoenix (1989), San Jose (1990 and 1992) and Cuyahoga County (1984). However, they were successful in Cleveland (1990), Denver (1990), and San Antonio (1989).

INCREASED COMMUNITY VISIBILITY

A professional sports franchise guarantees a significant amount of media coverage for the city in which it is located. The importance of this exposure was recognized by an official in Washington, DC when the Redskins were considering a move from that city to Arlington, Virginia (Corliss, 1992):

Officials in Washington could only fear that getting Skinned meant the town would be rubbed off the map. "Brooklyn has never been the same since the Dodgers left," said the D.C. council chairman whose own city lost two baseball clubs in the 1950s. "You don't even think about Brooklyn." (p. 51)

Some indication of the magnitude of exposure that occurs is given by the statistics cited in the following case study relating to media coverage of the Atlanta Falcons. Efforts are sometimes made to attribute an economic value to this exposure. For example, a study undertaken by Chicago's Department of Economic Development reported "that the championship-winning 1985-86 Chicago Bears football team produced publicity for Chicago equivalent to a $30 to $40 million promotion campaign" (cited in Baade & Dye, 1988, p. 46). The study does not describe the procedures used to derive this value, but a widely used method of obtaining a crude dollar value measure of media exposure is to use prevailing advertising rates in the media in which it appears. This approach is frequently used by companies to measure economic value of their sponsorship. The procedures involved and the merits and limitations of this approach are discussed later in the text in chapter 12 in the context of sponsorship.

The effectiveness of a sports event in raising awareness of a city was measured by Ritchie (1989). His context was the Winter Olympics held in Calgary in 1988. He used samples taken from a number of locations drawn both from Europe and the United States and traced changes in their awareness of Calgary during a 3-year period from 1986 to 1988. The changes were dramatic. The nearby city of Edmonton served as a control point against which the magnitude of changes in Calgary's level of awareness could be measured. Among the European sample in 1986 and 1987, Calgary obtained unaided-recall percentages of 10.1 and 12.0%, respectively, whereas comparable figures for Edmonton were 5.3% and 5.0%. The main impact of the Games is shown in the 1988 figures where Calgary's unaided recognition level jumped to 40.0%, while Edmonton's remained at just over 6%. Similar impacts were observed among the U.S. samples, although the growth in awareness of approximately 23 points was not quite so dramatic as the 28 point gain recorded by the European samples.

The instrumental purpose and value of high exposure has been articulated in the following terms in relation to the city of Adelaide's investment in its Grand Prix event (Van der Lee & Williams 1986).

This is the first step in marketing Adelaide to international markets. Any promotion to create market knowledge of what Adelaide has to offer as an international visitor destination can only be effective after potential visitors know it exists and where it is. Achieving this prerequisite awareness is a considerable hurdle to be overcome. The cost and effort in doing so for a new long haul destination is quite high. Therefore the Grand Prix influence (of which the first year is only part of a cumulative process) is quite valuable in that it would be difficult to achieve by alternative means. (p.54)

MEDIA EXPOSURE ACCRUING TO THE CITY OF ATLANTA FROM THE FALCONS FOOTBALL TEAM

CASE STUDY

On any given weekend last fall, the five major Atlanta-area newspapers devoted more than 1,000 column-inches to the Falcons and their opponents. The visiting team was mentioned prominently in each story.

When the Falcons travel, their coverage is at least as great, and probably larger, because they play in larger cities which are the homes of more publications than is Atlanta. Over the regular season, major stories featuring the Atlanta Falcons appear at least twice in the other three Western Division cities. These stories are circulated in the major metropolitan areas of the nation. And it is certain that the nation's 1,790 daily newspapers all carry at least the scores of professional football games, bringing the Falcons' name before countless readers and building Atlanta's image as a major-league city. With a 20-game schedule, 35,000 mentions of Atlanta are a certainty.

More than 130 radio stations in the Southeast carried the play-by-play action of all Falcons games, preseason and regular-season on the Mutual Broadcasting System. And a majority of the 7,000 radio stations across the nation broadcast daily sports reports with frequent mentions of the Falcons.

Nationwide television networks took the Falcons live into virtually every community in the United States, including the states of Alaska and Hawaii. Over 620 network affiliates (CBS, NBC, ABC) carry game reports including Atlanta scores. In the regular-season games, which were carried by either CBS or NBC on regional telecasts, the Falcons appeared on 364 television stations, and the ABC-TV Monday-Night Games of October 22 and November 5 appeared on 211 more stations. In addition, the four preseason games were televised to the Atlanta-area audience.

Four primary cable networks report sports extensively and frequently mention the Falcons during the season: Entertainment and Sports Programming Network (ESPN), in 37.5 million homes from the United Kingdom to Japan and Canada through Cental America; Cable News Network (CNN), in 31.4 million homes in all 50 states and 28 other countries; USA Network in 29 million homes in all 50 states; and Home Box Office (HBO) in 14.5 million homes in the 50 states and Puerto Rico.

These few observations make it quite clear that Atlanta benefits from her professional football team providing continued advertising and exposure to the rest of the world for the "next great. . . city." How much is this continued exposure worth? It is hard to say. So many factors are at work in determining a city's future that it is difficult to attribute success in growth to any one particular factor. However, every little bit helps, and few activities can yield the exposure produced by modern sports.

Note: From *Economic Impact of the Falcons on Atlanta: 1984* by W. Schaffer and L.S. Davidson, 1984, Atlanta, GA: Georgia Institute of Technology

ENHANCED COMMUNITY IMAGE

Increased exposure offers opportunities for more sharply defining or changing a city's image. The Mayor of Jacksonville, for example, perceived that a major league team in his city would provide "a real signature for the community" (Fulton, 1988, p. 34). It has been suggested that major sports events and teams are the new "image builders" for communities (Burns & Mules, 1986). In the construction years after

World War II, this role was performed by tall building tower skylines, large-span bridges, or manufacturing industries (for example, Motor City or Steel City). Today, as the economy has switched to a service orientation, major sports events and teams capture the imagination and help establish a city's image in people's minds.

This type of image change was documented by Ritchie (1989) in his study of the impact of the Winter Olympics on Calgary. In his 1987 surveys, the Calgary Stampede was the dominant image associated with the city, being mentioned by 26% of respondents, and the Olympics were second most frequently mentioned with 17%. In the 1988 surveys the Olympics were mentioned by 77% of respondents, with the Stampede falling to a mention of only 11%.

During the debate over construction of the Herbert H. Humphrey Metrodome in Minneapolis, the late Vice-President was asked if he thought keeping the Vikings and Twins in Minneapolis was important. "Yes," he retorted. "What do you want to become, a cold Omaha?" ("Suddenly," 1983, p. 110).

In Sheffield, England, the city's high public investment in facilities and in-kind assistance to host the World Student Games was justified on the basis of image improvement. The games were intended to be the "flagship" that management consultants had recommended the city seek to help scrub away Sheffield's "steel and grime" image ("Games," 1991). The city's chief planner stated

Sheffield has an image problem—Sheffield's smokey image acquired during the heydays of the steel industry, is proving difficult to shake off—Sheffield's image is obviously important if the city is to attract footloose industry. In a period when every town and city is extolling its local virtues Sheffield has something that is different. The World Student Games should raise the city's profile throughout the United Kingdom and hopefully much of the world. Indeed, some of those associated with the games have suggested that the attraction of footloose industry may be one of the most significant effects of the games. The legacy of excellent sporting facilities after the games should enable Sheffield to stand out from the clamor of towns and cities claiming to be different. (cited in Foley, 1991, p. 73)

THE ROLE OF THE GRAND PRIX ON CHANGING
THE IMAGE OF ADELAIDE

Promotion of the Grand Prix by both the organizers and the sponsors focuses on the action and the glamour aspects which dominate the image of the event. The event becomes recognized as part of the Adelaide tourism product and hence strongly associated with the City's image. The Grand Prix has made an immediate impact on the State's tourism image. People now associate the Grand Prix with South Australia and South Australia with the Grand Prix. Recent market research conducted in Melbourne supports this. Among Melbourne residents who said it was either extremely or highly likely that they would visit Adelaide during the next 12 months, 22% said the Grand Prix was a very important

factor in their decision to visit South Australia. The perceived excitement and action of the Grand Prix, aptly captured in the Grand Prix marketing slogan "Adelaide Alive" contrasts markedly with Adelaide's longstanding image in interstate markets as being "boring," "quiet," "City of Churches," etc. The existing image has acted to inhibit consideration of Adelaide as a travel destination for many would-be visitors. The Grand Prix influence in changing that image thus creates a greater market receptiveness to promotion of Adelaide as a travel destination.

The resources required to achieve such an impact on Adelaide's image by alternative means would be substantial, and hence the value of this tourism benefit is considerable. However, this is only a potential tourism benefit since if the opportunity is not effectively exploited then no tourism benefit is gained.

Note: from *The Adelaide Grand Prix* by P. Van der Lee and J. Williams, In: J. P. Burns, J. H. Hatch and T. J. Mules, 1986, The Grand Prix and tourism. Adelaide: The Centre for South Australian Economic Studies.

The accompanying description of the Adelaide Grand Prix is another example how a city used a sports event to change its image. The Grand Prix motor race was used to spearhead the "Adelaide Alive" image which was intended to replace Adelaide's traditional rather unexciting image. Expectations at both the Sheffield and Adelaide events were that a change in image would lead to increases in tourism and in businesses relocating from elsewhere. After the America's Cup races were held in Freemantle, Western Australia, it was observed: "based on the crowds which continue to come to Freemantle day and night, the town has become a major destination for tourists and local visitors in the year since it was 'discovered' by the Cup" (Newman, 1989, p. 55).

The image of prominent "first-tier" cities is molded by a host of symbols, events, people, and behaviors; thus, the incremental contribution of a sports event, facility, or team to the image of those cities is likely to be relatively small. Their contribution to the image of "second-tier" cities is likely to be proportionately more substantial (Fulton, 1988, p. 36).

While the largest cities viewed sports teams as an important piece of their overall cultural package, in many less populous cities the teams have become inextricably linked with the city's image. Cities such as Oakland, St. Louis, Kansas City and Cincinnati—none of them among the top 25 cities in population—all have proved to be great sports towns; in many cases, their sports franchises constitute validation that these cities were in the "big leagues."

"Sports means more to Oakland" says the former city manager. It makes less of a difference to New York, San Francisco, or Chicago."

Many believe the adage that "No place really can be considered to be a 'big town' if it doesn't have a professional team." This type of thinking was espoused by the mayor of San Jose when she was trying to persuade the Giants to move to her city (Fimrite, 1992):

She asserts that the Giants will also bring her city the recognition she feels it has earned as a big league metropolis. "The best kept secret in the country," says the mayor "is that San Jose, with a 1992 population of 803,000, not only is larger than San Francisco by 75,000 people, but also is the third largest city in the nation's largest state—behind only Los Angeles and San Diego—and the 11th largest in the country." (p. 51)

People frequently make judgments about the competence of a city's administration and its quality of life by extrapolating from snippets of information or from symbols. A sports teams is a highly visible symbol. Thus, another dimension of the image issue relates to perceptions of the level of competency of a community's governance. A sports franchise may be considered by some as a symbolic embodiment of the city as a whole (Euchner, 1993). (An analogous situation may also exist with major university sports today). If a city successfully negotiates and implements a major sports event or franchise agreement, then the inherent complexity of the task and the wide publicity these actions generate are likely to convey an aura of high competency upon the city's leadership. In contrast, if cities lose a sports franchise it may create the impression that local officials and politicians are incompetent. Those in leadership roles, for example, in cities that lost the Raiders, Colts, and Cardinals may be forever stigmatized in the eyes of many, irrespective of the intrinsic merits of their decisions. Further, those cities may be perceived as "declining," "losers", or "lacking in civic pride" because of the high profile loss. Baade and Dye (1988) note:

A mayor's political stock rises substantially if the mayor secures a professional sports presence and falls just as rapidly if his or her name is associated with the loss of a team. During Chicago's most recent mayoral campaign there was much speculation about what a White Sox move would do to Mayor Harold Washington's chances for reelection. Perhaps no one has stated as succinctly what underlies the fear of a franchise loss than the individual who headed Minnesota Governor Rudy Perpich's task force of revitalizing the state's economy. He commented: "It's almost worse for a city's image to lose a major league team than to have never had one at all." (p. 37)

Given the potential positive impact of a franchise on a city's image, those cities with most to gain from it are those that are in decline. They are most desperate to communicate signs of economic and social rejuvenation. Unfortunately, these struggling cities also are least able to make major investments.

STIMULATION OF OTHER DEVELOPMENT

The notion that a sports event or facility will stimulate additional development and thus contribute to expansion of a city's tax base is at least in part a consequence of the increased visibility and enhanced image cities believe will accrue from their investment. The types of development envisaged by proponents of this notion can be classified under three headings: complementary development, proximate development, and general development.

Complementary development refers to the upgrading or initiation of businesses as a result of the demand for their services that is directly created by the sport facility or event. For example, it was reported that the Adelaide Grand Prix "played a catalytic role in motivating some existing tourism operators to upgrade their business in terms of facilities and/or services" (Van der Lee & Williams 1986, p. 55). Demand for the event itself is concentrated on a week-long time period that makes it unlikely that such upgrading would be cost-efficient, but "the event raised expectations of higher tourism growth for the future" (Van der Lee & Williams, 1986, p. 55). The event provided a psychological boost and created an atmosphere of optimism that, in themselves, are sometimes sufficient to become a self-fulfilling prophecy. That is, the upgrading of amenities in the area may be a central factor in attracting increased visitation during the remainder of the year.

The America's Cup Challenge held in Freemantle, Western Australia, had the effect on the city of boosting development of both new marine-related industries and non-marine related high-technology businesses, such as computer systems, advanced metals technology, and synthetic fibers. These products were prominently publicized in the Australian media in the period of many months during which the media were preoccupied with the America's Cup. The frequent references to high technology products and Freemantle created a nexus in many people's minds (Newman, 1989).

Publicly sponsored professional sports facilities are increasingly conceptualized as being part of a total package incorporating *proximate development* that may include retailing, property development, and general leisure provision. The sports facilities are used to attract other businesses to the area. This was the thinking, for example, underlying development of Joe Robbie Stadium, the only private sector stadium developed in the past two decades. The stadium is on a 160-acre site that is part of a 430-acre parcel owned by developers. They leased the stadium site for a rental of $1 per year believing that the stadium would greatly enhance the value of the remaining property. They observed, "'The stadium is the catalyst. The business potential is fantastic'" (cited in Lowenstein 1985, p. 33). However, plans for development around the stadium were slow to materialize because of a downturn in the economy and lawsuits brought by opponents of development (Baker, 1992).

At the minor league level, Port St. Lucie, located north of Fort Lauderdale on Florida's southeast coast, appears to offer an example of successful development facilitated by baseball (Johnson, 1993):

In 1988, the New York Mets' spring training activities and minor league team were lured from St. Petersburg by a new, $10 million state-of-the-art stadium and training facility. The land for the stadium was provided by the city and funded through the county's tourist-tax revenues. The stadium developer, Thomas J. White Development Company of St. Louis, also is building a $2 billion residential and commercial project adjacent to the stadium. Mets team members are involved in the project's marketing strategy.

Port St. Lucie views this as a winning policy. The city nearly quadrupled its population, from 14,000 in 1980 to 55,866 by 1990. It has expanded its tax base, and baseball provides an amenity package to attract residents. The developer has a stadium located next to his development, which draws prospective buyers. The team uses a new premiere facility, subsidized by local government for spring training and its minor league team. (p. 158)

An element of a Virginia legislature study that investigated the case for subsidizing a new stadium for the Washington Redskins in Alexandria, Virginia, was a survey of the other 27 NFL stadiums. It concluded that 7 of them had served as magnets for development, but 5 of them were part of a convention center, were domed stadiums, or were part of multipurpose facilities (Baker, 1992). One of the stadiums where proximate development occurred was the Superdome in New Orleans. Its construction led to a revival of downtown with office buildings, hotels, and a shopping center being developed nearby. However, the Superdome's greatest attraction to other developers was its vast and inexpensive parking garage (Fulton, 1988).

The legitimacy of expecting a stadium to anchor revival of an urban neighborhood economy has been challenged (Baade & Dye, 1988). Proximate commercial ventures require visitor traffic, and stadium visitation typically is infrequent and seasonal. It seems likely, as the Virginia legislature study suggested, that if proximate development is to be stimulated, then the stadium should either be capable of multiple uses or be linked with other anchor facilities that can generate complementary traffic.

Proximate or complementary development does not accompany many new stadiums because they are not physically interwoven with other components of the urban fabric: These stadiums are designed for quick entry and exit of suburban fans with automobiles. Even though they are technically inner-city parks, their urban integration is limited to supplying parking facilities close to the downtown business district. Parks such as Pittsburgh's Three Rivers Stadium and New York's Shea Stadium fit this description. Another example is the new stadium in Chicago. As journalist Peter Richmond notes, "Never have city and stadium been so detached from each other: The garages will attach to the park by elevated walkways, and thus fans who arrive by car will have the privilege of never actually setting foot on the South Side of Chicago." (Euchner 1993, p. 70)

The large parking lots that surround many stadiums are "dead" space for most of the year, which mitigates against social and economic integration with other commercial entities. If a stadium is intended to stimulate other development, then fans should be channelled to it through carefully planned corridors to maximize secondary economic activity (Baade & Dye, 1988).

The antithetical goals of team owners and public officials who are seeking to use a new stadium to stimulate redevelopment of downtown areas are noted by Johnson (1991):

From the team's perspective the ideal location will be a site that is easily accessible, has visibility from major highways, and is compatible with the direction of existing and future population growth. It should not be surprising that the community goals of local officials often do not match the location criteria and business interests of team owners. As one interviewer commented, team owners are not in the urban redevelopment business. (p. 319)

In Indianapolis, the Hoosier Dome sparked the redevelopment of Union Station and was a major anchor for downtown development; therefore, it had a proximate development impact. An official also observed, "the best advertising this city has is that the dome exists—You never know who is watching an NFL game. Often viewers include promotion and convention planners. So the team really has proven to be a benefit for us." This type of optimistic statement exemplifies the belief that the "big-league" image will serve as a magnet and attract *general development*, which is neither complementary nor proximate, to the city.

Claims that general development is stimulated are easy to make but difficult to validate. Results from the only study reported in the literature that has tested the hypothesis that sports-based development acts as a magnet for new businesses were not encouraging (Baade, 1987). The study was conducted on data from eight different metropolitan areas and found there was no relationship between development of a stadium and manufacturing employment, manufacturing value added, or new capital expenditures.

Rosentraub and Nunn (1978) compared the impact of the stadiums of the Dallas Cowboys and the Texas Rangers on the local economies of Irving and Arlington, which are the teams' respective host cities, with those of seven other cities and towns. The analysis found that general economic trends and tax policy accounted for whatever economic activity had taken place and whatever economic benefits resulted spilled over into other cities in the region.

PSYCHIC INCOME

Frequently, benefits accrue to the collective morale of residents from a sports event or team, especially if it is successful, and these benefits may be termed "psychic income." Those involved in successfully organizing a major sports event are likely to grow in confidence and feel a sense of pride in their accomplishment. More generically, however, psychic income refers to benefits received by many community residents who are not involved in organizing and who do not physically attend the event, but, nevertheless, strongly identify with it. Lipsky (1979) writes that sports involvement can be

> a counterpoint to the decline of political effect and the widespread nostalgia for community in America. . . . The language of sports is the symbolic glue that holds the entire social lifeworld. It is the common idiom that links (heretofore male) Americans in the taverns, the living rooms, car pools and offices. . . . The team acts in many ways as the symbolic community that unites belief systems and authority structures with people's everyday lives. (pp. 67-68)

Elsewhere, Lipsky (1981) eloquently observed, "Sport is the magic elixir that feeds personal identity while it nourishes the bonds of communal solidarity" (p. 5).

This phenomenon is pronounced in all segments of the managed sport industry. A substantial proportion of a community emotionally identifies with "its" team or event and feels elation, anxiety, despondency, optimism, and an array of other emotions according to how the team performs. Some of these people may not understand the nature of the event or how the activity is performed. Nevertheless, the team constitutes "a common identification symbol, something that brings the citizens of the city together, especially during those exhilarating times when the city has a World Series champion, or a Super Bowl winner." (Quirk & Fort, 1992, p. 176). The emotional response of Atlanta residents to the news that the Olympic Games would be coming to their city illustrates the phenomenon of psychic income.

WORLD RECOGNITION GIVES ATLANTANS A NEW SENSE OF PRIDE IN THEIR CITY

Karen Twait was weaving her way to work through heavy eastbound traffic on Interstate 20 when the announcement came over the radio. "Suddenly horns started honking, and fists came out of car windows. Everywhere I looked people were screaming. It was incredible" said the 24-year-old financial analyst who moved here from Tampa three months ago. "I started screaming too. And tears just started streaming down my face. It was so dramatic. I never expected so much emotion to come over me."

On the other side of the city, Robert Clark, 52, an Atlanta native and downtown businessman, was watching TV, getting ready for work. "I was startled," Mr. Clark said. "I just broke down and cried when the guy said, 'Atlanta,' I don't know why. It's been more than 30 years since I cried. But I know I'll remember that day for a long, long time."

The instant the Olympic announcement was made Tuesday morning, a change swept through the city. The town rose up, rearranging a collective psyche that some say has long been subject to a Southern inferiority complex. Winning the Games seems to have finally ripened a town that's forever been on the edge of maturity.

Scores of people say they feel decidedly different now. They feel better about Atlanta, better about living here. Many people say they will never forget where they were and what they were doing when they heard the news, and they will long remember how they were moved. Anyone who has lived in a city that won the World Series or a Super Bowl will understand something of the feeling that swept through the city Tuesday. But Atlanta savored far more than a one-day seasonal victory.

Atlanta has long had an image problem. The town called Terminus that began as a transportation crossroads grew up as a drummers' town and remains one. It has always been a city where myths outstripped reality. Tourists still seek in vain to see vestiges of Scarlett's and Rhett's antebellum South, and must eventually confront the question: "What is there to actually see here?" In so many ways, Atlanta has been seen as Loserville, and not just in terms of sports.

"Atlanta has never become a city it wanted to be. Its history has been one of thinking it might have finally arrived, then finding it hasn't," said Albert Scardino, whose editorial writing won a Pultizer Prize in 1984 at the *Georgia Gazette* in Savannah.

"Atlanta itself has no real identity," Mr. Robinson said. "You never have to ask what makes New York a great city, or Boston or L.A. or San Francisco. You know why they're great. But Atlanta? The city has no real indigenous culture of its own. It's a city that has long been groping for its identity."

In the height of its most recent hoped-for glory, during the 1988 Democratic National Convention, the city was ripped again—called "The Big Hustle," a city built on lies, in *The Wall Street Journal.*

That changed Tuesday. With the Olympic Games, our Loserville became Lusterville. "Winning the Olympics says Atlanta is a real city," Mr. Robinson said. "It says to the people who live here, 'Finally, we're a place. We have an identity.' For a lot of people, this legitimizes the identity of their city."

Walking the streets in the days since the announcement, it is not hard to find people who say their image of the city has changed overnight. "The problem we've had is that we've always claimed to be an international city. But let's face it, we have not been one," said Tony Bulthuis, 45, accounts director at Comfort Inns, who moved here from Amsterdam 22 years ago. "Now we don't have to make excuses for ourselves any longer."

When Ann Crawford, 32, moved here from New York four years ago she thought it a sleepy town. "I had a sense of, "Oh, my God, what have I done," It was a big step for me, and it felt like a step backward.

"But today there is a real and new sense of pride," said Ms. Crawford, who works for the international exchange program American Field Service. "There's a sense that this is where it's happening. Everyone in the U.S. is envious of Atlanta today."

Debbie Lee, 25, a traveling businesswoman who has been in Atlanta eight years, put it this way: "I have a lot of friends that wouldn't visit me in Atlanta, friends from Florida, New York, California. But now they all want to come."

The new found optimism has spilled over to the city's most debated problems. "I'm hoping this will mean we'll finally do something about the homeless and needy," said Adrian Chester, 27, an Atlanta native who is a disc jockey at Dominique's nightclub. "Getting the Olympics is sort of like everyone's lottery ticket. It allows everyone to dream. And hopefully everyone will benefit."

Note: from *The Atlanta Journal and Constitution*, September 23, 1990 by S. Bronstein

The value of psychic income to an individual fan is illustrated by the following statement: "I'm a Lakers fan and pay nothing for it. If someone said, 'Give me $100 or the Lakers will fold,' I'd pay it" (Korman, 1989, p. 32).

Psychic income may be the major justification for public sector subsidization of private sports teams and events. It has been suggested that the subsidies sports managers negotiate from public sector officials through the political process can be conceptualized as a measure of the value of psychic income received by a community:

"Team owners deal with us collectively at the city level in selling major league status to cities. We're better off paying it than not having the team" (Korman, 1989, p. 32).

An indication of the extensity of the psychic income emerged from studies undertaken at the Adelaide Grand Prix. Researchers reported (Burns & Mules, 1986): "The most interesting result from the studies on traffic congestion, travel time lost, noise and property damage was the number of people who, while being affected by these problems, were nevertheless strongly in favour of the Grand Prix" (p. 26). The researchers went on to speculate about what could have generated the psychic income:

> For many, of course, there was the general air of excitement and the feeling that South Australians were participating in a world event. Perhaps for a while we secured for ourselves some of the glamour often associated with other Grand Prix venues such as Monza, Monaco and Brand's Hatch. Certainly it seems to be the case that people felt good about themselves. This feeling was increased with the winning of the award for the '1985' Grand Prix. (Burns & Mules, 1986, p. 27)

SUMMARY

It has been noted (Corliss, 1992) that "no city would erect a skyscraper and then hand it over gratis to IBM or AT&T" (p. 51). However, dozens of cities have erected stadiums and arenas, and leased them gratis or at very nominal rates to professional sport franchises. Trends over the past two decades suggest this is unlikely to change.

The apparent government largesse results from the imbalance of supply and demand of major sports events and teams. This gives managers and owners of these organizations substantial leverage for extracting public subsidy for their enterprises from existing or potential host communities. The external pressure exerted by franchises on a city frequently is reinforced by pressure from political elites within a city to attract or retain a franchise. Their access to financial, knowledge, and legal resources creates momentum that opponents are unable to stem. It has been estimated that the annual subsidy from cities and states to major league sports franchises alone is approximately $500 million. In recent years, increased elite seating has emerged as a major new revenue source, and franchises are likely to continue to pressure existing host communities to develop new facilities for them, which will enable owners to capture more of this revenue.

There are segments in a community who will vigorously oppose any public subsidy of private sports ventures because: (a) they have no interest in sports; (b) they object in principle to scarce government funds being used to provide entertainment for a segment of the community who are likely to be reasonably affluent, and that can afford the admission prices when there are other unmet pressing community needs; or (c) they resent government's directly subsidizing the very wealthy individuals who own professional franchises and who traditionally have made very substantial capital profits from these investments.

Public officials have to evaluate the returns they project will be received from hosting a sports event or team, and if they perceive the benefits exceed the cost investment, they then have to convince voters in their community that the investment is meritorious. There are five potential benefits that may accrue: first, increased community visibility will stem from media associating the community's name with the event or team; second, increased exposure offers opportunities for enhancing a city's image by more sharply defining or changing it. Third, the visibility and image benefits emanating from the sports team or event may stimulate other development. This development may be (a) complementary, which means it results from a demand for services that is directly created by the sports enterprise; (b) proximate, which means the enterprise attracts other businesses to the area; or (c) general, which refers to the belief that the sports enterprise is a sufficient magnet to attract business that is neither complementary nor proximate. Fourth, sports occupy a salient place in North American culture. They are often a source of civic pride and serve as a focal point that residents use to identify with the community. Residents identify with "their" team or event and receive psychic income from its presence, even though they may actively support it through the turnstiles.

Fifth and finally, community officials can justify a public subsidy in economic terms, by assessing the likely value of economic benefits that accrue to the community from money spent in it by visitors or investors who are attracted by the event or teams. In public debates, it is usually this economic justification that is given most prominence. For this reason, and because it is controversial, often misinterpreted, and frequently misapplied, the next chapter is devoted to a detailed discussion of economic analyses. However, for many residents, the first four justifications discussed in this chapter may appear to be more legitimate, substantive, and meaningful than are recommendations emerging from an economic analysis.

Questions for Study and Discussion

1. Explain, using examples, why the authors contend that justifying public subsidy for professional sport teams strictly on the basis of economic impact is so tenuous.

2. Discuss the two primary sources of momentum that compel cities to invest substantial public funds in attracting and/or maintaining professional sport teams. Are cities receiving fair return on their investment?

3. Discuss the circumstances under which the construction of a new stadium would *not* stimulate proximate or complementary development benefits.

REFERENCES

Baade, R. A. (1987). Is there an economic rationale for subsidizing sports stadiums? *Heartland Policy Study No. 13*. Chicago: The Heartland Institute.

Baade, R. A. & Dye, R. F. (1988). An analysis of the economic rationale for public subsidization of sports stadiums. *The Annals of Regional Science, 22*(2), 37-47.

Baker, D. P. (1992, August 22). Cooke would get good deal after he pays for stadium. *The Washington Post*, pp. C1, C3.

Bronstein, S. (1990, September 23). World recognition gives Atlantans a new sense of pride in their city. *The Atlanta Journal and Constitution*, p. 12.

Burns, J. A. & Mules, T. J. (1986). A framework for the analysis of major special events. In J. A. Burns, J. H. Hatch and T. J. Mules (editors). *The Adelaide Grand Prix*, pp. 5-36. Adelaide: The Centre for South Australian Economic Studies.

Corliss, R. (1992, August 24). Build it and they will might come. *Time*, pp. 50-52.

Euchner, C. C. (1993.) *Playing the field: Why sports teams move and cities fight to keep them*, Baltimore: The Johns Hopkins University Press.

Fimrite, R. (1992, June 1). Oh give me a home....... *Sports Illustrated* , pp. 50-52.

Foley, P. (1991). The impact of the World Student Games on Sheffield. *Environment and Planning C: Government and Policy 9*, 65-78.

Fulton, W. (1988, March). Politicians who chase after sports franchises may get less than they pay for. *Governing*, pp. 34-40.

Games people shouldn't play. (1991, April 6). *The Economist*, p. 58.

Ingham, A. G., Howell, J. & Schilperoort, T. S. (1987). Profession of sports and community: A review and exegesis. *Exercise and Sport Sciences Reviews, 15*, 455.

Johnson, A. T. (1989). *Local government and minor league baseball: Survey of issues and trends,* (Sports Consortium Special Report #1). Washington DC: International City Management Association.

Johnson, A. T. (1991). Local government, minor league baseball, and economic development strategies. *Economic Development Quarterly, 5* (4), pp. 313-324.

Johnson, A. T. (1993). *Minor league baseball and local economic development*. Urbana, IL: University of Illinois Press.

Korman, R. (1989, February 20). A matter of pride. *Sports Inc.* , pp. 32-37.

Lipsky, R. (1979). Political implications of sports team symbolism. *Politics Soc., 9*, 61-88.

Lipsky, R. (1981) *How we play the game: Why sports dominate American life*. Boston: Beacon.

Lowenstein, R. (1985, November 15). Miami Dolphins owner builds a stadium with private financing and fancy seating. *Wall Street Journal*, Section 2, p. 33.

Newman, P. G. (1989). The Impact of the America's Cup on Freemantle—an insider's view. In G. S. Syme, B. J. Shaw, D. M Fenton & W. S. Mueller (Eds). *The planning and evaluation of hallmark events* (pp. 46-58). Aldershot, England: Avebury.

Quirk, J. P. (1987). The Quirk Study: A close look at the two proposals. *St. Louis Dispatch*. January 18, Special Report p. 8.

Quirk, J. P. & Fort, R. D. (1992). *Pay dirt: The business of professional team sports.* Princeton, NJ: Princeton University Press.

Richmond, P. (1993). *Ballpark: Camden Yards and the building of an American dream.* New York: Simon and Schuster.

Ritchie, B. J. R. (1989, June 3). *Mega sporting events and their role in the development and promotion of international tourism destinations.* Keynote address to the 4th annual conference of the North American Society for Sports Management.

Roughton, B. (1990, September 23). Quebec, Montreal still owe $450 million in 1976 debt. *The Atlanta Journal and Constitution*, p. R20.

Schaffer, W. A. & Davidson, L. S. (1984). *Economic impact of the Falcons on Atlanta: 1984.* Atlanta, GA: Georgia Institute of Technology.

Suddenly everyone wants to build a superdome. (December 5. 1983, December 5) *Business Week* , pp. 110, 112.

Van der Lee, P. & Williams, J. (1986). The Grand Prix and tourism. In J.P.A. Burns, J.H. Hatch and T.J. Mules (Eds). *The Adelaide Grand Prix* (pp. 39-57). Adelaide: The Centre for South Australian Economic Studies.

CHAPTER 3

ECONOMIC IMPACT ANALYSIS

The primary argument for the substantial public subsidization that was identified in the previous chapter invariably focuses on a sport project's ability to generate economic benefits to a community that exceed the community's cost of investment in it. For example, when city managers were asked to identify the benefits that their communities derived from minor league professional baseball, 85% cited economic impact while other benefits were much less frequently cited (Johnson, 1989). Thus, Baade and Dye (1990) in the context of stadiums note, "In attempting to elicit taxpayer support, stadium proponents have emphasized the indirect economic benefit that stadiums create. In fact, much of the current debate on stadium economics is focused on the scope of indirect economic benefits" (p. 5). The magnitude of these indirect benefits is invariably measured by an economic impact analysis.

The scarcity of tax dollars has led to growing public scrutiny of their allocation, and in this environment there is likely to be increased use of economic impact analyses. Hence, this chapter is devoted to explaining the principles upon which the legitimacy and validity of economic impact studies depend. Particular attention is given to addressing the theoretical underpinnings of multipliers and their strengths, weaknesses, and limitations, because a review by the authors of a large number of economic impact analyses of sports facilities and events indicated that the multiplier was widely misunderstood and misapplied. A review of common mistakes and deliberate distortions that abuse the integrity of economic impact analysis is presented.

THE RATIONALE FOR ECONOMIC IMPACT ANALYSIS

Sports teams and events are business investments both for the individual entrepreneur or athletic department that organizes and promotes them and for the communities that subsidize and host them. Communities may invest public tax dollars into facilities or events for professional and college sporting entities for a variety of reasons, but economic benefits are likely to rank high among them. Civic leaders anticipate that sport events will attract visitors from outside the community whose expenditures represent an infusion of new wealth into the community. City officials are eager to promote economic development as a means of generating local tax revenues and providing jobs, because these issues are of prime interest to their constituents. A

ECONOMIC IMPACT ANALYSIS

Learning Objectives

After completing this chapter, the readers should be able to:

1. explain the concept of economic impact analysis and the principles which underlie its application.
2. explain the three interdependent elements which constitute total economic impact: direct, indirect, and induced impacts.
3. articulate pertinent economic impact analysis nomenclature including such terms as multiplier, leakage, and opportunity costs.
4. describe the most common sources of error in the conduct and interpretation of economic impact analysis.

sports stadium or franchise is a high-profile project that gives widespread visibility to their efforts, and thus they invariably commission a study to emphasize economic gains that can be tied to the project. While the entrepreneur or athletic department has a directly measurable bottom line that evaluates their economic performance, a community needs to assess benefits in a broader context.

Figure 3-1 illustrates the conceptual thinking that underlies the investment of public funds in sporting events and facilities for economic purposes. *Residents* of a community "give" funds to their city council in the form of taxes. The *city council* uses a proportion of these funds to subsidize production of an event or development of a facility. The *facility* or *event* attracts out-of-town *visitors*, who *spend money in the local community* both inside and outside the facility they visit. This "new money" from outside the community creates *income* and *jobs* in the community for *residents*. This completes the cycle: Community residents are responsible for creating the funds, and they receive a return on their investment in the form of new jobs and more household income.

Figure 3-1
Conceptualization of the Economic Investment and Returns Made by Residents in Communities that Subsidize Sports Events or Facilities

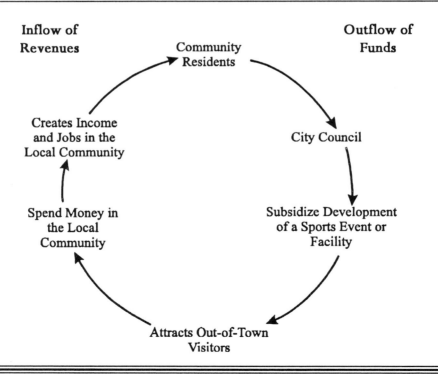

The purpose of economic impact analysis is to measure the broader economic benefits that accrue to a community. Sometimes the cycle shown in Figure 3-1 is perceived to start and end with the city council. This leads to a narrow definition of economic impact that includes only the taxes and revenues collected by local government from the event or facility. Such a narrow definition suggests the council should receive a satisfactory return on its investment from lease fees, admission revenues, increased sales tax revenues, or whatever. However, this approach is conceptually flawed because the money invested does not belong to the council, rather it belongs to the city's residents. Although it is efficient for the residents' investment to be funnelled through the council, it is the return which residents receive that is important, rather than only that proportion of the total return that filters back to the council. Thus, in the context of this chapter, concern is with how much residents receive in return for their investment, and economic impact is defined as the net economic change in a host economy that results from spending attributed to a sports event or facility.

THE MISCHIEVOUS APPLICATION OF ECONOMIC IMPACT ANALYSIS

"It's not what we *don't know* that hurts. It's what we *know* that just ain't true." Mark Twain's turn-of-the-century insight is remarkably appropriate today to an analysis of the techniques and tools employed by government officials in their policy-making roles. In this realm, the hurt can be measured in millions of tax dollars misspent on projects that in their planning stages appear beneficial. Much of the potential for real harm stems from what has become a common element in the evaluation of public works projects and economic development strategies: the Economic Impact Study (Hunter, 1988, p. 1).

The political reality of economic impact analyses is that they are usually undertaken to justify a position that either a sports organization or community-elected officials have adopted or are proposing. Their point is not to find the truth, but rather to legitimize something the sponsoring group wants to prove. The studies are seldom more than position papers for proponents or opponents of a particular project. Ostensibly, the people hired to conduct the studies appear to be both expert and neutral. However, "they are in truth the exact equivalent of an expert witness in a lawsuit who comes to testify in support of the side that is paying the expert's bill. An expert whose testimony harms his employer's case doesn't get much repeat business" (Curtis, 1993, p. 6). The same commentator suggests, "The fees for the study are like a religious tithe paid to a priest to come bless some endeavor" (p. 7).

Community officials invariably commission economic impact analyses in response to increasing pressures holding them accountable for demonstrating the efficacy of tax dollar allocations. They want to assure the public that government is making a "profit" in return for any subsidization it is giving to a private sports business and to convince taxpayers of the wisdom of the subsidy. Similarly, when such studies are commissioned by sport organizations, it is usually to demonstrate to public officials and taxpayers that the organizations are a substantive financial asset to the community and worthy of any public investment they receive or are requesting.

Too often, the motives of those commissioning an economic impact analysis appear to lead to adoption of procedures and underlying assumptions that bias the resultant analysis so that the numbers support their advocacy position. Consider the contrasting values placed on the San Francisco Giants in 1992 when it seemed probable they would leave Candlestick Park for a new stadium in San Jose. In San Francisco, which anticipated losing the franchise if voters in San Jose agreed to fund the stadium, the city's budget director reported she could only document a $3.1 million net gain to the city from the Giants. She placed this in the context of the city's gross economic product of $30 billion and pointed out this was 10,000 times as large, to emphasize how insignificant were the economic benefits. A professor of economics at nearby Stanford University was quoted as saying, " 'Opening a branch of Macy's has a greater economic impact' " (cited in Corliss, 1992, p. 52). In contrast, the Mayor of San Jose, who was trying to persuade the city's residents to approve a referendum allocating $265 million of public funds to a new stadium in which the Giants would play, announced that the same franchise would deliver to San Jose " 'somewhere between $50 million and $150 million a year in economic benefits' " (cited in Fimrite, 1992:52).

Baade and Dye (1990) cite a similar example of how the motives of those commissioning studies frequently lead to the generation of economic impact numbers that support their position:

A University of Pennsylvania researcher estimated that Philadelphia's professional sports teams contributed more than $500 million to the city's economy in 1983. In a contrasting study, a Baltimore area researcher estimated the overall economic impact the NFL Colts had on the Baltimore area as merely $200,000. Sharply different assumptions can compel sharply different results. The leverage on alternative assumptions is particularly troublesome where the sponsor of the research has an identifiable interest or point of view. The Philadelphia study was funded by a consortium of the city's professional teams, while the Baltimore study was conducted just after the Colts had bolted for the greener pastures of Indianapolis. (p. 6)

In making their case, supporters of minor league teams frequently refer to economic impact studies relating to major league teams in making their case. Such comparisons are fallacious:

A major league team is capable of attracting millions of fans to a stadium in one season, whereas even a successful minor league team rarely draws more than a few hundred thousand fans. A major league team attracts many fans from beyond its local jurisdiction, especially for postseason play, but this is not the case with a minor league team. Employee salaries of a major league team are significantly higher than those of a minor league team, most of whose employees are seasonal. A major league team brings national recognition to a city, but it is arguable that the average minor league teams brings even regional recognition to its host community. (Johnson, 1993, p. 7)

To convince voters of the worthiness of sports subsidies, city officials and private sector beneficiaries of the subsidies commission studies that invariably show that the subsidy will inject many millions of dollars a year into the local economy. In the context of stadiums, for example, it has been observed that "city leaders from Miami to San Francisco have summoned sound economic management as their star witness in defending plans to subsidize the renovation or construction of stadiums." The same economist goes on to ask, "Can this witness stand up to a stiff cross-examination?" (Baade, 1987, p. 1).

Unfortunately, the response to this question is frequently "no." Many of the studies are neither impartial nor objective. Rather they are mischievously concocted and used as advocacy documents that are intended to provide a public subsidy for a sports project with a convincing aura of economic legitimacy. The reason it is possible to have such widely divergent numbers as those given in the above examples is that economic impact analysis rests on many assumptions, the most important of which are discussed in this chapter. An executive of a major consultancy that conducts economic impact studies observed that if " 'you pick five consultants, you'll get five different numbers.' " Similarly, a partner in a major accounting firm who does these studies admitted, " 'It's a very inexact science' " (cited in Dunnavant 1989, pp. 31,32). Changes in the assumptions used can lead to dramatically different impacts being identified, and economic impact analysis should be best viewed as an "educated guess." However, advocates do not present findings as being tenuous: "This numerical guesswork is presented to the public—by local politicians and sports boosters—as indisputable proof that a city or state government should subsidize a sports team or a new stadium" (Fulton, 1988, p. 39). Consultants are hired in large measure to tell their clients what they want to hear, "And what they want to hear is that their event or team or whatever is going to generate a lot of money" (Dunnavant, 1989, p. 33).

The findings of those who have independently evaluated the economic impact of large public subsidies by local communities for sports teams, free from the pressures of a commissioning sponsor, are not encouraging. Lipsitz (1984) traced the evolution of public funding for three stadiums in Houston, Los Angeles, and St. Louis. He noted that voters in each city approved bonds for the projects in anticipation of widely distributed economic benefits, but found that the benefits never materialized. Lipsitz (1984) concluded, "Construction of new sports facilities does not significantly enrich cities...Rather, they typify the kinds of wasteful expenditures our society makes" (p. 14).

Baade and Dye (1990) used regression analysis to assess the impact of stadiums and professional baseball or football on the level of personal income for each of nine metropolitan areas: Cincinnati, Denver, Detroit, Kansas City, New Orleans, Pittsburgh, San Diego, Seattle, and Tampa Bay. Contrary to the claims of city officials, they found that sports and stadiums frequently had no significant impact on a city's economy. Indeed, they reported that in some of the cities with new or renovated stadiums there was a negative impact on local development relative to the region. They suggested this finding was consistent with the possibility that stadium subsidies might bias local development towards low-wage jobs. Another finding was that base-ball franchises had a more positive impact on area income than did football franchises. This was attributed to a typical home baseball schedule's being 8 to 10 times as expansive as that for football.

This chapter will identify 10 common sources of error in economic analysis that contribute to explaining the discrepancy between the claims of advocates and the findings of independent research. Several of these error sources stem from misinformed or mischievous use of the "multiplier effect" of government spending on the private sector, which is the principal economic theory embraced by economic impact studies. The concept of the multiplier was first noted during the latter half of the 19th century when it was recognized that changes in level of activity in one industry could bring about changes in level of activity in other industries and, therefore, create a *multiple* effect throughout the economy (Fletcher & Snee, 1989). Smith (1989) observes:

> Regrettably, extravagant claims for economic growth from visitor spending have been "supported" by pseudo-economic analyses based on the concept of economic multipliers. While the concept of an economic multiplier is quite legitimate and useful, it can be easily mishandled--either deliberately, or accidentally--because of the technical complexities associated with calculating multipliers and the need for large amounts of precise data. (p. 271)

Archer (1982), who is the leading authority on multipliers applied to visitor expenditures, attributes these abuses to three factors:

(1) A failure to explain adequately to noneconomists the theoretical basis and practical nature of multiplier analysis.

(2) The use of different and conflicting concepts of the multiplier itself.

(3) Researchers and practitioners who misuse the methodology in order to advocate or support a particular project.

Frequently, studies apply a multiplier to direct spending estimates without explanation as to how it was derived or how appropriate it is to that particular community; thus, the unwary reader is "left with the feeling that there is some magical process through which one dollar of spending eventually turns into two and perhaps even three" (Davidson & Schaffer, 1980, p. 16). The great danger in the multiplier and the way it is presented in research reports aimed at the policy maker is that its basic concept and application are deceptively simple. However, the data and analyses needed to measure a multiplier accurately are fairly complex. Because faulty calculation, presentation, or interpretation of multipliers will lead to nonsensical results with disastrous implications for policy making, this chapter is devoted first to explaining the multiplier concept and subsequently to describing some common abuses of it.

PRINCIPLES OF THE MULTIPLIER CONCEPT

If a group of spectators from another area come to see a sports event and spend $10,000 in a community, or if this money is spent by a visiting team coming to a city, then this initial direct expenditure stimulates economic activity and creates additional business turnover, employment, household income, and government revenue in the host community. The impact of this injection of outside money can be likened to the ripples set up in a pool if more water is poured into the system (Archer, 1973). The pool represents the economy, and the additional water symbolizes extra spending by the outside visitors. The ripples show the spread of money through the economy. This concept of a ripple effect in an economy is termed a multiplier by economists.

The host sports organization, restauranteurs, hoteliers, retailers, and others who receive the initial $10,000 are likely to spend it in five different ways (Figure 3-2):

1. With other private sector businesses in the same jurisdiction (local interindustry purchases) to restock their inventories to provide for future sales, to maintain their buildings, fittings and equipment, to pay insurance premiums, and for a myriad of other purposes;

2. With employees who reside within the jurisdiction of interest in the form of salaries and wages, which constitute personal income to them (direct household income);

3. With local governments as sales taxes, property taxes, and license fees (local government revenue);

4. With nonlocal governments as sales taxes or taxes on profits;

5. With employees, shareholders, businesses, organizations and others who reside outside the local jurisdiction (nonlocal leakages).

The last two categories of spending illustrate that the host city is part of a larger national economy, and some money leaks out of the city's economic system to pay taxes to, or buy goods and services from, entities outside the city. Only those dollars remaining within the host community after leakage has taken place constitute the net economic gain. The amount of the initial $10,000 expenditure that remains in the jurisdiction from local interindustry purchases, direct household income, or local government revenue is subsequently spent in one of the five ways listed above and thereby sets in motion a further chain of economic activity.

The process is shown diagrammatically in Figure 3-2 (Liu & Var, 1982). It assumes that the group of spectators or visiting team spent their $10,000 at four different types of establishments in a city. The figure shows the five different ways in which each of these establishments will disburse the money it receives. The hotel is used to illustrate the process, but the pattern would be replicated for each establishment. The three local depositories of funds receiving money in Round 1 and in successive rounds with the money that did not leak out of the community, will continue to spend this money in the same five ways. The spectators' initial $10,000 expenditure is likely to go through numerous rounds as it seeps through the economy, with portions of it leaking out each round until it declines to a negligible amount. These subsequent rounds of economic activity are termed *indirect* impacts.

Since local government revenue from taxes and fees is likely to be immediately expended back into the local economy for services it provides, this money is considered to remain a source of local economic stimulus. However, in the case of nonlocal government and other nonlocal leakages (Figure 3-2), the direct revenue leaks out of

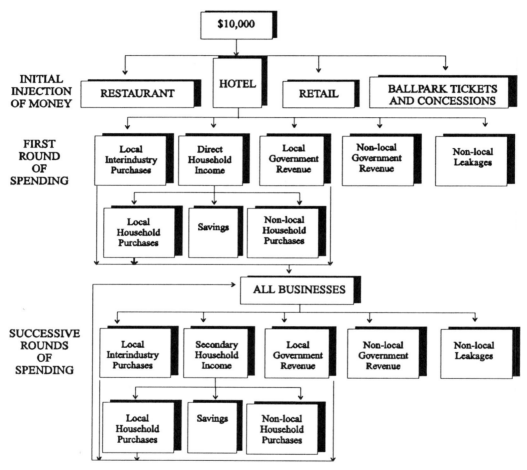

Figure 3-2
Illustration of the Multiplier Effect

Note: Adapted from Differential Multipliers for the Accommodation Sector. *Tourism Management* (p. 183) by Juanita Liu and Turgut Var, September, 1982.

the city and, thus, does not contribute any stimulus to the jurisdiction's economy. Also, some of the direct household income (i.e., salaries and wages) received by local residents may not be spent in the local economy. Rather, some of it may be saved, in which case it contributes nothing further to local economic stimulus, or it can be spent outside the local jurisdiction (Figure 3-2). As far as the community is concerned, saving the personal income received is similar to spending it outside the community. The effect is the same, in that the economic stimulus potential is lost. Savings only

become "useful" when they are used by financial intermediaries to fund local investment.

The proportion of household income (employees' wages and salaries) that is spent locally on goods and services is termed an *induced* impact, which is defined as the increase in economic activity generated by local consumption due to increases in wages and salaries. The *indirect* and *induced* effects together are frequently called secondary impacts. In summary, there are three elements that contribute to the total impact of a given initial injection of expenditures from out-of-town visitors:

Direct Impact: The first-round effect of visitor spending; that is, how much the restauranteurs, hoteliers, and others who received the initial $10,000 spend on goods in the local economy and pay employees who live in the jurisdiction.

Indirect Impact: The ripple effect of additional rounds of recirculating the initial spectators' dollars.

Induced Impact: Further ripple effects caused by employees of impacted businesses spending some of their salaries and wages in other businesses in the city.

Types of Multipliers

Three different types of multipliers are commonly used: sales, income, and employment multipliers:

A *sales or transactions multiplier* measures the direct, indirect and induced effect of an extra unit of visitor spending on economic activity within a host community. It relates tourism expenditure to the increase in business turnover that it creates and may be of some interest to officials in governmental entities as a means of approximating sales revenues that may accrue.

An *income multiplier* measures the direct, indirect, and induced effect of an extra unit of visitor spending on the changes that result in level of household incomes in the host community. It is operationalized as *the ratio of change in income to the initial autonomous change in expenditure that brings it about.* It most clearly demonstrates the economic impact on residents of the host community.

An *employment multiplier* measures the direct, indirect and induced effect of an extra unit of visitor spending on employment in the host community. It shows how many full-time *equivalent* job opportunities are supported in the community as a result of the visitor expenditure. This is the least reliable of the three multipliers (Fletcher & Snee, 1989) because it assumes that all existing employees are fully utilized; thus, an increase in external visitor spending will inevitably lead to an increase in level of employment. Clearly, this is not always the case because additional demand may be met by greater utilization of the existing labor force. This is particularly probable in the case of "one-time" sports events. They are unlikely to generate lasting employment effects because of their short-term nature. The hiring of extra staff is unlikely because the extra business only lasts for a few days. Rather, existing staff are likely to be released from other duties to accommodate this temporary peak demand or be requested to work overtime. At best, only some very short-term additional

assistance may be hired. Thus, the "full-time equivalent" jobs reported by the multiplier do not come to fruition, and the use of job creation as a measure of economic benefit in the case of one-time, rather than ongoing, sports events is suspect.

These types of employment adjustments were reported by Arnold (1986) and Bishop and Hatch (1986) after their interviews with managers in transportation and restaurant businesses immediately after the Adelaide Grand Prix. They found that companies in both types of businesses increased their labor requirements by increasing the hours of existing employees, although some restaurant establishments indicated they hired "casuals" to supplement this action. Arnold (1986) concluded, "There were virtually no new permanent jobs in the transport area generated as a result of the Grand Prix. In fact several companies had organized the increased work load in such a way that they did not pay overtime although this was not possible for all the extra work" (p. 81).

The sales, income and employment multipliers are complementary, but are not additive. For example, some studies the authors reviewed erroneously suggested that the employment effects were additional to the income effects. Hagan and Patterson (1989) commented appropriately on this in their economic analysis of the First Australian Masters Games in Tasmania:

> Other studies of major sporting events have addressed both their income and employment effects. It should be understood that the employment generated is not an additional benefit to the income effects. Rather, employment is a manifestation of income generation, the value of which is already expressed in income terms...The employment effects of the Masters Games were mostly marginal and short-lived and resulted in increased productivity rather than growth in State employment. (p. 43)

Table 3-1 reports the multiplier coefficients derived for an economic impact study undertaken by one of the authors on an event in San Antonio, Texas. The table illustrates two points that are crucial to properly interpreting and communicating the impact of a multiplier. First, the coefficients are different for each category of expenditure that is listed. Thus, in the city of San Antonio, a $1 expenditure by visitors on gasoline (private auto) yielded substantially less household income than a similar $1 expenditure in a night club (40 cents compared to 75 cents).

The second notable point illustrated in Table 3-1 is that the values of *sales* coefficients are substantially higher than those of *household income* coefficients. For example, the table indicates that, on average, each $1 expenditure by visitors on accommodations will generate 56 cents in income for residents of the city, but business activity in the city should rise by about $2 dollars. Because both of these multipliers are measured in dollars they are often confused. If it is not clearly defined which multiplier is being discussed, then there is a danger that inaccurate, spurious inferences will be drawn from the data.

In an economic impact analysis, sales multipliers are not useful. The point of interest is the impact of those sales on household income and employment. Residents are interested in knowing how much extra income they will receive from the injection of funds from visitors. They have no interest in value of sales per se because it has no

Table 3-1
A Comparison of the Sales and Household Income
Multipliers for an Event in San Antonio

CATEGORY	SALES MULTIPLIER				HOUSEHOLD INCOME MULTIPLIER			
	Direct	Indirect	Induced	Total	Direct	Indirect	Induced	Total
Food and Beverage	1	0.32	0.47	1.79	0.29	0.08	0.13	0.50
Admission Fees	1	0.25	0.46	1.71	0.36	0.07	0.13	0.55
Night clubs, Lounges, Bars	1	0.29	1.31	2.42	0.36	0.08	0.32	0.75
Retail Shopping	1	0.23	0.56	1.79	0.46	0.05	0.16	0.68
Lodging and Accommodatations	1	0.43	0.57	2.00	0.29	0.11	0.16	0.56
Private Auto	1	0.23	0.20	1.42	0.27	0.07	0.06	0.40
Commercial Transportation	1	0.22	0.29	1.51	0.52	0.05	0.08	0.65
Other Expenses	1	0.23	0.56	1.79	0.46	0.05	0.16	0.68

impact on their standard of living. Further, high sales multipliers may give a false impression of the true impacts of visitor spending because the highest income and employment effects are not necessarily generated from the highest increases in sales. The authors of a respected community guide to tourism development commissioned and endorsed by the U.S. Travel and Tourism Administration (University of Missouri 1986) observe:

> It is not uncommon to find, in the literature on tourism, statements to the effect that initial expenditures by tourists are multiplied many times over as a result of subsequent rounds of spending. Such statements may be misleading. We are concerned not with the volume of sales attributed to the tourist expenditure, but with the portion of that expenditure which ends up as local income. (p. 59)

As Fridgin (1991) correctly observes, it is misleading and valueless to multiply total visitor expenditures by a sales multiplier and refer to the product as the economic impact of that injected money on residents of the host community. Nevertheless, because sales multipliers are substantially larger than income multipliers, they tend to be attractive political tools for advocates to use in attempting to justify a particular public investment.

Calculating the Multiplier Coefficient

A household income multiplier is basically a coefficient that expresses the amount of income generated in a host community by an additional unit of visitor spending (Archer 1982). In other words, if visitors to the community spend $10,000 at a sports event and this generates $6,000 of income in that area, the income multiplier is 0.6. However, the coefficient of impact can be expressed in two different ways, and it is essential to understand the difference between them because available input-output analysis computer software produces both coefficient measures. Consider the following data (Archer, 1982):

External visitor expenditure injected $100

Direct income created $25

Secondary income created $20

Total income created $45

A coefficient derived by using the "incremental" (Vaughan, 1984) or "ratio" (Archer, 1982, 1984) approach expresses the income multiplier as

$$\frac{Direct + Indirect + Induced\ Income}{Direct\ Income}$$

In the above example this would be 45/25, giving a multiplier coefficient of 1.8.

In contrast, a "true," "normal," (Archer, 1982) "proportional" or "unorthodox" (Vaughan, 1984) approach expresses the income multiplier as:

$$\frac{Direct + Indirect + Induced\ Income}{Visitor\ Injection\ of\ Expenditure}$$

Using the above data, this would be 45/100 giving a multiplier coefficient of 0.45.

Occasionally, hybrids of these versions are used, frequently without comment or justification. For example, in a study charged with estimating the impact of a new baseball stadium in Tempe, Arizona, consultants used what they described as a "gross" multiplier, which was defined as:

$$\frac{Visitor\ Injection\ of\ Expenditure + Direct + Indirect + Induced\ Income}{Visitor\ Injection\ of\ Expenditure}$$

Using the numbers from the above example, would give a multiplier coefficient of 1.45. It is important to ascertain the formula used to derive coefficients. By not understanding how multipliers are derived or by using the wrong multiplier, decision makers could reach false conclusions.

A consensus has emerged in the multiplier literature that the normal approach should be used since it gives most guidance to policy makers (Vaughan, 1984). The incremental approach simply indicates that if $1 of direct income is created, a proportion of other income will be created in other parts of the economy. It does not give a true indication of impact because it does not include information on size of the initial leakage. The incremental multiplier puts the emphasis on the least important aspects of the impact, which are the indirect and induced effects. As Table 3-1 illustrates, in local or regional economies the direct effect is likely to substantially outweigh the other effects. Indeed, in rural economies where there is little industrial support, the indirect and induced elements of the multiplier are frequently insignificant in comparison with the direct element. "In fact, through purchases and income, the [direct effects] largely define the extent of the indirect and induced effects. Thus it is the direct effects which are of prime importance if the policy maker is to understand the nature of economic benefits" (Vaughan, 1984, p. 31).

The incremental approach does not yield a visitor-spending multiplier. Rather, it is only a measure of internal linkage within an economy. To multiply it by visitor expenditure is meaningless. Archer (1982) states that these types of incremental multipliers are misleading and should not be used. He advocates (1984) "general abandonment of the 'ratio' multiplier approach and consequent removal of the confusion which it creates. It is difficult to envisage how or why such an inappropriate approach has gained such wide usage. Unlike the [normal] multiplier, it has no basis in economic theory and it provides misleading policy prescription" (p. 518). Only "normal" or "true" multipliers should be used because they indicate income created by a given level of expenditure and also incorporate the incremental results.

Deriving Multipliers

Multipliers are derived from input-output tables that disaggregate an economy into industries and examine the flows of goods and services among them. In essence an input-output model is an elaborate accounting system that keeps track of the transactions and flows of new money throughout an economy (Fridgin, 1991). The process allows a separate multiplier to be applied for each of the major industry groups or sectors affected by the initial direct expenditure (Table 3-1).

> The multiplier for a particular sector traces all the induced impacts required from other sectors for a given change in output by the sector in question. These "backward linkages" allow the identification of the impacts of that sector on other sectors in the economy. (Roberts & McLeod, 1989, p. 244).

The availability of powerful personal computers has expedited greater use of input-output tables. There are a host of input-output models from which analysts can select. These models are conceptualized differently and constructed using different assumptions and statistical procedures. Hence, it is likely they would yield different measures of economic impact, even if the same expenditure data were entered into the models (Richardson, 1985). The choice among the menu of models depends on the trade-off between accuracy and cost, and this trade-off has led to two models being most widely used. The USDA Forest Service IMPLAN (IMpact Analysis for PLANning) system develops input-output models for all states and counties in the United States. It has been widely adopted as the regional impact analysis program-of-choice. An alternative is RIMS (Regional Input-Output Modeling System) developed by the U.S. Department of Commerce, Bureau of Economic Analysis (BEA), which also offers input-output tables down to the county level (Turco & Kelsey, 1992).

Defining the Impacted Community

The magnitude of a multiplier depends on the structure of the host community; that is, on the degree to which businesses at which visitors spend their money proceed to trade with other businesses within the host economy. It is generally assumed that a smaller community tends not to have the sectoral interdependencies that facilitate retention of monies spent during the first round of expenditures. Hence, much of the expenditure would be respent outside the local region leading to a low economic multiplier. Conventional wisdom posits that the larger the defined area's economic base, the smaller the leakage that is likely to occur and the larger the value added from the original expenditures. This principle is illustrated in Table 3-2, which records income multipliers associated with visitor expenditures that have been reported in the literature for countries, counties and cities (Fletcher & Snee, 1989). As the geographic entity gets smaller, the multiplier also tends to decrease.

The trade-off in defining the geographic area within which economic impact is to be assessed has been articulated by Burns and Mules (1989):

The smaller the area of focus the greater the number of those attending that would be classified as "visitors", that is, those attending from outside the region, and the greater would be the injection of new funds into the area's economy. Although the greater would be the leakage from any direct expenditures generated. (p. 173)

Most professional sports franchises are located in major metropolitan areas. However, it has been suggested that a substantial part of the income received by a sports organization may be spent outside the local community (Euchner 1993):

Most of a team's business and practice operations are conducted outside the city, and the player salaries that the fans pay do not usually end up in the city. Most professional athletes live outside the cities for which they play and even outside the state. (p. 72)

In contrast to this generalization, Schaffer and Davidson (1984) suggested that revenues which franchises receive from out-of-town visitors and other external sources, such as television, may tend to stay in the local area. They reported that 70% of expenditures by the Atlanta Falcons were made locally, stating that, "79 percent of the players and staff of the team live here all year; 39 of 58 players and 46 of 50 staff members live in Atlanta. Most field personnel are local residents, printing is local, the team uses Atlanta banks as well as an Atlanta based airline, and the team is locally owned" (p. 15). Much of the visitors' revenues received by the Falcons is respent inside the local region leading to a relatively high economic multiplier.

There has been a tendency for aspirants in inherently small market areas seeking a new professional franchise to expand the definitions of their traditional market area in order to strengthen their case with existing team owners and with city officials and residents who will be expected to subsidize the franchise. For example, promoters of Charlotte's NFL bid transformed the city of 396,000 into a region of 9.7 million people, despite the Charlotte metropolitan area's having only 1.2 million residents.

| Table 3-2 Income Multipliers Associated with Visitor Expenditures ||
GEOGRAPHICAL AREA	INCOME MULTIPLIER
COUNTRIES	
Turkey	1.98
United Kingdom	1.73
Irish Republic	1.72
Jamaica	1.27
Egypt	1.23
Dominica	1.20
Cyprus	1.14
Bermuda	1.09
Hong Kong	1.02
Mauritius	0.96
Antigua	0.88
Bahamas	0.79
Fiji	0.72
Cayman Islands	0.65
Iceland	0.64
British Virgin Islands	0.58
Gibraltar	0.57
COUNTRIES/REGIONS	
Door County, USA	0.55
Sullivan County, USA	0.44
Gwynedd, North Wales, UK	0.37
East Anglia, UK	0.34
CITIES	
Kendal, Cumbria, UK	0.30
Edinburgh, Lothian, UK	0.28
Brighton & Hove, UK	0.22
Winchester, Hampshire, UK	0.19
Bournemouth, Dorset, UK	0.18

Note: From Tourism Multiplier Effects. In *Tourism Marketing and Management Handbook* (p. 530), editors Stephen F. Witt and Luiz Moutintio, 1991, Hemel Hempstead, England: Prentice Hall International (UK).

Promoters counted everyone within 150 miles of Charlotte as a potential fan in order to attempt to persuade team owners that their market could generate the desired threshold of revenue ("Business Reports," 1992) and to persuade residents that substantial economic impact would be forthcoming. In fact, studies have consistently shown that at least 70% of fans are likely to come from the immediate metropolitan area (e.g., Crompton 1984; Schaffer & Davidson, 1975, 1984).

The geographic area of interest usually will be specified by those commissioning an economic impact analysis and is likely to relate, for example, to city boundaries. Clearly it is crucial that only visitor spending *within the defined area* be included in impact studies and *not total* visitor expenditures, some of which may have occurred outside the area. If more than one governmental entity is involved, for example, city, county and state, in subsidizing a sport organization, it may be necessary to develop separate economic impact analyses commensurate with the geographic boundaries of each entity. In this situation, visitors must be asked to recall or keep track of the place where they made their expenditures. An example of how this type of information may be collected is shown in Figure 3-3. By expanding geographic scope of the impact analysis, more of the linkages between businesses will be accounted for, and the magnitude of the multiplier is likely to increase.

Collecting Expenditure Data

A primary source of revenue for many sport organizations is television fees. For example, nearly one-half of an NFL team's revenue came from television contracts in 1989 (Peterson, 1989). Most of this is likely to be new money to the community and may be the major source of economic impact. It can be identified easily and entered into an input-output model. The other major source of new money comes from out-of-town visitors, participants, and media representatives. Their expenditures in the host community are more difficult to identify.

A prerequisite for accurate economic impact results is that the visitor expenditure data to which multipliers are applied be accurate. These expenditure data can be collected either by directly surveying visitors to the sports event who come from outside the community or by surveying the hoteliers, restauranteurs, retailers etc. who receive the expenditures. The latter approach is least preferred because the data are likely to be less reliable. Businesses will experience difficulty in assessing what proportions of their customers' expenditures were from visitors and from locals, and whether the sports event influenced visitors' decisions to come to the community. Nevertheless, this approach was used in a study of the economic impact of the Los Angeles Olympic Games, which relied upon information from the lodging and restaurant industry in southern California. It has been suggested that for a large, diverse event, such as the Olympics, surveying the recipients of the expenditures is the more efficient way of gathering data (Burgan & Mules, 1992). However, the accuracy of these data is likely to be highly suspect.

The preferred approach is to survey visitors at the sports event. *Visitors* refers not only to spectators but also to participants and officials who come from outside the community. It is beyond the scope of this chapter to discuss sampling methods and the relative merits of alternative data-gathering procedures. Rather, discussion focuses on appropriate questions and question formats for collecting data and estimating population expenditures.

Figure 3-3 shows the standard question format used by one of the authors to collect expenditure data from visitors to sports events. Using the same eight categories of expenditure at all events facilitates comparisons among them. Such comparisons provide a context for assessing whether the economic impact generated by a particular event is relatively low or high. It identifies which sectors of spending contribute relatively low and high amounts to the impact and thus offers guidance as to where future emphasis should be placed to increase economic impact.

It is critical to identify how much of visitors' expenditures was spent within the geographical area of interest. In the context of Figure 3-3, economic impacts on both Galveston and the State of Texas were sought. Hence, respondents were requested to report the amount spent on Galveston Island, Outside of Galveston Island but within Texas, and Outside of Texas.

Three other questions that must be asked in order to determine total visitor expenditures at a sports event are:

• To ascertain whether or not a respondent is a vistor to the defined area: *What is the ZIP code at your home address?*

• To ascertain spending per visitor or per group: *How many people (including yourself) were in your immediate group?*

• To identify "time switchers" and "casuals" who are discussed later in the chapter: *Would you have come to the community either now or in the next 3 months if the sports event had not been in progress? If YES, how many days longer was your stay (if any) than it would have been if the sports event had not been taking place?*

Table 3-3 summarizes the expenditure data reported by respondents to the questionnaire shown in Figure 3-3. Given this information, visitors' expenditures on Galveston Island for each category were calculated by using the following formulas:

(1)   Mean Expenditure Per Group   X   Number of non-Island   = $
       of non-Island respondents   respondents in the sample
       in the sample

(2)   *Total number of non-Island visitors*   X $ =   Total
       Number of non-Island   Average   estimated
       respondents in the   X   group   expenditure by
       sample   size   non-Island
                                                                      visitors

Thus, when applied to food and beverage expenditures on the Island shown in Table 3-3, the following numbers were inserted in the formulas:

Figure 3-3
An Instrument Used to Collect
Visitor Expenditure Data

To better understand the economic impact of this event, we are interested in finding out the approximate amount of money you and other visitors in your immediate group spent, including travel to and from your home. We understand that this is a difficult question, but please do your best because your responses are very important to our efforts.

TYPES OF EXPENDITURE	DURING THE COURSE OF YOUR VISIT, WHAT WAS THE APPROXIMATE AMOUNT YOUR IMMEDIATE GROUP SPENT IN EACH OF THE FOLLOWING CATEGORIES:		
	On Galveston Island	Outside of Galveston Island but Within Texas	Outside of Texas
A. FOOD & BEVERAGE (restaurants, concessions, grocery stores, etc.)	$ _____	$ _____	$ _____
B. ADMISSION FEES (sports event, other shows, etc.)	$ _____	$ _____	$ _____
C. NIGHT CLUBS, LOUNGES & BARS (coverage charges, drinks, etc.)	$ _____	$ _____	$ _____
D. RETAIL SHOPPING (clothing, souvenirs, gifts, etc.)	$ _____	$ _____	$ _____
E. LODGING EXPENSES (motel, hotel, etc.)	$ _____	$ _____	$ _____
F. PRIVATE AUTO EXPENSES (gas, oil, repairs, parking fees, etc.)	$ _____	$ _____	$ _____
G. COMMERCIAL TRANSPORTATION (airlines, bus, train, rental car, etc.)	$ _____	$ _____	$ _____
H. ANY OTHER EXPENSES Please identify _____	$ _____	$ _____	$ _____
	$ _____	$ _____	$ _____

Table 3-3
Expenditure By Visitors To Galveston Island

EXPENDITURE CATEGORY	ON GALVESTON ISLAND			OUTSIDE OF GALVESTON ISLAND, BUT WITHIN TEXAS			OUTSIDE OF TEXAS			TOTAL AMOUNT	PERCENT OF TOTAL
	Per Capita	Per Group	Total	Per Capita	Per Group	Total	Per Capita	Per Group	Total		
Food and Beverages	8.08	39.96	482,744	4.84	23.98	289,695	1.63	8.06	97,370	869,809	32
Admission Fees	3.76	18.58	224,459	0.29	1.46	17,638	0.42	2.10	25,369	267,466	10
Night Clubs, Lounges, Bars	0.77	3.80	45,907	0.25	1.23	14,859	0.60	2.96	35,759	96,525	4
Retail Shopping	10.49	51.90	626,988	0.76	3.78	45,665	1.27	6.29	75,988	748,641	28
Lodging Expenses	0.86	4.26	51,464	3.74	18.52	223,734	1.40	5.42	65,477	340,675	13
Private Auto Expenses	1.19	5.88	71,034	0.75	3.70	44,699	1.66	8.19	98,941	214,674	8
Commercial Transportation	0.34	1.69	20,416	0.11	0.57	6,886	0.55	2.74	33,101	60,403	2
Other Expenses	0.54	2.68	32,376	0.06	0.29	3,503	0.82	4.05	48,927	84,806	3
TOTAL	26.03	128.75	1,555,388	10.80	53.53	646,679	8.05	39.81	480,932	2,682,999	100

(1) 39.96   X   394   = $15,744.24

(2) *59,759.56*   % $15,744.24   = $482,744
  4.9465 X 394

The economic impacts of these expenditures when they were inserted into the IMPLAN model for Galveston County and subjected to the multiplier effect are reported in Table 3-4.

PREVALENT ABUSES IN ECONOMIC IMPACT STUDIES OF SPORTING EVENTS

A review by the authors of an extensive number of studies that have either been commissioned or completed in-house to assess the economic impact of sports events and teams on a community identified 10 sources of error that repeatedly occurred. Three of these have been discussed earlier in the chapter: use of sales rather than income multipliers; misrepresentation of employment multipliers; and use of incremental rather than normal multiplier coefficients. The remaining 7 abuses, which are discussed in this section of the chapter, are (a) inclusion of local spectators, (b) failure to exclude "time-switchers" and "casuals," (c) use of "fudged" multiplier coefficients, (d) claiming total instead of marginal economic benefits, (e) confusion of turnover

Table 3-4 Economic Impact of Visitors to Galveston Island			
Expenditure Category	Sales Impact	Employment Impact	Personal Income
Food and Beverages	1,258,612	31.5	357,485
Admission Fees	394,424	9.4	128,747
Night Clubs, Lounges, Bars	158,873	7.3	49,306
Retail Shopping	1,218,847	36.5	460,700
Lodging Expenses	554,772	16.5	156,533
Private Auto Expenses	157,929	2.1	44,187
Commercial Transportation	45,717	1.1	18,937
Other Expenses	65,013	1.9	24,574
TOTAL	$3,854,187	106.3 JOBS	$1,240,467

and multiplier, (f) omission of opportunity costs, and (g) measurement only of benefits, omitting costs.

The result of each of these abuses (many of which were used in multiple combinations!) is to exaggerate economic impact so that a study reports substantially higher numbers than are justified. Unfortunately, abuses incorporated in an economic impact analysis are contagious because when precedent has been established in one study, other sponsors feel compelled to perpetuate the abuse by incorporating the misleading procedures in their own analyses. If they fail to do so, then the economic impact attributed to their sports event is perceived to be lower than that reported by others, and thus less worthy of public investment. Hence, "taxpayers can sometimes be swayed by an economic argument that just doesn't exist" (Fulton, 1988, p. 39). Smith (1989) reports:

> The inevitable result of the misuse of economic impact methodology has been the growth of a backlash against the idea that tourism has any role to play in local economic development. Although this cynicism is rarely published in industry journals, it is expressed frequently in private conversations and sometimes even public addresses by officials. (p. 271)

Typical of this backlash are the comments made by Hunter (1988): "Economic impact studies based on the multiplier are quite clearly an improper tool for legislative decision-making." He argues that multipliers overstate the economic benefits of private businesses like sports stadiums, and the use of economic impact studies encourages government to invest taxpayers' money unwisely. The authors disagree with Hunter's unequivocal condemnation of the technique. They believe that despite its weaknesses and limitations, economic impact analysis is a powerful and valuable tool if it is implemented knowledgeably and with integrity. The only effective antidote to the backlash that Smith describes, and Hunter advocates, is to reject misleading and mischievous applications, some more of which are described in the following pages.

Inclusion of Local Spectators

Economic impact attributable to a sports event relates only to new money injected into an economy by visitors, media, external government entities, or banks and investors from outside the community. Only spectators who reside outside the jurisdiction and whose primary motivation for visiting is to attend the sports event, or who stay longer and spend more because of it, should be included. Gifts by host community businesses or individuals to out-of-town counterparts should not be included as new money because, although the visitors are from out of town, their bills are being paid by residents.

Expenditures by those who reside in the community do not represent the circulation of new money. Rather, they represent only a recycling of money that already exists there. It is probable that if local residents had not spent this money on the sports event, then they would have disposed of it either now or later by purchasing other goods and services in the community. Thus, their expenditure associated with the sports events is merely likely to be switched spending that offers no net economic stimulus to the community, and it should not be counted as economic impact. Attendance at a sporting event is one of many recreational activities available in the community. Baade and Dye (1990) observe: "Sports are just one kind of entertainment activity and as such compete for the local consumer's scarce disposable income and leisure time. Twenty dollars spent on football tickets may be merely twenty less dollars spent on theater tickets elsewhere in the city." (p. 6)

This widespread admonition from economists to disregard local expenditures is frequently ignored. The optimistic estimates of the Philadelphia study, described earlier in this chapter, incorporated local expenditures. The author of a study measuring the economic impact of the Denver Broncos on the Metropolitan Denver economy fully acknowledged that this procedure was inappropriate:

A limitation in most impact studies is in the implicit assumption that all first-round spending attributable to team or stadium activities is net new spending for the local area--either export sales or import substitutions. Spending on sports may merely redistribute pre-existing local spending. (Regan, 1991, p. 5)

Later in this Denver study the author noted:

The extent to which the money spent by local fans is "new money" and not simply a diversion of money destined for other local uses, is not known and cannot be determined. These local fan expenditures are an opportunity cost and an activity selected by the local population on which to spend a portion of their discretionary income. (p. 52)

Despite recognition of the inappropriateness of this procedure, local residents' expenditures were included anyway! Since 81% of Bronco spectators were revealed to be locals, presumably they accounted for a substantial portion of the $117 million "economic impact" reported in the study. Elsewhere in the study, the author accurately states what he is really doing: "The study determined the amount of dollars that circulate in the Denver Metropolitan Area as a result of the Denver Broncos Football Club" (Regan, 1991, p. 3). However, economic impact is not concerned with recirculation of existing dollars, only with the stimulus impact of new dollars. It is interesting to note that whereas this study of the Broncos identified an economic impact of $117 million, another study of the annual impact of a Major League Baseball team on Denver projected $16.5 million--and the baseball attendance is many times larger and the season many times longer than those of football!

One economist experienced in doing economic impact studies observed (Fulton, 1988):

Often either the consultant or the client really wants the economic impact to be a big number. They look at the dollars spent, and they say, "That's all new." And we say, "That can't all be new, people don't take money out of their savings accounts to go to ball games." (p. 39)

Getz (1991) has suggested:

There is some evidence to suggest that major events do keep some residents at home who otherwise would leave the area for a trip. And it is also probable that

a community with attractive events encourages more local spending for entertainment and merchandise. (p. 303)

Such expenditures could legitimately be considered new money in the sense that it is
money retained in the host community that otherwise would have been lost. Some
indication of the extent to which this occurs can be gained from including questions
which address this issue in an expenditure survey. For example, a survey conducted at
the Adelaide Festival of Arts indicated that 10.3% of the audience who were Adelaide
residents were actually "vacationing at home" to spend their vacation time and money
at the festival, which extended for a 4-week period. In addition, 7,000 residents indicated they would travel out of town more often to attend performances and exhibi-
tions, if the Adelaide Festival were not held. The incremental expenditure retained in
the community by these two groups was estimated at $3.4 million (Centre for South
Australian Economic Studies, 1992). In a personal communication to the authors of
this book, the Adelaide researchers stressed, "Without the evidence from the survey
we would not have included local expenditure." In most cases, these types of estimates are very tenuous, and economists invariably recommend that all expenditures
by local residents should be disregarded.

Failure to Exclude "Time-Switchers" and "Casuals"

Some nonlocal spectators at a sports event may have been planning a visit to the
community for a long time, but changed the timing of their visit to coincide with the
event. Their spending cannot be attributed to the event because it would have been
made without the event, albeit at a different time of the year. Other visitors already
may have been in the community, attracted by other features, and elected to go to the
sports event instead of doing something else. These two groups may be termed time-
switchers and casuals. Expenditures by these visitors would have occurred without
the event; consequently, income generated by their expenditures cannot be attributed
to it. It is necessary to distinguish between gross visitor expenditures and the net
increment of those expenditures, which is the spending attributable to increased length
of stay because of the sports event.

Questions to measure the extent of time-switching and casual attendance should be
included on expenditure surveys. For example, in the survey used as part of his
assessment of the economic impact of the Broncos on the Denver area, Regan (1991)
asked respondents the reason for their visit to Denver, and 91% reported, "To see the
Broncos play." In a survey of the economic impact of Chicago Cubs spring training
on Mesa, Arizona, many respondents reported they were out-of-state residents. However, the Mesa area is a prime location for "snowbirds." Large numbers of these
retired people lock up their homes in the Midwest for the four or five coldest winter
months and migrate south in a trailer home to spend the winter in the warmth of
Arizona. When respondents were asked, "If the Chicago Cubs were to relocate to
another state, would this affect your decision in visiting Mesa, Arizona?", approxi-

mately half of the out-of-state respondents indicated it would have no effect. Nevertheless, their expenditures were included in the economic impact as "new money" attributable to spring training, when it was clearly inappropriate to do this because they were "casuals."

Van Der Lee and Williams (1986) reported on how time switchers and casuals were identified at the Adelaide Grand Prix:

Survey respondents were asked to specify if their trip to South Australia was a special trip for the Grand Prix, (in addition to another planned trip to South Australia over the next two years) or whether they would not have come to Adelaide at all over the next two years, but for the Grand Prix. The expenditure generated by those who responded positively to these questions is a measure of the net visitor expenditure generated in South Australia by the Grand Prix itself (i.e., total direct visitor expenditure less any time-switching expenditure). (p.50)

Approximately 21% of visitors to the Grand Prix were time-switchers, who said they had rearranged the timing of an already proposed trip.

In a survey of respondents to an event in San Antonio, undertaken by one of the authors, it was found that

1. Thirty percent of nonresident respondents would not have come to San Antonio if the event had not been taking place.
2. Twenty-seven percent were time-switchers who would have come without the event, but the event was a reason that influenced their decision to come at that time. The event was instrumental in influencing when they came to San Antonio and in providing the incentive for them to initiate that action at that time.
3. Forty-three percent were casuals who would have come to San Antonio irrespective of the event. The event had no influence on their decision to visit the city at the time. They went to it because they were already in the community.

Thus, expenditures of the 43% who were casuals and the 27% who were time-switchers should be discarded in an economic impact analysis, because their expenditures would have entered the San Antonio economy even if the event had not been held. However, if some of these individuals extended their stay because of the event, then that increment of their expenditures should be included.

Time-switching of external funds is also an important issue in the analysis of construction expenditures for sports facilities. If some of that construction with external funds was intended for allocation to the host community in the future, but was brought forward to accommodate the timing requirements of a desired sports project, then its economic impact should not be attributed to the sports project. Indeed, it has been suggested it is possible that where large capital construction for special events is involved, on occasions the net economic impact may be negative (Burns & Mules, 1986):

This is because speculation flourishes in the hyped up atmosphere of such events and developers, acting on imperfect information, may embark on ventures which are basically unsound. If so, any extra activity generated at the time of the event may be more than offset by subsequent adjustments. (p. 6)

Use of "Fudged" Multiplier Coefficients

It is not desirable to take the results of an economic impact assessment from similar studies in other communities and apply it, because the combinations of business interrelationships in communities are structured differently; thus, linkages and leakages will be different. For the same reason, it is not reasonable to make a general statement of the form "Sports events have an income multiplier of 0.8." Each situation should be analyzed and assessed independently.

However, sometimes the budget is inadequate, or the expertise is not available to derive a multiplier coefficient from IMPLAN or a similar input-output model. Too often in these situations, project advocates step into the void and offer arbitrary coefficients that purport to be "conventional wisdom." Frequently, their assignment of those coefficients will be prefaced by the mischievous phrase, "A conservative estimate of the multiplier is ...." when what is put forward is, in fact, an outrageously high coefficient.

If it is not feasible to derive multiplier coefficients for a sports event, then there are two bases that could be used to suggest reasonable estimates. First, standard multipliers for most Standard Metropolitan Statistical Areas in the United States are available from the Bureau of Economic Analysis in the U.S. Department of Commerce. Second, "ball-park" estimates of income multipliers can be estimated using the following guidance (University of Missouri, 1986):

90 to 95% of United States county income multipliers, fall within a range of 0.4 to 0.8. Thus for most areas we expect a $100 (visitor) expenditure to increase local incomes by $40 to $80. Your multiplier will tend to be at the upper end of the range if:

- Your region is urban rather than rural
- [Visitors] buy products which require considerable local labor in production. (p. 57)

Claiming Total Instead of Marginal Economic Benefits

Burns and Mules (1986) state: "The most common source of error is in crediting all the stated benefits to only part of the costs" (p. 31). They argue that it is inappropriate to attribute all of the economic benefits received to the financial investment of the public entity. Thus, if a public entity contributes $1 million to a $3-million project, then it should be credited with one-third of the resultant economic benefits and not all of them. Burns and Mules (1986) suggest:

Where only part of the costs are funded by government, the analysis should either attribute all benefits to joint costs or else attempt to ascertain the marginal effect on benefits received by the additional funding made possible by the government. If all the benefits generated by joint private-public sponsorship of an event are attributed to the government contribution alone, the benefit-cost ratio may falsely appear very favourable. This is especially true if the government contribution is a relatively small amount of the total. (p. 10)

This viewpoint is conceptually logical, but it is not widely accepted by those involved in conducting economic impact analyses, possibly because it ignores the pragmatic reality of public-private sports partnerships. Proponents of attributing all the economic benefits to the government entity's contribution argue that it is the key to leveraging private-sector participation in a venture. In such cases, without the public investment there would be no private investment, and the sports event would not take place. Hence, it is appropriate to attribute total benefits to the public funding support.

Confusion of Turnover and Multiplier

Some tourism officials state in complete seriousness that the tourism multiplier for their city is 6 or 7 (Archer, 1982). This myth appears to have emerged from somebody somewhere having marked dollar bills and then tracing their movement through the business community. This procedure omits payments made by credit card or by check and fails to differentiate between income generation and sales transactions. It was noted earlier in the chapter that although it may take many rounds before all money leaks out of an economy, the substantial leakages that occur in each round make it unlikely that the income multiplier will exceed 0.8.

An additional issue related to turnover is the time frame over which the spending rounds occur. Schaffer and Davidson (1984) traced the rounds of spending associated with professional football in Atlanta. They reported that after 12 rounds, 99.7% of possible activity was identified. It has been reported that the entire process of expenditures rippling through an economy may take 15 to 20 years to complete (Fleming & Toepper, 1990) before all the initial expenditures leak out of an economy. This means that the real value of the multiplier effect is likely to be substantially lower than that estimated by the short-term input-output models, because $1 of visitor expenditure injected into an economy today will be worth only some fraction of that amount in real purchasing power after many years of working its way through the economy. Further, it has been shown that different multiplier values can arise from different estimates of how fast the resultant transactions occur within an economy (Archer, 1977).

Omission of Opportunity Costs

For an investment of public money to be justified, it must meet the criterion of "highest and best use." That is, it should yield a return to residents that is at least equal to that which could be obtained from other ventures in which the government entity could invest. Invariably, this criterion is ignored and economic impact analyses of sport events typically consider all factors of production as having zero opportunity costs to a community in terms of what they could produce if invested elsewhere in the economy. *Opportunity cost* is the value of the best alternative not taken when a decision to expend government money is made. Archer (1977) noted, "Any attempt to measure the benefits from particular economic activities requires some assessment of the real cost to society of devoting resources to that activity, and a comparison with the benefits to be obtained from the allocation of these resources to other activities" (p. 46). Consider the following situation (Dunnavant 1989):

> Politicians in Denver did not exactly drop their jaws in shock when a Brown, Bortz and Coddington study projected a $16.5 million annual impact were the city to get a Major League Baseball team. It was more like a yawn. "It's nice, but I can't say we were all that impressed," said a mayoral assistant. "We just finished approving a convention center that's going to generate $200 million." (p. 33)

The difference in economic impacts of these two types of facilities is attributable to who uses them. Sports teams primarily entertain local residents, whereas convention centers attract non-residents to the community. Ironically, it is the sports team that is likely to be more popular politically because its contribution to the host community's quality of life is likely to be more obvious to most residents. In the above example, the city was able to acquire both enterprises. If resources had been available for only one of them and community politicians had selected the baseball option, the economic impact analysis would have been positive so the city would probably have supported the baseball opportunity. From an economic perspective, this would have been an unwise investment of public dollars and would have occurred because the opportunity cost of not being able to invest in the convention center was not considered.

In his examination of the financial implications of two alternative proposals for developing a new stadium in St. Louis, Quirk (1987) pointed out another type of financial opportunity cost which would be incurred if the state's tax-exempt bonding authority was used to finance a new domed stadium in the city:

> The issuance of tax-exempt bonds to finance developments such as stadiums is now subject to strict federal limitations. The state of Missouri is allowed to issue only $750 million of such bonds a year (the limit gets tighter over time). The consequence is that issuing $150 million of other desirable state projects will have to be postponed or eliminated. The net benefits associated with the issuance of bonds to finance a domed stadium should include the costs ("opportunity costs") to the public of foregone net benefits from projects displaced by the funding of the stadium. (p SR8)

A similar example was provided by Euchner (1993):

> Stadium projects also can harm a city's already vulnerable capital spending program. At the same time Toronto debated whether to build a new domed stadium, which ended up costing close to $400 million, the city's budget for parks acquisition and maintenance was being squeezed. One city official esti-

mated that the city needed 700 new acres of parkland to keep pace with demand, but the city had a a budget of just $500,000 for parks acquisition. Other infrastructure needs that went begging included public transportation, housing rehabilitation, and expansion of the sewer system. (p. 67)

Switching money from other activities (e.g., road building, public housing, or a business park) does not make the economy better off. The efforts of the mayor of San Jose to persuade the city's residents to approve a referendum allocating $265 million of public funds to a new stadium in which the Giants would play were strenuously opposed by the CEO of a prominent major high-tech company in the city. He objected to "'subsidizing a multimillionaire [the ballclub owner] with a quarter-billion dollar asset. ...This is a terrible investment when we're losing jobs and we don't have enough teachers and police. [The owner's] no villain. He'd be a fool not to get the best deal he can. You look for suckers in these deals, which in today's world means government'" (cited in Fimrite, 1992, p. 52).

It is particularly galling to some that only total economic benefits are measured and the opportunity costs associated with their distribution are not considered. It appears that too often the economic rewards of sports projects tend to accrue to a small group of wealthy individuals, whereas similar public investments in health, education, or productive industry may lead to a wider distribution of benefits (Lipsitz, 1984).

Money used to subsidize sports events has been taken from community residents in the form of taxes. This represents an opportunity cost because residents are likely to have spent those funds in the community if the government had not taken them. In essence, the government may be perceived as spending it for them, so net gain to the community is zero (Hunter, 1988). The process merely substitutes public expenditures for private expenditures, and the resources allocated to a sports event or facility are denied to other sectors of the economy. This point was articulated by Burns and Mules (1986):

> While governments may like to believe that their contributions are "productive", unless total receipts from outside the region are increased by the government financing contribution, all that is happening is that public funding is being substituted for private funding and there is no net economic benefit to the State--just a public cost. (p. 10)

The authors go on to note that event and construction expenditures from outside a host community are benefits, because they cost the community nothing and extra income accrues to the economy. However, in contrast, expenditures by local governments are costs because they are financed by residents within the host community who therefore have to forgo something else, and there is no extra generation of income.

Thus, an expenditure on sports facilities by a local government cannot be considered an injection of new funds. If resources are injected into an economy from nonlocal governments, they can be considered as new money only if they would not have come to the community without the project. Thus, federal funds, such as Community Development Block Grants, which are awarded to communities on a formula basis and have been used in some communities to partially fund sports stadiums, should not be included in economic impact analyses. Fleming and Toepper (1990) note:

> The opportunity costs should include the monetary costs of development and maintenance of the site or area, along with an accounting of benefits lost by withdrawing the resource from its present or alternative uses. (p. 39)

Since stadiums are often constructed on valuable urban land, the opportunity cost of that land is sometimes substantial. Quirk (1987) commenting on financial aspects of a proposal to site a stadium on city-owned land in downtown St. Louis, states:

> The downtown stadium will use land that would be owned by the city and that has potentially valuable alternative uses. The true economic cost of the stadium should include foregone property taxes that would have been paid if the land had been sold or leased for private development, and it also should include foregone rents that could be earned from such alternative uses. (p. SR8)

The emphasis placed on multipliers in economic impact analyses dealing with sports events or facilities may lead the unwary to suppose that there was some unique property conferred on income and employment generation resulting from such events or facilities that was not shared by other sectors of the economy. Hughes (1982) observes, "It is the comparative size of the multiplier that is important, not simply the fact that a multiplier exists" (p. 171). He goes on to note that the empirical literature indicates visitor expenditure multipliers "at best probably reflect an average value added compared with other sectors. References to the multiplier as a significant advantage need to be seen in this context" (p. 172).

Similarly, Foley, (1991) calculated that the cost of each job created by Sheffield's investment in the World Student Games was £ 82,370. He states, "This figure is certainly high" and explains that this is because "sports facilities are generally vast structures with relatively few staff required to run them" (p. 76). Foley (199) concludes, "If an equivalent amount of money was spent on factories or offices, there would be far more jobs created (or accommodated) in the buildings provided" (p. 76).

Much of the employment associated with sports events is for food, beverage, and souvenir vendors; ushers; security personnel; bus and cab drivers; parking lot attendants; restaurant and hotel workers; and the like. Typically, these are low-paying jobs. Hence, Baade (1987) suggested that a city focusing on sports to foster its development may find that its economy compares poorly to that of other communities. His empirical findings appeared to lend support to this thesis. Using regression analysis he reported "a consistently surprising result" (Baade, 1987, p. 15). In seven of the nine cities he analyzed, stadium renovation or construction, or a city's adoption of a professional football or baseball team, was followed by a reduction in that city's share of regional income. Based on these results, Baade raised the possibility that jobs stemming from sports franchises or stadiums are not created, but rather they may be diverted from the manufacturing economy to the service economy, or from higher to lower paid occupations.

Displacement Costs. Displacement costs are a particular kind of opportunity cost. There is some likelihood that visitors from outside a community who are attracted by a sports event, may displace other visitors who otherwise would have come to the community but do not, either because they cannot obtain accommodations or because they are not prepared to mingle with crowds attracted by the event. Thus, an economic impact study done after the 1984 Los Angeles Olympic Games estimated that $163 million of out-of-region visitor expenditures did not occur in southern California during the period of the Games which would have accrued if the Games had not been held. This was attributed to two major factors:

- Widespread national media reporting of potential congestion at the 1984 Olympic Games, and of potential exorbitant visitor travel and accommodation pricing in early 1984, had negative effects on potential summer tourists and visitors.
- The 1984 Olympic games had been known to be scheduled for Los Angeles for six years, with resultant alternative vacation and visitation planning by out-of-town tourists and by regional residents, and some postponement of business trips. (Economics Research Associates, 1986, p. 7)

In calculating the economic impact of the Los Angeles Olympic games the $163 million was appropriately deducted from the gross economic impact in order to arrive at the net economic impact.

Measurement Only of Benefits, Omitting Costs

Unfortunately, sports events can generate substantial economic costs that often are forgotten in the euphoria surrounding an event. Roberts and McLeod (1989) note: "A common legacy of many past events has been a huge debt and a great deal of underutilized infrastructure" (p. 242). Similarly, Johnson (1983) in his review of franchise relocations concluded:

While there is no doubt that economic benefits are derived from a team's presence, it is unclear exactly how great these benefits are (especially in discussing basketball, soccer and hockey franchises), and it is possible that in some cities the public costs attendant to a franchise's presence outweigh its benefits. The point is that no comprehensive cost-benefit analysis has been done in any city. (p. 524)

Too often, only positive economic benefits associated with visitors are reported, and costs or negative impacts inflicted on a community are not considered. Thus, only gross benefits rather than net benefits are reported. If additional people are attracted to a community, then it will create extra demand on local services. Thus, the economic impact on Western Australia of the America's Cup when it was held in Freemantle was estimated at $454 million, but as Hall (1989) observed: "This figure is a measure of cup-related spending, not the outcome of a benefit-cost analysis. Opportunity costs, leakage from the state due to foreign and interstate investment, administrative and social costs were not taken into consideration" (p. 24). Negative or cost impacts may include such items as traffic congestion, road accidents, vandalism, police and fire protection, environmental degradation, garbage collection, increased prices to local residents in retail and restaurant establishments, loss of access, and disruption of residents' lifestyles. Translating some of these impacts into economic values is difficult, which may be one reason why they are usually ignored.

Even projecting reasonably accurate capital costs associated with major sports projects appears to be fraught with difficulty. In chapter 2 the egregious example of the Montreal Olympic Games was cited. Other illustrations of projections that were grossly inaccurate are provided by Euchner (1993):

> The original cost estimate for constructing Baltimore's Camden Yards stadium was $60 million; it eventually cost over $100 million, not including land acquisition and preparation. The variation can be greater for parts of projects. For example, the cost estimates for new parking lots for Busch Stadium in St. Louis ranged between $9.8 million and $52.3 million in 1985. The renovation of Yankee Stadium cost $120 million, almost five times the original $24-million estimate. (p. 67)

Among the major causes of these inaccuracies are political pressures to increase the project's quality after it has been committed and late changes in design to accommodate them.

Incorporating costs into a study changes it from an economic impact analysis to a benefit-cost analysis. Despite the difficulties associated with deriving accurate costs, in the authors' view decision makers should be using benefit-cost analysis when evaluating alternative investments. An economic impact analysis is designed to study the economic effect of additional expenditures attributable to a sports event and should be compared with equivalent investments designed to create economic stimulus in other sectors of the economy. In contrast, benefit-cost analysis is designed to identify the most sensible investment alternative. It considers the long term benefits that can be obtained from the sports investment, identifies the long term costs, and compares the net benefits with those likely to accrue if the same resources were employed in other options.

SUMMARY

Economic impact is defined as the net economic change in a host community that results from spending attributed to a sports event or facility. It has been noted that "*The* key stage in public campaigns for stadiums is the release of official studies that estimate how many millions of dollars a sports team 'contributes' to the city's economy" (Euchner 1993, p. 56). Most economic impact studies are commissioned by sponsors who seek numbers which will support their advocacy position. This often leads to those undertaking the studies adopting procedures and underlying assumptions that bias the results in a direction desired by the sponsors.

Three elements contribute to the total economic impact of out-of-town visitors. Direct impact is the first-round effect of visitor spending. Indirect impact is the ripple effect of additional rounds of recirculating the initial expenditures. Induced impact is the further ripple effect caused by employees of impacted businesses spending some of their salaries and wages in other businesses in the city.

The three most commonly used multipliers are those for sales, income, and employment. Sales multipliers are not useful for assessing economic impact, and household-income multipliers should be used for this purpose. The point of interest is the impact of the sales on household income and employment. Nevertheless, sales impacts tend to be used as *the* multiplier because they are substantially higher than income multipliers.

Popular input-output computer programs, such as IMPLAN and RIMS, calculate two types of multiplier coefficients that have been termed the incremental and the normal coefficients. The normal coefficient should be used and not the incremental coefficient. Even though it is inappropriate, the latter is frequently selected because it is a higher number.

The geographic area within which economic impact is to be assessed will be specified by those commissioning the study. The larger the area's economic base, the smaller the leakage that is likely to occur and the larger the multiplier is likely to be. Only expenditures made by visitors within the boundaries of the defined area should be included in an analysis, not total spending because some of this may have been expended in travel to or from the defined impact area.

Expenditures related to a sports event by those residing within the defined impact area should not be included in the analysis since they represent only a recycling of money that already existed there. Expenditures by time-switchers who were planning to visit the community for other reasons but scheduled their visit to coincide with the event, and casuals who attended the sports event but were in the community for other purposes and whose visit was not influenced by the event, should be excluded from an economic impact analysis. Only the net increment of those expenditures attributable to increased length of stay because of the sports event should be included.

If the budget or expertise is not available to empirically derive a multiplier coefficient for a particular economic analysis and a reasonable estimate of the household income multiplier has to be made, it should be between 0.4 and 0.8 because 90 to 95% of U.S. county multipliers are within this range.

Some economists have suggested that if a public entity contributes one-third of the cost of a sports event, then it should be credited with one-third of the economic benefits that accrue, rather than all of them. This viewpoint, however, has been challenged by others and has not received wide acceptance.

If a community subsidizes a sports event, facility, or franchise, then it cannot invest that money in another project. The return it could have received from the best alternative investment of the money is known as opportunity cost. This should be incorporated in an economic analysis. The multiplier coefficient of these alternative investments may be as high or higher than that associated with the sports investment.

Sports events will generally inflict economic costs on the host community as well as deliver economic benefits, but impact analyses invariably measure only the benefit impacts. Decision makers need information on both sides of the equation to make informed decisions.

We conclude this chapter by reproducing a critique of a study commissioned from a large consulting and accounting firm undertaken to estimate the economic impact of the 1994 Commonwealth Games. The review was undertaken by economists at the Centre for South Australian Economic Studies (1992). They highlight several errors in the analysis that have been discussed in the chapter.

CRITIQUE BY THE CENTRE FOR SOUTH AUSTRALIAN ECONOMIC STUDIES OF A REPORT: "ESTIMATED ECONOMIC IMPACT OF THE 1994 COMMONWEALTH GAMES"

The 1994 Commonwealth Games were held in the City of Victoria in the Canadian province of British Columbia. Victoria is located on Vancouver Island and is connected to the mainland by extensive ferry services. The Games' organizers contracted with consultants to carry out an economic impact study in 1990. Much of the work was speculative and based on "best guesses" at things before the event, like visitor numbers and their expenditure. It is interesting to note that no Commonwealth Games had ever had a proper economic impact study carried out with a full visitor survey.

The organizers' purpose in having this study conducted was to bolster flagging support for the Games in the local community of Victoria. Presumably they were keen to demonstrate as large an impact as possible, and the consultants did not let them down! This study makes every mistake in the book in overstating the economic impacts. To make matters worse, there was no mention of the cost to Victoria of putting on the Games, so the event appears to have huge benefits and no costs.

The study identifies four expenditure sources as giving rise to economic impacts:

1. pre-Games construction and organizing expenditure
2. visitor expenditure and expenditure by the organizers during the Games
3. corporate sponsor expenditure during the Games
4. post-games expenditure from increased tourism (both general and sporting).

All of the expenditures of the first three items were treated as if they gave rise to net additions to economic activity. The study made no effort to remove expenditure that was transferred from other activities, or from other periods of the same year, to the Games. No mention was made of whether the largest item of expenditure, construction expenditure on the facilities, was switched from other construction in Victoria or from funds granted from the Federal Government especially for the purpose. Mention was made of the possibility of switched visitor expenditure (i.e., expenditure by tourists who would have visited Victoria regardless, but who timed their visit in order to take advantage of the Games), but no attempt was made to measure it.

The capital and operating budget of the Games organisers accounted for 80 per cent of the total direct expenditure on the Games. Thus if all of this expenditure has been at the expense of, say, roadworks or education elsewhere in the province, the net economic impact on the provincial economy was zero. The critical issue is how the expenditure was funded. Expenditure that was funded by the Provincial Government could reasonably be assumed to be at the expense of other provincial expenditure. On the other hand, expenditure that was funded by grants from the Federal Canadian Government could be regarded as giving rise to a net increase in economic activity, unless such grants were at the expense of other grants to the Province. The consultants did not even consider this issue, and by assuming that all of this expenditure was "new" to the Province, they overstated the economic impacts.

A major problem with the study was that it provided no formal definition of the region on whose economy the impact of the Games was supposed to occur. Was it the City of Victoria or the Province of British Columbia? The study appeared to measure visitors with respect to Victoria, thus counting the residents of British Columbia from outside of Victoria as visitors. The estimated number of "visitors" was over 30,000, which compared with forward estimates of between 14,000 and 19,000 out-of-State visitors in this Centre's forward estimates for Adelaide's bid for the 1998 Commonwealth Games.

The big discrepancy suggests that the consultants were defining visitors with respect to the city. Yet they measured economic impact (using an input–output model) on the province of British Columbia, in which Victoria is a small part. (Vancouver is the largest city with a population of over one million.) Expenditure by residents of Vancouver in visiting the Games will obviously have switched from other activities within the province, leading to no net increase in economic activity.

A further problem was the estimate of visitor expenditure, which was based on an assumed average of $100 (Canadian) per visitor per day, when visitor surveys for Victoria showed an average of $60 (Canadian) per visitor per day. The consultants justified their use of $100 on the grounds that "certain types of visitors to the Games...will spend more than the average tourist" and "hotels/motels will receive higher average room rates during the event." Although both of these may be true, it is also the case that athletes and sports fans are not typically high spenders and there is likely to be a lot of "staying with friends and relatives" by visitors. All in all the economic impact of expenditure by visitors was greatly overstated.

The consultants estimated that in the long run, the Games would have a promotional effect on general tourism to Victoria. They put a figure of 1% (28,500 visitors) on this effect. No attempt was made to verify the 1%, despite there being numerous instances of large events where post-event tourism numbers could have been analyzed. Apart from this flaw, this part of the study was on safe ground, concentrating as it did on increases in tourism that were entirely attributable to the Games.

Not so sound was the treatment of sporting visitors. The consultants argued that the sporting facilities being built for the Games would attract major sporting activities to Victoria in the post-Games years. They estimated the effect to be

"81,840 out-of-town user-days" (including spectators). No discussion was given of how this rather large number was obtained. No attempt was made to net out those events that would have come to Victoria in any case. To make matters worse, the consultants included in their measure of expenditure in this area, the operating expenditure of running the facilities. They recognised that some of this would have been incurred in any case, but they did not recognize such expenditure as a cost, rather than a benefit of the use of the facilities.

This study is a good example of how *not* to do an economic impact study of a special event. The consultants could have avoided several of their errors had they taken two important steps prior to any analysis:

1. Define the region of interest
2. Identify which expenditures are costs to the region of having the event, and which are benefits in the sense of being new expenditures within the region due to the event.

If these two steps had been taken at the outset, many of the traps could have been avoided. As it stands, this study significantly overstated the benefits to Victoria of hosting the 1994 Commonwealth Games.

SOURCE: Adapted from the Centre for South Australian Economic Studies (1992). Estimated economic impact of the 1994 Commonwealth Games. Review of a report. *Sports Economics*, No. 3, February.

Questions for Study and Discussion

1. Assume you were asked to offer critical assessment of an economic impact study which reported a multiplier coefficient of 6. What issues would you examine to determine the legitimacy of a multiplier of that magnitude?

2. Why should the expenditures of each of the following groups be excluded from an economic impact analysis of sporting events?
   a. local residents
   b. time switchers
   c. casuals

3. Of the most prevalent abuses identified in the chapter, which *one* abuse do you consider to be the most serious error or omission commited in economic impact analysis, and why?

4. In general, which professional sport (baseball, football, etc.) in your opinion would produce the most positive economic impact for a community, and why?

REFERENCES

Archer, B. H. (1973). *The impact of domestic tourism.* Bangor: University of Wales Press.

Archer, B. H. (1977). *Tourism multipliers: The state of the art.* Bangor: University of Wales Press.

Archer, B. H. (1982, December). The value of multipliers and their policy implications. *Tourism Management,* pp. 236-241.

Archer, B. H. (1984). Economic impact: Misleading multiplier. *Annals of Tourism Research, 11*(3), 517-518.

Arnold, A.(1986). The impact of the Grand Prix on the transport sector. In J.P.A. Burns, J.H. Hatch and T.J. Mules (Eds.), *The Adelaide Grand Prix: The impact of a special event.* (pp. 58-81) Adelaide: The Centre for South Australian Economic Studies.

Baade, R. A. (1987). *Is there an economic rationale for subsidizing sports stadiums?* Heartland Policy Study No. 13. Chicago: The Heartland Institute.

Baade, R. A. & Dye, R. F. (1990, Spring). The impact of stadiums and professional sports on metropolitan area development. *Growth and Change,* pp. 1-14.

Bishop, G. & Hatch, J. (1986). The impact of the Grand Prix on the accommodation sector. In J.P.A. Burns, J.H. Hatch, and T.J. Mules (Eds.), *The Adelaide Grand Prix: The impact of a special event* (82-94). Adelaide: The Centre for South Australian Economic Studies.

Burgan, B. & Mules, T. J. (1992). Economic impact of sports events. *Annals of Tourism Research 19,* 700-712.

Burns, J. P.A. & Mules, T. J. (1989). An economic evaluation of the Adelaide Grand Prix. In G.J. Syme, B.J. Shaw, P.M. Fenton, & W.S. Mueller (Eds.), *The planning and evaluation of hallmark events,* (pp. 172-185). Aldershot, England: Avebury.

Business reports: Mid-size cities blitz NFL for new franchise. (1992, January) *American Demographics.* p. 9.

Centre for South Australian Economic Studies (1992). Estimated economic impact of the 1994 Commonwealth Games. Review of a report prepared by Coopers and Lybrand Consulting Group. *Sports Economics* No. 3, February.

Corliss, R. (1992, August 24). Build it and they will might come. *Time,* pp. 50-52.

Crompton, J. L. (1984). *The characteristics and spending patterns of visitors to Arlington, Texas in 1984.* College Station: Texas A&M University, Department of Recreation and Parks.

Curtis, G. (1993, September). Waterlogged, *Texas Monthly.* p. 7.

Davidson, L. S. & Schaffer, W. A. (1980, Winter). A discussion of methods employed in analyzing the impact of short-term entertainment events. *Journal of Travel Research 28*(3), 12-16.

Dunnavant, K. (1989, March 13). The impact of economics. *Sports inc,* pp. 31-33.

Economics Research Associate. (1986). *Community Economic Impact of the 1984 Olympic Games in Los Angeles,* Los Angeles.

Euchner, C. C. (1993). *Playing the field: Why sports teams move and cities fight to keep them.* Baltimore: The Johns Hopkins University Press.

Fimrite, R. (1992, June 1). Oh give me a home... *Sports Illustrated.* pp. 50-52.

Fleming, W. R. & Toepper, L. (1990). Economic impact studies: Relating the positive and negative impacts to tourism development. *Journal of Travel Research*, *29*(1), 35-41.

Fletcher, J. & Snee, H. (1989). Tourism multiplier effects. In S. F. Witt & L. Moutinho (Eds.), *Tourism Marketing and Management Handbook* (pp. 529-531) Hemel Hempstead, England: Prentice Hall International (UK).

Fridgin, J. D. (1991). *Dimensions of tourism.* East Lansing, MI: American Hotel and Motel Association.

Fulton, W. (1988, March). Politicians who chase after sports franchises may get less than they pay for. *Governing*, pp. 34-40.

Getz, D. (1991). *Festivals, special events and tourism.* New York: Van Nostrand Reinhold.

Hagan, J. H., E. & Patterson (1989, Winter). Manna and mammon--Appraisal of the First Australian Masters Games. *Australian Parks and Recreation*, pp. 40-45.

Hughes, C. G. (1982, September). The employment and economic effects of tourism reappraised. *Tourism Management*, pp. 167-176.

Hunter, W. J. (1988). *Economic impact studies: Inaccurate, misleading, and unnecessary.* (Heartland Institute Policy Study #21). Chicago, IL: The Heartland Institute.

Johnson, A. T. (1989). Local government and minor league baseball: Survey of issues and trends (Sports Consortium Special Report #1). Washington, DC: International City Management Association.

Lipsitz, G. (1984). Sports stadia and urban development: A tale of three cities. *Journal of Sport and Social Issues, 8*(2), 1-18.

Liu, J. C. (1979) The economic impact of tourism on an island economy: A case study of Victoria, B.C. Ph.D. Thesis, Department of Geography, Simon Fraser University.

Liu, J. & Var, T. (1982, September). Differential multipliers for the accommodation sector. *Tourism Management*, pp. 177-187.

Petersen, D. (1989). *Convention centers, stadiums, and arenas.* Washington DC: Urban Land Institute.

Quirk, J. P. (1987, January 18). The Quirk Study: A close look at the two proposals. *St. Louis Post-Dispatch*, Special Report 8.

Regan, T. H. (1991). *A study of the economic impact of the Denver Broncos Football Club on the Denver Colorado Metropolitan economy.* Unpublished doctoral dissertation, University of Northern Colorado, Greeley CO.

Richardson, H. W. (1985) Input-output and economic base multipliers: Looking backward and forward. *Journal of Regional Science, 25*(4), 607-661.

Roberts, E. J. & McLeod, P. B. (1989). The economics of a hallmark event. In G.J. Syme, B .J. Shaw, D. M. Fenton & W. S. Mueller. *The planning and evaluation of hallmark events,* (pp. 242-249). Aldershot, England: Avebury.

Schaffer, W. A. & Davidson, L. S. (1984). Economic impact of the Falcons on At-
     lanta. Atlanta: GA, Georgia Intitute of Technology.

Smith, S. L. J. (1989) *Tourism analysis: A handbook.* New York: Longman.

Turco, D. M. & Kelsey, C. W. (1992). *Conducting economic impact studies of recre-
     ation and parks special events.* Washington, DC: National Recreation and Park
     Association.

University of Missouri. (1986). *Tourism USA: Guidelines for tourism development.*
     Columbus, MO: University of Missouri, Department of Recreation and Park Ad-
     ministration.

Vaughan, D. R. (1984, December). The cultural heritage: An approach to analyzing
     income and employment effects. *Journal of Cultural Economics*, pp. 1-34.

SOURCES OF PUBLIC SECTOR FUNDING

Learning Objectives

After completing this chapter, the reader should be able to:

1. Identify and explain in some detail traditional tax sources used by public agencies to finance sport facilities and programs. More specifically:
   a. articulate property tax nomenclature.
   b. calculate property tax payments from tax rate and assessment information.
   c. explain the role of sales taxes as financing alternatives.
   d. discuss differences between general obligation and revenue bonds.
   e. explain the distinctive features of tax increment financing and special authority bonds.
   f. explain the requirements for obtaining a bond rating.
   g. discuss the substantial restrictions placed on the issuance of tax-exempt bonds for sport facility funding by the 1986 Tax Reform Act.

CHAPTER 4

SOURCES OF
PUBLIC
SECTOR FUNDING

Most public sector investment into the sport industry comes through subsidization and construction of facilities in which the sports teams play. The money to build these is usually obtained by issuing bonds. This chapter commences with a discussion of the property tax and the sales tax, because these are the sources of revenues state and local governments most frequently use to redeem the bonds they issue. The bulk of the chapter is then devoted to describing characteristics of the most common types of bonds that are used to fund major sports facilities, the rating systems that strongly influence the cost of those bonds, and the substantial limitations placed on the future funding of stadiums and arenas with tax-exempt public bonds by the 1986 Tax Reform Act.

THE PROPERTY TAX

For generations the property tax has been the backbone of local government finance. On average, approximately one-third of the income that municipalities receive is derived from this source although the average obscures wide variations among jurisdictions. The tax is borne by all owners of property except churches, charitable organizations, educational institutions, and other governmental entities, such as state and federal institutions.

Figure 4-1 shows a taxonomy of the types of property that may be subjected to taxation. The fundamental distinction is the difference between real property and personal property. Most variation across jurisdictions as to which of the property elements shown in Figure 4-1 should be taxed occurs in the personal property category, which includes everything that can be owned that is not real (i.e., land, buildings) property. It is difficult for appraisers to locate, inventory, validate and value both tangible and intangible personal property. Because of these difficulties it has been noted that sometimes personal property "is exempt by law; sometimes, by local practice. Seldom is taxation complete" (Mikesell, 1991, p. 292).

The value of real property is determined by estimating its taxable worth. These estimates are called "assessments." The task of determining these property values is assigned to an assessor, who is either appointed or elected. It is the assessor's respon-

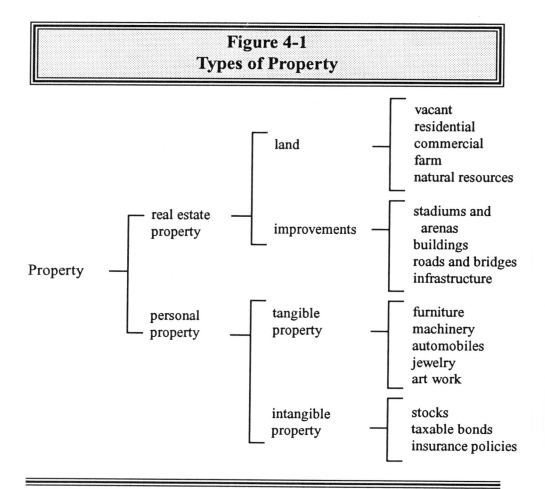

Figure 4-1
Types of Property

Property
— real estate property
  — land
    — vacant
    residential
    commercial
    farm
    natural resources
  — improvements
    — stadiums and arenas
    buildings
    roads and bridges
    infrastructure
— personal property
  — tangible property
    — furniture
    machinery
    automobiles
    jewelry
    art work
  — intangible property
    — stocks
    taxable bonds
    insurance policies

sibility to list on the tax rolls every parcel of taxable property within the jurisdiction and on a specified date each year, often January 1, to place a value on each parcel in conformity with assessment rules.

Current market value is defined as "the price at which the property would be transferred on the open market between a willing buyer and a willing seller, neither of whom is under any 'compulsion' to buy or to sell" (Oldman & Schoettle, 1974). A state's tax law may or may not assess property at the current market rate. Hence, assessed value is not necessarily the same as market value. In many states the practice is to assess property at much below prevailing market levels, typically between a range of 30% and 50% of fair market value. Thus, a home with a true market value of $100,000 assessed at 40% of value would have a taxable value of $40,000. The intent of this practice is to create an illusion. Because the assessed value of the property is below market value, property owners may believe that they are getting a concession and therefore be less inclined to challenge the assessor's judgment. In fact, the tax payment made by the homeowner is likely to be the same irrespective of whether all properties are assessed at 100% or 40% of their market value (Mikesell, 1991):

> Under normal circumstances the overall assessment ratio has little impact on absolute property tax burdens because assessment levels can be counteracted by differences in the statutory tax rate. For instance, suppose a municipality seeks $5 million from its property tax and that the market value of taxable property is $80 million. If the assessment ratio is 100 percent, a property tax rate of $6.25 per $100 assessed value will yield the desired revenue. If the assessment ratio is 50 percent, a property tax rate of $12.50 per $100 assessed value will produce the desired levy total. Low assessment ratios will produce compensating statutory rate adjustments.(p.293)

The aggregate value of all the assessed property within a particular jurisdiction is referred to as the *tax base*. Once the tax base has been determined by assessment, the local government sets a *tax rate* to meet its revenue needs. Tax rates are usually expressed in terms of dollars and cents per $100 assessed valuation. Tax rates are established by dividing the local government's budget (projected expenditures for one year), less anticipated income from nonproperty sources (e.g., sales taxes, fees, fines, federal and state funds), by the total assessed value of property.

For example, assume that the total assessed value of a community is $400,000,000 and the tax revenue needed by government units amounts to $50,000,000:

(a)   Tax Rate = $\frac{\$\,50,000,000}{\$400,000,000} = 0.125$

This may be expressed as a tax rate of 12.5 cents per $100 assessed value. The relationship between the budget and total assessed value always determines the tax rate. For example, if a city increases its budget expenditures and the assessed value total remains stable, the tax rate goes up:

(b)   Tax Rate = $\frac{\$\,60,000,000}{\$400,000,000} = 0.150$

Conversely, if the assessed value or tax base goes up and the city budget remains the same, the tax rate will go down:

(c)   Tax Rate = $\frac{\$\,50,000,000}{\$500,000,000} = 0.100$

The above equation (c) shows how it is possible, in communities where land values are escalating rapidly, for a government body to announce rather magnanimously to its taxpayers its plan to reduce taxes. Actually its claim is based on the fact that the assessed value of property has grown so much that the government body can afford to reduce the tax rate substantially without losing any property tax revenue. Hence, it is probable that the actual tax that the property owner is required to pay may well have increased.

When the tax rate has been established, it is a simple matter to determine the amount of taxes that will be collected. The calculation involves multiplying the approved tax rate by the assessed value of taxable property. This relationship is illustrated as:

Tax Rate X Assessed Value = Tax Revenue due from Property

Thus, if a property has an assessed value of $50,000 and a tax rate of $6 per $100 of assessed value, then the annual tax to be paid by the property owner would be $3,000.

Property owners are obligated to pay their annual tax bill. If they fail to do so, then a tax lien can be attached to the property. This gives the city the power to have the property sold and the proceeds from the sale applied to delinquent taxes, penalties, and accrued interest.

Tax Abatements

One of the strategies used by governments to stimulate private sector investment and create employment in their communities is to offer property tax abatements. Abatement programs exist in approximately two-thirds of the states (Severn, 1992). Typically, they are awarded whenever they are requested (Wolkoff, 1985); thus, they frequently constitute part of a city's incentive package in negotiations with professional franchises. A tax abatement will exempt the franchise's assets from property taxation for a given period of time. It may be for all or for a portion of the tax. The length of time varies according to state enabling legislation. For example, the norm in New York is 10 years whereas in Ohio it is 20 years (Wolkoff, 1985).

These abatements are substantial. For example, immediately after the New England Patriots' stadium was built in Foxboro, Massachusetts, the city of Foxboro received more than $250,000 a year in property taxes from the stadium's private owners, from land that netted only $628 in taxes before the stadium was built (Shnay, 1978). In financial projections prepared for the proposed Riverport Dome stadium in St. Louis in 1986, the abatement of real estate and property taxes for an extended period represented an annual subsidy to the facility of $2 million (Quirk, 1987).

A different form of tax abatement was given by the city of Colorado Springs to a real estate company in the area. The city had a parkland ordinance that required developers either to donate land to the city on a formula basis for use as a park or to pay a parkland dedication fee. The company authorized a stadium to be constructed on 15 acres of its land, and the city agreed that the use of the stadium for minor league baseball was in keeping with the definition of parkland use. Thus, it gave the company a $234,000 tax credit in lieu of requiring payment of the parkland dedication fee (Johnson, 1993).

THE SALES TAX

Sales taxes are generally the second largest source of tax revenues for municipalities after the property tax, but in some cities with large retail centers, sales tax receipts exceed those received from the property tax. Local sales taxes tend to piggyback on those levied by the states, and the combined general excise tax rates appear to range between 3% and 10%.

Most sales taxes are not applied to the sale of services, but are imposed on nearly all transactions involving tangible products at the retail level. Typically, food for at-home consumption and prescription drugs are exempted to reduce the regressiveness of the sales tax. In some states this has been expanded to exempt clothing. Purchase of these essential items constitutes a higher percentage of the income of low-income families than of high-income families. Thus, if these items remain in the tax base, the sales tax would be strongly regressive.

In the 1990s, voters in Arlington, Texas, and Denver passed increases in local sales taxes to fund new baseball stadiums. The San Antonio Alamodome, which opened in 1993, cost $174 million to build. The city adopted a pay-as-you-go approach to funding the project rather than issue bonds. Most of the money was raised by a 5-year surcharge of an additional half-cent on the local sales tax, which was approved by the city's voters in a referendum (Korman 1989).

> Holding down interest expense is the chief appeal of using sales tax revenue to pay the construction bills. "It's a prudent, clean, pay-as-you-go approach to financing" says the project director. He figured that raising the money with long term general obligation bonds would have cost the taxpayers $435 million in principal and interest over the years. That meant an annual debt service payment of $17 million, which would be equivalent to a 15 percent increase of the property tax. (p. 34)

In addition to general excise taxes, a surcharge sales tax may be imposed on selective items; consequently, differential tax treatment is applied to particular products or services. Such taxes are frequently applied to "sin" products, such as tobacco and alcohol, or to gasoline in order to raise additional funds for roads. Part of funding for the Metrodome in Minneapolis was obtained from a levy on alcoholic beverage sales. The mayor of San Jose proposed to pay most of the $265 million cost of the stadium she promised the Giants if they would move there by increasing the city's utility tax from 5% to 7%.

The Hotel-Motel Tax

The most frequently used selective sales tax for funding major sport facilities is the hotel-motel tax. Again, this is a state tax on which local jurisdictions piggyback, and the combined rate is in the range of 10 to 15% added on to the price paid for a hotel-motel room. Pledging part of this tax to redeem revenue bonds is politically attractive for three main reasons. First, it does not require voter approval in most states, whereas this is often required at the local level for general sales tax increases. Second, it transfers the costs of building (and sometimes also operating) a stadium or arena to out-of-town visitors. They do not vote on tax increases and are unlikely even to realize that the tax is underwriting those facilities. Third, ostensibly those who appear most likely to oppose the tax are a community's hoteliers because they are required to add it to their guests' bills and collect it. However, a major sports facility is likely to help fill rooms; therefore, hoteliers frequently support such taxes.

There are abundant examples of the key role of the hotel-motel tax in funding major sports facilities. Revenue bonds issued to finance the Indianapolis Hoosier Dome were redeemed by pledging proceeds from a 5% county admissions tax and certain cigarette tax revenues. Part of the funding for the Seattle Kingdome involved pledging proceeds from a 2% lodging tax. The Louisiana Superdome pledged proceeds from a 4% hotel-motel occupancy tax imposed in Jefferson and Orleans parishes, which constitute the principal population service area of the stadium. Revenues from this 4% tax have risen with the fourfold increase in hotel rooms in the New Orleans area that has occurred since the Superdome was built (Shubnell, Peterson, & Harris, 1985). Atlanta increased its hotel-motel tax to finance the $200 million Georgia Dome. The Dome's debt and related fees were projected at $18.3 million in the first year of operation and the hotel-motel tax was projected to raise nearly $11 million of this (Baldo, 1991).

Bonds

The expansion of public sector construction of major sports facilities that was noted in chapter 2 has depended primarily on the ability of municipalities to borrow money. Most of these capital outlays have been paid for through the sale of bonds. Bonds are formally defined as a promise by the borrower (*bond issuer*) to pay back to the lender (*bond holder*) a specified amount of money, with interest, within a specified period of time. The interest is expressed as a percentage of the principal (*face amount* of the bond) available for use during a specified period of time. Typically, the contract specifies that interest payments will be made semiannually.

The alternative to issuing bonds is to adopt a pay-as-you-go approach. This option was used to construct the Alamodome in San Antonio. Its major advantage is the substantial savings in interest charges that will accrue. However, there are two major disadvantages of pay-as-you-go that account for its relatively infrequent use. First, from a political perspective, the actions of many elected officials are guided by their desire to be reelected. Thus, they perceive it to be advantageous to build major facilities today, to reap the political rewards from their construction, and to shift the costs of facilities as far forward as possible so political penalties associated with paying for them become the problem of their successors. Second, from an equity perspective, pay-as-you-go is likely to be inefficient and inequitable. With population mobility, some residents will pay the full cost of a facility from which they will receive no benefits if they later leave the community. Conversely, others moving into the community will receive benefits from an asset to which they made no financial contribution (Mikesell, 1991).

To issue bonds a municipality obtains legal authorization, either from the voters or its legislative body, to borrow money from a qualified lender. The lender can be any individual, organization, or group with money to lend at interest. Usually, this is an established financial institution, such as a bank, an investment service, or sometimes an insurance company. When the financial institution lends the money to the public agency, the agency provides the lender with an appropriate number of engraved certificates (usually issued in $1,000 or $5,000 denominations). These redeemable certificates, or bonds, represent the legal obligation of the public agency (borrower) to pay back the bond holder (the lending institution) the amount borrowed, together with a fixed rate of interest.

A fundamental rule associated with issuing bonds is: Do not issue them for a maturity longer than the project's useful life. People should not be paying for a major sports facility after it is no longer in use: "If the debt life exceeds useful life, the project's true annual cost has been understated and people will continue to pay for the project after it has gone. If the useful life exceeds the debt period, the annual cost has been overstated and people will receive benefits without payment" (Mikesell, 1991, p. 408). In the context of major sports facilities, if a facility is being built to accommodate a franchise, then "useful life" effectively may be defined as the period of time for which a franchise occupies the structure. Thus, this rule counsels that the length of a bond's maturity should coincide with duration of the municipality's lease agreement with the franchise. The longer the maturity term, the higher the interest rate required to borrow for that period of time, because borrowers have to compensate investors for locking up their resources for a longer time.

There is a statutory limitation to the amount of borrowing that local governments can commit. These are state statutes and vary widely from one state to another. This restriction is generally referred to as the statutory "debt ceiling." In almost all cases, the debt ceiling is expressed as a percentage of the total assessed value of property within the particular jurisdiction.

Types of Bonds

A taxonomy of the types of bonds that government agencies may use to finance the building of a stadium or arena is shown in Figure 4-2. The most fundamental distinction in the type of debt that governments incur from issuing bonds is whether that debt is a full-faith and credit obligation or whether it is non-guaranteed. The discussion in this section is arranged under these two headings.

Full-Faith and Credit Obligations. Full-faith and credit obligations "have an unlimited claim" on the taxes and other revenues of the government entity issuing the bonds (Mikesell, 1991). In effect, the governmental unit makes an unconditional promise to the bondholder to secure or pay back the interest and principal owed, through its authority to levy taxes.

Bonds issued with this "full-faith and credit" provision are called *general obligation bonds*. Because of this provision they are considered by investors to be the safest and most secure form of long-term investment. They offer greater security that bond

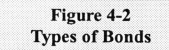

Figure 4-2
Types of Bonds

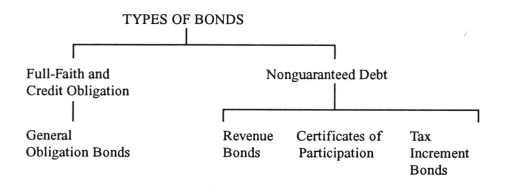

TYPES OF BONDS

Full-Faith and Credit Obligation   Nonguaranteed Debt

General Obligation Bonds   Revenue Bonds   Certificates of Participation   Tax Increment Bonds

principal and interest payments will be made on time than do other types of bonds that are non-guaranteed. Hence, they bear a lower interest rate than does equivalent non-guaranteed debt.

The burden of paying for these bonds is spread over all taxable property within the issuing government's geographical boundaries. Because the sale of general obligation bonds usually leads to an increase in local property taxes, the government body desiring to issue them must first obtain voter approval. There are many major sports facilities that have been constructed with general obligation bonds--Philadelphia's Veterans Stadium and the Pontiac Silverdome are examples--but these were constructed before the tax revolt movement impacted cities in the late 1970s.

The security provided by a government body's unconditional pledge of full tax support usually results in making the bonds easier to sell. The reduced risk, which comes with the almost certain probability of payback, increases the attractiveness of general obligation bonds to a greater range of potential investors.

The ease of sale and reduced cost of tax-guaranteed general obligation bonds are significant advantages. However, the requirement of obtaining majority voter approval for stadium or arena projects is an increasingly large hurdle (Baldo, 1991):

Taxpayers have grown weary of being held hostage by teams that threaten to move. Stadium referenda in San Francisco, Oakland and Miami have failed in recent years, and civic groups have opposed a new project in Detroit. "Municipal support will continue to dwindle because cities are basically going bankrupt," says the vice-president of a bank that has financed stadiums. (p. 34)

Another commentator noted, "It's difficult to pass a general obligation bond to build a stadium when cities are having trouble passing bond issues for schools and basic city infrastructure" (Shnay, 1978, p. 2). This observation is substantially more applicable today than when it was originally made. The immediate prospect of a change in this trend is not likely. Obtaining broad-based support from the electorate to pass general obligation bonds to finance major sports facilities appears to be an unlikely option.

Non-Guaranteed Bonds. Since the late 1970s, most public sector investment in major sports facilities has been in non-guaranteed funding mechanisms. These are not backed by the full-faith and credit of the government entity. Rather they are sold on the basis of repayment from other designated revenue sources. If revenue from the designated sources falls short of what is required to make debt payments, the government entity does not have to make up the difference.

Non-guaranteed bonds have three major advantages. First, in most states direct voter approval is not required. Second, they are not considered statutory debt and thus do not count against the government entity's debt capacity. Third, if the revenue accrues directly from the project, then those who most benefit from the facility pay for it.

Because they are not guaranteed, investors who buy these bonds incur more risk, which means these government entities have to pay higher interest rates to lenders than they would pay on general obligation bonds. The difference in rates between general obligation bonds and non-guaranteed bonds may be as much as 2%. In other words, it may cost 7% to finance a project using non-guaranteed bonds as opposed to 5% if general obligation bonds were used. The additional interest cost over the full period of the loan may be substantial. The difference between paying 5% and 7% on a 20-year, one-million dollar issue is almost $300,000.

A wide array of non-guaranteed funding mechanisms have been created, but the three that are likely to be most pertinent for development of major sports facilities are revenue bonds, certificates of participation, and tax increment bonds (Figure 4-2).

Revenue bonds can be backed exclusively by revenue accruing from the project, which means that a facility has to generate sufficient funds to cover both operating and maintenance expenses and annual principal and interest payments. Alternatively, in the context of professional sport facilities, a more common strategy is to back the revenue bonds with an income stream from other designated revenue sources, such as the hotel-motel taxes that were discussed earlier.

The Meadowlands hosts the New York Giants and Jets football franchises and the Nets basketball team. Both the stadium and the arena for these teams were financed by revenue bonds that were backed by revenues from the profits of the adjacent Meadowlands horse racing track. The City of Irving sold revenue bonds to all individuals purchasing season tickets to Dallas Cowboy games. Each ticketholder was required to buy a $250 bond, and those individuals with seats between the 30-yard lines had to buy at least four bonds (i.e., $1,000). This bond sale raised 60% of the capital needed to build the stadium (Rosentraub & Nunn, 1978). The Cowboy bonds are redeemable in the year 2008 at $300. They proved to be a good investment. The bonds and their seat options are routinely offered for sale at prices around $2,000.

Certificates of Participation are backed by revenue from lease-purchase agreements with the facility they are used to finance. Payments are subject to annual appropriations by the issuing government. There is a moral rather than a legal obligation to appropriate funds if lease payments are inadequate or if the lessee goes out of business. In the recession of the early 1990s investors in these certificates grew nervous as public officials questioned the requirement to continue appropriating funds to repay these certificates, because there was no legal obligation (Hildreth, 1993).

Over half the states now have enabling legislation authorizing *tax increment financing* (TIF), and although the rules and limitations associated with it differ, the basic concept is the same. If a major sports facility can serve as a magnet that attracts complementary or proximate businesses (chapter 2) to locate near it, then TIF may be a viable financing mechanism.

The first stage is to designate an area that is in need of urban redevelopment as a TIF district. The local development authority or city will then issue tax increment bonds and use the proceeds (Michael, 1987)

(1) to purchase or acquire by eminent domain several parcels of property containing substandard buildings or structures, (2) to clear the land and (3) to prepare the land for development by installing sewer, water or other public improvements. The property, then, is sold or given to a developer at less than the development authority's cost. This technique is commonly referred to as a land write-down. The bonds' principal and interest are paid by the tax increments, which are "captured" and dedicated to that purpose. (p. 17)

Tax increment bonds are secured only by projected increases in revenues from existing and new development in the TIF district. Repayment is contingent upon increases in the taxable value of the property in the district.

The distinctive feature of TIF districts is that they rely on property taxes created directly by revitalization projects in the district, projects that pay for redevelopment costs incurred by the public. The tax base of the property in the designated area is frozen at its current level before redevelopment. All entities that have taxing authority agree--cities, counties, and school districts, for example--to this freeze. (Only the tax base is frozen, not the tax rate.)

Since rejuvenation of the district is likely to increase the value of their assets, landowners and residents have every reason to support the district's establishment. Other jurisdictions like school districts, cities, and counties do not lose revenue by agreeing to freeze assessed property values because without rejuvenation this assessed value would decrease over time.

Although state laws vary, all include a provision that enables each of the taxing jurisdictions to continue receiving that share of the taxes it had collected in the past from the frozen tax base (see Figure 4-3A). Each taxing jurisdiction first applies its tax rate to the frozen value, then to the new property value. The revenues accruing from the difference between the two is the tax-revenue increment available that year for repaying capital debts accumulated by the project (see Figure 4-3B). These incremental dollars go to the special district that issued the bonds. As assessed valuation in the district increases above the frozen tax-base level, greater increments become available for retiring the redevelopment district's debts.

Figure 4-3A
Illustration of the Principle of
Tax Increment Financing

Frozen Tax Base

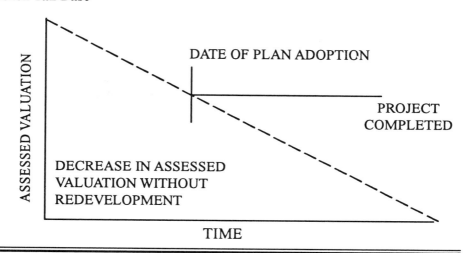

Figure 4-3B

Increased Assessed Valuation

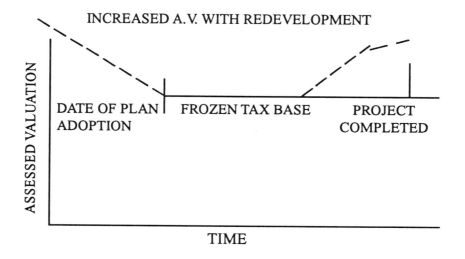

Decisions to buy TIF bonds are heavily influenced by the strength of any written agreement between the redevelopment agency and participating developers. If detailed agreements specifying proposed improvements, such as a major sports facility, their value, and a development timetable do not exist, the agency has less of a chance of selling the bonds.

From the perspective of a developer (Michael, 1987):

TIF is the economic equivalent of a capitalized property tax abatement. Although the development must continue to pay its regular property taxes, the increased taxes pay costs that the developer otherwise would have paid, such as land acquisition and public utilities for which special assessments would have been levied. Thus, TIF provides the economic equivalent of a property tax reduction or abatement. (p. 17)

Although non-guaranteed debt is secured by a revenue stream from a designated source, often the city will also accept a "moral obligation" to secure it. The city covenants to appropriate from its annual revenues amounts that may be required to meet full debt service on the bonds. This is done for two reasons. First, it reduces risk and, hence, rate of interest charged by investors. Second, even though a jurisdiction has no legal obligation to support non-guaranteed debt, a default would damage its reputation in the investment markets and make it more difficult and expensive for the jurisdiction to secure capital funds in the future.

Special Authority Bonds

Sometimes stadiums or arenas have been built with funds issued by special public authorities, which are entities with public powers that are able to operate outside normal constraints placed on governments. Primarily, this has been used as a way to circumvent public resistance to new sports projects and construct them without receiving public consent through a referendum. The Georgia Dome in Atlanta and Oriole Park at Camden Yards in Baltimore are among recent facilities built using authority financing. The authorities float the bonds that are sometimes guaranteed or accepted as a moral obligation by the state, without having to pass a voter referendum (Shubnell, et al., 1985):

The City of Pittsburgh financed Three Rivers Stadium through a conduit--The Stadium Authority of Pittsburgh--that was incorporated in 1964 by act of the city. Under state law, the authority may acquire, construct, improve, maintain and operate a stadium,; borrow money and issue debt; and collect fees and charges for stadium events. Conduit financing of this nature allows a municipality greater financing flexibility, as the powers legislated to a conduit agency bind it less strictly than city and state laws which are usually subject to stringent limitations on the type and amount of debt that they may incur.

The Stadium Authority of Pittsburgh first went to market in 1971 with a tax-exempt stadium lease-rental revenue bond. The bonds were used to retire temporary construction notes that had been issued to finance initial construction and certain start-up costs. Additional guaranteed stadium revenue bonds were issued in 1982 to provide improvements, including spectator lounge boxes and a new playing surface. (p. 8)

Bond Ratings

The interest rate that government entities will pay on their bonds is strongly influenced by the level of risk investors incur. To provide potential investors with information regarding the degree of risk involved in a bond issue, two major rating agencies--Moody's Investor Service, Inc. and Standard and Poor's Corporation--analyze an issue's risk of default and then assign a credit rating to the bonds. The rating is paid for by the bond issuer. The rating agencies prepare an opinion of the borrower's credit quality (for full-faith and credit issues) or of the particular bond issue (for revenue bonds). These opinions are widely distributed to the investment community and have a major influence on borrowing cost. An issue without a rating will seldom sell on national markets, but issues may be unrated if local markets will buy them (Mikesell, 1991).

The alphabetical rating systems used by the two agencies are generally considered to be equivalent, and the characteristics of a government entity that they consider when determining a bond rating are similar. An issue is assigned one of the ratings shown in Figure 4-4.

To impact their bond rating favorably many cities are now insuring bonds, a tactic that gives buyers more confidence and issuers lower interest rates. Effectively, the insurance guarantees against failure to pay when due; consequently, insured issues carry an effective triple-A rating (Figure 4-4). Insurance is typically priced at about one half of 1% of the total debt service to be paid over the life of the bond. The rate computes to about half the difference between the interest rate that a typical A-rated bond would pay and what an insured bond with a nominal triple-A rating would pay. The obvious rule is "to purchase insurance when the premium paid for insurance at the time of issue is less than the discounted interest savings resulting from the greater market acceptance of the insured issue" (Mikesell, 1991, p. 418). The tendency to use insurance is growing. In 1981 only 3% of new municipal bond issues were insured, whereas in 1991 this had increased to 30%.

EFFECTS OF THE 1986 TAX REFORM ACT

During the 1980s there was "an explosive growth in the use of nonguaranteed debt to fund public authorities and enterprises. Nonguaranteed debt went from 50 percent of total debt outstanding [among state and local governments] in 1970 to 71 percent in 1989" (Bahl & Duncombe, 1993, p. 31). Much of this growth was used by local and state governments to provide facilities or assistance on favorable terms for private businesses, as part of efforts to encourage economic development in their area.

A major advantage of most bonds issued by governmental entities is that they are tax exempt. The implications of this advantage are discussed in more detail in chapter

Figure 4-4
Credit Ratings by Moody's and Standard & Poor's

Moody's Investors Service	Symbol	Symbol	Standard & Poor's Corporation
Best quality, smallest degree of investment risk; referred to as "gilt edge."	Aaa	AAA	Prime: obligation of highest quality and lowest probability of default; quality management and low-debt structure.
High quality; smaller margin of protection or larger fluctuation of protective elements than Aaa.	Aa	AA	Higher grade: only slightly more secure than prime; second lowest probability of default.
Upper medium grade, many favorable investment attributes; some susceptibility to future risk evident.	A	A	Upper medium grade: safe investment; weakness in local economic base, debt burden, or fiscal balance.
Medium grade: neither highly protected nor poorly secured; adequate present security but may be unreliable over any great length of time.	Baa	BBB	Medium grade: lowest investment security rating; may show more than one fundamental weakness; higher default probability.
Judged to have speculative elements; not well safeguarded; very moderate protection of principal and interest, over both good and bad times.	Ba	BB	Lower medium grade: speculative noninvestment-grade obligation; relatively low risk and uncertainty.
Lack characteristics of desirable investment.	B	B	Low grade; investment characteristics virtually nonexistent.
Poor standing; may be in default.	Caa	CCC	
Speculative in high degree; default or other marked shortcomings.	Ca	CC	
Lowest rated class; extremely poor prospects of ever attaining any real investment standing.	C	C	Defaults.

5, but using them to construct stadiums and arenas enables facilities to be built at lower cost than if they were constructed directly by the owner of a sports franchise. Tax-exempt status means that investors do not pay federal income tax on the interest payments they receive from the bonds. A result of their rapid growth in the 1980s was that the federal treasury was annually foregoing billions of dollars through not being able to tax these investors' interest from bonds.

Hence, a key component of the 1986 Tax Reform Act was limitation on the types of projects for which governments could issue tax-exempt bonds. From 1984 onwards, it became obvious from Congressional hearings that there was strong sentiment among legislators to curtail the use of public tax-exempt bonds to develop facilities for private interests. Thus, many cities hustled either for their potential projects to be "grandfathered" into the legislation or to sell their bonds before the legislation was enacted. Some of the multitude of new sports buildings that were initiated in the early and mid-1980s (chapter 2) were the result of deals put together when the threat of changes in the federal tax law became apparent.

The 1986 act revoked the tax-exempt status for certain types of private-activity bonds, specifically naming those issued for pollution-control facilities, parking facilities, sports and convention centers, and industrial parks, if any of these facilities involved participation by the private sector (Bland & Chen, 1990). The most viable recourse for state and local governments wishing to satisfy these capital financial needs is now to issue taxable securities.

Although sports facilities were specifically cited as being ineligible for tax-exempt bonds if they were to be passed on to commercial franchises, the act did contain a number of loopholes. First, Representatives and Senators made provision for their favored projects, including a number of stadiums and arenas, to be grandfathered so that bonds for these specified projects received pre-1986 tax treatment. Second, stadium and arena bonds could still be tax exempt provided no professional sports team used the facility more than 10% of the time or made rental payments equal to more than 10% of the facility's annual debt service (Baldo, 1991).

SUMMARY

The property tax, which may be levied both on real and personal property, is the primary source of income for municipalities. The principal and interest payments incurred when bonds are backed by the full faith and credit of a jurisdiction are likely to be met by a commensurate increase in residents' property taxes. Both businesses and individuals are required to pay property taxes, but one of the strategies used by governments to encourage private sector investment in their communities is to exempt new businesses from property taxes for a given period of time. Professional sport franchises have benefited from these tax abatement incentives.

The second largest source of revenues that may be pledged to support bonds is the general sales tax. Non-guaranteed bonds issued to fund facilities often are redeemed by increases in sales taxes on selected items. The hotel-motel tax is frequently selected for this purpose, because there is a conceptual nexus between the new facility and generating additional traffic to fill hotel-motel rooms.

A bond is a promise by the borrower to pay back to the lender a specified amount of money, with interest, within a specified period of time. General obligation bonds are a full-faith and credit obligation and have an unlimited claim on the taxes and other revenues of the government entity issuing the bonds. These require voter approval through a referendum. The deteriorated financial status of municipalities in the past decade has made it increasingly difficult to obtain this approval for major sports facilities.

In recent years public officials have looked for ways to finance events and stadiums that would not use general-fund revenues or raise taxes. The pledge not to use taxpayers' funds has led to a focus on "off-budget" sources. Thus, most public bonds that have been issued for this purpose in recent years have been non-guaranteed, which means they are not backed by the full faith and credit of the government entity. Rather, their redemption is pledged from other designated revenue sources. In most jurisdictions voter approval for these bonds is not required. Three types of non-guaranteed bonds are most pertinent to the managed sports industry. Revenue bonds may be backed either by revenue accruing from the project or by an income stream from other designated sources such as the hotel-motel tax. Certificates of Participation are backed by revenue from lease-purchase agreements with the facility they are used to finance. Tax increment bonds are secured by projected increases in revenues from increases in the taxable value of property in the area that result from the initial investment.

All bonds that are sold on national markets are rated in terms of their level of risk to the investor by two major rating agencies. These ratings strongly influence the cost of borrowing. To reduce this risk, and lower interest rates, many jurisdictions now insure their bonds against default.

The 1986 Tax Reform Act revoked the tax-exempt status of public bonds issued to fund facilities where participation by the private sector was involved, and those issued for sports facilities were specifically cited. This is likely to inhibit future use of this funding source, but governments can still fund them through the use of taxable bonds. The act did grandfather a number of stadiums and arena projects that will receive pre-1986 treatment. In addition, bonds for stadiums can still be tax exempt if the private sector's involvement is minimal. This is defined as a professional sports team's using the facility for less than 10% of its use time or making rental payments that constitute no more than 10% of the facility's annual debt service.

Questions for Study and Discussion

1. What do the authors mean by their assertion that in many jurisdictions the intent of property tax assessment is to "create an illusion?"

2. Given the following information, how much could the government taxing authority expect to collect in property tax revenues. Show your calculations.

   Tax base = $100,000,000
   Assessment ratio = 80%
   Tax rate = 10 /$100 assessed value of property (AVP)

3. As a specialist on sport finance, you have been asked to advise a municipal sports commission on what type of government bonds should be sold to finance the construction of a proposed golf course. The commission is anxious to build the course to accommodate the ever-increasing demand for golf in the area. Describe the particular type of bond you would recommend. Be sure to provide a clear rationale for your recommendation.

4. Why did the 1986 Tax Reform Act limit the ability of cities and states to issue tax-exempt bonds? Under what restrictive conditions can tax-exempt bonds still be used to finance sport facilities?

REFERENCES

Bahl, R. & Duncombe, W. (1993). State and local debt burdens in the 1980s: A study in contrast. *Public Administration Review 53*(1), pp. 31-40.

Baldo, A. (1991, November 26). Ediface complex. *Financial World*, pp. 34-37.

Bland, L. & Chen, L. (1990). Taxable municipal bonds: State and local governments confront the tax-exempt limitation movement. *Public Administration Review, 50*(1), pp. 42-48.

Hildreth, W. B. (1993). State and local governments as borrowers: Strategic choices and the capital market. *Public Administration Review, 53*(1), 41-49.

Johnson, A. T. (1993). *Minor league baseball and local economic development*. Urbana, IL: University of Illinois Press.

Korman, R. (1989, February 20). A matter of pride. *Sports inc.*, pp. 32-37.

Michael, J. (1987, October). Tax increment financing: Local redevelopment finance after tax reform. *Government Finance Review*, pp. 17-21.

Mikesell, J. L. (1991). *Fiscal administration: Analysis and applications for the public sector.* Pacific Grove, CA: Brooks/Cole.

Oldman, O. & Schoettle, F. (1974). *State and local taxes and finance.* Mineola, NY: Foundation Press.

Quirk, J . P. (1987, January 18). A close look at the two proposals. *St. Louis Post-Dispatch.* Special Report, Section I, pp. SR5-7.

Rosentraub, M. S. & Nunn, S. (1978). Suburban city investment in professional sports. *American Behavioral Scientist, 21*(3), 393-415.

Severn, A. K. (1992). Building-tax abatements: An approximation to land value taxation. *American Journal of Economics and Sociology, 51*(2), 237-245.

Shnay, J. (1978, January 22). Many new stadiums facing financial problems. *Chicago Tribune*, Section 3, p. 2.

Shubnell, L. D., Peterson, J. E. & Harris, C. B. (1985, June). The big ticket: Financing a professional sports facility. *Government Finance Review*, pp. 7-11.

Wolkoff, M. J. (1985). Chasing a dream: The use of tax abatements to spur urban economic development. *Urban Studies 22*, 305-315.

CHAPTER 5

IMPLEMENTATION OF PUBLIC-PRIVATE PARTNERSHIPS

Learning Objectives

After completing this chapter, the reader should be able to:

1. discuss the complementary benefits that serve as the basis for joint-development arrangements between public sector and private sport organizations.

2. explain in detail, using appropriate illustrations, three joint-venture models for expanding sport facilities.

CHAPTER 5

IMPLEMENTATION OF PUBLIC-PRIVATE PARTNERSHIPS

This chapter is primarily concerned with exploring ways in which private sport organizations can cooperate with public-sector entities to their mutual financial benefit. The necessity of having to do more with less has required sport managers to explore creative ways in which to expand their resources. Increasingly, there are occasions when sport facilities or programs can be financially feasible only if some kind of joint-development arrangement can be established between a public-sector entity, such as a city or state, and the private event or sports team.

In chapter 1, it was noted that the costs of all professional sports are growing more rapidly than their revenues; that possibly one third of major league baseball teams and one quarter of NBA teams lost money in 1992; and that in the future, media revenues are likely to decline. One of the strategies used by owners to counter these trends is to seek new stadiums that incorporate skyboxes, club sections, and other amenities, which will enable them to substantially increase their in-grounds revenues. However, given their alleged lack of profit and their leverage power discussed in chapter 2, owners are looking for government entities to pay for a major proportion of new or extensively renovated facilities.

However, many local governments across the United States, especially in major urban areas are not in a strong financial position. According to the National Association of Counties, 40% of counties with populations of more than 100,000 suffered revenue shortfalls averaging $8.3 million in 1992. Similarly, more than 25% of the nation's cities reported budget deficits of at least 5% in 1992, according to the National League of Cities. The revenue crisis facing most communities has had a negative effect on the ability of cities to support and sustain sport and leisure facilities and services. Whereas counties, cities, and special districts reported spending more on park and recreation services in real dollar terms in 1990 than in 1980, these expenditures as a proportion of overall local government spending declined by 13% from 2.35% of total expenditures in 1979/80 to 2.06% in 1989/90 (Crompton & McGregor, in press). It appears that provision of recreation services, which includes investment in sporting amenities such as auditoriums and stadiums, became less of a priority for most local governments during the 1980s.

At the national government level, the primary federal grant program that is available to aid state and local governments in the construction of outdoor sport and recreation facilities is the Land and Water Conservation Fund. This provides matching grants to these entities of up to 50% of the cost of land acquisition, development, and construction. However, during the 1980s, funds from this source declined dramatically. In 1980 state and local governments shared $300 million from this source, but in 1988, 1989, and 1990 this was reduced to $20 million per year.

At the same time that it became more challenging for public entities to find money, the cost of developing specialized sport venues increased substantially. Quirk and Fort (1992) reported construction costs for stadiums and arenas over the last 30 years increased about 400%. Whereas the typical stadium built in the early and mid-1960s cost around $20 to $25 million--Dodger Stadium, 1962 ($23 million); Shea Stadium, 1963 ($24 million); Busch Stadium, 1966 ($25 million)--stadiums constructed in the early 1990s, such as Cleveland's Jacobs Field and Baltimore's Orioles park, cost around $150 million. The same kind of dramatic escalation in construction costs applied to arenas. In 1967 Jack Kent Cooke was able to build the Los Angeles Forum (17,000 capacity) for his NBA Lakers for $16.7 million. In 1994-95 it cost the Portland Trailblazers $262 million to complete their 20,340-seat sports/entertainment complex in downtown Portland.

Increasingly, the owners of professional teams have become less inclined to assume full financial risk for developments of such magnitude. This has been especially true in cities where local governments have been compelled to invest in replacing older facilities in order to keep existing teams. The leverage exerted by teams in all professional sports leagues was noted in Chapter 2 and this enables them to exert pressure on local governments to finance the building of new stadiums and arenas. The power of this leverage was demonstrated in Chicago in 1991, when the MLB White Sox threatened to move to St. Petersburg, Florida. The City of Chicago and State of Illinois spent $150 million to build a new Comiskey Park in order to keep the franchise. In addition, the city and state legislatures agreed to share operating losses on the ballpark up to a limit of $10 million a year (Zimbalist, 1992).

Most recent stadium or arena projects have involved joint participation, in which team ownership has shared to some degree the cost of development but, typically, the public sector's contribution is much greater than the amount contributed by a professional franchise. The Gateway development in Cleveland, Ohio, for example, is a $362-million combined stadium (Jacobs Field) and arena (Gund Arena) project, which involves three government jurisdictions (City of Cleveland, Cuyahoga County, and the State of Ohio) and two professional teams (Indians and Cavaliers). The public sector's contribution is estimated to be $220 million, whereas the teams' combined share is likely to approximate $140 million. Even when projects have been almost exclusively privately financed and entirely privately owned, such as Miami's Joe Robbie Stadium, public-sector contributions have been crucial to constructing the facilities.

In an environment in which sport franchise owners cannot or will not invest in new or extensively renovated facilities, and in which government entities are confronted with shrinking resources, increasingly the only way many sport projects may become reality is through cooperation in which both parties pool resources and share risks.

Critical to understanding the potential of joint ventures is a recognition that each sector has resources not possessed by the other. The essence of forging a collaborative agreement is finding a way to fuse the complementary benefits of each sector to the mutual advantage of all parties involved. Public sector organizations have access to a range of resources that can act as powerful enticements to private businesses. These resources include a substantial land bank, the ability to access low-cost development capital, control over zoning and permit applications, and the capacity to confer a number of tax incentives. On the other hand, the private sector offers an array of benefits which have proven to be attractive stimulants for public-sector cooperation. These inducements include specialized management expertise, reduced labor costs, and reduced liability risks. The complementary benefits that serve as the basis for public-private sector collaboration are summarized in Figure 5-1.

Figure 5-1
Complementary Assets of Public-Private Sector
Joint-Venture Agreements

Public Sector Assets	Private Sector Assets
• Substantial Land Bank	• Access to Capital
• Low-Cost Capital	• Specialized Management Expertise
• Tax Savings	• Reduced Liability Risks
• Control Over Zoning and Permit Process	• Reduced Labor Costs

PUBLIC SECTOR ASSETS

Land Bank

One of the most valuable assets a public agency possesses is the land it owns. It is common to find a substantial portion of a community's existing open space under the jurisdiction of a county, or municipal, park and recreation agency. Often, this inventory includes not only the largest tracts of potentially developable property but also some of the most attractive parcels with respect to location, access, and commercial value. A government agency may be prepared to offer some park land, open space, or existing facility to a private organization under a nominal lease arrangement (for example, one dollar a year) in order to encourage development of a resource that the public agency could not develop on its own. Without this incentive, the high cost of land would make the project economically nonfeasible for the private organization.

This type of incentive was key to the controversial movement of the Brooklyn Dodgers to Los Angeles in 1958 (Lipsitz, 1984):

- By the middle 1950s there had been an exodus of the Brooklyn population to the suburbs of Long Island and New Jersey. The neighborhood around the Brooklyn Dodgers' Ebbetts Field had deteriorated, and the ballpark appeared increasingly inaccessible and undesirable to the mobile sections of the population. Unhappy with a small old ballpark served by only one subway line, the team owner Walter O'Malley got the state of New York to authorize construction of a new stadium at a better location in the area. He sold Ebbetts Field and two minor league ballparks for $5 million and prepared to invest that sum in the new stadium. But land acquisition proved difficult in the face of rising prices and neighborhood opposition. At that point, the City of Los Angeles offered 315 acres of land to O'Malley as an inducement for him to move the team to Los Angeles and build a stadium on that site. The land occupied a choice location near downtown at the intersection of three major freeways. After complex negotiations, the city agreed to give O'Malley the land which was worth between $2 million and $6 million, mineral rights under that land, a ninety-nine year lease, all revenues from parking, concessions and tickets, $4.7 million in land preparation costs and $50,000 of free surveying. In return, O'Malley promised to provide the capital for a $20 million stadium. (p. 1)

A similar, more recent arrangement of this type was proposed between the District of Columbia and Washington Redskins owner Jack Kent Cooke to build a $206 million stadium:

- The arrangement calls for the city to lease the stadium site to the team for a dollar a year for 30 years. The Washington Redskins would pay for the construction and own the 78,600-seat facility for 30 years before turning it over to the city. In addition, the proposal guarantees the city $4.6 million a year in revenue for 30 years. The money, in part, would be used to redeem bonds issued by the city to pay for road repairs and alterations needed for the stadium. Mr. Cooke would retain all additional revenues from the operation of the stadium including ticket revenue, concessions and parking, and the leasing of luxury suites which alone could generate $25 million annually.

Low Cost Capital

A public agency is able to borrow money at a lower interest rate than is a commercial organization. If the public organization can make this relatively inexpensive money available to a private enterprise, this can constitute a substantial financial incentive. For example, a reduction of 3% in the annual rate of borrowing—the difference between the interest rate a private company is likely to have to pay if it were borrowing from a commercial lender compared to the interest payable on municipal bonds—may mean a reduction of $100,000 a year or more in annual debt payments on a $3-million loan. In effect, the public agency replaces the bank as the lender. By using this capacity, a local agency may be able to transform a nonremunerative project into a profitable venture. This arrangement was used recently as an essential component of the overall financing strategy for the development of a new downtown baseball stadium in Cleveland:

- Cuyahoga County, through its sale of tax-exempt revenue bonds, was able to furnish the Cleveland Indians baseball organization $30 million toward the construction of the $161-million stadium. Taking advantage of its excellent credit rating, the county was able to sell the variable interest bonds very inexpensively. In return for receiving the inexpensive development capital, the Indians agreed to repay the county an amount equivalent to the annual debt payments using revenues received from the sale of stadium luxury suites. As the beneficiary of the county's ability to borrow money inexpensively, the Indians will realize substantial savings in total interest.

The reason that local governments can borrow money at lower interest rates is that municipal bonds, unlike corporate bonds, are tax exempt. The interest paid is free from all federal income taxes, and usually from those in the state in which they are issued, if the state has an income tax. This results in substantial tax advantages for those in the highest income brackets. Thus, Table 5-1 indicates that an investor whose

TABLE 5-1
THE YIELD REQUIRED ON A TAXABLE INVESTMENT EQUAL TO THE YIELD ON A TAX-EXEMPT INVESTMENT FOR FOUR DIFFERENT TAX RATES

Tax-exempt yields	Taxable yield equivalents			
	28%	31%	34%	36%
2.00%	2.78%	2.90%	3.03%	3.13%
2.50	3.47	3.62	3.79	3.91
3.00	4.17	4.32	4.55	4.69
3.50	4.86	5.07	5.30	5.47
4.00	5.56	5.80	6.06	6.25
5.00	6.94	7.25	7.58	7.81

marginal tax rate is 36% (that is, $.36 on the last dollar earned, which currently is the highest level of taxation paid to the federal government) should be as willing to purchase a municipal bond offering 5.00% interest as to purchase a corporate bond offering 7.81%. Taking away the 36% federal income tax that would have to be paid on the 7.81% return would leave a taxable yield to the bond investor of 5.0%.

The tax-exempt provision allows governments to offer their bonds more cheaply than private firms can while providing investors equivalent **after-tax** returns on their investment. Although the cost of borrowing differs widely, depending on the fiscal position of a public agency and its credit rating, that cost invariably will be lower than the cost of borrowing from a commercial organization.

In his assessment of financial arrangements developed for financing a proposed domed stadium in St. Louis, Quirk (1987) calculated that if $120 million of tax free bonds were issued by the county, the bonds would

> sell at yields considerably less than what the bonds would have to pay if they were not tax-exempt and if they did not have county backing. A conservative estimate of the subsidy involved here is $4 million a year, assuming that county bonds will sell to yield 3.5 percent less than non tax-exempt bonds. (p. SR7)

Tax Waivers

The ability of the public sector to substantially reduce the tax liabilities of private investors can be a powerful inducement to encouraging their participation in a joint venture. Tax abatements were described in chapter 4. They are agreements between public jurisdictions and private organizations in which the jurisdiction agrees to forgo or postpone collecting at least some of the property taxes that a proposed new development would normally expect to pay. When Busch Stadium was constructed in St. Louis, the developers were able to take advantage of a Missouri law that was intended to encourage private development in run-down areas. Missouri's "353" Redevelopment Law allowed businesses engaged in redevelopment of "blighted" areas to avoid all taxes on their property for 10 years and to pay only half taxes for 15 years after that (Lipsitz, 1984).

The terms of a tax abatement often are negotiable and may range from a waiver of some proportion of taxes for a short period to absolution of all property taxes for an extended period of time. The conceptual rationale for tax abatements is that the overall public benefits created by the sports project (new jobs, appreciated property values, "major league" status for the city, civic pride, etc.) justify the tax relief extended to the private-sector interests. At the same time, these concessions again reflect the ability of franchise owners to exert strong leverage on cities.

- The Cleveland Indians and Cavaliers, professional baseball and basketball franchises, respectively, have been granted property-tax exemptions as principal tenants of a new stadium and arena in downtown Cleveland. The Indians occupy a $161-million, 42,000-seat ballpark (Jacobs Field) with a 30-year lease agreement. Under the arrangement, the baseball team will be absolved of all property tax obligations for both real property and the improvements made on the property (infrastructure, parking, stadium). The Cavaliers enjoy comparable property tax relief as primary tenants of the new $117-million, 21,000-seat arena. The savings in forgiven tax payments to both clubs, while not publicly disclosed, will amount to millions of dollars over the life of the joint venture.

Control Over Permit and Zoning Process

Nowhere is the adage "Time is money" more relevant than with respect to large-scale development projects. The faster a project can be built, the faster it can generate a return on investment. Invariably, one of the most challenging and often time-consuming aspects of the development process is meeting the various preconstruction permit requirements.

The ability to expedite permit applications has become increasingly important. The impact of government legislation and regulation is felt by the private sector from the initial planning of a project through to the development and operation phases. The development of a sport facility by a private company is subject to myriad regulations and requirements administered by a great number of government agencies. Obtaining all the necessary permits and permissions to proceed frequently is a frustrating process that discourages many developers. A public jurisdiction is likely to be able to assist in expediting this process. The public agency working from "within" the government system, can push much more effectively for rapid permit approval than can private firms operating "outside" the structure of government.

Land-use zoning substantially impacts the value of land. For example, if it is zoned for agricultural purposes, then the land's value is likely to be much less than if it is zoned for development because the income potential of agricultural land is substantially lower than if that same land is used to build houses, offices, or a stadium. Hence, changes in zoning that increase the amount of development allowed on a piece of land are likely to increase its value.

- After Sacramento voters rejected an initiative to construct a stadium on county land in 1979, private developers acquired 510 acres of rice farm land on the edge of the city that was zoned for agricultural use. In making this purchase, the developers gambled they could convince the city to rezone the site for commercial development. The developers purchased the Kansas City Kings NBA franchise in 1984 and brought it to Sacramento. This mobilized eager basketball fans who helped lobby for the rezoning so that a new arena could be built for the team on this land. The rezoning was granted, which meant that the value of the rice farm land and hence the developers' assets, increased dramatically. The sports project was used effectively to leverage the zoning change, which otherwise was unlikely to occur (Korman, 1989). The trade-out was described by Fulton (1988) in the following terms:

  Sometimes the cost of obtaining a team may not be money (which may be put up by business leaders, not taxpayers), but rather the sacrifice of a long term policy objective. This is what happened in Sacramento. The rapidly growing state capital of California has all the makings of a major-league town. (It's already the 21st-largest television market in the country.) But when local developer Gregg Lukenbill bought the Kansas City Kings basketball team, he and a few other landowners effectively traded their promise to bring the team to Sacramento (and also seek a baseball team) for permission to develop an area the city voters had previously set aside for agriculture. The City Council -- hungering for big-league status--eagerly went along with the deal. (p. 40)

PRIVATE SECTOR ASSETS

The most obvious contribution of the private sector to joint partnerships is an ability to provide funds for operation, maintenance, and/or capital development of a venture. However, there are three additional aspects of private sector involvement that may also be attractive to the public sector: management expertise, reduced labor costs, and reduced liability risks. Each of these is discussed in this section.

Management Expertise

Often, government agencies do not have personnel with the necessary training, experience, and/or equipment to effectively operate specialized sport facilities such as ice rinks, indoor tennis centers, arenas, golf courses, and ski areas. On the other hand, established private firms draw upon a depth of technical expertise that provides many advantages. These benefits include the ability to focus their work force and equipment more intensively to perform a specific function, coupled with the likelihood of owning more up-to-date specialized equipment.

The American Golf Corporation provides an excellent example of how one firm has parlayed its management expertise into becoming the world's leader in public golf course management.

THE AMERICAN GOLF EDGE
American Golf has been the world's leader in public golf course management for the past 20 years. We have provided excellence in every facet of our operations and continually strive to stay on the leading edge of all developments in the golf industry.

We are able to provide services like no other management company because of the expertise found in our corporate personnel and our management/operations techniques.

Some of our unique human resources are:

Construction Department – This department supervises all design and construction of new site facilities and renovation of existing buildings. Our staff has extensive experience in:

> • **Landfill Construction — One example is Mountain Gate Country Club, a 27-hole private country club located in Los Angeles.**
> • **Drainage Reconstruction — Inadequate drainage is a problem on many courses. We have had experience with every type of drainage problem across the country. One example of our redesign and construction can be found at Fullerton Golf Course in Fullerton, California.**
>
> *Agronomy Expert* **— Our in-house agronomy expert supervises and advises all Regional and Course Superintendents nationwide in the proper care of trees and turf.**
>
> *Training* **— This Department insures that all new employees are thoroughly trained in American Golf procedures, policies and philosophy.**
>
> *Employment Opportunities* **— Career opportunities are offered nationwide as well as competitive wages (based on nationally collected salary survey information).**
>
> *Marketing Department* **— All corporate marketing, advertising, promotion and public relations direction falls under this umbrella, as well as pro shop merchandise coordination. Central buying where possible, results in tremendous price savings for all American Golf pro shops.**
>
> Note: From the American Golf Edge, produced by American Golf Corporation., 1633 26th St., Santa Monica, CA 90404

As shown above, American Golf Corporation offers the public sector a range of "unique" services designed to enhance both operating efficiencies and the quality of the golf experience. Rarely does a government agency responsible for operating a golf course have the resources or expertise to furnish such a complete array of specialized services.

Founded in 1968, American Golf Corporation has grown to become the largest golf course management company in the world. The privately-held corporation currently operates 145 golf courses, with plans to manage 250 by 1996. The company specializes in revitalizing golf courses for which governments do not have capital funds. American Golf's approach involves initial investment (sometimes reaching $1 million) improving the course and related infrastructure, dramatically increasing rounds of play through enhanced service quality and vigorous marketing, and reducing costs largely through more flexible and cost-effective utilization of personnel. The company's recent takeover of four municipally owned golf courses in Detroit illustrates the benefits of private sector expertise.

- In 1990, American Golf Corporation entered into a 20-year lease agreement with the City of Detroit Recreation Department to operate four of the six city golf courses. The courses had consistently lost money for the city. In 1990-91, operating losses of close to $600,000 had to be covered by monies from Detroit's general fund. The contract requires American Golf to spend close to $2 million for improvements, including clubhouse renovations, new irrigation systems, landscaping, bunker restoration, and drainage work. In addition, the terms of the agreement stipulate that American Golf pay the city $50,000 in 1991 and 1992, increasing to $200,000 by 1995. In return, the possessory lease provides American Golf with exclusive operating rights to the four courses for nominal consideration ($1 a year). American Golf's Regional Director acknowledges the risks for his firm: "We'll lose money for six years." However, American Golf's strategy is to recoup losses as the dramatic changes in the courses draw people back. The company's goal is to attract 10,000 more golfers a year to each of the courses. The use of its own employees, who are paid considerably less than unionized city workers, sales from concessions, and equipment rentals will also offset payments to the city.

It is important to note that the City of Detroit excluded two of its six golf courses from the management agreement with the American Golf Corporation. Past experience has shown that jurisdictions that encourage some level of competition among service providers produce substantial savings from contractors. In this case, the city has induced competition between the American Golf Corporation-operated courses and those it maintained "in-house," which gives both service providers incentive to produce high levels of service.

Reduced Labor Costs

There is substantial evidence that private firms can offer services more cost effectively than can government agencies (Rehfuss, 1989). The key advantage is that private operators have greater control over payroll expenses. On average, government agencies pay 30-35% in "overhead" or fringe benefits to public employees. In effect, between 30-35 cents on every dollar paid to employees goes toward meeting the cost of such non-work related benefits as health insurance, retirement, sick leave, and maternity leave. Generally, government agencies are mandated by either civil service regulations and/or union bargaining agreements to pay for these employment benefits. On the other hand, many private business firms are not required to maintain such a high level of overhead. Federal and state laws may require commercial operators to pay Social Security and payroll taxes, but not employee medical or pension benefits. As a result, payroll overhead costs for private firms average around 12%. The approximately 20% overhead savings advantage enjoyed by many private-sector operators allows them to provide the same level of service much more economically than can public organizations. In addition, their exemption from civil service requirements provides them with greater flexibility in determining level of pay, fringe-benefit payments, and mix of full and part-time personnel. The example below illustrates how one public agency was able to overcome a difficult staffing problem by taking advantage of the flexibility afforded a private firm.

- A publicly-managed golf course in Alameda County, California, operated on a 13-hour summer schedule, opening at 6:00 a.m. and closing at 7:00 p.m. All maintenance activities were performed by public employees of a regional park and recreation authority. Early in the decade, employees formed a bargaining unit affiliating with the American Federation of State, County, and Municipal Employees (AFSCME), a public employee labor union. The labor contract established between AFSCME and the park authority stipulated a standard workday of 8 hours for full-time employees. Compliance with the contract required the park authority to commit two separate, 8-hour shifts of maintenance and operations personnel to the golf course. The park and recreation authority estimated that under this agreement, staffing costs at the golf course would increase as much as 21%. Faced with an intractable situation, the agency made the decision to contract out the operation of the golf course to a specialized management firm. An advertisement placed in the *Wall Street Journal* produced several legitimate bidders. A long-term lease (5 years with four 5-year renewable options) was awarded to a private firm with a successful track record in operating and maintaining golf courses. The agreement called for the management company to provide over $600,000 in capital improvements over the first 5 years of the lease. By applying a more flexible personnel schedule to accommodate actual work demands and, at the same time, not being obligated to pay as high an overhead (e.g., retirement, vacation, and hospitalization benefits), the park authority estimates the private firm has reduced labor expenses at the golf course by as much as 50%. The end result is that the golfing public benefited from an enhanced resource. At the same time, the park authority has freed approximately $400,000 a year in public monies previously committed to paying golf course personnel to apply to other areas of service concern.

Reduced Liability Risks

An increasingly attractive incentive for public agencies to enter working partnerships with private organizations is that such a collaboration can substantially reduce their liability risks. Most liability suits arise from careless or reckless acts (negligence) that result in unintentional harm to an injured party. Since the almost complete elimination in the 1980s of the doctrine of sovereign immunity, which historically prohibited units of government from being sued, cities, counties, and school districts have become increasingly vulnerable to negligence claims. Liability awards ranging from several hundred thousand to several million dollars are now commonly paid by public agencies. The increased threat of such catastrophic claims has necessitated that government agencies purchase expensive insurance premiums.

A key question, then, for public agency managers is how they can minimize the possibility of encountering a financially catastrophic claim against their agency. Because liability insurance premiums are based largely on the estimated degree of risk facing an agency, any actions that the agency can take to reduce level of exposure to risk should lead to reduced premium costs. Government agencies have found joint ventures to be an effective strategy for minimizing their liability risks, and, therefore, the costs associated with insurance protection. Increasingly, government agencies are structuring partnership agreements so as to transfer as much of the risk and responsibility for liability to the commercial or private operator. Typically, the transfer of liability risk is conferred in the lease agreement establishing a public-private partnership. The following sample is drawn from an actual lease agreement established between a municipality and a commercial operator for the maintenance and operation of a sports complex:

CLAIMS. The contractor shall hold harmless the City and all of its agents, employees and officers from any and all damages or claims of any kind or nature, that may be made or may arise directly or indirectly from the performance of duties by the Contractor, its agents and employees, including but not limited to any claims which may arise either directly or indirectly from the use of any equipment or tools which the City may lease or sell to the Contractor. The Contractor shall appear and defend any action or suit instituted against the City arising in any manner out of the acts or omissions defined herein above. The Contractor's duty to indemnify hereunder shall include all costs or expenses arising out of all claims specified herein, including all court, and/or arbitration costs, filing fees, and attorney's fees and costs of settlement.

The excerpt identifies two provisions key to effective transfer of liability risks. The first element establishes that the public agency will be "held harmless" in the event of a negligence claim. The intent is to release the public agency from all liability risks. However, while crucial, the hold harmless clause alone may not provide ironclad protection. A standard provision is to add an "indemnification" clause, which stipulates that if the hold harmless agreement is not completely adequate—for example, if the public agency is found liable of "contributory negligence"—any damages owed by the public agency would be paid by the commercial operator. Thus, responsibility and costs related to liability concerns are borne exclusively by the private contractor.

In a well-conceived public-private partnership, the exclusive costs and responsibility for liability borne by the private contractor are offset by benefits derived from the agreement. The potential savings realized by the contractor, who has to pay only nominal lease consideration ($1.00 a year) for access to a prime site, otherwise unaffordable, compensate for the potential additional liability insurance costs.

JOINT-VENTURE MODELS

It is evident that each sector has resources that could be of significant value to the other. To provide a framework for understanding how these assets can be forged into effective public-private partnerships, examples of joint-venture arrangements are presented in this section. They have been classified into three major categories: private-sector takeovers, public-sector pump priming, and joint-development agreements.

Private-Sector Takeovers

The first major category consists of situations in which a private organization takes responsibility for operation of a facility or service owned by the public sector. Most older cities throughout the United States and Canada have a large number of decaying, underutilized sports facilities desperately in need of rehabilitation. Given the fiscal constraints confronting most local governments, public funds are invariably inadequate or nonexistent for refurbishing tennis courts, athletic fields, ice rinks, and golf courses that have fallen into disrepair. The transformation of Louis Armstrong Stadium into a world-class tennis complex is an example of how a private sector takeover of a publicly-owned sports facility can benefit everyone.

USTA Take-Over of Louis Armstrong Stadium

It has been documented that a major problem facing most large cities is how to find sufficient funds to rejuvenate facilities that have been allowed to decay or fall into disrepair. The Louis Armstrong Stadium, located in Flushing Meadow Park in the middle of the Borough of Queens, was such a facility. It was left over from the 1964 World's Fair, was decaying, and had been virtually abandoned.

The United States Tennis Association (USTA) had outgrown its former home at Forest Hills, where it had held the U. S. Open Tennis Championships since 1924. It was looking for an alternate site in the New York City area. The USTA recognized the potential of this stadium and approached New York City with a proposal to develop a tennis center on the site.

The City agreed to lease USTA 16 acres for 15 years. As a result of this agreement, a deteriorating stadium, which the city could not keep up and could not rent, was redesigned. Within it were developed two separate tennis stadiums, one seating about 19,000 and the other, 6,000. In addition, there are 25 outdoor courts with lighting for night play and 9 air-conditioned indoor courts, as well as extensive areas for locker rooms, lounges, a pro shop, a restaurant, and administrative offices.

WHAT THE CITY GAINS

–The finest tennis facility in the East without having to pay anything. This $10-million stadium renovation is available to the city for public use for at least 305 days per year. The USTA receives exclusive use of the facility for no more than 60 days a year.

–A minimum annual payment of whichever is the greater: either $125,000, or a percentage based on rentals, concessions, food and beverages obtained at times other than USTA events.

–All parking revenues, including those at USTA events. This was not a part of the lease, since the city owns the Shea Stadium parking lot that is the one to be used. At a very modest $2 per car, the city will receive about $14,800 per day if the lot is filled. During the 12-day tournament period, this is likely to bring in close to $200,000.

–USTA is responsible for the cost of maintenance, operation, and security of the entire facility all year round. The USTA estimated its annual personnel costs alone for regular (that is, non-U.S. Open) security and maintenance to be $150,000.

WHAT THE USTA GAINS
- —Exclusive control for 60 days each year over scheduling and prices of tickets, food, programs, and merchandise.
- —All revenues from the U.S. Open that exceed $6 million.
- —All revenues from other special events that USTA will try to attract to the facilities, such as the Davis, Wightman, or Federation Cup tennis matches.

IMPLICATIONS
The *Fiscal Observer*, which reported the terms of this agreement, concluded its article by saying:

> The importance of the City-USTA partnership lies not in this one contract but in the precedent it may set for the future. The City owns hundreds of decaying, underused facilities throughout the five boroughs. It cannot even maintain them, much less rehabilitate them fully and bring them up to the standard of elegance contemplated by the USTA in Queens. The City must look around for new ways of using its facilities profitably, and its USTA partnership may well be the first of many deals. This partnership was brilliantly conceived and studiously implemented by the USTA.

Note: This example is adapted from a case study published in *The Fiscal Observer* Vol II, Number 16, August 3, 1978. It is used by permission of the Center for New York Affairs, 66 Fifth Avenue, New York, NY 10011

Pump Priming by the Public Sector

The second major type of joint-venture model requires a public agency to "prime the pump" to facilitate the development of new sport areas and facilities. Pump priming is the injection into a project of relatively small amounts of public resources to stimulate investment of much larger amounts of capital investment by the private sector.

- In 1987, the owner of the AAA Pacific Coast League Hawaii Baseball team was interested in relocating the team to Colorado Springs. The city needed a stadium for the team, but voters had previously rejected proposals to spend public money for a stadium. The owner was referred to a major real estate development company that was developing a 2,000-acre site, 8.5 miles from downtown. Believing it would give visibility to their development, the company agreed to donate the land for a stadium. The city agreed to pay the owner who was developing the new stadium $500,000 as its share of the project. This pump-priming contribution was crucial to bringing the stadium to fruition: "City financial participation was critical to the owner and was perceived by city officials as a potential deal-breaker" (Johnson, 1993, p. 238). Because the state's constitution forbade the use of public money for private interests, the city was required to receive something of value for its $500,000. Thus, a joint-use agreement calls for the stadium to be used by the city 180 days of each year through the year 2002. However, given the weather conditions in Colorado Springs outside baseball season, this use was much less generous than it may at first appear to be (Johnson, 1993).

The development of Joe Robbie Stadium in Miami in the late 1980s provides another good example of how a relatively modest contribution by the public sector can stimulate substantial private investment. In this case, the pump priming was achieved by contributing the land.

- The $90-million, 73,000-seat open air stadium on the northern edge of Dade County was financed almost entirely by Joe Robbie, owner of the Miami Dolphins. The financial feasibility of the project and, therefore, a key incentive for Robbie's investment, was greatly enhanced by Dade County's proposal to lease the 100-acre parcel of land on which the stadium was built to the Dolphins for 99 years at $1.00 per year. Freed from site acquisition costs, which would have run into the millions, the owner of the Dolphins was able to apply all of the revenues raised through the successful preselling of luxury suites and club seats as security on a 30-year, industrial revenue bond issue. Robbie pledged income from the leasing of 234 luxury boxes and 10,000 club seats. Leases on the luxury boxes averaged $45,000 to $50,000 per year for a period of 10 years. Club seats, also leased for 10 years, rent from $600 to $1,400 per year. Most of these exclusive seats were sold by the first year of the stadium's operation. Preconstruction deposits for luxury seating enticed a consortium of banks in the Miami area to back the project through their issuance of $83 million in industrial revenue bonds to finance the stadium's construction. To date, the stadium's profitability has ensured sufficient debt service. The benefits realized by the Miami area as a result of Dade County government's modest economic stimulus have been considerable. Since its opening in 1987, Joe Robbie Stadium has been the site of the 1990 Superbowl and 1994 World Cup Soccer. These two events alone have injected millions of new dollars into the local economy.

Pump priming may be implemented with in-kind resources rather than money. These resources may be used either to construct a new facility or to complement a developer's effort by assisting with development of infrastructure. There are many facets of a sports complex development, such as infrastructure (e.g., roads, utilities), which do not have revenue-generating potential. If the public sector takes responsibility for some of these costs, then development of a sports resource that is otherwise unprofitable may become financially viable to a team owner.

Joint-Development Agreements

In this category of joint ventures, public and private-sector organizations agree from the outset to share mutual responsibility for development and/or expansion of a sport resource. In joint-development arrangements, impetus for forming the working relationship can come from either sector. Historically, the public sector's level of involvement in bringing a project to fruition, and often its level of monetary contribution, have been more central than those of the commercial sector. More recently, however, the private sector has become more aggressive in seeking partnerships.

Two types of agreements are discussed. First, is the multiparty arrangement, in which a number of financial partners come together, from both private and public sectors to make a project feasible. The second type of joint-development agreement is the leaseback arrangement, by which a commercial developer agrees to finance and develop a sport facility and then lease it to the agency at a previously agreed rent.

Multiparty Arrangements. It is increasingly common for large-scale public-private sports partnerships to be complex arrangements involving multiple financial partners. Often they are spearheaded by an independent quasi-governmental body to facilitate collaborative exchange between the various private and commercial entities involved with the project. The Hubert Humphrey Metrodome, the Hoosier Dome, Pilot Field in Buffalo, and the Gateway Sports Complex are all examples of this type of arrangement.

In the case of the Metrodome in Minneapolis, the Metro Sports Facilities Commission (the Commission), a special authority created by the state legislature, was established to assemble the necessary financing ($75 million) from various private and public sources and to oversee the operation of the facility.

- Initially, the Commission negotiated with a group of Minneapolis land developers to have a 20-acre stadium site, valued at $9 million, donated to the Commission in return for the right to develop the surrounding real estate developers owned. However, the key to success of the project was the Commission's ability to broker an agreement between the City of Minneapolis and the downtown business community for the sale of $55 million of revenue bonds. The tax-exempt bonds issued by the City were purchased by five local corporations. To secure bond repayment, the Commission entered an agreement with the City of Minneapolis to collect an annual hotel-motel tax (2%) and liquor tax (2%). The revenues collected from these taxes are used to pay all the debt-service costs (principal and interest) on the revenue bonds. In addition, the Commission assesses a 10% admission tax on all events held at the Metrodome. Monies realized from this surcharge are used to cover annual operating expenses. The remaining $20 million was raised from $13 million in interest earned on the revenue bonds and $7 million from two of the Metrodome's principal tenants, the Minnesota Vikings and Twins football and baseball teams, respectively. The latter revenue came principally from the lease of luxury box suites.

    Crucial to establishing financial stability was the Commission's effort to negotiate long-term tenant lease agreements with the Twins, the Vikings, and the University of Minnesota. These agreements confirm a minimum of 100 dates per year for the next 20-30 years. The 30-year lease arrangement with the Vikings provides the Commission with 10% of the gross ticket sales. For 81 regular season games played in the Metrodome, the Twins surrender 7.5% of their gross gate receipts. To date, these revenues, along with admission tax proceeds from other events, have allowed the Commission to operate the Metrodome free from public subsidy of any kind.

Pilot Field in Buffalo is the home of the AAA Buffalo Bisons, which is the most successful of baseball's minor league teams. It was constructed in the late 1980s and is another example of a complex multiparty agreement with a host of different organizations contributing to its financing. The stadium has been called, "a minor league stadium with all the major league amenities," "the best ballpark in the minor leagues," and "the city's ticket to Glory Days" (Johnson, 1993, p. 91). The principal objectives of the project were to develop a facility designed to attract a major league baseball franchise and to act as a catalyst for downtown redevelopment. Contributions of the financial partners in the project are shown in Table 5-2.

- The largest contributor to Pilot Field was the New York State legislature,

Table 5-2
Financial Participation in the Construction of Pilot Field

Contributions	Amount (in millions)
City of Buffalo	
General improvement serial bonds	5.32
Downpayment on bonds	0.28
Three-year operation and maintenance budget	2.10
	7.70
New York State	
State Urban Development Corporation funds	22.50
ECIDA	
Revenue bonds	4.20
Other Contributions	4.00
Buffalo Development Companies	3.00
Buffalo Bisons	2.00
Buffalo Urban Renewal Agency (land credit)	0.75
Erie County legislature	9.75
Total Cost of Pilot Field	44.15

Note: From *Minor League Baseball and Local Economic Development* (p. 89) by Arthur T. Johnson, 1993, Urbana, IL: University of Illinois Press.

which in April 1985 appropriated $22.5 million in state Urban Development Corporation funds for the project. When these funds were approved, tripartite agreements were signed that delineated the responsibilities of the state, the city and the Erie County Industrial Development Agency (ECIDA), which was the developer of the project. The ECIDA was a public-benefit corporation created in 1970 to foster economic prosperity in Buffalo and Erie County. Under these agreements, the state must be repaid from any profits that may be realized after a maintenance reserve fund of up to $75,000 annually was established and after the debt service was paid on bonds issued by the ECIDA and the city. The agreements also required the city government to pay for all cost overruns. Under the terms of the tripartite agreement, the ECIDA was the owner of Pilot Field, and the city had a noncanceling, 15-year agreement with the agency. At the end of the lease, title to the stadium passes to the city.

The city was responsible for operation and maintenance of the facility. Its major source of revenue was a contract with the Buffalo Bisons, the principal tenant. The lease agreement was critical because it was the city's guarantee that it could operate and maintain the stadium without having to subsidize the operation with additional tax dollars. Since the project involved the construction of an expandable stadium so that it could accommodate major league baseball in the future, the council wanted an expandable base to ensure the city would benefit from the future growth.

To forge this partnership, a lease was developed that linked the rent to paid admissions. That is, the percentage of ticket revenues that the Bisons pay to the city increases as gross receipts increase. Any profit the city realizes from the operation of Pilot Field is to be applied toward the $800,135 it pays annually for principal and interest on the bonds issued by the ECIDA and the city for stadium construction. The term of these bonds is 15 years, corresponding to the term of the lease agreement the city has with the ECIDA. In 1988-89, the city enjoyed $158,405 in excess revenues over expenditures from stadium operations, if depreciation expenses are excluded. ECIDA's participation as project director was important because it had the ability to establish a construction price ceiling that the contractor was required to meet for the entire project. If the city had served as the developer, it would have been compelled by the city charter to bid each of the various aspects of the project and face the cost overruns that would occur with the inevitable change orders.

In July 1985 the city council authorized the sale of city bonds in the amount of $5.32 million to cover the city's share of the project. As Table 5-2 reports, several other groups also contributed. The Buffalo Development Companies, a consortium of local development agencies, contributed $4 million, including $150,000 in Urban Development Corporation handicapped-access funds. The Buffalo Urban Renewal Agency, an ancillary agency of city government, contributed the land. The Bisons contributed $3 million towards the purchase of the scoreboard and the construction of the concession areas, the restaurant, and team offices. The project also was aided when Senator Moynihan in the U.S. Congress included it as a "grandfathered" project in the 1986 Tax Reform Act; consequently, the stadium developers were allowed to finance the construction with tax-exempt bonds. This inclusion saved the project an estimated $17 million in interest payments over the 15-year life of the bonds.

Leaseback Arrangements. The leaseback joint-venture model may be implemented in a number of different ways. The following series of examples illustrates the possible diversity. A common approach to applying this joint-development alternative is for the public agency and commercial operator to enter into a long-term development and facility management contract. Typically, cost of construction is borne entirely by the private developer. Upon completion, exclusive or partial utilization rights are leased to the public agency at a previously negotiated, fixed or graduated annual rent for an extended period of time (often as long as 20-30 years). This type of leaseback arrangement makes increasing economic sense for communities hoping to expand facilities without paying large sums up front.

An example of this approach was the leaseback agreement established between the City of Dublin, Ohio, and Columbus Hockey, Inc., owners of the East Coast Hockey League franchise, the Columbus Chill:

• In 1993, the city and the hockey team agreed to collaborate on development of a $3.3-million indoor ice rink. The 60,000-square foot facility included two ice surfaces (one NHL size--190' x 85'--and one Olympic size--200' x 100'), a pro shop, skate rental area, video game room, public locker room, and a concession area. In addition, the ice arena will house offices for the Chill's management staff and a team locker room and training facility.

Impetus for establishing a new ice rink came from the Chill, who were finding it increasingly difficult to reserve adequate ice time for team practices at the one ice rink in the metropolitan area of 1.4 million residents. So great was the demand for ice at the single arena owned and operated by the local state university, that the Chill were limited to one-hour practices, often at 5:00 a.m. or 6:00 a.m. Analysis of the area's imbalance between supply and demand led management of the hockey team to develop a proposal for creation of a permanent facility, which could be utilized beyond the team's practice needs to accommodate the apparent demand for youth and adult hockey, figure skating, and speed skating in central Ohio. The Chill approached the City of Dublin with a joint-development proposal in which the hockey team would build and operate the ice arena but lease back initially up to 20% of the facility's ice time to the city. In return for utilization privileges, the city agreed to lease an eight-acre parcel of land (market value $400,000) to the Chill for 25 years at $1.00 per year.

The reciprocal benefits from this partial leaseback arrangement are extensive. The city received (a) a state-of-the-art community resource that will serve the ice-skating needs of its residents year-round at minimal taxpayer expense; (b) a regional attraction that will lure thousands of overnight and day-use visitors each year to the city to attend tournaments and annual events conducted at the ice arena (the economic benefits to the local economy will be considerable); (c) over 30 hours per week of exclusive ice time for programs conducted and supervised by the Dublin Parks and Recreation Department; and (d) complete possession of the facility when the lease expires in 25 years. On the other hand, benefits to the Chill include (a) substantially reduced development costs, in which acquisition expenses were borne entirely by the city, and many infrastructure costs, such as utility hookups and access roads, were shared (total savings could amount to well over $500,000); (b) a leaseback agreement that gives the Chill almost complete management autonomy. All income derived from concessions, video games, pro shop sales, rink rental (including the modest fee charged to the city for its exclusive use), and public skating will belong entirely to the hockey team; and (c) a permanent facility which completely accommodated practice and office personnel needs.

Another particularly innovative version of leaseback was utilized by Country Clubs of the Southwest, Inc. (CCSW) (Howard & Crompton, 1980):

• CCSW purchased land suitable for golf course purposes and then donated the land to a local government jurisdiction. The city or county in turn leased the land back to CCSW, which assumed responsibility for building, operating, and maintaining the public golf course. CCSW also collects all revenues related to golf course operations. Private memberships are made available, entitling members to preferred tee times and special rates in the pro shop. After 50 years, the entire operation will be turned over to the public agency free of all encumbrances. The benefits to Country Clubs of the Southwest are no property taxes and the ability to offer both public and private memberships. Benefits to the public agency are: a facility provided to meet public recreation needs, no capital expenditures, expert management, no operation and maintenance expenses, and a golf facility free and clear after 50 years.

SUMMARY

The alleged lack of profit claimed by professional sport organizations is causing them to exert pressure on governments to pay a major proportion of costs associated with new or extensively renovated facilities. However, it has also become much more difficult in recent years for public entities to fund the high-quality facilities incorporating many new types of amenities that sport organizations seek. Increasingly, the two sectors are having to pool their resources and enter partnerships to bring these large improvements to fruition.

Public sector organizations have four major assets to which the private sector is likely to seek access. They are a substantial land bank, ability to borrow money at a lower interest rate, an authorization to waive a proportion or all property and other local and/or state tax payments, and control over both permit and zoning processes. None of these resources require governments directly to raise taxes. Hence, officials can use these assets to negotiate with private sport organizations, without being subjected to the scale of controversy and criticism that invariably surrounds proposals to use tax dollars for this purpose.

In addition to their ability to provide funds for operation, maintenance, and capital development if there is likely to be a satisfactory return on those invested funds, the private sector has three other assets likely to appeal to government entities. They are management expertise in specialized areas; the potential to pay lower fringe benefits to employees, which reduces labor costs; and a willingness to take over the government's liability risks that are associated with many ventures of this type. The essence of forging a collaborative agreement is determining ways in which government and private sport organizations can integrate these complementary assets to the advantage of both parties.

It is possible to categorize the wide array of joint-venture agreements into three broad categories: private-sector takeovers, pump priming by the public sector, and joint-development agreements. The last category is distinguished by parties from the two sectors agreeing from the outset to share in the development in a major way. Joint-development agreements can be classified into multiparty arrangements or leaseback arrangements. The complex multi-party arrangement is emerging as the dominant model. This involves multiple financial partners making contributions because the costs are too great for only two entities to meet them. Leaseback involves the private sector's building a facility and subsequently leasing it to a public agency.

Questions for Study and Discussion

1. Assume you're the Executive Director of the City Sports Commission. You are attempting to convince the owners of a sports development corporation to locate one of their new state-of-the-art commercial softball complexes in your community. What inducements could you provide to influence the owners to build the sport complex in your city?

2. As the owner of a minor league hockey franchise, you're interested in building a new, expanded arena. Recognizing the costs would be too great for your club to bear alone, develop a detailed proposal for encouraging the city to enter into a joint development arrangement. Specifically, explain how you would structure the joint development agreement.

3. Describe the essential features of each of the three joint-venture models: private-sector takeovers, pump priming, and joint-development agreements. Use examples to illustrate how such partnerships may actually work.

REFERENCES

Crompton, J. L. & McGregor, B. (in press). Trends in the financing and staffing of local government park and recreation services. *Journal of Park and Recreation Administration.*

Fulton, W. (1988, March). Politicians who chase after sports franchises may get less than they pay for. *Governing*, pp. 34-40.

Howard, D. R. & Crompton, J. L. (1980). *Financing, managing and marketing recreation and park resources.* Dubuque, IA: Wm. C. Brown.

Johnson, A. T. (1993). *Minor league baseball and local economic development.* Urbana, IL: University of Illinois Press.

Korman, R. (1989, February 20). A matter of pride. *Sports Inc.* pp. 32-37.

Lipsitz, G. (1984). Sports stadia and urban development: A tale of three cities. *Journal of Sport and Social Issues, 8*(2), 1-18.

Quirk, J. P. (1987, January 18). The Quirk Study: A close look at the two proposals. *St. Louis Post-Dispatch*, Special Report 8.

Quirk, J. & Fort, R. D. (1992). *Pay dirt: The business of professional team sports.* Princeton, NJ: Princeton University Press.

Zimbalist, A. (1992). *Baseball and billions.* New York: Basic Books.

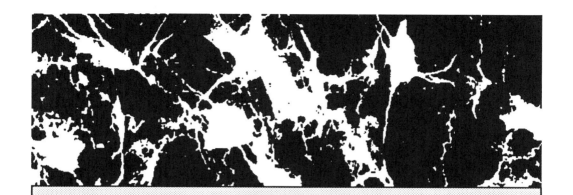

SECTION 2

FINANCIAL RESOURCES ACCRUING DIRECTLY FROM THE ENTERPRISE

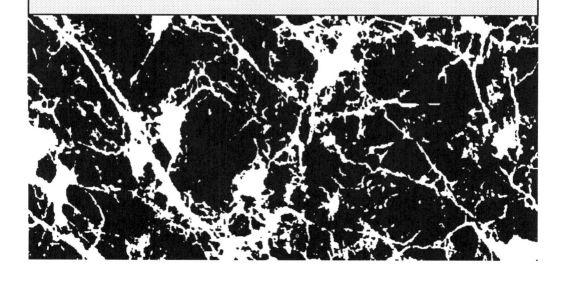

CHAPTER 6

CHARGED ADMISSIONS

ATTENDANCE TRENDS
   PROFESSIONAL SPORTS
   COLLEGIATE SPORTS
PRICING TICKETS FOR SPORTING EVENTS
   SOME PRICING CONSIDERATIONS
   PSYCHOLOGY OF PRICING
      Expected Price Threshold
      Increasing the Sport Consumer's Willingness to Pay
      Tolerance Zone
      Price Impact on Sport Fans
MAXIMIZING PER FAN REVENUES
   LUXURY SEATING
ORGANIZING TICKET SALES
   TYPES OF TICKETS
      Season
      Mini-Plans
      Individual Game Tickets
      Complimentary Tickets
      Student Tickets
   PRE-SEASON SALES
   METHODS OF SELLING
      Incentives
   DURING-SEASON SALES
      Group Sales
      Consignment
      Discounts
ACCOUNTING SYSTEMS
   TICKETING
   PRINTING
   ACCOUNTING PROCEDURES FOR TICKET REVENUE
      Ticket Records
      Game Day
      Post-Game
SUMMARY

Learning Objectives

After completing this chapter, the reader should be able to:

1. discuss attendance trends for professional and collegiate sports.

2. explain several key psychological concepts and their impact on consumers' willingness to pay for sporting events.

3. discuss, citing appropriate examples, several strategies for maximizing in-stadium per-fan revenues including luxury and club seating.

4. discuss the basic principles and procedures for organizing and administering ticket sales before, during, and after a sporting event.

CHAPTER 6

CHARGED ADMISSIONS

This chapter examines a number of issues facing sport managers with respect to the selling and pricing of tickets for sporting events. First, the chapter provides a perspective on attendance trends for collegiate and professional sport and their implications for increasing revenues from charged admissions. Next, the opportunities and problems sport managers face in establishing a price for admission to a sporting event are discussed. Pricing is one of the least understood aspects of sport management. The chapter also includes a description of the latest methods used by managers of collegiate and professional sport organizations to generate more cash flow per ticket sold. Strategies such as priority seating and luxury suites, have allowed managers to greatly amplify their overall gate receipt revenues. The chapter concludes with an in-depth discussion of the organization and administration of ticket sales. The intent is to provide the reader with a basic understanding of various kinds of ticketing plans and methods. Appropriate accounting procedures as well as current computerized ticketing systems are described.

A recent marketing survey estimates that U.S. consumers spend about $2 billion a year buying tickets to sporting events (Brown, 1993). As shown previously in chapter 1, the importance of ticket sale revenue to professional sport varies considerably from one league to another. Whereas the NHL and NBA are largely dependent on gate receipts as their single greatest source of income, the media-rich NFL and MLB receive less than one-third of their overall revenues from ticket sales. Gate receipts, however, are the lifeblood of minor league baseball. A former general manager with the Class A Everett Giants notes, " 'The core of a (minor league) team's existence is the admission ticket' " (cited in Pajak, 1990, p. 27). Data provided by Johnson (1993) indicates that about half the total revenues generated by minor league teams comes from ticket sales. Johnson (1993) further points out that

> high attendance is desirable not only for the ticket revenue, but also for the revenue from the sale of concessions and novelties. The size of the concession revenues greatly influences whether a team is profitable. In many cases, concessions account for more than 25 percent of a team's revenues. (p. 25)

__Daniel Mahony__ has made a substantial contribution to this chapter. Mr. Mahony is currently working on his doctorate in Sport Management at The Ohio State University and formerly served as Assistant Ticket Manager in the University of Cincinnati Athletic Department.

At the collegiate level, ticket sales are a primary source of revenue. An examination of the most recent NCAA study on the financial condition of intercollegiate athletic programs shows that income from the sale of tickets comprises a significant share of overall revenue (Table 6-1). Reliance on gate receipts is particularly prominent for the largest athletic programs, in which on average, 38% of an athletic department's annual revenues are derived from ticket sales. At major Division I schools, such as Ohio State and Michigan, ticket sales to football games in 1993 alone earned each athletic department $9,535, 200 and $9,916,000, respectively (Eichelberger, 1994). The prominence of ticket revenues diminishes for smaller programs. At the Division II and III levels, student activity fees replace gate receipts as the single most important source of revenue. A crucial concern for many of these schools, however, is the degree to which the generally declining financial health of colleges and universities may erode current levels of student and government support for athletic programs. It appears with few exceptions that sport managers will be faced with increased pressures to generate additional revenues from the sale of tickets to sporting events.

Table 6-1
Principal Revenue Sources for Large, Medium and Small Collegiate Athletic Programs

Percentage of total revenues by size of athletic program

Source of Revenue	Large (Div.IA,	IAA)	Medium (Div. II)	Small (primarily Div. III)
Ticket Sales	35%	18%	13%	13%
Student Fees	7	32	32	38
Donations	15	11	11	12
Bowls, TV	14	3	1	0
Govt. Support	5	18	25	20
Guarantees	8	6	2	1
Other	16	12	16	16

Note: data compiled from *Revenues and expenses of intercollegiate athletic programs: Analysis of financial trends and relationships 1985-1990.* M. Raiborn, Overland Park, KS National Collegiate Athletic Association, pp. 23-39

ATTENDANCE TRENDS

Professional Sports

Sport managers face a daunting challenge. Increasing gate receipts can result from either selling more tickets or raising the unit cost or price of tickets sold. The first alternative of increasing sales volume depends on a number of factors. One obvious determinant is the amount of surplus seating capacity or number of available (unsold) seats. For three of the four major professional leagues--basketball, football, and hockey--peddling more tickets is *not* the answer to generating more revenue. NBA, NFL, and NHL teams in general already sell more than 90% of their available seats. When a sellout is defined as attendance at a game that exceeds 90% of capacity, 20 of 28 NBA teams had virtual season-long sellouts in 1992, whereas 16 or 21 NHL franchises sold out more than 75% of their home games.

Entering the 1993 season, only three NFL teams had attendance difficulties: the New England Patriots, Phoenix Cardinals, and Tampa Bay Buccaneers. However, both the Patriots' and Cardinals' season ticket sales had improved appreciably over the previous season.

The near-capacity profiles of these three leagues is reflected in the attendance figures shown in Table 6-2. The generally modest growth of attendance over the past decade, particularly for the NFL and the NHL, is explained by the fact that the current capacity for live gate attendance has reached its maximum for most teams. The NBA has more recently achieved the same level of consistent near or at-capacity demand, prompting Commissioner David Stern to look in new directions for additional revenue. " 'Our arenas are full, our ticket prices will moderate, so we've got to grow new TV audiences and deal with global opportunities' " (cited in Saporito, 1991, p. 86).

In contrast to the NHL, NBA, and NFL, where sellouts are the rule rather than the exception, professional baseball at both the major and minor league levels sells on average only half its available seats. In 1992, major league baseball sold only 50.4% of its capacity, a 2% decline from 1991's record attendance of 56.8 million. However, in 1993 major league baseball rebounded to post all-time attendance highs. Boosted by the addition of two expansion teams, the Colorado Rockies--which shattered all existing single-franchise attendance records--and the Florida Marlins, overall attendance increased by 22.5%. Interestingly, even when deducting the two new teams, fan attendance in the "old" National League was still up 4.5% over 1992 (Chass, 1993). Despite the increased number of fans attending games, most baseball teams over the course of the season have been unable to sell from one-half to one-quarter of their available seating inventory. Two factors explain the low number of sellouts in baseball: (a) stadium capacity and (b) length of the playing season. According to Quirk and Fort (1992), most MBL teams play in stadiums with capacities designed to accommodate football, not baseball. Good examples are the Philadelphia Phillies, who play in Veterans Stadium (65,000 capacity). Recent projects, such as Jacobs Field in

TABLE 6-2
Attendance at Selected Professional and Collegiate Sporting Events During the 1980s

Sport	1981	1985	1989
Baseball			
Major Leagues	26,544,376	46,838,819	55,173,096
Minor Leagues	16,559,704	18,380,000	23,103,593
Collegiate	8,370,377	11,668,916	14,282,547
Basketball			
NBA	10,308,879	11,490,944	16,531,561
Collegiate	30,935,117	32,056,673	33,020,286
Football			
NFL	13,606,990	13,345,047	13,625,662
Collegiate	35,807,040	36,312,022	36,406,297
Hockey			
NHL	11,692,588	12,741,230	13,745,183
Minor & College	7,369,134	10,138,266	15,824,600

Note: compiled from 1981, 1986 and 1990 Surveys on Sports Attendance, *Daily Racing Form*, Highstown, N.Y.: News America Publication Inc.

Cleveland (1994) and Baltimore's Camden Yards (1992), indicate that the ideal capacity for a facility built for baseball only is around 45,000 seats, well under the 65,000-plus capacity suitable for the NFL. In addition, the MLB's 162-regular season game schedule is much longer than those of all other professional sport leagues (NBA, 82; NHL, 84; and NFL, 16 games), making it extremely difficult to sell out a large proportion of all 81 home dates.

Collegiate Sports

As Table 6-2 reveals, overall attendance at college football and basketball games has been stagnant, particularly over the last half of the 1980s. From 1985 through 1990, the number of fans attending collegiate football games grew imperceptibly (+0.3%). During the same period, basketball attendance increased only moderately (+3.0%).

The flat attendance profile of college football has placed great pressure on many athletic departments, particularly those with big-time football programs. Football alone accounts for almost 80% of the total gate receipts generated by many Division IA schools (Raiborn, 1990). Given that many of these programs are almost completely dependent on self-generated revenue, stagnant or declining attendance has led many athletic directors to focus on raising the cash flow per seat. Typically, at the collegiate level, generating additional revenue per ticket sold has come from either raising ticket prices or instituting what is now commonly referred to as "priority seating."

The concept of priority seating ties preferred seating locations to additional donations to the athletic program. In order for fans to purchase the best seats in the stadium, they have to make an extra contribution to the athletic department for the "right" to buy those seats. This privilege may cost a season ticket purchaser at a big-time school as much as $5,000-10,000 for two season tickets worth at face value $264 (6 games @ $22 per ticket). Generally, the greater the donation, the better the seat. First introduced in the early 1980s, priority seating has become the norm at the Division I level, with about 90% of Division I schools currently implementing the concept.

Pricing Tickets for Sporting Events

When it comes to establishing ticket prices, it appears that sport managers at all levels operate largely by the seat of their pants. Quirk and Fort (1992) concluded that "ticket prices for professional sport teams are the best-informed *guesses* [emphasis added] of management" (p. 144). Historically, sport managers have relied almost exclusively on their own judgment as to what ticket prices would be most acceptable to fans. The prevailing approach has been to raise prices incrementally by some

---

Figure 6-1
Average Ticket Prices for Professional Sports

Major League Baseball (1993)		$9.57
National Basketball Association (1992-93)		$25.16
National Hockey League (1992-93)		$25.96
National Football League (1992)		$27.19

Note: data compiled from *Team Marketing Report*, A. Friedman, Editor, Chicago, IL.

arbitrary percentage or flat rate. Although prices have consistently increased for admission to most professional and collegiate events, pricing decisions seem to be based loosely on two considerations, either the perceived revenue needs of the organization or management's assessment of what the market will bear.

Some Pricing Considerations

Before examining current trends in pricing sporting events, we discuss some of the issues and concerns sport managers should consider in attempting to find the *right* price for the entertainment services they provide. In establishing the price of admission to sport events, managers should take into account several factors. It is first important to consider the price a fan pays for a ticket in its broadest context. Normally, price is conceived of as simply the direct amount of money sacrificed to acquire access to a desired service or event. However, the monetary price of buying a ticket is only one way in which people pay for attending sporting events. In fact, it may be a small part of the overall direct monetary expenditure made by a fan. Bernard Mullin, a baseball executive with the Colorado Rockies, estimates that only a third of the cost of attending a game is spent on tickets. Fans pay considerably more--67 cents of every dollar--for such things as transportation to and from the game, parking and ballpark concessions (Fichtenbaum, Rosenblatt, & Sandomir, 1989). Available data support Mullin's assertion. As the next chapter illustrates, fan expenditures on concessions alone have grown to a substantial level, with fans who attend major league baseball games spending as much as $8.50 on food and beverage concessions.

Access costs are such a large and important part of the total cost of attendance that they cannot be ignored. The actual cost of transportation necessary to attend an event is a function of mode of transportation, travel distance, and often for those using private transportation, the fee for parking at a stadium or arena. The magnitude of these expenses varies substantially. It is increasingly common, however, to find the fee for parking adjacent to a crowded sport venue as expensive as the admission charge itself. In addition to these direct expenses, individuals may incur extensive nonmonetary costs associated with traveling to and from sporting events. There are two types of nonmonetary time costs that sport managers should be cognizant of: travel time and waiting time. The amount of travel time that makes a barrier to attending events obviously varies according to the individual and the event, but apparently even small travel times will inhibit attendance. Substantial effects have been reported for travel times of 30 minutes and less (Crompton & Lamb, 1986).

The cost of waiting time--for example, in long lines to purchase tickets prior to a game or to use a bathroom stall in the women's restroom--may be substantial, substantial enough for some people to reach the judgment that the nonmonetary costs associated with attendance are too steep even though the direct ticket charge may be entirely acceptable. In these instances, fans not able to see a favorable balance between the nonmonetary and monetary costs associated with attendance are likely to seek alternative forms of entertainment. The important point is that sport managers should consider all of the costs of attending sporting events. The investment that fans make includes not only the direct charge of purchasing a ticket but also the monetary and nonmonetary opportunity costs (travel and waiting time) associated with attendance. These access costs may involve more personal sacrifice than money for some people and, therefore, may be more influential than monetary costs in determining whether or not these individuals attend.

Psychology of Pricing

Establishing a price that will be accepted by sports consumers requires consideration of several psychological dimensions of pricing. The most important of these as they apply to the attendance of sporting events and the purchase of sport products and services are discussed in the following paragraphs.

Expected Price Threshold. Research has shown that consumers have an expected range of prices that they are willing to pay for a particular program or service. Monroe (1971) confirmed through several experiments that consumers have acceptable ranges of prices for various products. He found that people refrain from purchasing a product not only when the price is considered too high but also when the price is perceived to be too low. If a price is set above a threshold price, they will find it too expensive. If a price is set below the expected level, potential consumers will be suspicious of the quality of the service. The upper and lower boundaries of this zone of acceptance may have been formed from an individual's recollection of prices asked or paid in the past.

An important factor in establishing the Expected Price Threshold may be the initial price the organization charges for admission to an event or for a particular service. If consumers have not previously attended this type of sporting event or have no previous exposure to the service, the initial price may become the reference price. This first price firmly establishes in the consumer's mind the fair price for the service. Hence it becomes the reference price against which subsequent price revisions are compared. An organization is likely to have more flexibility in the first pricing decision than in any subsequent decisions, which will always be constrained by consumers' relating their sense of appropriateness and fairness back to the former price. The first pricing decision, therefore, usually has a strong determining impact on the level of price that can be charged for that service throughout its life.

The function of the initial pricing decision in formulating a reference price point emphasizes the risks involved in pricing an event or service too low when it is first offered so that potential fans or patrons will be enticed to try it. This objective can best be achieved by offering a promotional price that is recognized by all potential users as being temporary. A fixed, relatively short period during which the special low promotional price will apply should be established. This should be communicated *together* with the regular price that will be charged for the service at the end of this "introductory" period.

Understanding sport consumers' expected price threshold is critically important for athletic directors concerned with attempting to generate revenue from what have been commonly labeled "nonrevenue" sports. Although deriving substantial gate income from many of these sports may not be possible or even intended, some of these sports appear to have considerable potential for expanded revenue production. Good prospects, for example, are women's basketball and men's baseball and hockey.

The challenge facing many financially strapped programs is how to induce people to pay either at all, or more, for something that historically has been provided free or at a nominal cost. Currently, in the Big Ten Conference, for example, the general public can attend three-fourths of all sporting events sponsored by the member institutions at no direct cost (Masters, 1992). This same pattern of generally free admission is common at all institutions across the United States and Canada.

Athletic directors hoping to generate more from nonrevenue sports face a challenging dilemma. Whereas establishing the first price is crucial to setting the standard for any subsequent price adjustments--and, therefore, the first price should not be artificially low--at the same time, any new or abrupt increase in price may exceed consumers' price thresholds. The existing price threshold may be quite low, with a reference price conditioned by years of free or nominal admission. The amount of flexibility available in fixing the price, however, may also be at least partially influenced by fans' perceptions of what they have or would have to pay for a comparable experience. Some fans may transfer price expectations from one sport or type of event to another. At present, the extent to which fans generalize price cues or discriminate price-quality relationships between men's and women's basketball, for example, is not well understood. It is crucial, therefore, that prior to the initiation of any price hike, market surveys that assess consumers' levels of price tolerance be conducted to ensure that the new price falls within a potential target market's expected price threshold.

Increasing the Sport Consumer's Willingness to Pay. If a price is to be charged for the first time or if a relatively large price increase beyond the expected threshold is to be made, fan resistance may be reduced by raising their perception of the value of the event or service. If consumers think that the value of the event they are purchasing is commensurate with the price being charged, then they are less likely to react adversely to the price increase.

Directly conveying the existing benefits or attributes of attending a sporting event may bring to consciousness aspects of the overall experience that otherwise may have been ignored or taken for granted. Providing a detailed description of all an event's attributes and the benefits it offers may assist in raising its perceived value. McCarville and Crompton (1987, McCarville, Crompton & Sell, 1993) in a series of experiments have demonstrated that consumers' willingness to pay for selected recreation and sport activities could be raised substantially by offering information that directly communicated the personal benefits consumers would derive from the activity.

Another way to produce changes in perceived value and increase an individual's willingness to pay is to use price comparisons with other substitutable or nonsubstitutable events or services. Comparisons with other suppliers' similar activities or services may help to convey the impression that although an increase in price has occurred, the new price is still very reasonable. The intent is to communicate excellent value relative to competitive options. For example, "for $2 you get the best in college baseball at less than half the cost of attending a professional game in the area." Comparisons with nonsubstitute services may provide individuals with a point of reference with which to favorably compare a price: "For less than the cost of a hamburger and fries at your favorite fast food outlet, you can spend an afternoon watching the best in college baseball."

Tolerance Zone. The concept of tolerance zone suggests that if price increases are within a sufficiently small range or zone, they will not adversely impact attendance at an event or the purchase of a service. For example, an increase in admission charge to a collegiate men's hockey game from $1.25 to $1.50 may be noticed by consumers, but it is likely to be small enough that it will not alter their pattern of attendance. Perceptions of price increases and decreases are relative to the original price. An increase in price of an event from $2.50 to $5.00 may arouse vigorous protest, whereas an increase in the price of a different service from $7.50 to $10.00 may raise no comment. Even though the increase in each case is $2.50, the first is a 100% change whereas the second is only a 25% increase.

A series of small incremental increases in price over a period of time--all which fall within the tolerance zone--are less likely to meet consumer resistance than is a single major increase. Sport managers should consider increasing their prices regularly rather than holding back increases until a large relative change in price is required. Given the frequency with which costs change, a systematic review of prices should be conducted at least on an annual basis; otherwise, prices will not keep pace with costs. The best time to review prices is probably at the end of the season or during the annual budget review process.

Price Impact on Sport Fans

A recent study conducted by *USA Today* (Brown, 1993) offers some insight into how price influences attendance at major league sporting events. Two-thirds of *USA Today's* Sports Team, a representative panel of 305 sports fans throughout the United States, reported that expenses related to attendance (tickets, concessions, parking) kept them from attending major league games more often. Sixteen percent indicated that they would attend no games at all in the future due to the costs associated with attending major league sports events. The findings suggest that, for many fans, a definite ceiling or expected price threshold exists beyond which they will resist or refuse payment. Interestingly, the cost of concessions, particularly food, rather than the price of admission, was perceived to be the most overpriced element of the experience.

Maximizing Per-Fan Revenues

Facing limits on the total volume of tickets that may be sold as well as on the amount fans are willing to pay for them, a number of sport managers have turned to a new strategy that focuses on raising the total cash flow per seat. Rather than focusing solely on selling more tickets, the emphasis turns to maximizing per-fan revenues. Applying what former baseball executive Peter Bavasi refers to as the "Las Vegas" approach, the Oakland A's have purposely kept ticket prices among the lowest in the major leagues. According to Bavasi, the A's intent is to " 'invite patrons in inexpensively and have them buy their way out' " (cited in Mulligan, 1992). The A's strategy is to minimize the price of a ticket as a barrier to attending games. Once at the ballpark, fans are offered a variety of enticements including baseball-related entertainment--batting cages, photo booths with cutouts of players, and an array of specialty food and beverage items, such as Chinese food, fruit salads, bottled and imported beer. The A's estimate that fan spending on these attractions has increased expenditures at ball games by as much as $10 to $12 per fan.

Luxury Seating

A critical element of the strategy to maximize cash flow per seat has been the sale of luxury seats. Alternatively called luxury boxes, executive suites or skyboxes, the concept involves selling preferred seating at a premium price. The premium can be considerable. The 161 Toronto Sky Dome luxury boxes, for example, were priced between $100,000 to $250,000 per season when originally leased in 1989. The relatively few tenants, primarily corporations, occupying these boxes contribute over $25 million a year to the Blue Jays' coffers.

Although the physical features of luxury suites may vary from one stadium or arena to another, generally all will include basic amenities, such as carpeting, wet bar, restroom, and seating ranging from 12 to 24 seats. The illustration (see Figure 6-2) of a premium suite in Cleveland's new Jacobs Field displays the deluxe features and services typical of luxury suites.

The revenue-generating capacity of luxury seating is enormous. Hoffman and Greenberg (1989) declared the sale of luxury boxes the fastest growing source of income in sports. Recent evidence supports their assertion. Proceeds from the sale or lease of luxury seats have financed almost completely the construction of the NBA Pistons' new arena at Auburn Hills, Michigan, the NFL Cowboys' Texas Stadium at Irving, Texas, and Joe Robbie Stadium in Miami. The revenue streams generated from the long-term leasing (generally 10 years) of VIP seating in these facilities has been sufficient to retire the revenue bonds used to finance their construction. For example, the $12 million-a-year income from suite rentals (up to $120,000 per season) at the Pistons' "Palace at Auburn Hills" will allow the team to retire all of its $70-million construction debt within 6 years. Joe Robbie, the owner of the Miami Dolphins and namesake of the new $100-million stadium he built in 1990, grosses close to $20 million a year--more than half the NFL team's annual income--from leasing 216 luxury suites.

A number of collegiate athletic programs have also reaped great financial benefit from the sale of luxury seating. Auburn University, for example, incorporated 71 executive suites into a $15.5-million stadium-renovation project. The 68 revenue-

Figure 6-2
Luxury Seating at Cleveland's
Jacobs Field

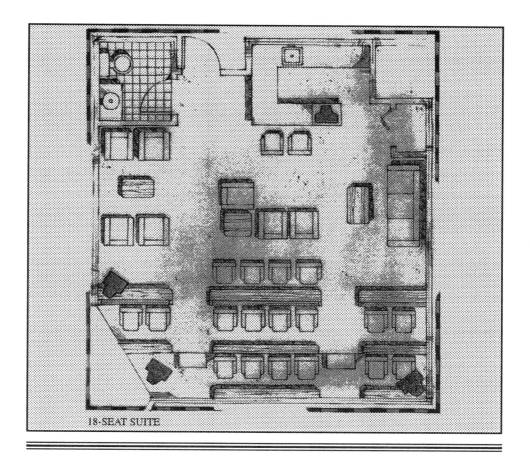

18-SEAT SUITE

producing suites each sold for as much as $862,865, completely offsetting the $1-million-plus annual debt incurred by the expansion project. When the debt is retired in 2002, Auburn will realize an annual profit of $1,776,000 (Rosenblatt, 1988). Other notable examples of schools that have financed recent stadium expansions from luxury suite proceeds are Boston College, the University of Tennessee, and Clemson University.

A less extravagant option to luxury suites or boxes are what have become generally referred to as "Club Seats." Typically, this preferred seating arrangement provides fans with chair-back, wide-bottom, cushioned seats and immediate access to a variety of specialty services and amenities. The proposed Jack Kent Cooke Stadium in Washington, DC offers its 15,000-club seat fans private carpeted concourses, lounge, and bar facilities, as well as waiter and waitress service. As Hoffman and Greenberg (1989) aptly point out, "The extra seat width helps to accommodate a wallet large enough to handle the $2,000 to $4,000 each occupant is charged" (p. 171).

Figure 6-3 provides an example of leasing options offered by the Cleveland Indians for the 2,000 Club Seats they offer at their new park. The prepaid provision in the 10-year membership alternative is common to many preferred or luxury seating plans. The intent is to generate as much cash up front as possible to meet the financing maxim that "a dollar received immediately is preferable to a dollar received at some future date" (Weston & Brigham, 1974, p. 252).

Changes in the U.S. tax structure over the past 10 years apparently have not dampened enthusiasm for luxury seating. The 1986 Tax Reform Act and President Clinton's 1993 economic program have progressively reduced the tax benefits corporations can receive for business entertainment. Prior to the 1986 tax reform legislation, businesses could fully write off expenses related to leasing luxury boxes. With the adoption of the Clinton Administration's tax plan, the deduction has been slashed from 80% to 50% (Kirshenbaum, 1993). Zimbalist (1992) attributes the continued popularity of luxury seating despite restricted deductions to the dramatic growth of after-tax real income in the top 20% of the American wage earners from 1977 through 1991: "The principal patrons of luxury boxes have seen their incomes soar in recent years, despite overall economic malaise" (p. 57).

It is important to recognize, however, that not all luxury seating projects have been completely successful. Several teams, most notably, the NFL's Detroit Lions and the MLB Seattle Mariners, had difficulty in the early 1990s selling more than half of their luxury suites. The Milwaukee Brewers' efforts to build a new stadium have been jeopardized by their inability to presell enough skyboxes to secure ample construction financing. Despite these disappointments, it appears as though luxury seating will continue to be a popular revenue-generating strategy. Fourteen stadiums containing 1400 skyboxes are currently on the drawing boards (Ozanian & Taub, 1992).

ORGANIZING TICKET SALES

Types of Tickets

Season. A major focus for many sports organizations is the sale of season tickets. Season ticket sales provide a guaranteed source of revenue before the season starts and are not dependent on variable factors, such as weather, quality of a particular opponent, and team record. The money received from sales can be invested and begin earning interest. Season tickets can also be distributed before the beginning of the season. Mailing tickets for 81 home major league baseball games at one time is easier than selling and distributing tickets for each of the 81 game individually.

Figure 6-3
Club Seat Leasing
Options at Cleveland's Jacobs Field

Three-Year Membership-Lease	Five-Year Membership-Lease	Ten-Year Membership Lease Prepaid
◆ Initial lease payment of $1,215 for first year, excluding the cost of tickets.*	◆ Initial lease payment of $1,215 for first year, excluding the cost of tickets.*	◆ Priority seat selection
◆ Locked in at a seven percent annual lease escalator in years two and three.	◆ Locked in at only a five percent annual lease escalator in subsequent years.	◆ One-time lease payment of $13,770, excluding the cost of tickets.*
◆ Guarantee your personally selected seat for three years.	◆ Guarantee your personally selected seat for five years.	◆ Avoid annual lease price escalators for life of lease.
◆ Optional on-site parking available for term of lease.	◆ Optional on-site parking available for term of lease.	◆ Guarantee your personally selected seat for 10 years.
		◆ Optional on-site parking available for term of lease.

*Tickets are not included in lease price, and will be billed to you annually. The Club Seat ticket price will not exceed field level box seat price.

Note: information provided by the Cleveland Indians

Some NFL, NHL, and other sports organizations have been able to sell all their seats on a season-ticket basis. Although this may appear to be a perfect scenario, there are some disadvantages with this situation. Fans who are never able to watch their team in person may lose interest. The interest of these fans may be needed to increase television ratings, to buy tickets if support for the team declines, or to fill seats if the team moves to a larger facility. Also, season ticket holders will probably spend less money on programs and merchandise on a per-game basis than would a once-a-year attender. Therefore, it may be advisable to sell about 10% of the tickets on an individual basis even in situations where a season sell-out is possible.

One creative approach to this situation was used by the Columbus, Ohio, Chill minor league hockey team. The Chill played their games in a 5,200-seat facility. In the early 1990s, the team became very popular and found it could easily sell all their seats on a season basis. Instead of confining its fan support to the first 5,200 to purchase full-season tickets, Chill management devised a strategy intended to expand its fan base. The Chill set a limit for full-season ticket sales (all 32 games) at 2,500 seats. The remaining 2,500 seats were sold as part of two mini-plan packages, one for 15 games and the other for 10. The organization still had 9 other games for which the 2,500 seats were available to the general public. The Chill also set up 700 floor seats for each game to be sold to the general public. This strategy was used to increase the number of fans who could come to games, without decreasing the amount of per-game ticket revenue. Rather than simply selling 5,200 full- season tickets, the ticket-ing strategy utilized by the Chill allowed them to maintain their consecutive sellout streak but with an expanded fan base of 7,500 season ticketholders plus furnishing single-game purchase opportunities to 25,000 additional Chill fans.

Season ticket sales generally involve the sale of a particular seat in the stadium for an entire season for a one-time fee. When attendance is expected to be low, season passes may be sold for general seating. Although there are exceptions, season tickets are often discounted as compared to the individual game price. Both professional and collegiate ticket offices focus their efforts on selling certain types of season tickets. At the professional level the focus is on box seats, whereas donation club seats are the priority at many colleges.

Box seats are usually the best seats available. Sports organizations concentrate on selling these "choice" seats because they are generally the most expensive and be-cause they will be viewed as more valuable when they are always sold out. The organization will try to sell them to the prior holders first, then to season ticketholders in the "non-choice" sections and finally to new season ticketholders. However, the ticket manager should never sell all of these tickets before the season. Some choice seats need to be kept for players' and coaches' families and special guests of the organization. Organization administrators expect that ticket managers will have some choice seats available for "last-second emergencies."

As previously discussed, at many colleges payment for some of the seats also involves a donation to the alumni association or the athletic fund. Although some schools require every season ticketholder to donate additional money, most only re-quire donations from those who want the best seats. Even when choice seats are not clearly identified as donation club seats, donors are generally given first priority in seating. Because studies have shown that donations to athletic departments are often related to priority seating (Hammersmith, 1985; Isherwood, 1986), donation club seating can be an effective means for encouraging donations and increasing revenue. In fact, the size of the average donation is usually much greater than the face value of the tickets.

Mini-Plans. Because most sports organizations cannot sell all their tickets on a season basis, many offer a variety of mini-plans. Mini-plans allow fans to purchase tickets for a portion of the total season. They provide an easier step for individual-game ticketholders who wish to become more active fans, but are not ready to purchase season tickets. Similar to season tickets, these plans are beneficial to the sports organization because they provide a source of revenue before the season and allow a large number of tickets to be sold and distributed at one time.

The mini-plans require the consumer to purchase tickets for a specific number of games. One type of plan specifies exactly which games are being offered. Generally, when these "set" plans are being used, the organization will present a few different options from which the sports consumer may choose. For example, the University of Akron offers two mini-plan packages in addition to various season ticket plans (see Figure 6-4). Plan B features all the conference games, whereas Plan C includes all Saturday games. A second type of mini-plan is flexible and allows the fan to list which games he or she wishes to attend. Although it is better for the customer, this type of plan will be far more difficult for the ticket office and will not help to sell the less popular games. Also, flexible plans make it virtually impossible to guarantee the fan the same seat for every game.

A third plan involves a combination of a number of specified games and a number of games that are chosen by the fan. For example, an eight game mini-plan may specify four games and allow the consumer to choose the other four games. The fourth type of mini-plan involves the sale of ticket books. These books include coupons that can be used for any games that the fan chooses throughout the year. Ticket books are best suited for situations where sellouts are rare. The coupons may allow direct admittance to the sport facility or may have to be exchanged for a ticket.

Individual Game Tickets. Many seats are sold on a game-by-game basis. In professional basketball and baseball, the tickets may be priced differently based on location in the stadium. Some colleges price each game based on the perceived quality of the opponent. Individual game tickets may also be discounted before or during the season.

Complimentary Tickets. Complimentary tickets are those that are given to the customer at no cost. Players and coaches are allowed to give a specified number of tickets to friends and family. The organization may also give tickets to employees, politicians, important businessmen, potential donors, and charitable organizations. Some clubs that have many empty seats will give out a large number of complimentary seats to increase attendance.

Complimentary tickets must be accounted for very carefully. The documentation for these tickets will be audited at year end and will be closely examined. Because of the strict NCAA rules regarding "comp" tickets, documentation is especially important at the college level. Many schools have been penalized and placed on probation, at least in part because of the improper use of complimentary tickets.

Student Tickets. Colleges and universities generally have a specific number of seats available for students. Although the tickets are usually discounted, some larger schools with popular athletic teams require students to pay for tickets. However, many schools admit students without charge to the athletic events. Schools may

Figure 6–4
Example of Mini-Season Ticket Plan

5 Ticket Plans to Choose From

Plan A
Full Season
All 13 Games

College of Wooster
Mississippi Valley State
Lamar
Tennessee State
Northern Illinois
Wisconsin-Green Bay
Western Illinois
Eastern Illinois
Youngstown State
Wright State
Valparaiso
Illinois-Chicago
Cleveland State

$78

Plan B
Conference Special
8 Conference Games

Northern Illinois
Wisconsin-Green Bay
Western Illinois
Eastern Illinois
Wright State
Valparaiso
Illinois-Chicago
Cleveland State

$48

Plan C
Saturday Night Special
All Saturday Games

Mississippi Valley State
Lamar
Northern Illinois
Western Illinois
Wright State
Valparaiso

$36

Plan D
Faculty/Staff
(with UA I.D.)
Limit 2 Season Tickets

College of Wooster
Mississippi Valley State
Lamar
Tennessee State
Northern Illinois
Wisconsin-Green Bay
Western Illinois
Eastern Illinois
Youngstown State
Wright State
Valparaiso
Illinois-Chicago
Cleveland State

$36

Plan E
Family Plan
Children 18 Years of Age
and Under Get Free
Ticket

College of Wooster
Mississippi Valley State
Lamar
Tennessee State
Northern Illinois
Wisconsin-Green Bay
Western Illinois
Eastern Illinois
Youngstown State
Wright State
Valparaiso
Illinois-Chicago
Cleveland State

$156

require that students pick up tickets before the game to control crowd size and to allow the athletic department to sell unclaimed student tickets. However, some schools have enough room to allow general seating in the student section, and they admit all students who come to the game. The athletic department generally receives money from student fees, and this is considered to be full or partial payment for the student tickets. Most schools require that students show their student I.D. when being admitted to prevent them from selling these tickets to "scalpers."

Preseason Sales

The ticket sales campaign should begin a minimum of 3 months before the season. The ticket office is likely to need 3 months to ensure that the orders are recorded, the seats assigned, all the tickets are printed (if done by the office) and mailed at least 2 weeks before the season. However, the organization should try to take advantage of any increases in enthusiasm. If the team just completed a very successful season, the organization may want to begin selling tickets as soon as the season is completed. Also, the signing of a superstar player or the hiring of a new coach can lead to increases in optimism and sales. It would be a mistake to ignore such opportunities and wait until 3 months before the season to begin ticket sales.

Before the campaign begins, the ticket office needs to be prepared. First, all brochures should be ordered and received for the direct mail campaign. Second, the ticket stock or printed tickets should be ordered and received. Ticket office employees need to remember that state institutions must go through a bidding process before ordering these materials, and this will take additional time. Third, open seats should be identified so that ticket office personnel can be knowledgeable when talking to potential ticketholders. Fourth, a schedule needs to be clearly outlined, including starting dates for the sale of each type of ticket (season, mini-plans, individual games, etc.), deadlines for renewal, date on which final seat assignments will be made, and deadline for mailing tickets to customers. The schedule should be realistic because failure to follow it will help erode sports consumers' confidence in the ticket office and its procedures.

Seat assignment is one procedure that will be very important to the average ticket purchaser, and the assignments may be based on a variety of criteria. Organizations may use longevity, the date the order was received, or donation level. Some colleges use complicated point systems that base seat assignments on a combination of the size of donations and the number of years of giving. (See the "Point System" in Chapter 13 for more information about how some athletic ticket offices assign preferred seat locations on the basis of a point system.) Although the method used may vary among teams, it is critical that a clearly defined system for assignment be documented and followed. Season ticketholders are concerned with being treated fairly and need to be assured that a system for assignment has been established.

Methods of Selling

Ticket offices can use a combination of methods to sell tickets. This section will describe a few of the most common: (a) direct mail, (b) follow-up phone calls, (c) telemarketing, (d) direct sell, and (e) outlets. Each of these methods is most effective when it is combined with a targeted advertising campaign.

Many sports organizations use direct mail campaigns to begin selling tickets. Brochures are sent to past and potential customers presenting the various options available. Although the most difficult task often is obtaining the mailing list, this has become easier now that most ticket offices are at least partially computerized. Ticket office personnel should add potential customer names to the customer database whenever possible so that any person who orders tickets will receive a brochure the next year. The ticket office also needs to be aware of the team's critical trading radius and the groups they are targeting when determining to whom brochures will be mailed. General mailings that are not targeted are likely to be costly and inefficient.

Sports organizations can use follow-up phone calls after the mailing. They should, at least, call all season ticketholders from the previous year who have not been heard from after a reasonable period of time. These calls can be used to encourage renewals and to discover which seats will be open. In addition, the phone calls can provide valuable customer feedback. If the staff is available, the organization can also call others who received the mailing. Colleges have access to an inexpensive source of labor in work-study students, and some professional organizations have used volunteer fan groups to make these calls.

Telemarketing has been used extensively by many sports organizations to encourage purchases by customers who were not contacted during the direct mail campaign. Again, many organizations have been able to find inexpensive sources of labor that allow telemarketing campaigns to be cost effective. However, the increasing disdain for such campaigns and the use of answering machines to screen phone calls have decreased the effectiveness of telemarketing. The campaign will also be less successful if the organization does not determine target groups in advance. For example, the Los Angeles Clippers have achieved some success in telemarketing by targeting mostly business executives, who are more likely to be able to afford season tickets (Mulligan, 1992).

In order to compensate for the decreasing effectiveness of telemarketing, some sports organizations have used aggressive direct sales campaigns. The Oakland A's employ "a force of full-time, commissioned salespeople who knock on doors in commercial buildings, industrial parks, and even dentists' offices" (Mulligan, 1992, p. E1). They work on straight commission, 10% of sales; thus, the campaign costs the organization almost nothing if the sales personnel are not successful. The A's management believes "that it is easier to hang up a phone or toss a brochure in a wastebasket" than it is to get rid of a member of their salesforce (Mulligan, 1992, p. E1). The A's combined their direct sales campaign with telemarketing, direct mail, and other sales methods to attract the fourth highest attendance in MLB in 1991. Many members of the sports industry consider the A's to be a model organization in terms of marketing and ticket sales.

Ticket outlets, such as Ticketmaster, are used by many sports and entertainment organizations to sell all or some of their tickets. The outlets are convenient for the consumer and decrease the amount of work for the ticket office. These outlets have computers that are programmed to find and print the best ticket available. However, Ticketmaster and other outlets charge the customer and the sports organization service fees for each ticket sold. Although the fee paid by the organization is usually a small percentage of the ticket price, the service fee paid by the fan is generally $2-$3 per ticket. The service fees may decrease sales by pushing the tickets beyond the fan's price range. The increase could be kept by the sports organization if the tickets were not sold at the outlets.

Incentives. The sports organization can use a number of incentives to encourage purchases. One of the most popular incentives is a tax deduction. Businesses can deduct a portion of the price of the tickets as a business expense. However, recent changes in the tax law have progressively decreased the percentage that can be deducted. Individuals and businesses can also deduct any donation to the alumni association or athletic department that is related to the purchase of college tickets. The ticket office needs to be careful, however, to separate the cost of the tickets from the donation package. The payment for tickets is not a charitable donation, and deducting it as such is an IRS violation.

The ticket office can offer discounts to increase sales. Most season-ticket or mini-plan packages are at least moderately discounted from the individual game price. The organization will often offer individual game discounts for specific games or for groups of a certain size.

Some organizations guarantee season ticketholders that they can renew the same seats for the rest of their life. Even though "seats-for-life" can be very effective in helping to encourage sales, there is a disadvantage to this offer. Once the tickets are promised to the holder for life, the flexibility and future revenue-increasing efforts of the sports organization may be seriously damaged. The "seats-for-life" offer may actually become detrimental over the long term and should be used very cautiously.

During-Season Sales

For most sports organizations, the ticket sales campaign does not end with the mailing of season tickets and the beginning of the season. After the season starts, the ticket office now knows how many tickets are available on an individual-game basis and its personnel have a number of means available to try to sell these seats. An advertising campaign is one method that can be used to encourage individual-game ticket sales. It is important that the ticket office be equipped with enough phone lines and employees to handle all the last-second orders in a timely and friendly manner. Offices that are not able to handle this rush can benefit from the services of outlets. In addition to general advertising, four methods are examined for increasing sales and filling seats: (a) group sales, (b) consignment, (c) discounts, and (d) complimentary admission.

Group Sales. Sports organizations that have excess capacity may offer group rates. Group sales allow the ticket office to sell a large number of tickets at one time and can help to fill an empty section of the stands. Some teams have a group sales department that actively solicits groups and may even offer a package including transportation and lodging. Sports organizations sometimes give these groups seats that are in an empty and poorly located section. However, this strategy will probably hurt repeat business and decrease group sales over the long term.

Consignment. Ticket offices will sometimes consign tickets to another group or organization, which will then sell the tickets. The most common groups to which tickets will be consigned are the visiting team (common in college) and charitable organizations. Visiting teams often want at least a small consignment of tickets in order to make sure tickets are conveniently available for their loyal fans or large donors. Charitable organizations will generally receive a portion of the ticket price as a donation to their organization. There are two critical items to remember when consigning tickets. First, the ticket office should maintain written documentation for all consignments and require someone from the other organization to sign for the tickets and accept responsibility for them. Second, a deadline for the return of unsold tickets by the other organization should be clearly set and should be early enough to allow the ticket office to account for the money and sales before the game (these tickets may still be sold on the day of the game).

Discounts. The sports organization may also decide to discount tickets for specific games. The ticket office should be cautious, however, not to use discounts in a last minute panic situation. First, this will decrease the perceived value of the tickets and will make the organization look desperate. Second, the fans will begin waiting longer to buy tickets if they know the team will probably discount the tickets on game day. This increases the amount of work on an already hectic day and may decrease the amount of revenue. Third, fans who already purchased tickets may become upset and ask for refunds. One sport organization found that a late discount increased their workload (they had to process numerous refunds), and they actually refunded more money than they made by selling the discount tickets.

One of the best examples of an effective discount system is used by the Cincinnati Reds. The Reds sell the top six rows of the stadium at a discount on game day, if those seats are still available. This provides the team the opportunity to try to sell the tickets at regular price, but still allows them to discount unsold seats on game day. Because the discount is well publicized by the organization, the fans are not surprised and do not feel cheated.

Complimentary. Ticket offices may give away more complimentary tickets than normal in order to increase attendance. The advantage of this strategy is that the larger crowd will improve the game atmosphere, and the team will receive more money for concessions and parking. Also, the tickets can be given to charitable organizations, which is good for public relations. However, the disadvantage is that these giveaways will decrease the perceived value of the tickets. Many struggling leagues have tried to increase attendance by giving away complimentary tickets and selling tickets at a great discount. Of course, the downside of this approach, as discussed earlier in the section on the psychology of pricing, is that the heavily discounted price may become--particularly for those fans attending for the first time--the consumer's reference price. Teams that indiscriminately give away or deeply discount tickets to the general public run the risk of the discounted price's becoming the reference price against which subsequent price revisions are compared. The team trying to achieve a "quick fix" at the gate may be unwittingly eroding the long-term price tolerance of many of its potential consumers. Once an expected price threshold of $5 is established in the consumer's mind, it may be very difficult in the future to get that individual to purchase a ticket at normal price levels of $10 or $15. For that reason, complimentary tickets are most successful when they are given to charity, or they are advertised as a special one-time-only deal.

ACCOUNTING SYSTEM

Ticketing System

The sophistication of computerization in ticket offices has increased tremendously over the past decade. The days of shoe boxes full of season ticketholder cards, large handwritten seating charts, and multicolumn spreadsheets completed by hand are over. With one personal computer, an organization can purchase relatively inexpensive programs that will allow it to maintain a database of ticket holders and produce all necessary documentation including spreadsheets and record of sales.

As mentioned previously, Ticketmaster and other outlets use computers to locate the best seats, to maintain a record for each seat in the facility, and to print all tickets. After the athletic venue is entered in the system, selling tickets for any event at the facility is relatively easy. Also, point-of-sale printers can be used to print the tickets as they are sold so that there are no printed, but unsold tickets (these tickets are referred to as "deadwood"), and reconciling tickets to receipts is much easier with the use of daily printouts from the computer. The system also allows the ticket-office worker to view a "map" of the facility, which shows which seats are open, which are sold, and which are on hold for a particular reason. However, the use of an outside outlet costs money in service fees and does not allow for the control that many ticket offices seek.

Recently developed specialized computer systems, such as *Paciolan* and *Select-A-Seat*, allow ticket offices to store all their records into a computer's memory. For example, *Paciolan* maintains perpetual records on everyone who purchases tickets, including their ticket orders, payment history, seat assignments, and donation levels. Computer systems can be used to assign seats more rapidly and to print all the tickets in the office. Generally, point-of-sale printers are also available for sales at the ticket window. The ticket office will still need to keep order forms and other "paper" documentation for the annual audit and for investigating any discrepancies. However, most of this can be disposed of after a few years.

The computer systems can be somewhat expensive. *Paciolan's* ticket software package costs about $30,000, in addition to all the computer hardware costs. *Paciolan* also offers software packages for other areas of the sports operation, including a general ledger system, a support group package, and a facility-scheduling package. Although the costs can become large, these systems allow the ticket office to be more efficient, maintain accurate records, and better serve the customer.

Printing

Tickets may be printed by an outside company or by the ticket office. Even when the tickets are printed internally, the ticket stock will have to be ordered. Each ticket that is printed externally must be counted and checked to assure that there are no duplications. When season tickets are mailed, each seat for each game must be pulled from the stacks, double-checked, and then placed into the envelope before mailing. It is easy to see how long and difficult this process can be for the ticket office. Also, every ticket for every game must be printed before the season, even though many will not be sold for some games. This system is costly and time consuming, especially for a large organization.

The ticket office has much more control when its personnel order the ticket stock and then print all their own tickets. Specialized computer systems allow the organization to print complete season-ticket packages (a ticket for each game for a specific seat) with mailing labels attached. Employees then separate each season-ticket order and place it into an envelope for mailing. Internal printing also enables the ticket manager to control how many tickets are printed for each game and will decrease the amount of deadwood. Printing tickets internally is preferable for the organization that can afford this type of computer system.

Accounting Procedures for Ticket Revenue

The ticket office will be receiving payments throughout the year and must have a system to maintain accurate records of receipts, deposits, and accounts receivable. Employees must record both the amount received and the reason for the receipt. When the deposits are recorded, every dollar must be attributed to the game or event for which it was received. Money received for outstanding accounts should also be attributed to the paying customer. Although deposits should be made daily, the deposit is not ready to be sent to the cashier's office or the bank until the ticket manager is sure that everything has been accurately recorded. Mistakes will be easier to find on the day of the receipt than they will be days or weeks later. The deposit should be kept in the vault until it can be taken to the bank.

Many ticket offices allow, and sometimes encourage, customers to order tickets without immediate payment. The ticket office must maintain accurate records and pursue payments for these outstanding accounts. Although allowing customers to order now and pay later is temporarily good for customer relations, there are several disadvantages. First, some of the money will be uncollectible. Second, the ticket office may have to become a pseudo collection agency. This unpleasant task can be time consuming. Third, relations with customers may be damaged when they begin to view the collection calls and letters as harassment. Because of these problems, some sports organizations have instituted policies that require payment to be received before the tickets will be mailed or distributed. This is similar to the policy used by many retail businesses and is not difficult for the customer to comply with due to the availability of credit cards. Regardless of the type chosen, the ticket office must have a documented policy that is clearly understood by customers and employees.

Ticket Records

The ticket office must maintain records that account for every ticket. For each game, the organization should know the number of tickets that have been (a) sold at each price, (b) consigned and the organizations that have them, and (c) distributed as complimentary with an explanation and approval for these giveaways. The ticket office should maintain records that include signatures for consigned tickets and complimentary approvals. The records relating to tickets will be audited at the end of the year, and the office will need to account for every ticket and every dollar. If the records are accurate and detailed, the audit will be easy for all parties involved. However, an audit can quickly become a nightmare for the ticket office that is not prepared and has maintained poor records.

Game Day

Pre-game preparations. The ticket office must be prepared and must follow established procedures to assure that all necessary tasks are completed in a timely and efficient manner on game day. Many preparations must be done before the ticket windows are open (usually 90 minutes before game time). First, the ticket office must assign a small "bank" to each ticket seller from the petty cash fund. Both the sellers' banks and the petty cash fund should include the type of change needed for that event. For example, plenty of quarters should be available if the ticket price is $3.25.

Second, the ticket office must assign a sufficient number of tickets to each seller when pre-printed tickets are going to be used. When possible, the tickets assigned to the seller should be easily accessed from his or her ticket-selling location. If there are ticket printers at the seller's station, plenty of ticket stock should be available. After counting their tickets and money, each seller must sign a sheet to acknowledge that he or she is accepting responsibility for both. Tickets should also be assigned to the ticket manager so that he or she has them available for the sellers if they sell their allotment.

Third, a ticket-office employee must complete a pre-game reconciliation to account for all tickets printed and pre-game receipts (see Part 1 of Figure 6-5a and Part

```
┌─────────────────────────────────────────────┐
│              Figure 6-5a                      │
│         Men's Basketball Game                 │
│           Toledo vs. Topeka                   │
│      February 28, 1995 at 8:00 PM             │
└─────────────────────────────────────────────┘
```

Part 1: Pre-Game Ticket Reconciliation

	Paciolan	Ticketmaster	Student
	11500	500	3000
Season Adult	5000		
Season Youth	500		
Mini-Plan	250		
Individual Game			
$10	1300	400	
$ 8	700	100	
$ 6	250		
Complimentary	1500		
Visiting Team	200		
Student			2000
Sellers:			
#1	300		150
#2	300		150
#3	300		150
#4	300		150
#5	300		200
Ticket Manager	200		125
Control	100		75
	11500	500	3000

Part 2: Deadwood (Seller Checkout)

	Paciolan	Ticketmaster	Student
Control	100		75
Seller #1	200		50
Seller #2	0		25
Seller #3	150		25
Seller #4	200		50
Seller #5	250		50
Ticket Manager	100		25
	1000	0	300

Note: The ticket manager assigned 100 more Paciolan tickets to Seller #2 and 100 more Student tickets to Seller #1

```
┌──────────────────────────────────────────────────┐
│ ╔══════════════════════════════════════════════╗ │
│ ║            Figure 6-5b                        ║ │
│ ║      Men's Basketball Game                    ║ │
│ ║       Toledo vs. Topeka                       ║ │
│ ║   February 28, 1995 at 8:00 PM                ║ │
│ ╚══════════════════════════════════════════════╝ │
└──────────────────────────────────────────────────┘
```

Part 1: Pre-Game Sales

	Tickets	Receipts
Season Adult ($8)	5000	$ 40000
Season Youth ($6)	500	3000
Mini-Plan ($8)	250	2000
Individual Game (Ticketmaster)		
$10	400	4000
$ 8	100	800
Individual Game (Paciolan)		
$10	1300	13000
$ 8	700	5600
$ 6	250	1500
Student	2000	4000
	10500	$ 73900
Visiting Team Sales ($10)	200	2000
Total Pre-Game Sales	10700	$ 75900

Part 2: Game Day Sales (Seller Checkout)

	$10	$8	$6	Student	Total Receipts
Seller #1	50	20	30	200	$ 1240
Seller #2	300	50	50	125	3950
Seller #3	100	30	20	125	1610
Seller #4	20	50	30	100	980
Seller #5	25	0	25	150	700
	495	150	155	700	$ 8480

Pre-Game Sales	$ 75900
Game Day Sales	8480
Total Sales	$ 84380

1 of 6-5b). This reconciliation can be done early in the morning, or the night before, so the employee has time to investigate any discrepancies before the day becomes hectic.

The employee should start with Part 1 of Figure 6-5a. The amounts at the top of each column are equal to the number of tickets printed in each category. The numbers for season tickets, mini-plan tickets, individual-game tickets, complimentary tickets, visiting team tickets, and student tickets should be available from a computer printout or daily sales log totals. The totals for each seller and the ticket manager are on the assignment sheets. The control tickets are generally assorted singles that will probably not be sold and can be counted in the vault. If the total of each column is equal to the top (number of tickets printed), this part is complete. If these two figures are not equal, ticket office personnel must then recount tickets assigned and control and recheck their logs or printouts to find the discrepancies.

After this section is complete, the employee must then complete Part 1 of Figure 6-5b. The number of tickets sold in each category is available in Part 1 of Figure 6-5a. These totals are then multiplied by their respective prices to determine the amount received. The total receipts should be equal to the ticket office records of the total game receipts plus the accounts receivable for that game. If this is not true, further investigation is needed. The pre-game reconciliation will assure that everything is balanced at that point, and problems with the post-game reconciliation can be attributed to a mistake made during game day.

During Game. Although game day is almost always difficult for the ticket office, there are some strategies to help the operation to run more smoothly. First, the organization should hire a sufficient number of experienced ticket sellers. Although a cheaper source of labor may be available (i.e., students), experienced sellers are quicker, more professional, and less likely to make mistakes. Although most fans will arrive close to game time, long lines and unhappy fans can also be avoided if extra sellers are hired.

Second, the ticket office should have a clearly identified window(s) at which fans can pick up prepaid tickets, complimentary tickets, or tickets being held for someone (this is referred to as the "will call windows[s]"). The ticket office should also have enough workers to distribute tickets quickly. Teams may separate the will call alphabetically and hire more workers to decrease the length of the lines. Some organizations require advance payment, so that time-consuming cash transactions can be avoided at the will call window. The ticket office should have a separate player and coach's will call area so that these special guests do not have to wait in long lines. Also, the NCAA rules regarding players' comps require that an established procedure be followed that is different from the normal will call policy.

Third, the organization should have as many employees as possible without preassigned responsibilities to deal with situations that may arise. Even the best prepared organization will have at least some last-second problems. It would be a mistake if there were not employees available to serve the customer and to handle these sometimes complicated situations.

Post-Game. The ticket office's job is not done when the ticket sales are finished. The office must first check the ticket sales and receipts for each seller to make sure his or her records are accurate. Proving a mistake is difficult after the seller has signed out. The sales figures for each seller are then recorded on Part 2 of Figure 6-5b. The total receipts (in this case $8,480) should be equal to the money received from the sellers minus the "bank" they received before the game. The number of unsold tickets, or deadwood, is recorded in Part 2 of Figure 6-6a. The total deadwood should be equal to the number of tickets now being stored in the vault (these tickets must be kept for audit purposes).

Sometime before the game is completed, the ticket office must give an attendance figure to the media. Contrary to popular belief, this number is not arrived at "scientifically." It is usually an estimate based on tickets distributed and turnstile counts. The organization should be cautioned against overestimations. This will lead to a decline in trust and respect from the fans and media that may never be recaptured.

The office must also do a post-game reconciliation (see Figure 6-6). This final reconciliation should be easy if the pre-game reconciliation and seller check-outs have been done accurately. The middle section is completed by adding the pre-game sales figures in Figure 6-5b (Part 1) with the game sales in Figure 6-5b (Part 2). The total receipts figure is then compared with the total receipts at the bottom of Figure 6-5b to ensure that all the figures in Figure 6-6 are accurate. The total complimentary tickets figure (from Figure 6-5a) is then added to total sales to determine the Total Tickets Distributed. This amount is used with the Turnstile Count to determine the Attendance to Press. The last check is at the top of Figure 6-6. All the figures are available in Figure 6-6 or Figure 6-5a, except the total for Paciolan Purchased Tickets. This amount can be computed using the middle section by adding all Paciolan tickets sold.

The final game report should include the pre- and post-game reconciliations and information, such as turnstile counts, attendance to the press, weather, team records, and comments that will make this report more useful to the ticket office in future years. Reports from previous years can help in determining the number of tickets to print and sellers to hire. The report should be placed in a file that also includes all documentation related to the game (signed consignment sheets, complimentary approval forms, etc.) Using the information in the game file, the ticket office could now answer any questions an auditor may have regarding the tickets printed and the game receipts.

SUMMARY

Charging for admission to sporting events has long been a key source of revenue for collegiate and professional teams. At the big-school level of collegiate sport, ticket sales are a vital source of revenue comprising 35% of the total income generated by Division IA athletic departments. The prominence of gate receipts diminishes greatly, however, for smaller college athletic programs. At the Division II and III levels, ticket sales contribute less than 10% of athletic programs' total revenue. The importance of gate receipts to professional sport also varies considerably. The NHL, NBA, and all

```
┌─────────────────────────────────────────────────────┐
│ ┌─────────────────────────────────────────────────┐ │
│ │                  Figure 6-6                      │ │
│ │            Post-Game Reconciliation              │ │
│ │             Men's Basketball Game                │ │
│ │               Toledo vs. Topeka                  │ │
│ │          February 28, 1995 at 8:00 PM            │ │
│ └─────────────────────────────────────────────────┘ │
└─────────────────────────────────────────────────────┘
```

	Total	Paciolan	Ticketmaster	Student
Purchased Tickets	12200	9000	500	2700
Complimentary	1500	1500	0	0
Deadwood	1300	1000	0	300
	15000	11500	500	3000

	Tickets	Receipts
Season Adult ($8)	5000	$ 40000
Season Youth ($6)	500	3000
Mini-Plan ($8)	250	2000
Individual Game (Ticketmaster)		
$10	400	4000
$ 8	100	800
Individual Game (Paciolan)		
$10	1995	19950
$ 8	850	6800
$ 6	405	2430
Student ($2)	2700	5400
Total Sales	12200	$ 84380
Complimentary	1500	
Total Tickets Distributed	13700	
Turnstile Count (attached)	12000	
Atendance to Press	12500	

Weather: 45°, Rain

Score: Toledo 56, Topeka 54

Comments: Bad weather, both teams undefeated and nationally ranked, many students came to buy tickets the morning of the game, west ticket window #2 was very busy

Signature:

minor league sports rely on ticket sales as their principal source of income. The media-prominent NFL and major league baseball still depend on gate admissions for more than a third of their overall revenues.

Understanding how price influences attendance at sporting events is an increasingly important responsibility of sport managers. Knowledge of key psychological concepts of pricing such as Expected Price Threshold and Tolerance Zones is critical for increasing sport consumers' willingness to pay. Recently, sport managers have adopted strategies designed to optimize total cash flow per seat sold. Premium seating plans and various luxury seating arrangements have been effective in boosting per-fan revenues.

Although every ticket office operates in a slightly different manner, there are some key fundamental commonalities. First, the ticket office should be proactive instead of reactive whenever possible. Some last-second emergencies cannot be avoided, but extensive preparation can help to lessen the number and severity of these problems. Second, the office must maintain accurate and complete records. This documentation will be needed for the annual audit and to investigate any discrepancies. Third, the ticket office is also a customer- service department. A ticket office employee is often the initial customer-contact representative for the organization. A customer-service orientation is crucial to building a positive public image of the organization and sustaining a high level of repeat sales.

Questions for Study and Discussion

1. **Research suggests that a number of psychological perceptions influence consumers' willingness to pay for an event or particular service. What pricing strategies should sport managers consider in order to take advantage of these psychological perceptions?**

2. **Describe the current strategies used by managers of collegiate and professional sport organizations to generate more cash flow per ticket sold.**

3. **Why is it inadvisable for sports teams to sell all their seats on a full-season ticket basis even in situations where a season sellout is possible?**

4. **What are the advantages of selling miniplan ticket packages?**

5. **Describe some of the fundamental record-keeping procedures ticket offices should establish to document sales.**

REFERENCES

Brown, B. (1993, May 11). Supply and demand sets ticket prices. *USA Today*, p. 8C.

Chass, M. (1993, August 8). Call it baseball or call it business, it's still booming. *New York Times*, p. 2E.

Crompton, J. L. & Lamb, C. (1986). *Marketing government and social services.* New York: John Wiley & Sons.

Eichelberger, C. (1994, July 31). CU sports sacked for financial loss. *Rocky Mountain News*, p. 9B

Fichtenbaum, P., Rosenblatt, R. & Sandomir, R. (1989, January 2). How golden is the goose: Sports in the '90s. *Sports inc.*, pp. 29-31.

Hammersmith, V. A. (1985). The development of a survey instrument to profile donors to athletics. *Dissertation Abstracts International, 46,* 09A. (University Microfilm GV350H34)

Hoffman, D. & Greenberg, M. (1989). *Sportsbiz: An irreverent look at big business in pro sport.* Champaign, IL: Leisure Press.

Isherwood, A. C. (1986). A descriptive profile of the fund raising programs in NCAA Division I-A. *Dissertation Abstracts International, 47,* 08A.

Johnson, A. (1993). *Minor league baseball and local economic development.* Urbana, IL: University of Illinois Press.

Kirshenbaum, J. (1993, March 24). Running up the tab. *Sports Illustrated,* pp. 22-24.

Mason, J. G., & Paul, J. (1988). *Modern sports administration.* Englewood Cliffs, N.J.: Prentice Hall.

Masters, M. (1992). *Business and ticket managers' manual.* Chicago, IL: Big Ten Conference.

McCarville, R. E. & Crompton, J. L. (1987). An empirical investigation of the influence of information on reference prices for public swimming pools. *Journal of Leisure Research, 19*(3), 223-225.

McCarville, R. E., Crompton, J. L. & Sell, J. A. (1993). The influence of outcome messages on reference prices. *Leisure Sciences, 15*(2), 115-130.

Monroe, K. (1971, November). Measuring price thresholds and latitude of acceptance. *Journal of Marketing Research,* pp. 460-464.

Mulligan, T. S. (1992, July 2). Sports teams pitch hard to generate ticket sales. *Los Angeles Times*, p. E1.

Ozanian, M. & Taub, S. (1992, July 7). Big leagues, bad business. *Financial World*, pp. 34-42.

Pajak, M. (1990, March). Every fly ball is an adventure. *Athletic Business*, pp. 26-28.

Quirk, J. & Fort, R. D. (1992). *Pay dirt: The business of professional team sports.* Princeton, NJ: Princeton University Press.

Raiborn, M. (1990). *Revenues and expenses of intercollegiate athletic programs: Analysis of financial trends and relationships 1985-1989.* Overland Park, KS: National Collegiate Athletic Association.

Saparito, B. (1991, July 1). The owners' new game is managing. *Fortune*, pp. 86-90.

Weston, J. F. & Brigham, E. (1974). *Essentials of managerial finance* (3rd ed.). Hinsdale, IL: Dryden Press.

Zimbalist, A. (1992). *Baseball and billions.* New York: Basic Books.

CHAPTER 7

SALE OF LICENSED PRODUCTS AND SERVICES

Learning Objectives

After completing this chapter, the reader should be able to:

1. articulate pertinent sport licensing nomenclature.
2. recognize the potential of sport licensing as a promising source of revenue.
3. identify and explain the 3 Ps of licensing: Protection, Promotion and Profit.
4. discuss the relative advantages and disadvantages of organizing a licensing program "in house" or employing the services of an outside licensing agent.
5. explain the basic conditions and terms stipulated in a licensing contract.

CHAPTER 7

SALE OF LICENSED PRODUCTS AND SERVICES

Dickie Van Meter, President
Licensing Resource Group, Inc.

INTRODUCTION

Revenues realized from the sale of licensed sports merchandise have become an increasingly important source of revenue for professional sports franchises and inter-collegiate athletic programs. In 1992, total sales of products bearing the logos of the four professional sports leagues in North America exceeded $6 billion (Table 7-1).

The growth of retail sales of licensed sport products has been meteoric. National Football League souvenir revenues have increased nearly 400% since 1980. Econo-mists projected the sale of NFL logo merchandise would exceed $3 billion by 1993 (Compte 1989). Gross sales of goods licensed by major league baseball grew from $200 million in 1987, the year in which Major League Baseball Properties was estab-lished, to $2 billion in 1992. With licensing revenues being split evenly among each major league club, Zimbalist (1992) estimated that each team's share amounted to $3.7 million. Seeing the great potential for raising revenue, minor league baseball became involved with licensing in 1992. The $15 million in total retail sales netted the 152 participating minor league clubs around $1.3 million in royalty revenues (Beradino, 1993). Colleges and universities are relative newcomers to the sports licensed logo business as well. A recent survey of Division 1A athletic programs suggests that licensing revenues are becoming a significant source of new revenue for collegiate athletic departments, with about 20% of the responding schools reporting annual licensing income exceeding $250,000.

It is evident that despite the significant income already being realized from the sale of licensed sports products, sport administrators are just beginning to scratch the sur-face of licensing's full potential. The survey of Division 1A schools found half the "big-school" programs receiving less than $50,000 a year from the sale of products bearing their logo. One-fourth reported receiving no licensing revenues at all. The vast majority of amateur, interscholastic, and public sport organizations have yet to begin to explore the potential of licensing.

Dickie Van Meter is President of Licensing Resource Group, Iowa City, Iowa, a full-service consulting and licensing management firm. Phone 319/351-1776; FAX 319/351-1978.

Table 7-1	
Total Retail Sales of Licensed Products for the Four	
Major Sport Leagues in North America	

LEAGUE	TOTAL SALES
National Football League	$2.5 billion
Major League Baseball	$2.0
National Basketball League	$1.0
National Hockey League	$0.5
TOTAL	$6.0 billion

Note: From "What's next: Raider's deodorant?" by Elizabeth Lesly, November 30, 1992, *Business Week*, p. 65.

The intent of this chapter is to provide the reader with a thorough understanding of what trademark licensing is and how licensing programs are organized. The initial portion of the chapter provides definitions of the many specialized terms essential to understanding the fundamental components of a licensing program. A key element of the chapter is the sample licensing agreement found in the chapter appendix. This contract is a sample designed to provide an overview of the content and structure of a licensing agreement. Actual contracts vary widely, but include the basic elements found in the sample contract.

Licensing Terminology

The licensing industry has its own terminology. Listed below are some of the most common terms.

Advance Fee - The money paid by a licensee to a licensor that may be required to obtain a license.

Copyright - An original work of authorship fixed in any tangible medium of expression, now known or later developed, from which they can be perceived, reproduced, or otherwise communicated, either directly or with the aid of a machine or device; this includes, but is not limited to, literary and graphic works. Indicated by a ©, "Copyright" or "Copy."

Cross-Licensing - The use of more than one licensed mark on the same product. Royalties generated as a result are divided between the owners of the marks.

Exclusive License - A license that grants the licensee exclusive permission to use a specific trademark on specific products for a specific period of time and/or in a specific territory.

Guaranteed Minimum Royalty - The minimum amount a licensee promises to pay a licensor. This may be covered by royalties generated or represent the difference between royalties generated and the guaranteed minimum.

Licensee - The entity granted permission by contract to use the trademark or service mark under the holder's (licensor's) supervision and control.

Licensor - The name given to the owner of a particular mark or marks; one who authorized commercialization of their trademark through licensing.

Non-exclusive License - A license which does not grant exclusive rights to a certain trademark, product or territory. More than one licensee may offer the same product in the same territory.

Patent - Protects a functional or design invention.

Premium - Merchandise that is given without charge or is sold at a discounted price as an inducement to purchase another product or service. Example: A glass given away by a gas station with a fill-up of gas.

Promotional Licensing - An advertising or publicity campaign that may involve licensed marks.

Registration - A trademark filed in the United States Patent and Trademark office or the appropriate state office, with the necessary description and other statements required by the act of congress, and there duly recorded, securing its exclusive use to the person causing it to be registered. Indicated by a ®.

Royalty - A fee that a licensee pays a licensor for the use of specific marks on specific products in a designated territory. Royalties are determined by multiplying the royalty rate (a percentage which may range from 6-10%) times gross sales at wholesale.

Service Mark - Any word, picture, number, letter or other symbol which indicates a service comes from a particular source or origin which may include institutions. Example: ABC University Printing Service.

Trademark - Includes any word, name, symbol, or device or any combination thereof adopted and used by a manufacturer or merchant to identify his goods and distinguish them from those manufactured or sold by others. Indicated by a "TM."

The basic difference between patents/copyrights and trademarks is that the first protects new ideas and technologies and the latter protects established names and marks. Federal registration provides the maximum protection if litigation is necessary. If no effort is made to protect the marks, the license may be considered "naked" and not upheld in court. Periodically federal registrations will need to be renewed if they are in continuing use. Additionally, an owner has common law protection for trademarks that are not federally registered. Common law rights arise from mere usage of the marks.

The first step in the registering of trademarks at the federal level is a search to determine whether anyone has previously registered the mark in question. As might be expected, many schools have duplicating mascots or initials. For example, the University of Texas considers the capital letter "T" an important mark. However, the University of Tennessee also considers the letter "T" as an important symbol of its institution. Both schools are correct in their geographic areas. Trademark law allows for the definition of geographic areas if both parties agree. If a university were to attempt to register the word "bear" or "panther," it is highly likely that the application would be blocked. In that case, it is recommended that the schools' name be included in the registration application. For example, one could register the "University of XYZ Panthers." The character or illustration of a mascot may be registered if the design is original and associates itself directly with the university. Once it is determined a mark or name is to be registered, then appropriate classes need to be selected. Each mark must be registered in those classes covering the product categories that will likely bear the marks.

Some recommended classes for marks include:

1. Class 6 - Metal Goods
2. Class 16 - Paper Goods and Printed Matter
3. Class 18 - Leather Goods
4. Class 21 - Housewares and Glass
5. Class 24 - Fabrics (pennants and banners)
6. Class 25 - Clothing
7. Class 26 - Fancy Goods (patches for clothing buttons)
8. Class 28 - Toys and Sporting Goods
9. Class 41 - Education and Entertainment Services

Ownership is indicated by the following marks:

TM - Trademark notification.
® - Federally registered mark.
© - Copyright notification.

In addition, the professional leagues, character licensors, and universities require that products be clearly marked with labels or tags that identify goods as "Officially Licensed". These labels help in the policing of the marketplace (see Figure 7-1).

Licensing administrators often refer to the three P's of licensing: protection, promotion, and profit. Successful licensing programs aggressively "protect" their marks and image, are interested in "promoting" their name through its controlled use on products, and are interested in increasing bottom line "profit." Permission to use those marks, whether they belong to character licensors, professional leagues, or colleges and universities, is given through formalized licensing contracts. These contracts require that manufacturers meet certain standards, pay advance fees, and guarantee royalties for use of the marks.

Figure 7-1
Samples of "Officially Licensed" Sports Products

THE DEVELOPMENT OF SPORT LICENSING

Licensing is a fairly recent phenomenon on college campuses. The first license was granted to R. Gsell, a watch manufacturer, in 1973 by the University of California at Los Angeles (UCLA) bookstore. Many people credit the UCLA Bookstore for the birth of merchandising emblematic goods. UCLA's success quickly prompted several other prominent institutions to initiate licensing programs. In 1974, The Ohio State

University and the University of Southern California actively began to protect their marks by registering their names and logos as trademarks and developing programs that protected the marks and collected royalties for their use. By 1993, according to Anne Chasser (personal communication, May 18, 1993), Director of Trademark Licensing Services, Ohio State had licensed 500 products—75% on wearing apparel—which generated over $40 million in gross sales .

The NCAA had an opportunity to control and organize collegiate licensing in the late 1970s. Many schools looked to the NCAA for guidance, but the resources available were not prepared to organize schools into a formal licensing program. The NCAA has concentrated its licensing efforts on the annual men's basketball tournament and the incredible phenomenon known as the Final Four. The NCAA operates a licensing and merchandising program for all its championship events. They contract with a concessionaire who sells at all championship events, which include everything from fencing to the Final Four. Many feel that the NCAA could have changed the course of collegiate licensing if it had taken steps earlier, but the nature of its highly political structure prevented an aggressive effort to organize a coordinated licensing presence for its member institutions.

The collegiate licensing industry has not been without controversy. Many of the early manufacturers maintained that the use of schools' marks should fall in the public domain. The University of Pittsburgh continued for 2 years to pursue its claim against Champion Products, one of the largest sports apparel manufacturers in the country. Champion claimed that it had created the market, and the university claimed that it had the right to require a license for the use of its marks and collect royalties. Other schools, including Ohio State, DePaul, and UCLA, took action against Champion. Champion found itself in the unenviable position of suing its customers, a decision that came to haunt the company. Although the Pittsburgh-Champion case was actually settled out of court, the legal system has supported a school's right to control the use of its name and marks. At the same time, the NFL won its lawsuit against Wichita Falls Sportswear, establishing the league's right to control its marks. These major legal victories gave universities the courage to consider litigation, and Champion quickly moved to settle with universities and sign contracts. Other companies watched the progress of litigation and began to negotiate licensing agreements with the schools with which they wished to work.

Successful legal action, coupled with the explosion of the "fleece business" in the 1980s, stimulated many colleges and universities to initiate formal licensing programs. (*Fleece* is the term for the actual material from which sweatshirts, pants, and shorts are made.) By the early 1990s, more than 250 institutions had established licensing programs. In many cases, these programs are reactive and offer little more than a token response to the request by a company for permission to use the college's name or logo. However, a growing number of institutions have moved well beyond a protection position to the development of a comprehensive licensing program. In these instances, the university has either maintained its own full-time licensing staff or contracted with an outside licensing management company to aggressively administer and promote

TABLE 7-2
Licensing Survey

In an effort to provide some perspective on the nature and scope of licensing and its financial impact on intercollegiate athletics, a selective survey of schools sponsoring both Division 1A basketball and football was conducted in March 1993. Forty athletic departments from the original sample pool of 85 returned questionnaires for a response rate of 47.1%. At least half the member schools from the Big Ten, Mid American, PAC 10, Southeastern and Western athletic conferences are represented.

Q1. In what area is the licensing program housed at your school?

Administrative Area	Percentage
Athletic Department	27.5
Vice-President - University	12.5
Campus Bookstore	17.5
Other University Administration	35.0
Athletic Foundation	5.0
No Licensing Program	2.5

Q2. Is your licensing program handled in-house or by an outside agent?

Locus of Control	Percentage
In-House	40.0
Outside Agent	52.5
No Response	7.5

Q3. Does your athletic department participate on a licensing committee or partici-pate directly in licensing decisions?

Yes	52.5%
No	37.5%
No Response	10.0%

Q4. Does your athletic department share in revenues realized from the licensing program? If so, what is the athletic department's relative share (%)?

Relative Share (%)	Percentage
0% (no licensing revenues)	25.0
Less than 10%	7.5
10-25%	7.5
26-50%	12.5
51-75%	20.0
76-99%	7.5
100% (all revenues)	20.0

Table 7-2 cont'd.

Q5. Approximately how much revenue does the athletic department receive annually from licensing?

Amount of Revenue	Percentage
$1 million plus	2.5
$500,000 - $999,999	10.0
$250,000 - $499,999	7.5
$100,000 - $249,999	15.0
$ 50,000 - $ 99,999	15.0
$ 10,000 - $ 49,999	17.5
less than $10,000	7.5
$0 (no licensing revenue)	25.0

their licensed products. In the early 1990s, about 50% of those schools with formal licensing programs are represented by an outside agent.

The survey data in Table 7-2 provide perspective on the current state of licensing programs in major universities across the United States. The survey of selected schools sponsoring both Division IA football and basketball was conducted in March 1993 by Dennis R. Howard, Director of Sport Management at The Ohio State University. The intent of the survey was to sample representatives from each of the major or "big school" conferences. Forty athletic departments from the original sample pool of 85 completed the questionnaires for a reponse rate of 47.1%. At least half the member schools from the Big Ten, Mid American, PAC 10, Southeastern and Western Athletic conferences are represented.

It is interesting to note that only about one-third (32.5%) of the athletic departments or their affiliated support groups (i.e., athletic foundations) reported having direct administrative control for licensing at their institutions. Administrative authority was most often located within the university's central administration, typically under the jurisdiction of the contract administration office or the vice-president for administration. The pattern of administration for licensing programs has obvious implications for the athletic department. In those institutions where the athletic department has no direct administrative authority for licensing, generally the athletic department will have little or no influence over licensing decisions. The survey indicated that 37.5% of the responding athletic programs had no involvement at all in the operation and development of licensing at their universities. Unfortunately, in these instances, this generally means that the athletic department receives none or very few of the proceeds generated by the licensing program. One of every four athletic programs responding to the survey reported that they received no annual licensing revenues. Ohio State University is one of the institutions that fall into this category. In 1992, the total retail sale of licensed goods by The Ohio State University exceeded $35 million, netting the school $1.5 million in royalty fees (A. Chasser, personal communication, May 18, 1993). All of these monies were committed to a general university scholarship fund. Whereas a significant share of these revenues were derived from the sale of athletic apparel (team jerseys, shorts, etc.), the university's centrally administered licensing program, located within the Office of Trademark and Licensing Services, shares approximately 25% of its annual income with the university's athletic department.

In Canada, the University of Calgary was the first to develop a trademark licensing program. The 1988 Winter Olympic Games, which were hosted by Calgary, accelerated the establishment of the licensing program in an effort to optimize the many merchandising opportunities offered by the Olympics. The Calgary program became a model for other Canadian institutions.

In 1986, the Association of Collegiate Licensing Administrators (ACLA) was formed in Orlando, Florida, during a national college bookstore meeting. ACLA is a professional association that sponsors annual and regional meetings and publishes a directory, newsletter, and other educational publications. Members are either licensing administrators on a university campus or an associate member, which might include manufacturers or other businesses providing services (trademark attorneys, agents, etc.) to the licensing industry.

Licensing in Professional Sport

Professional leagues have effectively maximized licensing opportunities, and as a result, the popularity of licensed products has grown. In each league, proceeds from sales of team merchandise are pooled and divided evenly among the league teams. In the four major professional leagues, merchandising is coordinated by a central "properties" division, which licenses hundreds of products from sweatshirts to dog dishes.

Professional baseball established Major League Baseball Properties (MLBP) in 1987 as its licensing and marketing arm. Prior to centralizing baseball licensing in one office, retail sales of baseball merchandise consisted primarily of trading cards, T-shirts, caps, and a multitude of low-end products sold at stadium concession stores and sporting good stores. By the early 1990s, MLBP had tightened up its licensing requirements and introduced a new line of high-quality products, such as authentic reproductions of team jerseys and jackets, silk camisoles, bow ties, scarves, and event boxer shorts with prints of baseball scenes or team logos. Currently, MLBP has extended licenses to over 300 licensees that market over 3,000 products decorated with baseball team logos and designs (Lubove, 1991). Applying a standard royalty rate of 8.5% on net sales of approximately $2 billion, MLBP generated close to $170 million in licensing royalty revenues for major league teams in 1992.

Professional football's licensing branch is National Football League Properties, Inc. (NFLP). NFLP has taken a very aggressive approach to merchandising licensed league products and souvenirs. Rather than waiting for manufacturers to bring goods for licensing approval to them, NFLP has developed "in-house" a wide variety of new products and licensees. They have successfully developed more than 30 different merchandising programs. Two such enterprises include "NFL Kids" and "NFL Spirit" specialty apparel lines targeted to children and women, respectively. In the early 1990s, NFLP introduced "NFL Throwbacks" featuring clothing items from classic teams, such as the Canton Bulldogs, the Acme Packers, and the Oakland Raiders. These initiatives have reaped great rewards for the NFL. Total sales of team and league-related products contributed an estimated $2.5 billion to the league's coffers in 1992 (Pasquarelli, 1992).

The National Basketball Association and National Hockey League have enjoyed success in marketing licensed products, but have a long way to go to catch up with the NFL and MLB. Other sports properties have aligned themselves with those experienced in sports licensing to produce successful lines. They include

- Minor League Baseball - licensed through MLB Properties
- World Cup '94 - licensed through Warner Sports Merchandising
- USA Basketball - licensed through NBA Properties
- Negro League - licensed through MLBP (pro bono)

Amateur sports associations and recreational leagues are also in the process of exploring how the licensing of their name and marks will provide both protection and revenue opportunities to their organizations.

THE ADMINISTRATION OF LICENSING PROGRAMS

Organizations contemplating the development of formalized licensing programs have basically two alternatives available to them. They can either decide to appoint or employ their own "in-house" staff to oversee the program or procure the services of an outside licensing agent or management company.

The decision on whether to administer a licensing program strictly in-house or to rely on outside resources depends largely on circumstances, such as the scope and potential for the sale of licensed products and budget, as well as the availability of specialized expertise. Those organizations with limited staff resources, modest expectations--perhaps, initially limited to protection--may find it practical to contract with outside resources. Sport organizations which may have the need for more comprehensive services, yet lack the necessary staff expertise, may want to utilize the resources of a full-service management company. Specialty licensing firms can take responsibility for all aspects of a licensing program on behalf of the organization they represent. Their responsibilities include qualifying licensees, the negotiation of licenses, review of insurance certificates, reconciliation of quarterly royalty reports, information management, and trademark enforcement.

Typically, full-service licensing management firms provide their services for a fixed percentage of the royalties generated by the program or for a flat fee for specific services. Although the outside agents' percentage of royalties vary considerably, their fees average 20% of gross royalty revenues.

In the early 1990s, two full-service licensing specialty firms are the primary agents to colleges and universities in Canada and the United States: The Collegiate Licensing Company (CLC), established in 1984, and the Licensing Resource Group (LRG), established in 1991.

As discussed previously, most professional sports leagues have established their own centralized properties divisions that, in effect, act as their own in-house merchandising arms. In each case, these league-specific licensing divisions control, regulate, and aggressively market licensed products for their respective leagues.

Unlike professional sports, no common pattern for the organization of in-house licensing programs exists on college campuses. Schools that have made the decision to take responsibility for administering their own licensing programs have housed their on-campus licensing administrator generally in one of three areas: (a) the campus bookstore (22%), (b) the contract administration office (21%), or (c) the department of intercollegiate athletics (20%) (Association of Collegiate Licensing Administrators, 1993).

Sadly, from the perspective of many collegiate athletic directors, only about 25% of the approximately 300 licensing programs on college campuses are administered by athletic departments or independent athletic support groups such as athletic foundations. For many intercollegiate athletic programs, this may mean they receive no direct revenues from the sale of athletic products. Although the athletic department may not run a campus licensing program, it is critical its interests be represented. Many campuses have established licensing committees to support institutional licensing programs. Commonly, this committee is composed of representatives from the bookstore, the alumni association, legal affairs, and contract administration. Unfortunately, representation from the athletic department is not always assured. The licensing survey (see Table 7-2) shown earlier in the chapter revealed that only half the athletic departments participate directly on their school's licensing committee. Although participation on such a committee will certainly not guarantee that the athletic department will receive its fair share (or any share) of licensing revenues, the opportunity to provide input into policies that protect and enhance the quality of products representing the image of the school's athletic programs is vitally important.

The Licensing Contract

The cornerstone of any licensing agreement is a contract between the licensee and the owner of the trademark or copyright, the licensor. The contract agreement specifies the marks to be licensed and licensed products to be sold, establishes the basis for royalties to be paid to the licensor, defines the length of the contract, and stipulates the basis for terminating the contract. The sample license agreement included in the appendix of this chapter provides a comprehensive example of the conditions and terms that are typically established in a contract between a university, sports organization, or league and a company wishing the use or sales of its marks or logos.

The hypothetical licensing agreement between Minnesota State University (MSU) and College Products, Ltd. grants the corporation the non-exclusive right to manufacture and sell T-shirts and sweatshirts using the name, logo and nickname ("Screaming Eagles") of the university for one year (see Schedule A). Common to most licensing agreements, the sample contract requires College Products, Ltd. to make an up-front financial commitment to MSU in the form of a $500 Licensing Fee and a nonrefundable $1,000 advance against anticipated royalties. In addition, the agreement specifies a guaranteed minimum royalty payment of $5,000 to MSU regardless of what revenues College Products may realize from selling the university's licensed apparel.

The contract stipulates a royalty rate of 10%, which would place it at the high end of current royalty rates, which typically range from 6 to 10%. In our example, for every T-shirt or sweatshirt sold, 10% of the "net sale" price would be paid to MSU. The net sale price is carefully defined [see Section 3(e)] to allow only prescribed deductions, such as customer discounts and bona fide "returns" of merchandise. College Products is required to certify in a written royalty statement a detailed quarterly accounting of all deductible discounts and allowances.

Other important provisions of the contract assure MSU quality control over licensed products by requiring College Products to submit samples for review and approval prior to their manufacture and sale [see Section 6(a) - (h)]. Sections 12 and 13 of the contract protect MSU from liability claims that may result from any defects in the licensed MSU apparel distributed by College Products, Ltd. Schedule A requires the licensee to purchase a minimum of $1 million in product liability insurance to assure adequate coverage in the event of a liability claim. It is important that licensors entering into licensing agreements require proof of product liability insurance from licensees and maintain copies of insurance certificates that name licensor as an additional insured.

Enforcement

What does enforcement mean to a licensing program? Those failing to show good faith efforts to enforce the authorized use of their marks may risk the legal right to license those marks and collect royalties. Enforcement means taking action to insure that those companies that use an organization's marks and logos have secured permission and/or a license to do so and unauthorized use is policed and eliminated. Enforcement efforts may take place at local, regional, and national levels.

Local. A strategy is necessary that allows for the identification of all local retail outlets around a campus venue that sell merchandise bearing licensed marks. In addition, universities need to be prepared to take action in the case of a special event, which may include game days or a university's participation in a bowl game, basketball tournament, or other special opportunity. In many cases, local trespassing and vending ordinances will support enforcement efforts and control sales of emblematic merchandise.

By far the biggest problem for colleges and universities is locally owned retail outlets that screenprint and/or sell products with school logos. In the initial stages of licensing program development, university community businesses producing such items should be identified and licensed. If a university commits to a licensing program, it must consistently require the collection of royalties for all use of its name(s) and marks. Many manufacturers of collegiate products have expressed concern that they have become licensed, yet find as they sell in the local marketplace that they are competing with unlicensed suppliers. This dilutes the value of the license and reflects badly on the credibility of the institutional licensing program. Well-run licensing programs have an ongoing program that has "shoppers" reviewing what is being sold in the local retail stores. Merchandise should be clearly identified as to origin (producer) and license. In the case of university licensing programs, retailers are often pleased to be working with the university and promoting the sales of licensed merchandise that helps support the institution and in many cases the athletic programs.

In some cases, a local retailer or screenprinter will test a licensing program by defying the requirements. An institution should be prepared to take action. Taking action sends a clear message not only to those testing a university but also to good faith supporters of the program.

All universities are highly sensitive to public relations and are hesitant to make waves in the local community by censuring those businesses that are not cooperating. However, local enforcement is a necessary element in a university licensing program. Historically, those universities that have been proactive in their enforcement efforts have benefited by demonstrating their commitment to operating a quality licensing program.

Regional. In some cases, universities, professional leagues, and licensees join to bring a manufacturer or screenprinter into compliance. Infringers, in most cases, are using a screenprinter that is more than likely using the marks of more than one property. By joining forces, collective clout is exercised. In some areas of the country, swap meets or flea markets are popular. Group efforts and shared costs allow for "sweeps" that confiscate unlicensed merchandise bearing registered trademarks. A group can collectively take legal action if needed. Typically, once the products are confiscated, it is rare that a vendor will appear in court to plead his or her case and collect the confiscated goods.

National. Professional leagues and many renowned universities have struggled with counterfeiters on a nationwide basis for years. These counterfeiters capitalize on the success of a university that has enjoyed great market popularity across the country. Professional leagues continue to develop strategies to shut down these professional and highly sophisticated counterfeiters. Many universities with national visibility benefit from working with the NFL, NBA, Disney, etc.

National counterfeit operations are often well organized, and it is recommended that schools work with legal firms experienced in this type of action. In recent years, professional leagues, character licensors, and universities have joined in seizures. These efforts have resulted in some dramatic actions, but the counterfeiters are so clever that they will soon set up in another area and continue to counterfeit marks that are not being enforced.

SUMMARY

Licensing sport program names and marks is the most recent and, perhaps, most promising source of new revenue. All four major professional sports leagues in North America have made significant commitments to the sale of licensed apparel and souvenirs. The model used by major league baseball (MLB), football (NFL), basketball (NBA), and hockey (NHL) has been to establish their own in-house licensing program or properties division to protect and promote their logo merchandise. The result has led to annual royalty revenues of $6 million for the four major professional leagues.

Colleges and universities have also begun--just within the last two decades--to realize substantial returns on their licensed goods and products. Many institutions have established comprehensive licensing programs that involve recruiting and qualifying licensees, collecting royalties, and enforcing trademarks. The three alternative approaches to organizing collegiate licensing programs have been for universities to (a) oversee the administrative requirements "in-house," (b) contract for the services of an "outside" specialized licensing firm, or (c) combine some level of in-house administration with the contracting out of selected services. Regardless of how institutions have elected to organize their licensing programs, a substantial number of athletic departments--approximately 25%--do not receive any licensing revenues. A potential opportunity for athletic administrators in this situation is to seek membership on a campus-wide licensing committee. Many institutions have established committees to oversee and coordinate their licensing programs. At the very least, the athletic department should strive to have its interests represented on such a committee.

Unfortunately, the majority of amateur, public recreation and interscholastic sports organizations have yet to investigate the potential of licensing. The sample licensing contract found in the appendix of this chapter has been included to provide a sample for sports organizations interested in establishing a licensing program. An experienced trademark attorney should be consulted in the development of a licensing contract. The content and structure can be adapted to fit the circumstances of any organization that sees the potential of protecting and promoting the sale of its logo apparel and souvenirs.

QUESTIONS FOR STUDY AND DISCUSSION

1. What is the essential difference between a copyright and trademark?
2. What are the 3Ps of licensing? Explain, using appropriate examples, how licensing programs can achieve these desired ends.
3. Assume as a finalist for an Assistant Director of Athletics position at a Division I (basketball only) school, you are appearing before an interview panel. The school has had very little exposure to licensing, and is interested in establishing a licensing program to protect its marks and image as well as generate additional revenue. You are asked:
   "Tell us what you know about collegiate licensing programs. Specifically, share with us what you know about (a) the purpose or functions of licensing programs, (b) approaches to organizing them, and (c) their potential for generating additional revenues for collegiate athletic programs."
4. Review the Sample Licensing Agreement between Minnesota State University and College Products. Provide, in your own words, a description of the essential conditions stipulated between the two parties for the following sections: compensation, inspection, termination, indemnity, and insurance.

REFERENCES

Association of Collegiate Licensing Administrators. (1993). *ACLA 1993 Industry Study*, Orlando, FL.

Beradino, M. (1993, February 7). MLBP sails smoothly through unchartered waters. *Baseball Weekly*, pp. 24-25.

Comte, E. (1989, October 30). NFL Properties values booming. *Sporting News*, p. 64.

Lesley, E. (1992, November 30). What's next: Raider's deodorant? *Business Week*, p. 65.

Lubove, Seth (1991, October 14). Going, going, sold! *Forbes*, p. 180.

Pasquarelli, Len (1993, January 7). Cracking the NFL properties line-up a tough deal. *Atlanta Journal and Atlanta Constitution* , p. D6.

Zimbalist, A. (1992). *Baseball and billions*. New York: Basic Books.

APPENDIX

LICENSE AGREEMENT

THIS AGREEMENT is entered into this 1st day of October, 1994 by and between MINNESOTA STATE UNIVERSITY, whose address is 1 University Drive, East Minneapolis, MN 55555 by and through its authorized agent, UNIVERSITY LICENSING AGENT, INC., a New York corporation with offices at 227 Park Avenue, New York, New York 10017 (hereinafter "MSU") and COLLEGE PRODUCTS, LTD., a Delaware corporation with offices at 122 Smith Drive, Los Angeles, CA 99999 ("LICENSEE").

WITNESSETH:

WHEREAS, MSU has established and desires to preserve, protect, enhance and promote its national and international reputation and prestige as a public/private institution of higher education, research, public service, cultural and intercollegiate sports activities, and LICENSEE acknowledges and recognizes this reputation and prestige; and

WHEREAS, MSU is the sole and exclusive owner of the trademarks, logos, copyrights and other intellectual property rights more fully described in Schedule A attached hereto (the "Licensed Properties"); and

WHEREAS, MSU has the power and authority to grant to LICENSEE the right, privilege and license to use, manufacture, and sell those types of licensed products which incorporate or are otherwise based on the Licensed Properties as identified in Schedule A attached hereto (the "Licensed Products"); and

WHEREAS, LICENSEE has represented that it has the ability to manufacture, market and distribute the Licensed Products in the countries identified in Schedule A attached hereto (the "Licensed Territory");

WHEREAS, LICENSEE desires to obtain from MSU a non-exclusive license to use, manufacture, have manufactured, and sell Licensed Products in the Licensed Territory; and

WHEREAS, both LICENSEE and MSU have agreed to the terms and conditions upon which LICENSEE shall use, manufacture, have manufactured, and sell Licensed Products.

NOW, THEREFORE, in consideration of the promises and agreements set forth herein, the parties, each intending to be legally bound hereby, do promise and agree as follows:

1. LICENSE

(a) MSU hereby grants to LICENSEE, for the Term of this Agreement, the non-exclusive right and license to use, manufacture, have manufactured, sell, distribute and advertise the Licensed Products in the Licensed Territory. The license includes a license under all trademarks and copyrights and any applications and registrations therefore with respect to the Licensed Properties. It is understood, however, that this license grant and LICENSEE's obligation to pay royalties hereunder are not predicated or conditioned on MSU seeking, obtaining, or maintaining any trademark or copyright protection for the Licensed Properties.

(b) All rights not specifically granted to LICENSEE under this agreement are retained by MSU.

(c) LICENSEE may not assign its rights under this agreement or grant sublicenses to third parties without MSU's prior express written approval.

(d) LICENSEE shall not make, use or sell the Licensed Products or any products which contain the Licensed Properties or any marks or artwork which is confusingly or substantially similar to the Licensed Properties outside the Licensed Territory and will not knowingly sell the Licensed Products or such other products to persons who intend to or are likely to resell them outside the Licensed Territory.

(e) LICENSEE shall not, without prior written permission from MSU, manufacture, sell, or distribute Licensed Products as premiums or promotions, nor in connection whatsoever with lotteries, games of chance, firearms, tobacco or alcoholic beverage promotion.

(f) LICENSEE shall not, without prior written permission from MSU, advertise, sell or otherwise marked Licensed Products through direct mail or catalogue sales to a list of students, parents of students, faculty, staff, alumni, contributors, or similar group maintained or compiled by MSU.

2. TERM

This Agreement shall be effective as of the date of execution by both parties and shall extend for the term recited in Schedule A unless terminated by operation of law or in accordance with the provisions of this Agreement (the "Term"). This Agreement shall be automatically renewed for additional one (1) year term(s) immediately upon expiration of the then in-effect Term unless either party shall give written notice of termination within ninety (90) days prior to the end of the then in-effect Term. All provisions of this Agreement shall remain in full force and effect throughout all subsequent renewal periods.

3. COMPENSATION

(a) In consideration for the licenses granted hereunder, LICENSEE agrees to pay to MSU, upon execution of this Agreement and upon commencement of any Renewal Term, a non-refundable, non- creditable License Fee in the amount recited in Schedule A hereto (the "License Fee"). In addition, LICENSEE further agrees to pay to MSU a royalty on its Net Sales of License Products at the royalty rate recited in Schedule A (the "Royalty"). LICENSEE agrees to pay to MSU, upon execution of this Agreement and upon the commencement of any Renewal Term, a non-refundable Advance against Royalties in the amount recited in Schedule A which may be credited against LICENSEE's actual royalty obligation to MSU.

(b) The Royalty owed MSU shall be calculated on a quarterly calendar basis (the "Royalty Period") and shall be payable no later than thirty (30) days after the termination of the preceding full calendar quarter, i.e., commencing on the first (1st) day of January, April, July and October, except that the first and last calendar quarters may be "short" depending on the effective date of this Agreement.

(c) For each Royalty Period, LICENSEE shall provide MSU with a written royalty statement in a form acceptable to MSU. Such royalty statement shall be certified as accurate by a duly authorized officer of LICENSEE reciting, on a country by country basis, the stock number, item, units sold, description, quantity shipped, gross invoice, amount billed customers less discounts, allowances, returns and reportable sales for each Licensed Product. Such statements shall be furnished to MSU regardless of whether any Licensed Products were sold during the Royalty Period or whether any actual Royalty was owed.

(d) During each calendar year during the Term of this Agreement, LICENSEE agrees to pay MSU a Guaranteed Minimum Royalty as recited in Schedule A which may be credited against LICENSEE'S actual royalty obligation to MSU. The Guaranteed Minimum Royalty shall be calculated at the end of each calendar year. In the event that LICENSEE's actual Royalties paid MSU for any calendar year are less than the Guaranteed Minimum Royalty for such year, LICENSEE shall, in addition to paying MSU its actual earned Royalty for such Royalty Period, pay MSU the difference between the total earned Royalty for the year and the Guaranteed Minimum Royalty for such year.

(e) "Net Sales" shall mean LICENSEE's gross sales (the gross invoice amount billed customers) of Licensed Products, less discounts and allowances actually shown on the invoice (except cash discounts which are not deductible in the calculation of Royalty) and, further, less any bona fide returns (net of all returns actually made or allowed as supported by credit memoranda actually issued to the customers) up to the amount of the actual sales of the Licensed Products during the Royalty Period. No other costs incurred in the manufacturing, selling, advertising, and distribution of the Licensed Products shall be deducted nor shall any deduction be allowed for any uncollectible accounts or allowances.

(f) A Royalty obligation shall accrue upon the sale of the Licensed Products regardless of the time of collection by LICENSEE. A Licensed Product shall be considered "sold" when such Licensed Product is billed, invoiced, shipped, or paid for, whichever occurs first.

(g) If LICENSEE sells any Licensed Products to any affiliated or related party at a price less than the regular price charged to other parties, the Royalty shall be computed at the regular price.

(h) The receipt or acceptance by MSU of any royalty statement or payment shall not prevent MSU from subsequently challenging the validity or accuracy of such statement or payment.

(i) Upon expiration or termination of this Agreement, all Royalty obligations, including the Guaranteed Minimum Royalty, shall be accelerated and shall immediately become due and payable.

(j) LICENSEE's obligations for the payment of Royalties shall survive expiration or termination of this Agreement and will continue for so long as LICENSEE continues to sell the Licensed Products.

(k) All payments due MSU shall be made in United States currency by check drawn on a United States bank, unless otherwise specified by MSU.

(l) Late payments shall incur interest at the rate of ONE PERCENT (1%) per month from the date such payments were originally due.

4. RECORD INSPECTION AND AUDIT

(a) MSU shall have the right, upon reasonable notice, to inspect LICENSEE's books and records and all other documents and material in LICENSEE's possession or control with respect to the subject matter of this Agreement. MSU shall have free and full access thereto for such purposes and may make copies thereof.

(b) In the event that such inspection reveals an underpayment by LICENSEE of the actual Royalty owed MSU, LICENSEE shall pay the difference, plus interest calculated at the rate of ONE PERCENT (%) per month. If such underpayment be in excess of ONE THOUSAND UNITED STATES DOLLARS ($1,000.00) for any Royalty period, LICENSEE shall also reimburse MSU for the cost of such inspection.

(c) All books and records relative to LICENSEE's obligations hereunder shall be maintained and made accessible to MSU for inspection at a location in the United States for at least two (2) years after termination of this Agreement.

5. WARRANTIES & OBLIGATIONS

(a) MSU represents and warrants that it has the right and power to grant the licenses granted herein and that there are no other agreements with any other party in conflict with such grant.

(b) MSU makes no warranties or representations with respect to the validity of the intellectual property for the Licensed Properties.

(c) LICENSEE represents and warrants that it will use its best efforts to promote, market, advertise, sell, and distribute the Licensed Products in the Licensed Territory.

(d) LICENSEE shall be solely responsible for the manufacture, production, sale, and distribution of the Licensed Products and will bear all costs associated therewith.

(e) LICENSEE shall introduce the Licensed Products in all countries in the Licensed Territory before the Product Introduction Date recited in Schedule A and commence shipment of Licensed Products in all countries in the Licensed Territory before the Initial Shipment Date recited therein. This is a material provision of this Agreement.

(f) LICENSEE shall not be entitled to materially modify or change the Licensed Properties without the prior written consent of MSU. LICENSEE agrees that any additional artwork or properties which it may create or develop and use in conjunction with the Licensed Properties (the "Additional Works") shall be deemed to have been done on behalf of MSU as a "work made for hire" as that phrase is understood under the copyright laws and that all rights in such Additional Works shall be owned by MSU and may not be used by LICENSEE without the prior express written consent of MSU. In the event that it should be determined that such Additional Works do not constitute works made for hire, LICENSEE agrees to assign to MSU all of its rights in such Additional Works for no additional consideration. In no event may LICENSEE, either during the Term of this Agreement or thereafter, use such Additional Works without the prior express written consent of MSU.

6. NOTICES & SAMPLES

(a) LICENSEE shall fully comply with the marking provisions of the intellectual property laws of the applicable countries in the Licensed Territory.

(b) The Licensed Products and all promotional, packing, and advertising material shall include a notice designating such product as an official licensed product and all appropriate legal notices as required by MSU. LICENSEE agrees that, unless otherwise expressly approved in writing by MSU, each usage of the Licensed Properties shall be followed by either the TM or the R Trademark Notice symbol, as appropriate, and initially the following legend shall appear at least once on each Licensed Product and on each piece of promotional, packaging and advertising material:

Copyright or © MINNESOTA STATE UNIVERSITY 1993
TM and ® Designate Trademarks of MINNESOTA STATE
UNIVERSITY and are used under license by LICENSEE.

(c) The Licensed Products shall be of a high quality which are at least equal to comparable products manufactured and marketing by LICENSEE and in conformity with a standard sample approved by MSU.

(d) Upon completion of all artwork for use with the Licensed Products and any advertising or promotional copy, LICENSEE shall submit one (1) complete set of all such artwork and copy to MSU for approval. LICENSEE may not use any artwork or advertising or promotional copy without receiving approval from MSU.

(e) Prior to the commencement of manufacture and sale of the Licensed Products, LICENSEE shall submit to MSU, at no cost to MSU and for approval as to quality, six (6) sets of sample of all Licensed Products which LICENSEE intends to manufacture and/or sell, and one (1) complete set of all promotional and advertising material associated therewith. Such approval by MSU shall not be unreasonably withheld. Failure of MSU to approve such samples within ten (10) working days after receipt thereof shall be deemed disapproval. Once samples have been approved by MSU, LICENSEE shall not materially depart therefore without MSU's prior express written consent, which shall not be unreasonably withheld.

(f) At least once during each calendar year, LICENSEE shall submit to MSU an additional six (6) samples of the Licensed Products.

(g) If the quality of a class of the Licensed Products falls below such a production run quality, as previously approved by MSU, LICENSEE shall use its best efforts to restore such quality. In the event that LICENSEE has not taken reasonable steps to restore such quality within thirty (30) days after notification by MSU, MSU shall have the right to terminate this Agreement.

(h) LICENSEE agrees to permit MSU or its representatives to inspect the facilities where the Licensed Products are being manufactured and/or packaged.

7. NOTICES
Any notice required to be given pursuant to this Agreement shall be in writing and mailed by certified or registered mail, return receipt requested or delivered by a na-

tional overnight express service. Notices and payments to MSU shall be addressed to its authorized agent at the following address:

UNIVERSITY LICENSING AGENT, INC.
227 Park Avenue
New York, New York 10017

8. PATENTS, TRADEMARKS AND COPYRIGHTS

(a) MSU may seek, but is not obligated to seek, in its own name and at its own expense, appropriate trademark or copyright protection for the Licensed Properties. MSU makes no representation or warranty with respect to the validity of any trademark or copyright which may be granted with respect to the Licensed Properties.

(b) It is understood and agreed that MSU shall retain all right, title and interest in the original Licensed Properties and to any modifications or improvements made to the Licensed Properties by LICENSEE, including but not limited to the copyright rights relating to any Additional Works used in connection with the Licensed Properties.

(c) The parties agree to execute any documents reasonably requested by the other party to effect any of the above provisions.

(d) LICENSEE acknowledges that all legal rights and goodwill associated with the Licensed Properties are owned by MSU and that the Licensed Properties are unique and original to MSU. LICENSEE further agrees that any goodwill generated as a result of its use of the Licensed Properties on the Licensed Products shall inure to the benefit of MSU. Unless otherwise permitted by law, LICENSEE shall not, at any time during or after the effective Term of the Agreement, make any claim to the Licensed Properties nor shall LICENSEE dispute or contest, directly or indirectly, MSU's exclusive right and title to the Licensed Properties or the validity thereof.

9. TERMINATION

The following termination rights are in addition to the termination rights which may be provided elsewhere in the Agreement:

(a) *Immediate Right of Termination.* MSU shall have the right to immediately terminate this Agreement by giving written notice to LICENSEE in the event that LICENSEE does any of the following:

(1) if LICENSEE fails to obtain or maintain product liability insurance in the amount and of the type provided for herein; or

(2) if LICENSEE fails to meet the Product Introduction Date or the Initial Shipment Date recited in Schedule A; or

(3) if any Licensed Products are subject to a recall by the Consumer Product Safety Commission or any other governmental agency; or

(4) if LICENSEE discontinues or dissolves its business.

(b) *Right to Terminate on Notice.* Either party may terminate this Agreement on thirty (30) days written notice to the other party in the event of a breach of any provision of this Agreement by the other party, provided that, during the thirty (30) days period, the breaching party fails to cure such breach.

(c) *No Fault Right to Terminate.* Either party shall have the right to terminate this Agreement at any time on six (6) months written notice to the other party, such termination to become effective at the conclusion of such six (6) month period.

10. POST TERMINATION RIGHTS

(a) Not less than thirty (30) days prior to the expiration of this Agreement or immediately upon termination thereof, LICENSEE shall provide MSU with a complete schedule of all inventory of Licensed Products then on-hand (the "Inventory");

(b) Upon expiration or termination of this Agreement, except for reason of a breach of LICENSEE's duty to comply with the quality control or legal notice marking requirements, LICENSEE shall be entitled, for three (3) months (the "Sell-off Period") and on a non-exclusive basis, to continue to sell such Inventory. Such sales shall be made subject to all the provisions of this Agreement including the payment of a Royalty which shall be due within thirty (30) days after the close of the Sell-Off period. At the conclusion of the Sell-Off Period, MSU may require that the LICENSEE either destroy any product still on hand or, alternatively, purchase it from LICENSEE at a price equal to 50% of LICENSEE's Net Selling Price.

(c) Upon the expiration or termination of this Agreement, all rights granted to LICENSEE under this Agreement shall forthwith terminate and immediately revert to MSU and LICENSEE shall discontinue all use of the Licensed Properties and the like.

(d) Upon expiration or termination of this Agreement, MSU may require that the LICENSEE transmit to MSU, at no cost, all material relating to the Licensed Properties including all artwork, screens, color separations, prototypes and the like with respect to the Licensed Properties.

(e) In the event of termination or expiration of this Agreement for any reason, all monies paid to MSU shall be deemed non-refundable and LICENSEE's obligation to pay the Guaranteed Minimum Royalty for the year in which such termination becomes effective shall be accelerated and shall immediately become due and payable on a pro rata basis depending upon the effective date of such termination or expiration.

11. INFRINGEMENTS

(a) LICENSEE agrees to promptly notify MSU of any known use of the Licensed Properties by others not duly authorized by MSU. MSU shall have the right, in its sole discretion, to prosecute lawsuits against third persons for infringement of MSU's rights in the Licensed Properties.

(b) Any lawsuit shall be prosecuted solely at the expense of MSU and all sums recovered shall be retained by MSU.

(c) The parties agree to fully cooperate with the other party in the prosecution of any such suit.

12. INDEMNITY

LICENSEE agrees to defend, indemnify and hold MSU, its officers, directors, agents and employees, harmless against all costs, expenses and losses (including reasonable attorney's fees and costs) incurred through claims of third parties against MSU based on the manufacture or sale of the Licensed Products including, but not limited to, actions founded on product liability.

13. INSURANCE

LICENSEE shall, throughout the Term of the Agreement, obtain and maintain at its own cost and expense from a qualified insurance company licensed to do business in New York, standard Product Liability Insurance naming MSU, its officers, directors, employees, agents, and shareholders as an additional insured. Such policy shall provide protection against all claims, demands and causes of action arising out of any defects or failure to perform, alleged or otherwise, of the Licensed Products or any material used in connection therewith or any use thereof. The amount of coverage shall be as specified in Schedule A attached hereto. The policy shall provide for ten (10) days notice MSU from the insurer by Registered or Certified Mail, return receipt requested, in the event of any modification, cancellation or termination thereof. LICENSEE agrees to furnish MSU a certificate or insurance evidencing same within thirty (30) days after execution of this Agreement and, in no event, shall LICENSEE manufacture, distribute or sell the Licensed Products prior to receipt by MSU of such evidence of insurance.

14. JURISDICTION & DISPUTES

This Agreement shall be governed by the laws of Minnesota and all disputes hereunder shall be resolved in the applicable state or federal courts of Minnesota. The parties consent to the jurisdiction of such courts, agree to accept service of process by mail, and waive any jurisdictional or venue defenses otherwise available.

15. AGREEMENT BINDING ON SUCCESSORS

This Agreement shall be binding upon and shall inure to the benefit of the parties hereto, their heirs, administrators, successors and assigns.

16. ASSIGNABILITY

The license granted hereunder is personal to LICENSEE and may not be assigned by any act of LICENSEE or by operation of law without the prior express written consent of MSU.

17. WAIVER

No waiver by either party of any default shall be deemed as a waiver of any prior or subsequent default of the same or other provisions of this Agreement.

18. SEVERABILITY

If any provision hereof is held invalid or unenforceable by a court of competent jurisdiction, such invalidity shall not affect the validity or operation of any other provision and such invalid provision shall be deemed to be severed from the Agreement.

19. INTEGRATION

This Agreement constitutes the entire understanding of the parties, and revokes and supersedes all prior agreements between the parties and is intended as a final expression of their Agreement. It shall not be modified or amended except in writing signed by the parties hereto and specifically referring to this Agreement. This Agreement shall take precedence over any other documents which may be in conflict therewith.

IN WITNESS THEREOF, the parties hereto, intending to be legally bound hereby, have each caused to be affixed hereto its or his/her hand and seal the day indicated.

MINNESOTA STATE UNIVERSITY   COLLEGE PRODUCTS, LTD.
  by its authorized agent
University Licensing Agent, Inc.

By: By:
Title: Title:
Date: Date:

_____   _____

SCHEDULE A

Licensee: COLLEGE PRODUCTS, LTD.
Licensee Address: 123 Smith Drive
                             Los Angeles, CA 99999
Licensee Contact: John Jones
Licensee Telephone: 213-555-1234
Licensee Telefax No.:   213-555-1235

1. Licensed Properties
The Licensed Properties are defined as follows:

Trademarks: **MINNESOTA STATE UNIVERSITY**
            MSU LOGO
            SCREAMING EAGLES

Copyrights: VA12345 for Screaming Eagle
             artwork

2. Licensed Products
The Licensed Products are as follows:
        Men's, Women's and Children's T-shirts and Sweatshirts

3. Licensed Territory
The following countries shall constitute the Licensed Territory:
United States of America and Mexico

4. TERM
This Agreement shall commence on the date executed by both parties and shall extend for an initial Term of One (1) Year.

5. Licensee Fee and Royalty Rate
The License Fee shall be $500 due upon execution of this Agreement and $1,000 due upon the commencement of any Renewal Term(s) thereof.
The Royalty Rate is as follows: TEN PERCENT (10%)

6. Advance
The following Advance shall be paid upon execution of this Agreement: One Thousand Dollars ($1,000.00).

7. Guaranteed Minimum Royalty
During each year during the Term of this Agreement, LICENSEE hereby guarantees that MSU shall receive a minimum royalty of Five Thousand dollars ($5,000).

8. Product Liability Insurance

One Million Dollars ($1,000,000) combined single limit, with a deductible amount not to exceed Twenty Five Thousand Dollars ($25,000), for each single occurrence for bodily injury and/or for property damage.

9. Product Introduction/Initial Shipment

The Product Introduction Date for all Licensed Products in the United States shall be Super Show, 1995.

The Initial Shipment Date for all Licensed Products in the United States shall be March 15, 1995.

SALE OF FOODSERVICE
AND
SOUVENIR CONCESSIONS

Learning Objectives

After completing this chapter, the reader should be able to:

1. discuss the historical development, current state and economic importance of concession operations in sport settings.
2. understand the revenue and cost structure of concession operations.
3. explain the respective advantages and disadvantages of contracting out concession services versus self-operation.
4. understand the key elements that should be included in a concession service contract.

SALE OF FOODSERVICE
AND
SOUVENIR CONCESSIONS

Chris Bigelow, Principal
The Bigelow Companies

INTRODUCTION

Although the concession industry has long played an integral role in sport operations, it has historically been relegated to back-room, behind-the-scenes dealings that the public rarely saw or heard about. Team owners offered their concessionaires long-term low-commission contracts in return for large cash grants, loans and advances. As one team executive stated, "Without the concessionaires' loans, major league baseball may have never survived the thirties, forties, or fifties!"

Today that financing source is still available, but there are few secret deals or one-sided contracts. Sports owners now have teams of accountants and lawyers and comply with detailed banking and Securities Exchange Commission rules covering the financing of partnerships and corporations. The competitive nature of the concession industry has all but eliminated those back-room deals.

Perhaps the most dramatic change for the concession industry came, however, in 1987, when Joe Robbie Stadium opened. Privately financed through the preopening sale of luxury suites and previously-unheard-of club seats, Joe Robbie Stadium offered its customers a new level of service never before available in a sports facility: waiter and waitress service at their seats, and a fully air-conditioned and carpeted private concourse featuring complete buffets from gourmet sandwiches to homemade pasta and freshly carved prime rib. Team owners now spoke in terms of a fan's entertainment experience, not just their team's win and loss record. A new level of culinary expertise would now be required of the concessionaire, and the concessionaire's skill would be instrumental in the success of the customers' total entertainment experience at the sports venue.

Chris Bigelow is a principal of the Bigelow Companies, Independence, Missouri, and foodservice and merchandise consultant offering management, advisory and design services to stadiums, arenas, and convention centers. Phone 816-795-7157; Fax 816-795-1739.

Concessions had now entered a new era. Before we discuss in detail this new role of the concessionaire, let us briefly examine the industry in general.

Historical Perspective

The concession industry is a U.S. phenomenon. Even today in Europe and Asia, foodservice and merchandise sales play a minor role in sports. International sports like football (U.S. soccer) are a concessionaire's nightmare--no time-outs.

In 1887, a young man decided to print a program for a baseball game in Columbus, Ohio — because "you can't tell the players without a scorecard." From that venture young Harry M. Stevens expanded to other venues, hawking soft drinks and sausages to the enthusiastic crowd. A local New York cartoonist observing Stevens selling red hots in a bun at New York's Polo Grounds soon drew a cartoon showing the sausages styled with faces and legs and Stevens barking the sales. The cartoonist coined the phrase "Hot Dog." Those events ushered in the beginning of the concession industry and the start of the H.M. Stevens Concession Company.

Around the same time, three brothers named Jacobs began popping popcorn during intermissions at a theater in upstate New York. They began serving more theaters and soon thereafter a minor league baseball park. That marked the beginning of the Sportservice Company. Other local and regional companies entered the field, but few survived. It was not until the early 1960s that most of today's major competitors of H.M. Stevens and Sportservice entered the marketplace.

Industry Profile

It is difficult to quantify the concessions industry because there are so many components. Souvenirs and foodservice, licensed merchandise and nonlicensed merchandise, professional sports facilities, community civic centers, arenas, college, university and other amateur sports venues, even amusement parks and convention centers are all a part of the so-called concession industry. Although merchandise often is sold by a separate party in concert venues, in the professional sports venue the foodservice concessionaire is typically the merchandise concessionaire as well.

In 1992, *Restaurants and Institutions Magazine* estimated that the recreation foodservice industry serves over 31,000 locations, and generates $4.4 billion. Seven companies dominate the field in North America, controlling approximately $1.1 billion of those sales dollars. The remainder of the sales would be divided between smaller regional or local companies and facilities that operate their own concessions. The seven major concessionaires are:

- ARA Services, Inc., Philadelphia, PA, based, Versa Services, Ltd., in Canada. Major accounts: The Spectrum, Oriole Park at Camden Yards, Soldier Field.
- Fine Host Corporation, Greenwich, CT, based. Major accounts: Joe Robbie Stadium, Portland Memorial Coliseum, Great Woods Amphitheatre.

- Ogden Entertainment Services, New York City based. Major accounts: The Great Western Forum, Philadelphia Veterans Stadium, The Kingdome.
- Service America, Stamford, CT, based, Servomation in Canada. Major accounts: Jack Murphy Stadium, BC Place Stadium, Cleveland Municipal Stadium.
- Sportservice Corporation, Buffalo, NY, based. Major accounts: Boston Garden, Comisky Park, Busch Stadium.
- H.M. Stevens, New York City based. Major accounts: The Meadowlands, Fenway Park, The Astrodome.
- Volume Services, Spartanburg, SC, based. Major accounts: LA Coliseum, Yankee Stadium, Truman Sports Complex (Kansas City).

Sportservice probably has the longest relationship of any concessionaire with a single client. It began providing concessions for the Detroit Tigers in the 1920s and still serves Tiger fans to this day.

Ogden Entertainment Services was formed from the acquisition of several old-line concessionaires: Berlo Vending, ABC, and Cabinet Confectionery Company. As mentioned, other than Stevens, Sportservice, and Ogden, the remaining concessionaires did not enter the field until the 1960s and 1970s, corresponding with the boom in sports facility construction. Most of these concessionaires represent the recreation divisions of larger contract foodservice companies.

To further quantify the industry, *Amusement Business* in 1993 polled 200 arenas, stadiums, amphitheaters, convention centers, fairs. and amusement parks with the following results.

1. Food and Beverage Sales as a percentage of your facility's total revenue: 28%

2.

Food & Beverage Operator	Total Industry	Stadiums, Arenas, Convention Centers	Fairs	Parks
In-house	38%	32%	19%	82%
Contracted	46%	68%	47%	17%
Combination	15%	0%	34%	0%

3.

Food and Beverage Per Capita Sales	$3.64	$3.70	$4.00	$3.27

Economic Impact

As the above data indicate, concessions sales account for 28% of a facility's total revenue. However, concessions revenues play a larger role in some facilities than others. For an NFL team that receives millions of dollars from network television or a convention center that receives revenues from a large hotel bed tax, concession revenues may represent only 10% of total receipts. However, for many sports franchises, stadiums, and arenas, concessions income is one of the top three sources of revenue along with ticket sales and advertising income.

In minor league sports such as minor league baseball, in which the major league team pays the players' salaries and ticket prices are relatively low, concessions profits are often the difference between a profitable and an unprofitable team. For years the theater industry has publicized that it breaks even on film costs through ticket sales, but makes its profits from the concession stands. Those same economics are in place at many sports venues and hundreds of stock-car tracks throughout the United States, where the owners break even on ticket sales and advertising, requiring foodservice and souvenirs to produce the profits.

Creative facility managers at all types of venues now review all of their revenue sources, including concessions and parking, before negotiating leases or facility rental agreements with a sports team or promoter. By knowing their potential profits from concessions as well as their operating costs for such items as security, ushers, ticket takers, parking lot attendants, and clean-up crew, they can establish an equitable rental structure for the building.

Just like the movie theater owner, a facility manager today may offer the stadium or arena at a reduced rental fee in order to book an event and profit only from the additional concession sales. Municipal facilities with a structured rent schedule may lose events or even sports franchises or have to persuade their politicians to step into the negotiations to save a potential sporting event because they are not allowed to offset one revenue stream (rentals) with another (concessions).

One of the best illustrations of the value of the concession operation to a facility is the Charlotte Coliseum's original lease with the NBA Hornets. The Hornets leased the facility for one dollar per year and retained all revenue sources, *except concessions*, which the facility retained. Although that appeared to be a favorable deal for the team, within a year the team was also asking for a piece of the concessions to remain profitable.

Many teams have formed their own concession companies to maximize their revenues as well as control the level of services. The Wirtz family, owners of the Chicago Blackhawks and The Chicago Stadium, and co-owners of the new United Center, own Bismarck Foods, a Chicago concessionaire. Michael Ilitch, owner of the Detroit Tigers, Detroit Red Wings and Little Caesar's Pizza, formed a concessions division to operate the foodservice in the arenas in which his teams play. The Portland Trailblazers and St. Louis Blues will manage their own concessions while contracting their upscale restaurant and club foodservice, and the Atlanta Hawks continue to manage their own foodservice at the Omni. Table 8-1 provides perspective on the extent to which the four primary professional sports leagues and major college athletic programs either utilize an outside contractor or manage their own concessions.

In amateur sports, foodservice plays a smaller financial role than it does in professional sports for two primary reasons: the disposable income of the fan and the lack of beer sales. Beer sales often account for 35 to 55% of a concessionaire's sales, depending on the event. Because most colleges do not allow beer sales at their facilities, and no high schools allow alcoholic beverage sales, concession volumes are at a minimum 35% less than at professional sports.

It is a misconception that alcoholic beverages are banned by the NCAA. The NCAA has no authority over sales during regular season play, only in postseason/

Table 8-1 Contracted Versus Self-Operated Services		
Sport	**Contracted**	**Self-Operated**
Major League Baseball	100%	0%
National Football League	89%	11%
National Basketball League	77%	23%
National Hockey League	55%	44%
Major Universities (estimated)	75%	25%

Note: data compiled by The Bigelow Companies, Independence, MO

postconference play. The individual schools and sometimes the conference dictates alcoholic beverage sales policies during regular season events. Many colleges that do not allow beer to be sold to the general public do have private clubs, alumni rooms, and athletic booster rooms where beer and liquor are readily available.

Schools that play their games in off-campus facilities often find that the sale of beer can affect their rental costs of that facility. Obviously if the facility cannot generate any income from beer, it must charge the university a greater rental for the use of the stadium or arena.

The value of beer sales to a concessionaire was best illustrated when one concessionaire even established a scholarship fund in exchange for allowing beer sales at a conference postseason tournament. The colleges that are most willing to allow beer sales are usually ones that attract a large alumni following from a metropolitan area. The alumni are both of age and used to a higher level of service at other professional sporting events. Also, universities that are business oriented and interested in maximizing their revenues will often allow sales of alcoholic beverages.

The other reason mentioned for lower concession sales at collegiate sports events is that generally they attract a larger number of younger individuals with less disposable income than that of professional-sports spectators. Concessions are an impulse buy and perceived as high priced, not necessarily high value. Therefore, as will be seen in the next section, consumers at college and amateur events spend less than do consumers at professional events.

CONCESSION INDUSTRY STANDARDS

Per-capita sales are the primary standard that a concessionaire uses to analyze an event. Per-capita sales, or the "per cap," are determined by dividing the actual turnstile attendance into the gross (total receipts less sales tax) concession sales. This number indicates the average expenditure per customer.

It is important to know the actual turnstile attendance for an accurate per cap rather than use the announced attendance, estimated attendance, or even the number of tickets sold. Many minor league sports will publicize an announced attendance that they use for public relations purposes. In baseball the American League announces paid ticket sales whereas the National League announces turnstile attendance. Paid ticket sales do not reflect "no shows" (ticket purchasers who failed to attend) or "freebies" (individuals using free tickets from a charity, sponsor or promotional plan).

All facility managers should have a turnstile attendance; otherwise, they will be unable to verify their ticket takers' accuracy at not allowing anyone in the event without a ticket. This confidential information is used by concessionaires to measure their ability to serve the customer and would never be published or used to discredit a fledgling franchise or athletic program. The per cap allows a facility manager and a concessionaire to measure the concessionaire's performance against industry standards and against its own past performances.

It would not be logical to compare the gross concessions sales of a baseball game with a sellout crowd on a hot summer evening to those of an early spring game with just a small crowd. Likewise, each sport has peculiar eating habits, such as the number and length of intermissions, the weather, and whether or not it is played indoors or out. Domed stadiums traditionally have lower per capita sales than do outdoor stadiums in the summer, but the reverse is true in the winter in bad weather.

The following table (8-2) offers a range of per caps that can be considered industry standards. The range is necessary because of the many differences indicated above, as well as items such as the number of concession service lines at a venue, menu pricing,

Table 8-2
Foodservice Per-Capita Spending- Industry Standards

Event	Low	High
High School Basketball & Football (without Beer)	$ .25	$ 2.00
College Basketball (without Beer)	.60	1.50
College Football (without Beer)	1.25	2.50
Minor League Baseball	2.75	6.00
NBA Basketball	3.75	6.75
NHL Hockey	4.00	7.50
MLB Baseball	4.50	8.50
NFL Football	4.50	9.50
Championships/Super Bowls	10.00	25.00

Note: data compiled by The Bigelow Companies, Independence, MO

portions, and geographic spending habits. These per caps should increase as pricing increases and as the concessionaire serves the customer more efficiently.

Many concessionaires will break down their sales even further with a beer per cap and a per cap by seating level. In the premium seating section offering wait-staff service and more upscale concessions, such as the club level concepts, per-capita spending is often 50-100% greater than the traditional concession levels. In stadium/ arena club restaurants and luxury suites, food and beverage per caps can range from $20 to $35.

Concessionaires will monitor the spending for merchandise and programs as well. The following table (8-3) indicates the ranges that are more affected by the win/loss record of the team and the popularity of the team colors, designs and fashions than anything else.

Operating Costs

To anticipate what a team owner or facility manager can expect financially from a concessionaire, it is important to understand the concessionaire's operations in terms of both sales and expenses. A popular misconception, even by experienced facility directors, is that concessionaires earn huge profits from their operations. This belief stems from the appearance of product mark-ups that are much greater than those of traditional retailers, stories of historic profit levels of concessionaires in the 1950s, 1960s and early 1970s, and from the concessionaires' ability to pay large commissions. However, it is due to those mark-ups and their operating efficiencies that the

Table 8-3
Merchandise Per Capita Spending- Industry Standards

Event	Low	High
High School Basketball and Football	N/A	N/A
College Basketball	.25	.50
College Football	.25	.75
Minor League Baseball	.25	1.00
NBA Basketball	.50	1.75
NHL Hockey	.50	1.25
MLB Baseball	.50	2.00
NFL Football	1.00	3.00
Championships/Super Bowls, etc.	5.00	20.00

Note: data compiled by The Bigelow Companies, Independence, MO concessionaires can pay their clients those large commissions. Due to those large commissions, made available by the competitive nature of public bids and proposals, the concessionaires are operating on razor-thin margins.

There are two major controllable costs in a concession operation: product cost and payroll. The other expenses, such as repairs, maintenance, office supplies, licenses, telephone, and marketing, while partially variable and partially fixed, rarely exceed 10% of gross sales. Likewise, depreciation and commissions, which will be discussed later in the chapter, are fixed by contract. Therefore, a successful concessions manager must concentrate on maximizing sales while properly managing the two controllable costs, product and payroll.

Product cost is the total cost of the item sold. That would include the souvenir or food item (e.g., hot dogs, buns), condiments, wrappers, napkins, serving implements, and containers. A concessionaire can control the product cost first by purchasing the proper quality product at the best available price. Next, a weighted product cost must be established, projecting unit sales and individual product cost. Selling prices are then set to provide an overall or weighted product cost based on the concessionaire's budget.

Typical concession food costs range from 15% to 25%, or in other words, menu items are marked up 4 to 7 times above the product cost. Typical catered food costs range from 28% to 38%.

Sports novelty costs range from 25% to 40% for traditional souvenirs; however, the increasingly popular high-ticket items, such as jewelry or leather jackets, may have as high as a 50% to 70% product cost.

Payroll costs are divided into two categories: salaried and hourly. Salaries are fixed costs that the concessionaire can only change by permanently hiring or firing employees. The hourly wages, however, can and should be managed for each event.

The concessionaire projects each event's potential per capita sales, multiplied by the box office's estimated attendance, to determine the projected concession sales. Multiplying that number times the budgeted payroll percentage gives the amount of payroll dollars that the concessionaire should spend for that event. Divide the payroll dollars by the average shift pay, and the concessionaire has the number of employees he or she can afford to schedule for that event.

Typical Payroll Costs

Concession Stand Workers...... 8-12% of concession sales
Food and Beverage Vendors.....15-20% of vending sales
Catering/Restaurant Workers....18-30% of catering/restaurant sales
Sports Souvenir Vendors...........12-17% of sports souvenir sales

A conflict often arises when a facility manager wants a higher level of customer service than the concessionaire's budget allows. This is often the case when concessionaires are paying extremely high commissions and need to minimize all of their operating expenses to produce a profit. The result can be too few concession stands open, slow customer service, long lines, and potentially lost sales. That is why it is important that the concessionaire and the facility manager meet regularly to discuss reasonable payroll costs and staffing levels. This information should also be shared between facility management and the concessionaire prior to contracting with any foodservice concessionaire.

Concession Revenues

The concessions department in any facility exists equally as a customer service function and as a major revenue center for the facility. The most successful venues find the proper balance between those two functions. The recommended strength of each function is most dependent on the type of facility and the types of events that the facility hosts.

The majority of sports venues do view the revenue production of their concessions department as the most critical issue. Facility managers seek to determine the best financial deal for their facility. In order to determine that, they need to examine their operation the way a prospective concessionaire would examine it. A concessionaire will prepare an operating pro forma analyzing the potential sales and expenses that a facility can generate. The level of revenues (commissions) that concessions generate for a facility are dependent on:

1. Attendance at each event.
2. Event types and degree of riskiness of sports franchises.
3. Investment made by the concessions department.
4. Contract term (if services are contracted).
5. The initial capital costs (the greater these costs, the smaller the commissions).

If the concessions are operated in-house, there is no minimum acceptable profit level. However, for contracted accounts, concessionaires rarely will operate an account unless it can generate a minimum of $75,000 profit after all of their on-site expenses, including commissions. That number can be reduced if the concessionaire has a large base of operations already existing in the market area. If one assumes that at the $75,000 profit level the concessionaire is earning 10% of gross sales, it would follow that a major concessionaire would not be interested in serving an account grossing less than $750,000 annually. Smaller accounts should consider either self-operation or contracts with a local or smaller regional firm.

Typical Facility Commissions Range

Sales Category	Commissions Range
Concession Sales	35% to 55%
Catering/Suite Sales	15% to 35%
Restaurant Sales	0% to 15%
Sports/Souvenir Sales	30% to 45%

CONCESSIONS AS A FINANCING TOOL

As discussed earlier, the concessionaire was often a silent partner in the financing of a sports franchise in the first half of the century. In the 1960s and 1970s there was a tremendous growth in facilities. Most of these sports facilities were built by governmental agencies, and concession contracts were awarded by public bids. By the late 1980s and early 1990s, taxpayers were deciding that financing stadiums was not an appropriate use of their money and they began rejecting governmental proposals to construct such facilities. Team owners who had been assuming more control of operating these sports venues realized that in order to maximize their revenues, they had to have state-of-the-art facilities with luxury suites, private club seats, private restaurants, and adequate points of service for concessions. The owners also realized they would have to develop these buildings with private funds because cities, counties and states no longer had the revenues. Once again owners looked to their suppliers, such as the concessionaire, to assist them with financing. Owners solicited proposals from concessionaires for both their services and financial input into the project.

The income from concessions or from a concessionaire may appear in several forms. A signing bonus or grant can be provided by the concessionaire for the privilege of contracting with the team for the concession rights. This bonus may range from one to millions of dollars and is viewed and depreciated by concessionaires just like any other investment they may make into equipment, smallwares (i.e., pots, pans, utensils) or leasehold improvements.

A team owner may also pledge the projected revenue stream of concessions commissions to the team's loans in order to satisfy bankers and investors in the project. The loan or bond repayment can be even more secure if the concessionaire offers an annual minimum guarantee of commissions regardless of sales volume.

The concessionaire may be asked just to equip the foodservice and souvenir sales areas, which are constructed by the facility owner. This is a typical requirement in a concessions contract. The concessionaire may construct and equip the sales areas or even construct and equip both the foodservice and souvenir sales areas and other non-concession-related areas as well. This investment reduces the total capital commitment required of the facility owner. However as stated earlier, the larger the capital commitment by concessionaires, the less they are willing to pay in commissions to the facility.

A very important financing tool of the facility ownership is advertising rights. Signage, scoreboards, scoreboard spot ads, program ads, exterior message boards, and naming rights of the facility can all provide both up-front signing bonus capital and annual rental revenue. A key link to many of those deals is that a potential facility sponsor wants its product to have exclusivity and be offered for sale at the venue as the soft drink, dairy product, or beer. In order to do that, the facility owner must have the contractual rights to direct the concessionaire to use those sponsored products.

Sponsorship is one of the reasons that branded foods, such as Pizza Hut, TCBY Yogurt and Subway, have become so prevalent in sports facilities. Due to federal and state laws in the United States, there can be no tie between advertising and the exclusive sale of alcoholic beverages. This is not the case in Canada or other countries. These "brand name" restauranteurs are interested in expanding into sports venues for several reasons: their traditional growth areas are now saturated, and the demographics of a particular sport are also their ideal demographics. For those reasons, these traditional advertisers are willing to advertise in the stadium and arena, offer customers the products that they enjoy, and potentially increase per-capita spending. The facility, the customer, and the concessionaire can all win in these negotiations.

Concession agreements are becoming more sophisticated to allow the facility and concessionaire to develop more of a partnership approach to managing the concessions. This improved working relationship can allow the facility to earn more commissions as more events are developed and to lessen the concessionaire's commissions or operating costs if attendance or the number of events is below projections.

All of these financing tools can affect the concessionaire's commission structure. When a facility or team uses a concessionaire as a source of capital, they do have to pay that money back in contract terms, commissions, or actual loan repayments. Concessionaires must earn a return on their investment, and as a rule that return is 10-25% of the investment. That return may be greater than a traditional banker would realize, but often concessionaires are the only parties willing to invest in a new sports project or provide an investment above what the traditional investment sources would provide.

Facilities financed with tax-exempt bonds may find that the Internal Revenue Service codes do not allow them to enter into a traditional contract with a concessionaire. That is because the IRS does not allow a private firm to share the profits or loss of a facility developed with these bonds. The firm may earn only a flat management fee. That eliminates all of the incentive for the concessionaire to operate efficiently, and it also means the facility owner must assume all of the risk to make a profit even though the owner has contracted with a concessionaire. Incentives on sales development by the concessionaire are allowed with tax-exempt funding although the incentive cannot exceed the annual flat fee.

One final form of investment made by concessionaires is a loan repaid over the life of the contract with set interest terms, a floating rate above or below prime, or even a repayment triggered by sales volume. These loans are often a separate agreement from the concessions agreement. This type of agreement usually occurs in private facilities where the terms of the agreement are not made public. It frequently provides a team or facility owner with a ready line of credit and ensures the concessionaire a contract equal to the repayment terms of the loan.

Obviously utilizing the concessionaire's capital provides a selling point for working with a concessionaire. However, as we will discuss later, many owners have felt that they can maximize their revenues in the long run by not using the concessionaire's capital. This is possible when the owner has access to other less expensive forms of capital.

DESIGN PROGRAMMING

In order to ensure that a facility has the potential to maximize both services and revenues, a foodservice and merchandise specialist should work with the architect or as part of the architect's team from the time when space is being allocated and the operational program is being developed.

Several facilities have set the blueprint for what a state-of-the-art sports complex must have. The simple and efficient twin design of the sports complex in Kansas City of Arrowhead Stadium for football and Kauffman Stadium for baseball is still the basic infrastructure used for most modern stadiums. Joe Robbie Stadium and the SkyDome illustrate the importance of luxury services, such as club seats, destination restaurants (e.g., Hard Rock Cafe), and multi-event capabilities. The Palace at Auburn Hills and the American West Arena in Phoenix clearly show the capacity of luxury suites and concessions in an indoor arena. Finally, Oriole Park at Camden Yards in Baltimore illustrates the success a new facility can enjoy when all of the functional elements of high levels of customer services are combined and surrounded by a unique building facade that creates a nostalgic baseball feeling and adds to the customer's overall entertainment experience.

The common theme of all of these facilities is the high level of customer services. These services allow the concessions department and the team to maximize revenues. In order to achieve these levels of customer service, the facility must be designed to operate efficiently. Conveniences, such as restrooms, information booths, and security, must fit the typical patron's needs. More importantly, the revenue producers, such as concessions, vending rooms, suites, retail souvenir stores, portable stands, club wait-staff kitchens, dining rooms, parking, and ticket offices, must be placed in the proper quantity and location to maximize potential operating revenues.

The following guidelines are used by foodservice consultants and architects in today's newest stadiums and arenas.

Design and Program Criteria

Concession Stands with Beer in Stadium	1 point of service per 200 seats Locate by seating patterns.
Concession Stands without Beer in Stadium	1 point of service per 250 seats
Vending Rooms	2 food and soft drink vendors per 1,000 seats 3 beer vendors per 1,000 seats 1 vending room per 8,000 seats
Portable Concession Stands	• Place as needed throughout concourse. Varies by event.
Club Seats	1 server or combination of server and runner per 40 seats 1 service kitchen/bar per 2,000 seats 1 concession point of service per 150-175 seats

Suites	1 service steward/captain per 5-8 suites
	1 service pantry per 25 suites
Restaurant/Lounge	• Requirements vary by facility.
	• Restaurant should not be less than 150 seats, nor more than 600 seats, depending on facility size. Lounge not less than 25 seats, no maximum size. Banquet facilities are advisable.
Picnic/Group Sales Area	• Multipurpose rooms or tents capable of serving banquets from a remote kitchen or picnic areas with commercial grills and preparation equipment are essential for expanding group sales business.
Press/Employee/Backstage Dining	• Varies by team requirements
Souvenir Stands	• Portable or permanent one point of service per 1,000 to 1,500 seats for professional sports, one point of service per 1,500 to 5,000 for amateur and minor league sports. Locate by exits and entrances.
Souvenir Retail Stores	• Number and size vary by team's popularity. Locate centrally and adjacent to advance ticket window if planning to be open on both event and nonevent days. In larger outdoor stadiums, locate one per level or multiple smaller sized stores.

CONTRACTING VERSUS SELF-OPERATION

Most of this chapter has made reference to a concessionaire, as the majority of larger professional sports venues do contract their services. However, the majority of smaller professional and collegiate venues either operate the concessions in-house or use a local concessionaire. There is also a trend developing in which several team owners are considering or have developed their own concessions division. Several of the reasons for using a concessionaire have already been discussed, but what are the advantages of self-operation?

For most facility directors who operate their own concessions, the reason is control. They want to decide if prices are too low or too high or if a concession stand should be open for an event even though ticket sales are light, and they want to be able to determine the quality of products purchased without having every decision become a negotiating session with the concessionaire.

Self-operators also feel they are maximizing their revenues by cutting out the middle man, the concessionaire. They will admit that the decision to self-operate does mean a time commitment on their part of up to 40% of the day devoted to foodservice issues, but they feel the extra 3% to 6% profit is worth it.

The contracting proponents point out that they use a concessionaire because they do not want the headaches and hassles that a foodservice operation brings. Scheduling of hourly part-time employees, purchasing perishable foodstuffs or imported souvenirs, determining what stands are open, whether or not the sanitation policies are enforced, and who might be stealing cash are all items that these managers do not want to oversee, even with a qualified concessions manager on staff. In addition, many of these facility managers do not have the necessary resources (e.g., budget, personnel) to run a concessions department effectively and do not have the freedom to establish autonomous purchasing and personnel offices.

Of course both types of managers are absolutely correct. There are advantages and disadvantages to both systems. A good concessionaire working with a fair contract should act as though it were a department within the facility manager's organization. At the same time, a well-qualified in-house concessions manager can operate just as efficiently as a large corporation and many times be much more flexible when local events require it.

Concessionaires do provide proven systems of operations and a network of facilities that help each other out with new menu ideas, management trends, and training techniques. As mentioned earlier, a concessionaire can provide its own capital, thereby freeing the facility's money for other projects.

The financial issues are also correct on both sides. A large in-house operation can certainly operate as efficiently as a national concessionaire, thereby saving the management fees. Locally bid products, such as soft drinks, meat, and bread, can often be obtained at or below a concessionaire's national price in a large venue, and beer — the single largest product purchased — is typically priced by state law; consequently, everyone buys at the same price. Although concessionaires do have national purchasing contracts for equipment, which helps when replacing a single item, their price will not be significantly different from that of an in-house operator who develops a public bid for any major purchases such as new construction or major remodeling.

The real key to the successful concession operation, whether contracted or self-operated, is the on-site concessions manager. The concessionaire can offer that manager a career path of being promoted to larger and larger facilities, whereas the in-house operator must find other duties for the manager or risk stagnation if he or she stays in the job too long. Likewise, a concessionaire has other trained managers with new ideas to replace the current manager when he or she is ready for a promotion, whereas an in-house operator will have to recruit outside the facility or promote an assistant when replacing the manager. However, even the best concessionaire can assign a bad manager or one who does not fit into a facility's culture. A bad manager will negate any benefits of either system and needs to be replaced immediately.

The decision to contract or self-operate needs to be evaluated both quantitatively and qualitatively. The answer will be dependent on the facility's unique requirement and on the management staff's capabilities and desires.

Contract Negotiations

One reason many facility directors self-operate today is that they had a bad experience with a concessionaire in the past. "They were uncooperative," "they were penny-pinchers," "they were too interested in their own bottom line and not the good of the facility" are often-quoted phrases heard in the sports facility industry. When investigating the problem, normally it is discovered that the concessionaire was as unhappy as the facility director, and the reason was a contract that did not work.

Although facility/concessionaire agreements do not give equal rights to both parties, they should clearly establish the parameters by which concessionaires should operate and should provide concessionaires with an equitable return for their work. For that reason it is recommended that sport managers understand a concessionaire's financial objectives (pricing strategies, product, payroll, operating costs, and profit projections) before entering into an agreement. They should make sure that those expectations are reasonable and obtainable based on the facility's event and attendance schedule. A knowledge source or consultant should be used to evaluate the information that prospective concessionaires say they will provide. In fact, most facilities are now employing a consultant from the development of the Request for Proposal document, into the evaluation and selection process, and right through to the final contract negotiations.

Sport managers are in a buyer's market. Concessionaires are hungry to expand and are willing to agree to a director's demands to secure the contract. Sport managers should check with other facility directors. Does this concessionaire live up to marketing promises? Does the company exceed service expectations?

The following issues should be addressed in a concessions contract:

Foodservice Contract Demands

- Exclusions - Itemize Potential Exclusions
  Community Festivals
  Religious Conventions
  Ringling Brothers Circus
  Disney on Ice
  Luxury Suites
  Open Catering

- Definitions - Gross versus Net
  Gross Sales
  Gratuities
  Off-Premise Sales
  Subcontracted Sales
  Novelty Sales
- Product Control - Capitalize on Advertising
  Brand
  Variety
  Quality
  Portion
  Pricing
- Management Control - Treat Contractor as Department Head
  Interviews with management candidates
  Authority to dismiss management
  Staffing levels
  Training Involvement
- Investment - Leasehold, Equipment, Smallwares
  Approval of all investments
  Approval of depreciation/amortization
  Buyout provisions
- Insurance - Insulate your Liability
  Hold harmless
  Product liability
- Audit Controls - Constant Supervision
  Daily event summaries
  Monthly profit and loss
  Annual audit
  Unannounced audits
- Miscellaneous
  Computerization
  Cash Registers
  Operational Audits
  Repairs and Renovations
  Marketing
  Utilities
  Default
  Bankruptcy
  Mechanic's Liens
- Quality Assurance
  Management
  Staffing
  Product
  Service

There are two basic contract types: the traditional commission agreement and the management fee agreement, which has been growing in acceptance in recent years. Each contract type offers some benefits and some risks.

The commission agreement provides for the concessionaire to pay the venue operator a percentage of the concessionaire's gross receipts. The concessionaire supplies and pays all costs for payroll, product, and operating supplies, and the concessionaire retains all profits after the above costs are deducted.

The management fee agreement provides for the concessionaire to receive a management fee, typically stated as a percentage of gross receipts and a profit incentive, which is likely to be stated as a percentage of *net* profits. The concessionaire supplies all personnel, product, and operating supplies, and the facility operator reimburses the concessionaire for those costs. The facility retains all profits after the above costs are deducted.

The advantages of the commission agreement are as follows:
- It eliminates the risk of financial loss to the facility.
- It simplifies the auditing of the concessionaire's operation.
- It insulates the facility from daily operating decision.

The advantages of the management fee agreement are as follows:
- It develops a partnership of mutual interest between concessionaire and facility.
- It provides the potential for increased revenues to the facility
- It provides the facility with greater control and flexibility for foodservice operating decisions.

The management fee arrangement eliminates the typical adversarial relationships found in so many foodservice contracts. Many times the facility makes demands that cost the concessionaire additional payroll or product cost. The client makes these decisions for the overall good of the facility, but the concessionaire sees it as a negative financial influence to its profits while still having to pay the same commissions to the facility.

Under the management fee agreement, both contractor and facility share the costs of operating and in the profits. The management fee arrangement reduces the risk a concessionaire may have on low-volume events to provide quality service, but rewards the facility even more for high volume sales and efficient operations.

The management fee arrangement encourages regular input from the facility manager on items, such as product quality, staffing levels, and special pricing for unique events.

The Hubert H. Humphrey Metrodome, Louisiana SuperDome, Hoosier Dome, Arrowhead Stadium, Kaufman Stadium, Anaheim Stadium, and the Palace at Auburn Hills are all facilities utilizing the management fee agreement. Fees typically range from 0-7.5%, depending on sales volume and profit. Splits range from 3 to 25%. The SuperDome is an example of a facility that switched to a management fee arrangement after 15 years under a commission agreement. The reasons were to allow the facility manager more input into the concession operation and provide for increased revenues to the facility as sales increased.

Financial and Operational Quality Assurance

The successful sport concessions operation is one in which the facility and concessionaire function as partners. Each party is aware of the other's requirements, and each party understands the other's financial constraints. To maintain this mutual respect, it is important for the facility to know that the concessions department is maintaining the highest level of financial and operational integrity.

Annual financial audits and regularly scheduled operational audits provide a facility director with the confidence that the concessionaire is maximizing the building revenues. The use of secret shoppers, comment cards, season ticketholder direct mailings, a fan accommodation booth, and even regular appearances on the local sports call-in radio show help facility managers evaluate the concessions, and other customer service departments, from the customer's point of view. Although every comment is important, if a complaint is repeated several times by several customers, chances are it is real, or equally important, its perception is real, and it must be corrected immediately. Some large venues are developing quality assurance managers who have no function other than to identify potential problems before the customers experience them.

It is recommended that managers of sport venues act as customers for a day each month. They should drive to the facility during rush hour, wait in line to pay to park, wait in line to purchase tickets, ask lots of questions of the service employees, wait in line to purchase concessions, and even to go the restrooms. They should sit in the cheap seats. How is the view? Are there any vendors up there? One manager even did all of this in a wheelchair to check his ADA compliance and accessibility. The closer sport managers get to their customers, the higher the level of services they can provide, and the more time and money customers will want to spend at their stadiums and arenas.

SUMMARY

Developing a concessions department or contracting with a concessionaire is one of the most important decisions a sport manager makes to ensure the highest level of customer service and maximum operating revenues for the venue. This chapter has detailed many of the critical issues a manager must analyze before initiating a concession program, and while overseeing a concessions department or contract.

Managers should remember that the foodservice and souvenir industry is now very popular, and in order to maximize both customer service and revenues, their concessions manager must capitalize on the customers' impulse-spending habits. When managers design the correct facilities and deal with a flexible concessions department, new menu items can be introduced, slow-moving items repackaged or showcased, and new services tried, and all for very little investment.

If an item does not sell, it should be taken off the menu. To find out how high a per cap can be generated without decreasing profits due to excessive payroll, managers should keep adding portable carts and service lines. If a local restauranteur is getting all of the facility's pre-event business, that operator should be brought into the building as a subcontractor, or the facility should produce their product better than the original restauranteur. In other words, managers must keep experimenting and analyzing those per-capita spending trends and operating costs.

Currently, customers want higher levels of service and products and are willing to pay a premium for them. Managers might package the first 10 rows of seats with VIP parking and charge a premium or package a pre-game meal, VIP seats, and valet parking and charge a premium. Computerized hand-held order terminals should be used by the in-seat wait staff. Customers are impressed by the fast service. The facility can feature the city's native products, foods, and services. Managers should offer valet parking and a season ticket-holders' lounge. A premium can be charged for parking spaces closest to the building. Managers can develop a sponsors' lounge where the building sponsors can entertain their customers. None of these ideas is new. They have all worked at other facilities, and those facility managers all agree: Customers are willing to spend more when they are offered a higher level of service, when their expectations are exceeded, and when they can purchase an exclusive service or be part of an exclusive club that others cannot join.

Questions for Study and Discussion

1. What kind of dramatic impact did the opening of Joe Robbie Stadium have on the sport concessions industry?
2. Provide a descriptive profile of the economic contribution of concessions to the overall revenue generated by sport teams. Distinguish the relative impact between professional and amateur teams. What factors account for the differences?
3. What are the two controllable costs in concession operations and how can they be controlled?
4. What are the respective advantages and disadvantages of operating concessions in-house versus on a contracted basis?
5. Describe the two basic types of concession contracts. What contract arrangement is preferred by the author and why?

SECTION 3

RESOURCES FROM
EXTERNAL SOURCES

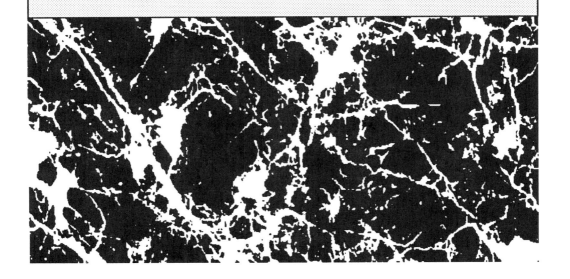

CHAPTER 9

NATURE OF THE SPONSORSHIP EXCHANGE

Learning Objectives:

After completing this chapter, the reader should be able to:

1. define the concept of sponsorship exchange
2. discuss the historical evolution of sport sponsorship and those factors which have stimulated sponsorship growth.
3. discuss the principal benefits sport organizations seek from corporate sponsors including: financial investment, media exposure, and in-kind services.
4. articulate the key benefits business sponsors seek from sport organizations including: increased awareness, image enhancement, product trial and hospitality opportunities.
5. discuss how sponsorship benefits from sporting events can be achieved at each stage of the product adoption process.

CHAPTER 9

NATURE OF THE SPONSORSHIP EXCHANGE

In the course of developing this book some argued with us that sponsorship belongs in a sport marketing rather than a sport financing text. We disagree. From the perspective of a sport manager, sponsorship is viewed primarily as a source of additional financial resources. Indeed, it has been estimated that sport sponsors, "contribute five times as much as fans to stage U.S. sports events" (Hiestand, 1993, p. 1c), and some have argued that "without the support of corporations, the world of sports, as we know it today, would collapse" (Irwin, 1993, p. 11). For the most part, sport managers do not seek sponsorship for the purpose of communicating their product to a target audience (media tie-ins may be exceptions to this generalization). Rather, it is companies that seek to communicate with target audiences by linking with a sports event or facility through sponsorship. The sport manager's role is to understand how companies use sponsorship in their marketing programs, to be responsive to company needs, and then to charge the maximum fee companies are prepared to pay for providing them with these communication opportunities.

The discussion of financing sport through sponsorship is divided into four chapters. This chapter considers the nature of the sponsorship exchange. Chapter 10 discusses the controversial issue of sponsorship by tobacco and alcohol companies, whereas chapter 11 focuses on the pragmatic issues of implementing a sponsorship partnership. Finally, in chapter 12, techniques for measuring the impact of sponsorships are presented.

This chapter starts by differentiating between sponsorship and donations, which are discussed later in the book in Chapter 13. The evolution of sport sponsorship to its current ubiquitous presence in major professional sports is briefly traced and its penetration into the college and high school levels is noted. The major factors contributing to sponsorship's current high profile and its role in a company's overall marketing communications effort are discussed.

The essence of successful sponsorship is the exchange in mutual benefits which occurs between the business and sports organization. It is a reciprocal relationship. The organization is likely to seek financial, in-kind and media benefits, while the benefits which may be sought by businesses can be classified into four categories: #5 increased awareness, image enhancement, product trial or sales opportunities, and hospitality opportunities. These are described together with the key role played by media in enhancing sponsors' benefits.

DIFFERENTIATING SPONSORSHIPS AND DONATIONS

Voluntary exchange is the central concept underlying both sponsorship and donations. The concept requires something of value to be offered in exchange for something else of value. Before an investment or donation is made the contributor is likely to ask two questions, "What is in it for me?" and "How much will it cost me?" The trade off is weighed between what will be gained and what will have to be given up. Both sponsorship and philanthropy offer sources of funds, resources, and in-kind services to sports organizations, but they differ in the nature of what they expect in exchange.

In the context of this book, sponsorship is defined as a business relationship between a provider of funds, resources, or services and a sports event or organization which offers in return some rights and an association that may be used for commercial advantage (Sleight, 1989). The distinctive terms in this definition which differentiate sponsorship from philanthropy are *business relationship* and *commercial advantage*.

A sport organization offers a variety of potential opportunities to businesses that they may perceive to be of value. These may include increased awareness, image enhancement, product trial or sales opportunities, and hospitality opportunities (Figure 9-1). Companies in return may offer support through investments of money, media exposure, and in-kind services.

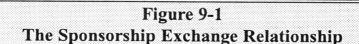

Figure 9-1
The Sponsorship Exchange Relationship

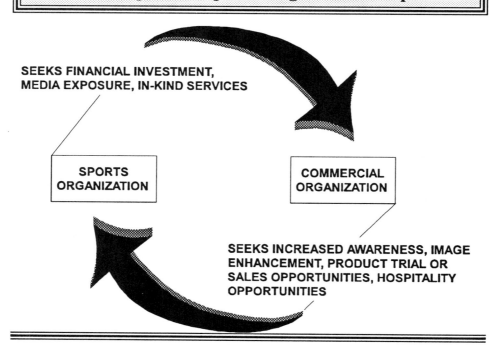

SEEKS FINANCIAL INVESTMENT, MEDIA EXPOSURE, IN-KIND SERVICES

SPORTS ORGANIZATION

COMMERCIAL ORGANIZATION

SEEKS INCREASED AWARENESS, IMAGE ENHANCEMENT, PRODUCT TRIAL OR SALES OPPORTUNITIES, HOSPITALITY OPPORTUNITIES

Although donors may offer similar types and amounts of support, the benefits they seek in return for their contributions are different. The key motive in philanthropy is the satisfaction of knowing that good is being done with the donated resources. The motives underlying philanthropic donations are altruistic rather than commercial, because the donors are concerned with humanistic or community concerns rather than with a commercial return on the investment.

In the early days of sponsorship, often it was not differentiated from philanthropy. Decisions to support a particular sport or sporting event frequently reflected the personal interests of senior management, rather than a careful assessment of the benefits that were likely to accrue to the company from its investment. Today, this type of decision is unusual. Accountability for an investment has to be shown by demonstrating its potential for increasing a company's profitability. At the same time, sponsoring sports, like many other corporate innovations, is more likely to come to fruition if it is championed by a senior-level decision maker. The champion's commitment may be stimulated by personal interest. One company executive responsible for sport sponsorships observed:

> There certainly must be corporate interest. It may be employee interest that precipitates the event interest. It may of course be a key executive, an agency recommendation, or the outcome of a marketing plan. To make the event work there must be a champion. The champion must have the interest, authority, and single minded vision to make the event work. (cited in Copeland, 1991, p. 212)

EVOLUTION OF SPORT SPONSORSHIP

> The first sponsor of sport was probably a Roman patrician currying favour with his Emperor by underwriting a day of blood-letting in the Colosseum. He would have regarded himself as the patron of the games but since he was seeking a return on investment, he was being no more philanthropic than any of today's commercial sponsors. (Wilson, 1988, p. 157)

The first businesses in the United States to be associated with and invest in sports events were in the transportation industry (Brooks, 1990). In 1852 a New England railroad transported the Harvard and Yale teams to a crew competition and vigorously promoted it. The company profited from the rail tickets sold to thousands of fans who travelled to the site. By the late 1890s in many cities, streetcar and rail companies had developed close links with baseball teams and generated special services from downtown areas to the ballparks.

Similar pioneering sponsorship arrangements were instigated elsewhere. For example, two expatriate Englishmen, Felix Spiers and Christopher Pond, who had established a substantial catering business in supplying refreshments to the Melbourne and Ballarate Railway in Australia, underwrote the cost of the first tour of an English cricket team to Australia in 1861. Referring to this investment, Wilson (1988) notes, "It might be stretching the definition to classify as a sponsor a company who walked away with $11,000 in profit" (p. 157). Spiers and Pond capitalized on the publicity they received from this very successful venture by returning to Britain to establish a famous catering company. Similarly, in France the magazine *Velocipide* sponsored an early automobile race in 1887 (International Advertising Association, 1988).

Coca-Cola was the first company to perceive the value of being associated with the Olympics (Brooks, 1990). In 1928, it contributed 1,000 cases of the soft drink to the U.S. team at the Amsterdam Games and claimed the title of Official Olympic Supplier.

In marked contrast to these early, rather isolated examples, sponsorship in the past two decades has grown exponentially, so that by 1994 it was estimated that 4,500 companies spent $4.7 billion on event sponsorship (International Events Group, 1994). Two-thirds of this sponsorship was invested in sports events (Figure 9-2). Among sports, professional baseball attracts a larger number of sponsoring companies than

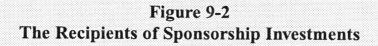

Figure 9-2
The Recipients of Sponsorship Investments

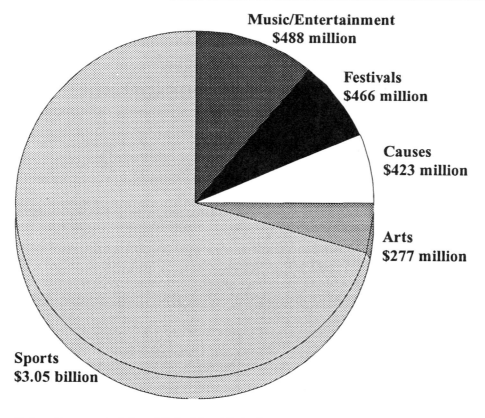

Music/Entertainment
$488 million

Festivals
$466 million

Causes
$423 million

Arts
$277 million

Sports
$3.05 billion

Note: From materials published by *I.E.G. Sponsorship Report* (1994, December). *13* (24). Reprinted with permission.

does any other sport. There are at least four reasons for this. First, there are more major and minor league teams than in any other professional sport and teams play more games in a season. Second, "it's a product that is aligned with some of the peak selling seasons of products like soft drinks and beer, which are probably the two biggest categories putting money into professional sports" (Cohen, 1993, p. 16). Third, the natural breaks between innings offer opportunities for sponsors to communicate their messages. Fourth, the slow pace of the game enables spectators to look around: "The action doesn't move quite as quickly as it does in the other sports and your eye wanders, making the signs in the outfield or on the scoreboard that much more visible" (Cohen, 1993, p. 16).

Another indicator of growth is the increasing number of sports marketing companies. The managing director of a prominent North American sports marketing firm claimed that in 1979 there was nobody in the sports marketing business in the United States, but that by 1992 there were 450 agencies that claimed to represent the interest of sponsors in sports marketing (Cunningham, Taylor & Reeder, 1992).

Figure 9-3 lists the companies involved in sponsorship arrangements with the major professional sports leagues in 1992. These estimates suggest that 123 companies spent an average of $830,000 each on sponsorships with the four major North American professional team sport leagues, three major professional golf tours, and two professional tennis tours. This figure includes only ties to the leagues themselves; not team and event sponsorship which exceeds that acquired by the sanctioning bodies. Thus, for example, in 1988 more than $150 million was invested in NFL football sponsorships by more than 100 major corporations, but most of it was negotiated with individual teams rather than with the NFL (Kaufman, 1988). For example, the Minnesota Timberwolves in the NBA had 33 sponsors in 1991, and 15 of the team's 40-person marketing staff worked with sponsors ("Target Sponsors," 1990).

Increases in Olympic Games corporate sponsorship fees offer perhaps the most dramatic indicator of sponsorship growth. In 1984, the Los Angeles Olympic Organizing Committee conceived the idea of acquiring a substantial proportion of funding for the Games from corporate sponsorship. The Committee charged $4 million for each of its 30 major sponsorships. In 1992 eight corporations paid at least $23 million each to be joint partners with the Barcelona Games organizers. At the 1996 Atlanta Games, the organizer's goal was to sell $500 million worth of corporate sponsorships, most of which were to be forthcoming from 10 national "Partners" in different commercial categories, such as automobiles, fast food, telecommunications, insurance and beer. The cost to each Partner was $40 million in cash, services, or equipment, and Partners were guaranteed exclusivity in their market category (Johnson, 1993). Thus, the Olympic sponsorship fee has increased tenfold in the 12-year period, but in return there has been an attempt to remove "clutter" by having fewer sponsors involved.

Sponsorship now extends far beyond professional sports and the Olympic Games. A recent survey of 150 NCAA Division I and II colleges and universities reported that 90% of the schools surveyed had established some type of corporate sponsorship program (Irwin, 1993). For example, in 1991 The Pennsylvania State University

---

Figure 9-3
Companies Involved in Sponsorship Arrangements
With the Major Professional Sports Leagues, 1992

Property	Sponsors, Categories and Length of Agreements
Ladies Professioanl Golf Assn. Tour Minimum term: Two years Estimated '92 sponsorship: $2.7 million	**Budget Rent A Car Corp.** Official car rental company since '91. **Centel Corp.** Official telecommunications provider since '90. **Continental Airlines.** Official airline since '90. **Coppertone**/Schering-Plough, Inc. Official sun-care product since '88. **du Maurier Ltd.** (tobacco) since '90. **Eastman Kodak Co.** Official film and photographic consultant since '88. **Gatorade**/The QuakerOats Co. Official sports beverage. *Golf Magazine.* **Hilton Hotels Corp.** Official hotel since '90. **Kinder-Care Learning Centers, Inc.** Official child care. **MCI Communications Corp.** Official long-distance company since '90. **Mead Corp.** Official trash receptacle since '92. **Oldsmobile**/General Motors Corp. Official car. **Panasonic**/Matsushita Electric Corp of America. Official consumer electronics supplier since '92. **Pert Plus, Secret**/The Procter & Gamble Co. Since '88. **Rolex Watch U.S.A.** Official timepiece since '81. **Royal Caribbean Cruise Line.** Official cruise line since '91. **Ryder System Co.** (transportation).
Major League Baseball Estimated '92 sponsorship: $18.1 million	**Chevrolet, Chevy Trucks**/General Motors Corp. Official car and truck '91-'93, since '86. **Coca-Cola Classic**/The Coca-Cola Co. Official soft drink '91-93, since '89. **Frosted Flakes, Rice Krispies**/Kellogg Co. Official breakfast food, cereal '91-'95. **Gatorade**/The Quaker Oats Co. Official sports beverage '91-'95. **IBM Corp.** Official information system '90-'92, since '87. **Leaf, Inc.** Official candy and gum '91-93, since '88. **MCI Communications Corp.** Official telecommunications and long distance company '91-'93. **The Procter & Gamble Co.** Official health, beauty aids, paper '92-'93. **Rolaids**/Warner-Lambert Co. Official antacid '91-93. **The Sherwin-Williams Co.** Official paint '92-'94. **United Airlines.** Official airline '91-'93. *USA Today*/Gannett Co. Official newspaper '90-'95.
National Basketball Assn. Minimum term: Three years Estimated '92 sponsorship: $16 million	**American Airlines.** Official airline '91-'94, since '81. **Big G Cereal Division**/General Mills, Inc. Official hot and cold cereals '90-'93. **Coca-Cola Classic**/The Coca-Cola Co. Official soft drink '89-93. **Dutch Boy Paints**/The Sherwin-Williams Co. Official paint '90-'93. **Edge Shave Gel, Aftershave**/S.C. Johnson & Son, Inc. Official shave gel, cream and aftershave '89-'93. **Gatorade**/The Quaker Oats Co. Official sports beverage and thirst quencher '89-'94. **IBM Corp.** Official computer '91-'94. **ITT Sheraton Corp.** Official hotel '89-'92. **Jeep/Eagle/Chrysler Corp.** Official car and vehicle through '93, since '85. **McDonald's Corp.** Official quick-service restaurant '90-'93. **Miller Genuine Draft**/Miller Brewing Co. Official malt beverage '90-'94. **Nestle USA, Inc.** Official candy bar '92-'93. **Norwegian Cruise Line.** Offical cruise line '91-'94. **Schick Razors and Blades**/Warner-Lambert Co. Official razors and blades '89-'92. **Wheaton Van Lines, Inc.** Official mover '91-'94.
National Football League Minimum term: Two years Estimated '92 sponsorship: $14.6 million	**American Express TRS Co.** Official travel company. **Anheuser-Busch Cos. Paul Arpin Van Lines, Inc.** Official mover. **Avis, Inc.** Official car rental company of the NFL and member clubs since '91. **Coca-Cola Classic**/The Coca-Cola Co. Through '93, since '84. **Delta Air Lines, Inc.** Offical airline since '92. **DHL Worldwide Express.** Official worldwide express carrier since '91. **Eastman Kodak Co.** Official film. **Fuji.** Official videotape. **Gatorade**/The Quaker Oats Co. Official sports beverage since '86. **Glidden Co.** Official paint. **GTE Corp.** Telecommunications consultant. **Miller Lite**/Miller Brewing Co. Since '88. **Toshiba America, Inc.** Official fax. **Zenith Data Systems Corp.** Official personal computer.

Figure 9-3 cont'd.

Property	Sponsors, Categories and Length of Agreements
National Hockey League Minimum term: Three years Estimated '92 sponsorship: $7.5 million	**Alka-Seltzer Plus**/Miles Inc. Official cold medicine '91-'92, since '90. **Bud Light/** Anheuser-Busch Inc. Official malt beverage, U.S. only, '91-'92, since '87. **Canada Post**, '91-'92. **Coca-Cola Classic**/The Coca-Cola Co. Official soft drink '91-92, since '89. **Esso Petroleum Canada**. Official gas and oil, Canada only. '91-'92. **Fiberglas Canada, Inc.** Official building products, Canada only. '91-'92, since '90. **Gatorade**/The Quaker Oats Co. Official sport drink '90-'96. **Gillette Canada, Inc.** Official razor, blade and shave cream, Canada only, '91-'92, since '89. **Kellogg Co. of Canada**. Official ready-to-eat cereal, toaster products and waffle, Canada only, '91-'92. **McDonald's Corp**. Official quick-service restaurant '90-'92. **Molson Breweries of Canada, Ltd.** Official malt beverage, Canada only, '91-'92, since '88. **Owens-Corning Fiberglas Corp**. Official building products, U.S. only, '91-'92, since '90. **Palm Dairies Inc.** Official dairy, ice cream, Canada only, '91-'92. **Pro Set, Inc.** Official trading card '91-'92, since '90. **Thrifty Rent-A-Car System, Inc.** Official car rental company '91-'92, since '87. **Upper Deck Co.** Official trading card '91-'92, since '90.
PGA Tour Estimated '92 sponsorship: $8.5 million	**Advil**/Whitehall Laboratories. **Coca-Cola Classic**/The Coca-Cola Co. Official soft drink '91-2000. **Coppertone**/Schering-Plough, Inc. **Delta Air Lines, Inc.** Official airline. **Easman Kodak Co.** Official copier, film, diskette. **Foot-Joy, Inc.** Official athletic/fitness shoe. **Gatorade**/The Quaker Oats Co. Official sports drink '91-'92. **Hilton Hotels Corp.** Official hotel since '91. **IBM Corp.** Official computer scoring and information system '92-'94, since '91. **MasterCard Int'L** Official credit card. **MCI Communications Corp.** Official telecommunications and long distance company. **Merrill Lynch. Murata Business Systems.** Official fax machine. **National Car Rental System.** Official rental car company. **Nikon, Inc.** Official Camera. **Oldsmobile**/General Motors Corp. Official car since '92. **Philips Business Systems Co.** Official audio/video products. **Royal Caribbean Cruise Line.** Official cruise line. **Sharp's**/Miller Brewing Co. Official non-alcoholic brew.
Senior PGA Tour Estimated '92 sponsorship: $9.4 million	**Advil**/Whitehall Laboratories. **Cadillac**/General Motors Corp. Official car since '90. **Coppertone**/Schering-Plough, Inc. **Delta Air Lines, Inc.** Official airline. **Eastman Kodak Co.** Official copier, film, diskette. **Foot-Joy, Inc.** Official athletic/fitness shoe. **Hilton Hotels Corp.** Official hotel since '91. **MasterCard Int'L** Official credit card. **MCI Communications Corp.** Official telecommunications and long distance company. **Merrill Lynch. Murata Business Systems.** Official fax machine. **National Car Rental System.** Official rental car company. **Nikon, Inc.** Official camera. **Philips Business Systems Co.** Official audio/video products. **Royal Caribbean Cruise Line.** Official cruise line. **Vantage**/R.J. Reynolds Tobacco Co. Since '87.

Note: From Status Report: Pro Sports League Sponsorship, *I.E.G. Sponsorship Report* (p.4), July 27, 1992, Volume 11, Number 14. Reprinted with permission.

announced a sponsorship agreement with Pepsi-Cola which was projected to generate revenue of about $14 million over the next decade. The partnership gave Pepsi primary scoreboard advertising rights in the new Academic/Athletic Convocation and Events Center and in Beaver Stadium, as well as exclusive rights to sell Pepsi products at all Penn State football games and in vending machines and soda fountains on the university's 22 campuses. Another approach was initiated by Georgia Tech, which sought individual game sponsors (Maxie, 1989):

- To boost revenue Georgia Tech invited sponsors to pay $75,000 per game for five games at Bobby Dodd Stadium, $100,000 for a Thanksgiving weekend game with Boston College and $175,000 for the season finale against Georgia. The school estimated that after expenses, it could make about $500,000. As part of the package, each corporation that sponsored a football game was permitted to sponsor a basketball game at no extra cost. In return for their fee, the sponsor received the following benefits:
  - 15 seats in the executive suite, 250 priority seating tickets and 10 parking spaces;
  - a corporate tent with catering;
  - full-page advertisement in *The Atlanta Journal-Constitution*, Georgia Tech's student newspaper, the school's media guides, and the game-day programs;
  - 100 regional television spots promoting the game;
  - a substantial number of radio spots;
  - appearances by Tech cheerleaders and Buzz the mascot at promotions during the week before the game;
  - its logo on signs posted at the stadium for the game and on posters of the football team.

Once this type of local corporate sponsorship has been widely accepted and exploited by universities, it seems likely that attention will turn to involving national sponsors. There have been proposals to form a corporate consortium of college athlete departments in which 50 to 100 schools would band together and negotiate with national sponsors (Millet, 1989). In the professional leagues, such as NBA, NFL, and NHL, major multinational corporations are able to go to a single office for a "buy" of that league. This has not been possible in college athletics, and individual universities cannot make an impact on national sponsors. Under the proposed arrangement, universities control all local corporate sponsorships but must agree to commit to the national program a proportion of scoreboard recognition, program recognition, newspaper advertisements, billboard advertisements, radio and television tags, press guides, public announcements, and banners. Distribution of revenues to schools in the consortium would be based on a formula reflecting attendances at games, extent of media coverage and other factors. It was estimated that such a national consortium program would yield revenue to participating universities of $300,000-$650,000 per year.

At the high school level, an increasing number of school districts are unable to provide the funds needed to offer a full range of high school athletic programs. More high schools are moving to a "pay-for-play" system in which athletes pay a fee for each sport in which they participate. High school tournaments are becoming more expensive to organize, and gate receipts in those sports for which there is a charge are insufficient to cover the costs of all the tournaments. These conditions have created interest in soliciting sponsors, although much of the sponsorship is with governing bodies rather than with individual schools. It was reported that in the 1992-93 school year, at least 23 state high school associations had sponsorship (International Events Group, 1993b). Thus, the New Hampshire Interscholastic Athletic Association (NHIAA) signed sponsorship agreements with McDonald's, True Value Hardware, New Hampshire Sweepstakes, and Coca-Cola. Coca-Cola, for example, contributed $300 to NHIAA for every high school that allowed a Coca-Cola soda or juice machine in its building, and this amounted to over $20,000 per year (Reinert, 1989).

Similarly, Pizza Huts Nevada/Utah district office committed $370,000 over a three year period to high school sports in both states. Details of this agreement are described in the shaded box below. In California, Reebok and Coca-Cola provided a total of $1.6 million to support state high school championships over 3 years from 1990 to 1993. The sponsors were attracted by the exposure they obtained to California's nearly half-million high school athletes and their parents ("Spectrum," 1989). However, this sponsorship was not renewed. A spokesman reported, "We got good exposure and the sponsorship made us feel good, but we didn't see enough of an increase in product sales to warrant such a significant marketing expenditure" (International Events Group 1993b). In addition to the two statewide sponsors, the Southern section which is the largest of the state's 10 sections had 10 sectional sponsors: Gatorade, Round Table Pizza, Jack in the Box, Ford, the California Angels, Sunny Delight, Wilson, Herff Jones, the Army National Guard and Conlin Brothers Sporting Goods. Sponsors were given prominent signage while the major backers received title sponsorship on several events, the CIF-Reebok State Wrestling Championship, for example, and, even more cumbersome, the Southern Section CIF Reebok/Jack in the Box Football Championship.

HIGH SCHOOLS RAISE SPONSOR DOUGH FROM PIZZA HUT

Pizza Hut Inc's Nevada/Utah district office committed $370,000 over a three year period to high school sports in both states. The chain, first sponsor of the Nevada Interscholastic Activities Assn., will title play-off and championship events in 18 sports. "The tie opens an avenue for us to work with booster clubs," said Ric Starnes, market manager for the district. "It's a bridge between us and the kids." Pizza Hut will pay $60,000 for the '91-'92 school year and $65,000 and $70,000, respectively, for the next two seasons, said Don Baird, president of School Properties U.S.A., Inc., the sponsorship and licensing agency hired by NIAA.

The chain will promote the NIAA/Pizza Hut State Championships in its 32 Nevada restaurants. NIAA is earmarking about $20,000 of the company's fee to reimburse teams for meals eaten at Pizza Huts while traveling to and from state championships. Another $3,000 will pay for awards to the three schools presenting the most Pizza Hut receipts at the end of the school year.

NIAA's logo incorporates Pizza Hut's and will appear on banners in Nevada's 70 high schools, attended by 70,000 students. The chain also has rights to sell pizza at game venues except those with prior vendor commitments. Pizza Hut

received about three minutes of radio time on each of three divisional football championship game broadcasts last month and mention on public TV's broadcast of two of those games. Starnes said it was too early to gauge results. "We'll have a better read in basketball season."

Pizza Hut will pay the Utah High School Activities Assn. $40,000 for official product status at 84 tournaments in 1991-92 and $67,500 for each of the following two years. The chain has 46 stores in the state. Sponsorship accounts for more than 25 percent of UHSAA revenues. First Security Bank of Utah signed a new one-year, $150,000 title deal when its initial three-year, $325,000 agreement expired. About 103,000 students attend Utah's 106 high schools.

Pizza Hut's package includes mention in five 30-second PSAs daily, starting 10 days out, and at lest two 30-second PSAs during each game telecast on media sponsor KXIV, which covers football and basketball championships at two levels and track at all levels. The PSAs are equivalent to $250,000 in ad time, according to Baird.

The district office also co-ops local stops of the PEPSI/PIZZA HUT HOOP-IT-UP. "Every store in the district will be involved in some sponsorship activity, whether it's a booth at a founder's day fair or whatever," Starnes said. "Area managers work with each store manager on sponsorship."

Note: from *IEG Sponsorship Report 10*(23), December 9, 1991.

EXTERNAL FACTORS THAT STIMULATED SPONSORSHIP GROWTH

Nine major changes have taken place in the external environment affecting sports sponsorship that have contributed to its sustained growth over the past two decades. The first four of these relate to television.

1. Rapid increases in the numbers of television channels, radio stations and magazines meant that the number of advertising messages vying for attention made it difficult for a particular message to make an impact. In the case of television, the problem of clutter arising from media proliferation was accentuated by an increase in the growth of 15-second spots and in the commercial time inserted into programs by the networks. "The constant clutter of traditional media is like a roomful of people talking. If you cannot separate your voice, then you are wasting your money" (Morse, 1989, p. 4). Sponsorship was seen as an alternative means of gaining exposure that avoided this clutter and was sufficiently distinctive that the associated message was likely to be seen and heard.

2 . The cost of television advertising escalated while the influx of new cable channels reduced the viewing audience a program could deliver. The proliferation of sports events shown both on the networks and on cable systems fragmented the viewing audience. The impact on these smaller audiences was further reduced by the introduction and widespread use of the "zapper," which enabled

people to tune out commercials without leaving their arm-chairs and of the videocassette recorder which enabled them to fast-forward commercials. Sponsorship was perceived to be a more cost-efficient alternative medium for gaining exposure.

Ironically, among the main reasons cited by companies for terminating their involvement with sponsorship of a sport are that the profusion of sponsorships associated with televised sports has created clutter and that the demand by companies interested in such sponsorships has caused the costs to escalate too high! For example, Sunkist which was an early sponsor of the Fiesta Bowl in 1985, withdrew after the sponsorship fee rose to $1.6 million in 1990. Not only did the company consider the cost to be too high, but also the entry of a dozen other companies to bowl sponsorship since Sunkist pioneered it created clutter and diminished Sunkist's impact (McCarthy, 1991).

3. The introduction of color television increased the viewer appeal of televised sport, and together with the proliferation of channels created by cable, this led to substantial growth in the amount of televised sport produced. Thus, many more opportunities for sponsors interested in television exposure were created. Sport attracts a relatively high percentage of television air time because sport is inexpensive to produce and widely popular. Certainly, it receives substantially more television exposure than does any other potential sponsorship vehicle.

4. With the banning of tobacco and liquor advertisements from television in the early and mid-1970s, companies making these products had to seek alternative promotion avenues. Sponsorship partnerships with sports were appealing for three main reasons. First, the association gave these potentially harmful products an aura of public respectability. Second, the extensive television coverage of sport provided them with access to that medium from which they were technically banned, even though their messages had to be indirect. Third, sponsorship partnerships enabled these companies to access the youth market. These firms recognize that inducing adolescents to smoke is crucial to the future viability of the cigarette industry in the United States. As a result, companies making these two products have emerged as the leading sources of sponsorship.

5. Commercialization of sport has become increasingly accepted by organizing bodies. One of the authors recalls participating in a meeting in the early 1970s with the chairman of a leading English professional soccer club who was also chairman of the Football League which is professional soccer's organizing body in England. He was genuinely outraged and scornful of the idea of sponsorship saying, "You'd have all our players running round with Texaco on their shirts." Ten years later, all major British soccer clubs were doing just that! In the United States a similar "acceptance curve" of sports sponsorship appears to be percolating down from professional sports organizations, through colleges, to the high school level.

6. The success of sponsorships associated with the 1984 Los Angeles Olympic Games received high visibility and helped legitimize sponsorship to the corporate sector as an effective promotional medium. Thirty U.S.- based corpora-

tions advanced or guaranteed $4 million each in cash, products or services for the right to be designated an official corporate sponsor of the Games. Another category of companies (some 50 in all) was granted licenses to sell goods that carried the Olympic logo, and these companies paid $500,000 for the rights. Two points from these Games emphasized the potential viability of partnerships between sports and business organizations: The sponsoring companies attained substantial media exposure and a measure of positive image building, and the Games were an unprecedented financial success.

7. Acceptance and implementation of the concept of marketing segmentation was not widespread until the late 1970s (Brooks, 1990). Market segmentation is the process of partitioning large markets into smaller homogeneous subsets of people with similar characteristics who are likely to exhibit similar purchasing behavior. In the 1960s most companies were moving products by mass marketing. By the 1980s, successful companies recognized that a mass market did not exist, but rather the market place consisted of segments or clusters of potential customers with different propensities to purchase particular products and services. Acceptance of segmentation was accelerated by the high-profile documentation provided by demographers of the fragmentation of society into yuppies, single-parent families, dual-income households with children, and so on. This fragmentation made a company's potential consumer more elusive and difficult to reach.

Sports fans are spread widely across the full range of demographic and psychographic types; thus, sponsors can target specific audiences by their choice of sport. This has been reflected in the growth of more narrowly focused media outlets that cater to special interests. For example, 30 years ago sports magazines were dominated by generic publications, such as *Sports Illustrated*, and were relatively few in number. Today, there are likely to be between two and six magazines catering to each individual sport, such as golf, running, or baseball. Their readership profiles offer the potential for sponsors to reach a large proportion of their target market through association with events conveyed as news by these media. The advent of cable and satellite dishes has created similar targeting opportunities for sponsors in the television media. Sleight (1989) notes, "Sponsorship works because it fulfills the most important criterion of a communications medium -- it allows a particular audience to be targeted with a particular set of messages" (p. 42).

8. The proliferation of products and services and the increased competition that has characterized the market place in the past decade have been accompanied by a consolidation of companies through mergers and take-overs. Thus, in many industries fewer but larger companies exercise more control and influence in distribution channels. This has made it more critical for producers to enhance relations with distributors. Sponsorships offer entertainment and communication opportunities to do this. A related stimulus has been the evolution of large national food and drug chains that stock their own "No Name" and

house brands. This has persuaded some consumer goods companies to invest more heavily in sponsorship promotional tie-ins which offer incentives for the trade and "push" volume through trade channels to consumers (Cunningham, et. al., 1992).

9. The financial difficulties experienced by many cities and counties are causing more of them to charge for city services, such as police, garbage collection, and fire and ambulance standbys, which are used in association with an event. This has raised the costs of staging sports events and stimulated a more intensive search for sponsorship. This trend was documented in annual surveys undertaken by the International Events Group (1992). In 1983, 76% of events received free city services. This declined to 50%, 31% and 25% in 1990, 1991 and 1993, respectively.

The Role of Sponsorship

In addition to the external environmental changes that have facilitated growth in sponsorship, there has been increasing recognition of unique qualities that give it intrinsic merit. The marketing mix consists of four components: product, price, distribution, and promotion. Promotion is basically an exercise in communication. Its role is to facilitate exchange with present and potential clients by informing, educating, persuading, or reminding them of the benefits offered by a company, its products, or services. Traditionally, messages have been communicated through some combination of four vehicles: personal selling, advertising, publicity, and incentives (sometimes termed sales promotions). Sponsorship offers a fifth vehicle that can contribute to the total communication effort of a company. It complements the other four vehicles, rather than supplanting any of them.

The question "Which of these five vehicles is the best to use?" is the wrong question to ask. The correct question is, "How can each of these vehicles link with the others to achieve our communication objectives?" Sponsorship offers a way to focus attention on a specific target market that can then be accessed by the full range of a company's communication tools. It is likely to be most effective when its use is integrated with the other four vehicles. Sleight observes (1989), "Without a cohesive approach to communication no company can successfully integrate sponsorship with the other marketing activities" (p. 30). In the Los Angeles Olympic Games, Fuji spent millions of dollars as an official Olympic sponsor, but failed to tie that role in with a strong promotional effort beyond the sponsorship itself. Research showed Americans were more likely to associate Kodak with the Games because Kodak sponsored the U.S. Olympic Team and spent heavily on television advertising during the network's coverage (Gross, Traylor & Shuman, 1987).

Sponsorship has two special strengths. First, positioning has become a central concept in marketing strategy, and corporate and brand image development are key factors in positioning. Image is used to differentiate and position products that are essentially similar. Sponsorship is particularly suited to image enhancement. Second, in many situations sponsorship may offer opportunities for a company to establish a more intimate and emotionally involved relationship with its target audience than is feasible with the other four communication vehicles. A company's relationship with most of its audiences is usually rather distant and obviously commercial, whereas sponsorship enables a target market to be approached through activities in which they are personally interested. The intent is to communicate with audiences through their interests and lifestyle activities. In the context of sport, sponsorship allows a company to deliver its message to consumers who are relaxed, in a state of mind and in an environment that makes it likely they will be receptive. It may facilitate potential customers' spending quality time with a company and its products: "When you reach prospects who are interested in or are attending an event, they are yours. They are there because they want to be. They're part of the event and in a receptive mood" (McCabe, 1989, p.4).

Sponsorship's potential contributions are not limited to these two special strengths. Indeed, its role in a company's total communications effort is likely to vary widely in different industries (Meenaghan, 1983):

When used by tobacco companies its function is similar to that of advertising. In the case of building companies using sponsorship for guest hospitality purposes it can be regarded as related to personal selling. When used by the large multinational oil and banking groups its function lies broadly within the realms of public relations, while its usage in motor sport by oil companies and car manufacturers may be regarded as promoting sales. (p. 7)

BENEFITS SOUGHT FROM SPONSORSHIPS BY SPORT ORGANIZATIONS

A sports manager is likely to solicit three types of sponsorship benefits: financial, media and in-kind. It is often best to secure media sponsorship first. Having print and air sponsors commit to the dollar value of their support and to agree to promote other major sponsors is likely to make securing financial sponsorships easier (Cicora, 1991). Often, the first question asked from a potential financial sponsor relates to how much media promotion will be forthcoming. However, sponsorship by a newspaper or television station is likely to result in its competitors' avoiding any significant coverage of the event.

In-kind sponsorship with media is more difficult to obtain than it used to be. The amount of space available has shrunk considerably. Media realized that many sports managers, after negotiating the in-kind media assistance, were collecting revenues from it by selling the in-kind space to other cosponsors. Instead of allowing events to broker this space, the media now do it themselves or else write into agreements that mention of cosponsors in that space is precluded.

There are four main types of in-kind benefits that a business sponsor may provide: (a) product support, which could include equipment, and food and beverages; (b) personnel support, for example, assistance from staff who may have computing expertise the sports organization needs; (c) communication resources and expertise to increase awareness and interest; (d) the intangible benefit of "institutional clout" conferred on the sports organization by associating with a sponsoring business company of high reputation.

If a sponsor invests in extending the promotion accompanying a sports event because of a desire to increase awareness of the sponsor's linkage to it, this also widens the market for the event. The potential benefits to a sports organization of this type of investment are illustrated by the case of snooker in the United Kingdom (Gratton & Taylor 1985):

> In the early 1970s, snooker was a low interest sport with little media coverage. Sponsorship allowed the sport to move from smoky rooms to lavish surroundings for big competitions (most notably the Crucible Theatre, Sheffield). These surroundings attracted more media, in particular television coverage, which itself attracted more sponsors, giving higher prize money. The higher prize money and media coverage generated much wider interest which further encouraged the television companies and the sponsors, thus giving another boost to the upward spiral. Sponsorship then was a necessary condition for the promotion of the sport itself. By 1983, snooker was the fourth most televised sport in Britain, and had the second highest participation rate for an indoor sport. (p. 227)

Sometimes it is easier for companies to invest in in-kind sponsorship because it can be "hidden" from shareholders or employees who may be skeptical of the value of sponsorship. Thus, an executive from Target commenting on his company's sponsorship of the NBA Minnesota Timberwolves' new basketball arena observed: "We were concerned about negative reaction from the press, public and employees. The Wolves reportedly were asking more than $1 million for title rights. Try telling your employees you can afford to put the company's name on an arena when they are receiving only minimal raises'" (cited in Eaton, 1991).

One of the most widely cited sponsor successes in sport was the Cornhill Insurance Company's sponsorship of English international test cricket games, which is described later in this book in Chapter 12. However, Head (1981) recalls:

> One retains the memory of Cornhill staff pickets parading outside the Oval Cricket Ground in London during a Test match. Their banners pointed out that, while the company was spending £400,000 a year on cricket, it was, so they alleged, being less than generous in current wage negotiations with its own employees. The fact that sponsorship funds, even if diverted into wage packets, would have little effect on them, or that, as part of a marketing campaign, the money is better spent in promoting business and thus underpinning salaries in the long term, is an esoteric argument that cannot compete with emotive banners, especially at a time of rising unemployment. (p. 77)

Image association with a sports event is a primary reason for sponsors' investing in the event. However, the potential for positive association may be equally important to a sports organization. If the organization links to a sponsor with a strong, positive public image, then this "institutional clout" may help legitimize the organization and improve its public persona.

Associated Costs

These investments may require the sports organization to accept some costs. Two of these types of costs are likely to be controversial. First, in return for their support, sponsors may insist on changing the sporting event. Often, changes may be implemented to make the sporting event more exciting, entertaining, and attractive to television, or to better fit the media's programming format so that the sponsor's audience is expanded. Tennis is an example of this type of influence. The method of scoring was changed by the introduction of sudden death tie-breakers to shorten the length of matches, and the traditional all-white apparel was replaced by multicolored outfits.

A second type of cost that may be controversial in the context of amateur sport organizations and colleges/high schools is a perception by existing clienteles that the ancillary commercial needs of a sponsor have become more important than the intrinsic merit of the sporting event itself. The Olympic Games is perhaps the forum in which this debate reaches its apex, but the issue is debated in many other contexts at lower levels of sport. Commercial ties to the Olympic Games date from the beginning of the century. One writer described the early Olympics as "nothing more than `sporting sideshows'" for the Universial Exhibition in Paris (1890), the Great Exhibition and Fair in St. Louis (1904), and the Anglo-French Exhibition in London (1908). The Exhibitions promoted the products of industrial capital and provided venues for the seduction of new custom" (Lawrence 1986, p. 205). However, such commercial linkages were subtle--far removed from the ostentatious sponsorship links that emerged in the Los Angeles Games and that led to one writer concluding, "Who won the L.A. Olympics? It is clear from this analysis that commercialism ran away with the Gold" (Lawrence, 1986, p. 204).

In the context of college athletics, Georgia Tech's decision to solicit sponsorships for each of its seven home games brought forth the following comment (Kinder, 1989):

> After selling games, what's next? How long before we hear Georgia Tech's stadium announcer say, "Wake Forest's Bell South extra-point try was blocked by Tech's Coca-Cola linebacker Wood Woodson, and now the Georgia-Pacific scoreboard shows Wake Forest with 20 Marriott points to Georgia Tech's 17 Domino's Pizza points"? (p. 96)

In an attempt to ameliorate the impact of this type of backlash many sports organizations, including the NCAA, NFL, and NBA, have imposed rules limiting the size of corporate logos that can be displayed on team uniforms (Stotlar, 1989). Established in 1983, the NCAA's Rule 43 limits the size and number of manufacturers' logos on team uniforms and equipment to "a single manufacturer's logo not to exceed 1 1/2 inches square."

BENEFITS SOUGHT FROM SPONSORSHIPS BY BUSINESS ORGANIZATIONS

Companies seek to communicate with groups other than their customers. Other groups that may be affected by sponsorship decisions include employees, shareholders, and financial institutions. For example, a particular sponsorship may create a sense of pride and unity among employees. Thus, it was reported in a study of sponsor decision makers, "Many respondents mentioned that they sponsor sport to assist staff recruitment. A company having wide exposure in the media can get the reputation of being a dynamic firm which people would like to join" (Abratt & Grable, 1989, p. 353). However, in this section the discussion is focussed primarily on how businesses use sponsorship to communicate with customer publics, because this is likely to be the predominant concern when sponsorship decisions are made.

A large number of relatively narrowly focussed benefits may be sought by businesses from sponsorship, but they can be classified into four broad categories: increased awareness, enhanced image, product trial or sales opportunities, and hospitality opportunities. It is assumed in this discussion that businesses are seeking product benefits from their sponsorship. The profusion of multiple product companies led many corporations to recognize a need to raise their profile with financial institutions, shareholders, and other key publics. This has led some businesses to seek to communicate messages through sponsorship about the corporation as well as its products. Hence, the benefits listed in the following exhibit may be applied to corporate entities as well as their products.

BENEFITS THAT MAY BE SOUGHT BY BUSINESSES FROM SPONSORSHIP

1. INCREASED AWARENESS:
   a) Create awareness of a new product.
   b) Increase awareness of an existing product in new target markets.
   c) Bypass legal prohibition on television advertising imposed upon tobacco and liquor products.

2. IMAGE ENHANCEMENT:
   a) Create an image for a new product.
   b) Reinforce the image of an existing product.
   c) Change public perceptions of an existing product.
   d) Counter negative or adverse publicity.
   e) Build pride among employees and distributors for the product.
   f) Assist employee recruitment.

3. PRODUCT TRIAL OR SALES OPPORTUNITIES:
   a) Offer product trial to potential new customers.
   b) Induce incremental sales increases through promotional giveaways, couponing tie-ins, sweepstakes, and point-of-purchase displays.

c) **Create on-site sales opportunities.**
d) **Promote a different use of an existing product.**
e) **Reinforce the image of an existing product.**
4. **HOSPITALITY OPPORTUNITIES:**
a) **Develop bonding with key customers, distributors and employees.**
b) **Develop in-house incentive opportunities.**

There is some evidence suggesting that companies evolve through a progression of the benefits shown above. Armstrong (1988) conducted in-depth interviews with representatives of 17 international electronics companies that had major investments in sports sponsorship. He reported that initially sponsorship was primarily viewed as an alternative to advertising and as a way of getting media exposure. However, over time the emphasis shifted to image and public relations benefits. If these interviews were conducted today, it is reasonable to hypothesize that those companies would have progressed further through the benefit sequence. In 1992, the sponsorship director of a major event (Cherpit, 1992) commented, "Companies want a greater return for their dollar and quick impact. Corporate image building and visibility are at the bottom of the priority list" (p.5). Similarly, the Director of Corporate Sponsorship and Events at the Eastman Kodak Company stated (Diggelmann, 1992):

As a sponsor, I look to the promoter to come to us with ideas on how the property can, in our case, sell film. Like most other companies today, we are no longer satisfied with enhanced image; give us opportunities for on-site sales, well-developed hospitality packages, dealer tie-ins, etc., and we'll listen. (p. 5)

Three of the four benefit categories constitute longer term strategic components of sponsorship that contribute to a company's overall strategy for encouraging potential customers to purchase. In contrast, the creation of product trial or sales opportunities is a short-term tactical action designed to culminate in immediate product trials or purchases. There is some parallel with the roles of the other marketing communications vehicles, because advertising, publicity, and to a lesser extent, incentives, could be viewed as strategic mechanisms, whereas only personal selling is likely to result in immediate sales.

A sponsorship is likely to have the potential to yield multiple benefits involving all, or some combination of, the four categories. For example, sponsorship of a single sports event may lead to increased awareness of the sponsor's product; stronger bonding by extending hospitality to existing key clients, potential clients, distributors, and decision makers; the use of hospitality privileges to create staff and dealer incentives; and induced product trial by potential new customers. A corporate sponsor is likely to devise as many benefit opportunities as possible from a sponsorship in order to optimize return on the investment.

THE RELATIONSHIP BETWEEN SPONSORSHIP BENEFITS AND THE CONSUMER'S PURCHASE DECISION PROCESS

A variety of decision-making paradigms that model the stages through which potential consumers pass before purchasing a product have been proposed. A review of their similarities, differences and relative merits is provided by Reid and Crompton (1993). The most widely accepted of these models is the AIDA concept (Lamb, Hair & McDaniel, 1992). The acronym stands for Awareness-Interest-Desire-Action. In the model of the product adoption process shown in Figure 9-4, an additional stage, Reinforcement, has been added to the end of the AIDA sequence. It has been noted that

> What the company does to nurture the relationship with the customer, to build it, to strengthen it, is crucial to the company's marketing effectiveness and efficiency. To work hard to attract new customers and then to be complacent in strengthening the relationship makes little sense (Berry & Parasuraman, 1991, p. 132).

Hence, customer retention as well as attraction of new customers is likely to be a primary objective of some businesses sponsoring sport. This involves reinforcing, reassuring, and confirming to customers that they made a wise decision in purchasing the company's product.

The product adoption model shown on the left side of Figure 9-4 suggests that potential purchasers of a product pass through a process that consists of five stages from initial awareness to committed loyalty. These stages are defined as follows:

Awareness: An individual becomes aware of the existence of a particular product and acquires some limited knowledge of its attributes.

Interest: More detailed knowledge of the product's benefits is acquired. Interest in it and a preference for it develop as a favorable attitude emerges. A distinctive image of it evolves.

Desire: An appraisal of the product's merits is made through a mental or actual trial. If it is perceived to meet an individual's needs better than alternative offerings, then there is a desire or intent to purchase.

Decision Action: This is the culmination of all that has gone before and the product is purchased or rejected.

Reinforcement: This reassures and confirms to purchasers that a wise decision was made and consolidates loyalty to the product.

The product adoption model emphasizes that a purchase decision is usually the culmination of a process that starts long before an actual purchase takes place and continues long after an initial purchase is made. A company's challenge is to design sponsorship benefits that will move potential customers from their present stage in the adoption process on to the next stage toward committed loyalty. Figure 9-4 illustrates how the four main benefit categories available to businesses from sponsorship may be

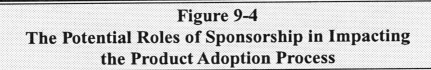

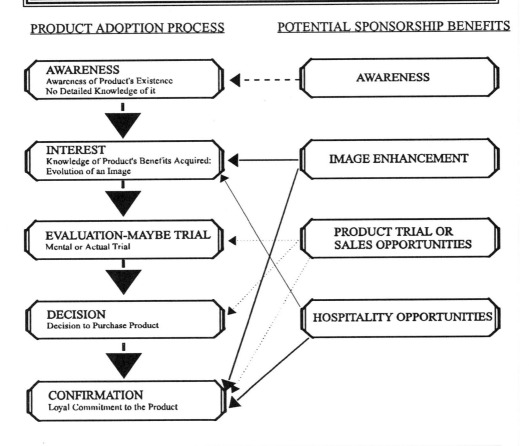

Figure 9-4
The Potential Roles of Sponsorship in Impacting
the Product Adoption Process

used to facilitate the product adoption process. The broken, dotted, and continuous lines in Figure 9-4 indicate the stage in the adoption process at which each of the sponsorship benefits may be targeted. For example, the two solid lines emanating from hospitality opportunities indicate that this benefit may be targeted at two groups: to reinforce and consolidate links with existing customers and suppliers; and/or to nurture interest in the company and its products from those individuals who have been identified as strong, future prospects. In the following subsections, the potential role in facilitating the product adoption process of each of the four categories of sponsorship benefits is described and illustrated.

Increased Awareness. Sponsors who seek awareness benefits are trying to move potential consumers on to the first stage of the adoption process (Figure 9-4). Thus, if a sponsor is a well-known company whose products already have high levels of awareness, then this benefit will not be sought, because sponsorship could only marginally increase awareness. For this reason, most major sponsors who have a high profile with their target markets tend to use sponsorship to effect other stages of the product adoption process   (Figure 9-4). However, in cases where the awareness level is low, sponsorship can have an impact in expanding the number of potential consumers, which then provides a broader base at which to target communication strategies aimed at more advanced stages of the adoption process.

- Fortis Inc. of New York developed a medical insurance plan for the U.S. Olympic Committee to cover its elite core of athletes. This was useful to the company "because of the awareness that could be generated among our agents and group brokers, giving them the ability to promote the fact that Fortis is protecting Olympic-caliber athletes... When an agent or broker calls on a client carrying the same program that USOC has it has an impact. It energized our brokers and helped get a new group insurance product off the ground. (Schlossberg, 1992)

The Cornhill Insurance case, which is described in detail in chapter 12, offers a good example of a product with low visibility using sponsorship effectively to create awareness.

Image enhancement. Image is the sum of beliefs, ideas, and impressions that a person has of a business or its products (Kotler & Andreasen, 1991). It may formally be defined as the mental construct developed by an individual on the basis of a few selected impressions. Images are ordered wholes built from scraps of information, much of which may be inferred rather than directly observed or experienced, and these inferences may have only a tenuous and indirect relationship to fact.

Image benefits are most frequently sought by companies that are striving to create interest and a favorable attitude towards their products by "borrowing" the image of a sport and using it to enhance the product's image with its target audience (Figure 9-4). This is likely to be particularly effective when a relatively new product or one with low awareness is involved. Because few or no competing impressions of the product currently exist, the company hopes that by associating with a sport, the sport's image attributes will be associated with its product. Sports do have distinctive images: For example: cricket is English, baseball is American; polo is upper class, basketball has mass appeal; tennis is clean and safe; motor racing is dirty and dangerous (Meenaghan, 1983). Consider the image enhancement products gained from the following linkages with sports:

- In England, Gillette, a U.S. company, was in competition with Wilkinson, a British company that makes razor blades. Through its involvement with cricket, a traditional English sport, Gillette effectively erased its American image in the U.K. market (Meenaghan, 1983).
- Subaru's sponsorship of the U.S. ski team was intended to emphasize the snow- and ice-handling capabilities of its four-wheel drive compact car (Brooks, 1990).

- Timberland sponsored the Alaskan Iditarod. As manufacturers of rugged outdoor footwear, the choice of a sled race across harsh Alaskan conditions offered a strong association between brand image and the sports event (International Advertising Association, 1988).
- The banning of tobacco advertising on television in the United States and in many other countries caused tobacco companies to invest more heavily in sponsorship as an alternative means of gaining media exposure. Marlboro cigarettes elected to sponsor Formula 1 auto racing. The key factors in this decision were   (a) the glamorous image associated with the sport in terms of the color, personality, impact and excitement associated with the Grand Prix circuit; (b) its "winning identity" showing Marlboro as being "ahead of all the others"; and (c) its provision of an internationally glamorous, yet masculine platform for the brand on which to sell the product in its many markets world wide (International Advertising Association, 1988).
- K-Mart Corporation became involved with professional golf to upgrade the department store chain's stodgy, blue-collar image. Golf is an upscale sport and K-Mart felt the link would help reposition the stores to appeal to a higher economic sector of the population (Brooks, 1990).
- Olympic athletes' indulging in Evian Waters at the Albertville and Barcelona Olympic Games were intended to reinforce the product's fitness life-style positioning with existing and potential customers (Schlossberg, 1992).

The initial description of image in this section noted that it may be only tenuously related to fact. A prime example of this is the remarkable adeptness of the cigarette companies at creating positive images for their products often through sports, even though when used as intended tobacco products will harm the user. This issue is considered in the next chapter.

Image is not static. It is amended by information received from the environment. However, it is unlikely to change easily. Once people develop a set of beliefs and impressions about a product, it is difficult to change them. (Consider the probable success of the K-Mart strategy of associating with golf in the above example, in the light of these comments!) This relative permanence exists because once people have a certain image of a product, they tend to be selective perceivers of further data. Their perceptions are oriented toward seeing what they expect to see. Hence, it is likely to be difficult for sponsorship to be effective in changing image. Thus, in addition to impacting the interest stage of the adoption process by borrowing a sport's image, many companies use image enhancement to reinforce existing product image, give existing purchasers good feelings about purchasing it, and encourage their loyalty towards it (Figure 9-4) Cadillac, for example, has an established image and the company's sponsorship objective is "to reinforce and enhance Cadillac's image among the general public--to use our name as a metaphor for excellence: 'The Cadillac of its class'" (Perelli & Levin, 1988, p. 4).

Product Trial or Sales Opportunities. Product trial or sales opportunities may be used to impact the desire, purchase action or reinforcement stages of the adoption process (Figure 9-4). Product trial opportunities are particularly valuable because moving people from interest in a product to the desire stage, which involves seriously evaluating the merits of the product to determine whether a purchase should be made, is a difficult communications task (Figure 9-4). There are likely to be many products in which individuals may have an interest and toward which they are favorably disposed but that they have never tried, especially products for which the cost of trial is high in terms of money, time, potential embarrassment, or whatever. Sponsorship offers a vehicle for encouraging trial, which frequently is the most effective method by which potential customers can assess a product's merits:

- The makers of Ultra Fuel high-carbohydrate energy drink and Hydra Fuel fluid-replacement drink sponsored 75 multisport and 6 cycling events, soon after the drinks were launched. A spokesman observed, "We're not like Gatorade, with a big ad budget that allows us to go after everybody. Our objective is to get our drinks into the hands of premier athletes and the people who follow the sports in which they compete. Brand identity for the two drinks is not there right now. Fewer than 10 percent of triathletes and biathletes have tried the products. Our goal is to sample 50,000 people this year." At each event, the drinks are poured at all aid stations on the course, at a booth at the finish line, and the company receives signage and the right to display an inflatable balloon (International Events Group, 1992a, p. 6).

- Converse launched a new tennis shoe, the Converse Classic, by sponsoring the Converse Classic Tennis Tournaments, which comprised the largest U.S. Tennis Association sanctioned series for local players. The series involved 3,500 players from 37 U.S. cities. The players represented the top level of tennis at the "grass roots" level. All of them received a free pair of Classic shoes. Thus, the tournaments provided Converse with product-trial opportunities for a new product with a targeted group of opinion leaders across the country. An executive commented, "We decided to take the shoe to the consumer who is the toughest critic —the local player. We wanted to put shoes on the feet of players to see if we could create an implied endorsement from the enormous player pool. What these players wear is very important to their peers at the club level" (Moritz, 1980).

- BMW's main sponsorship goal was to increase the number of prospective buyers visiting their dealerships to evaluate the merits of BMW automobiles. They wanted to reach women who were successful in the business world, and they determined that triathlon sponsorship was one way to do this. Thus, BMW became a cosponsor of the Danskin's Women's Triathlon Series which was comprised of seven triathlons held in different cities. Series participants received coupons that could be redeemed for the Danskin products, if they test drove a BMW. Approximately 25% of participants visited dealers (International Events Group, 1992b).

An event may be used to identify prospects for product trial. In such cases, subsequent tailored packages can be developed to induce the trial:

- Bell Cellular Inc's primary sponsorship goal is sales, so it uses its on-site presence to generate targeted leads. These are followed up with tailored pitches. For example, the entry form to win a car includes questions on earnings and other key demographics (Lavelle, 1991).
- Manufacturers Hanover Bank sponsored Corporate Challenge races in 12 U.S. cities and in Oslo and Stockholm. The runners' release form asked entrants if they owned or rented their homes and if they would consider switching banks. This enabled the bank to target prospects with tailored follow-up actions. (Bleakley, 1991).

Sometimes product trial means demonstrating the excellence of a product's technology to potential consumers rather than inducing them to test it personally. For example, for its role in sponsoring the winning yacht in an America's Cup race by contributing expertise and computing equipment, Data General Computers claimed kudos for "our" win in subsequent advertising lauding its information-networking system. Similarly, the sails were "new generational" designed to utilize the high strength characteristics of Kevlar/Myler laminates (James, 1986).

Computer companies frequently seek to use this demonstration approach by offering in-kind assistance to sports events. This often means that when viewers see a score, statistic or graphic related to a sporting activity they are watching, they also see the name of the company whose computer provided the data. Consider the investment made by Olivetti (Long, 1993):

- Olivetti has been providing a timing service to Formula One motor racing for 13 years. Olivetti says it has processed 2 million race times, more than 500,000 laps, and calculated 700,000 top speeds. The computer team comprises 15 engineers, 10 kilometers of cable, and a dozen 386 PCs, which make up the timing systems. The race and lap timer, based on a photocell at the finish line, feeds one set of PCs, while the telemetric system (whereby a small transmitter on the car sends the team confidential data on how it is running to antennae embedded in the track) supplies another. Two further systems stationed at other points on the circuit provide top speeds and intermediate times for all of the drivers. In 1992, at the Imola Grand Prix in Italy, Olivetti introduced a new system that takes timings from 15 points on the track, which provides TV companies with even more statistics to push at the viewer. All of this represents a major investment, but the payoff is Olivetti's opportunity to demonstrate its technical excellence and have it recognized by name on millions of TV screens around the world.

Earlier in the chapter, the linkage between Pennsylvania State University and Pepsi-Cola was described. A key benefit of this sponsorship to Pepsi was the exclusive rights to sell soda products at the university's campuses and sporting venues. On a smaller scale, Fratelli's ice cream company sponsors events in order to have exclusive rights to sell ice cream at them: "A quarter of a million people and the exclusive right to sell ice cream can translate into a lot of tangible benefit" (Morse, 1989, p. 4).

An example of a situation in which sponsorship was used to induce direct purchase action (Figure 9-4) was provided by G.I. Joes' sponsorship of the Portland Trail Blazers NBA team. G.I. Joes is an eleven-store general merchandise chain in Oregon (Stotlar, 1989):

- "Our biggest days are the traditional big-spending days like the day after Thanksgiving and the day after Christmas" said G.I. Joes' vice-president of marketing. We have added three big shopping days, however, that our competition don't have. They are the three days of the Portland Trail Blazers/G.I.Joes Scorecard Days. For each quarter that the Blazers outscored their opponent in this once-a-month promotion Blazer fans received a 5% discount off any regularly priced products in a G.I.Joes store. If the Blazers won all four quarters, the fans received a 20% discount (plus a bonus discount of 10% for a total of 30% off).

    Now a 30% discount is a nice discount, but in January and February newspapers are filled with "store clearance" ads featuring higher discounts. Would a 30% discount tied to a Blazer victory create a shopping madness when normal store clearance discounts received yawns? The first full 30% discount arrival in February and its impact were gauged by measuring sales on the 3 corresponding days the previous years. Sales increased 208%.

G.I. Joes Store Sales

Previous Year		30% Discount Year
Feb. 8	$ 81,500	$134,000
Feb. 9	$ 82,500	$172,000
Feb. 10	$116,000	$278,000
	$280,000	$584,000

Product trial may also be used to reinforce the favorable feelings that existing users have towards the product (Figure 9-4). When a beverage company or its distributors sponsor races, the availability of complimentary beverages at the end is intended to remind runners of the beverages' refreshing, recuperative qualities and to consolidate loyalty towards them.

Hospitality Opportunities. Hospitality opportunities may be used either to interest targeted individuals in a product or to strengthen bonds with existing customers and reinforce their commitment to the company and/or its products (Figure 9-4). "Guest hospitality refers to those opportunities whereby the company can make face-to-face contact with select publics in a prestigious social context, thereby strengthening and personalizing relationships with decision makers, trade channels and business associates" (Meenaghan, 1983, p. 37). Hospitality is a key element in many companies' relationship marketing strategy. Relationship marketing concerns attracting, developing, and retaining customer relationships. Berry and Parasuraman (1991) state that its central tenet is

the creation of "true customers"--customers who are glad they selected a firm, who perceived they are receiving value and feel valued, who are likely to buy additional services from the firm, and who are unlikely to defect to a competitor. True customers are the most profitable of all customers. They spend more money with the firm on a per-year basis and they stay with the firm for more years. They spread favorable word-of-mouth information about the firm, and they may even be willing to pay a premium price for the benefits the service offers. (p. 133)

Establishing this kind of relationship requires the building of social bonds with customers, "staying in touch with them, learning about their wants and needs, customizing the relationships based on what is learned, and continually reselling the benefits of the relationship" (Berry & Parasaraman 1991, p. 138). The objective of offering hospitality at a sports event to existing or prospective customers is not to conduct business, but rather to use a relaxed informal context outside the normal business environment to create a personal interactive chemistry that will be conducive to doing business later. The role of hospitality opportunities at the interest stage of the product adoption process (Figure 9-4) in facilitating sales was well articulated by Bentick (1986), who observed:

An invitation to discuss trade is often counter-productive because the target audience is wary that acceptance of the invitation to discuss trade will be interpreted as a commitment to actually trade. Moreover, in the case of a meeting which has as its sole objective the investigation of opportunities for trade, embarrassment is the only result where one party wishes to trade but the other does not. This contrasts with a situation where any non-professional common interest--stamp collecting, social drinking or sporting event--is either the pretext for a meeting, the real object of which is to investigate opportunities for trade, or is the main attraction where trade is discussed only incidentally. In these cases both parties can avoid loss of dignity in the event that they are unable to reach agreement about prospects for trade, and can meet again in the future to discuss other projects without rancor. (p. 176)

Hospitality can be facilitated without sponsorship, and this occurs at most major sports events through the sale of boxes, suites, and similar options. For example, at the 1993 U.S. Open Golf Tournament, 46 corporations paid a fee of $125,000 to have hospitality tents set up for their use (Mihoces, 1993). However, guests are likely to be more impressed and feel more important if they are invited to a sporting occasion for which their host is a sponsor. Hospitality linked with sponsorship is differentiating. It enables a company to differentiate itself from other companies offering hospitality by conferring on the business the added value of being seen to be part of the event. The uniqueness of the hospitality opportunity is becoming more important. One sports marketer observed:

The average trade manager now receives five invitations to NASCAR events. Five years ago, he would only get one. Obviously, he will look for the best package, the one that takes care of his kids and spouse... People want to do more than just attend an event, it has to be made special. ("Changing Role," 1990a)

Most major sports events receive large revenues from selling space for hospitality, but there is a potential downside to this: "The fight for tickets needed by the hospitality operators reduces those available to true sports fans and pushes up the black-market price. The sight of row after row of identical hospitality marquees disfigures many major sports venues" (Sleight, 1989, p. 166). Further, if hospitality opportunities are offered that are not tied to sponsorship, companies that have paid the more expensive fee to be a sponsor see their presence ambushed or diluted by hospitality buyers. All of these concerns suggest that the nature and capacity of the hospitality package are likely to form a key part of a sponsorship agreement.

It is possible that sponsorship may become sufficiently intrusive that it induces a backlash from the general public. For example, some cynics have called the Atlanta Olympic Games the Coca Cola Games. This exemplifies their belief that the primary function of the Games is now to facilitate the sale of products, rather than the prime function of the product sponsorships' being to facilitate the Games. They argue that the emphasis of primary purpose has shifted. Consider the preliminary hospitality plans for major sponsors of the Atlanta Olympics:

Each sponsor will have access to as many as 400 hotel rooms, as many as 800 tickets for the opening and closing ceremonies, as many as 1,600 tickets for daily events, and a "Plantinum VIP Hospitality Package" that includes four chauffeured sedans. Three "hospitality villages" are also scheduled to be built at three primary sporting venues so that sponsors can wine and dine guests (Ruffenach, 1992).

The magnitude of investment in hospitality is illustrated by Alcan's linkage with the British Open Golf Championship. Over a 4-year period, the company invested over £1 million in providing hospitality at this event for over ,1000 business associates whom Alcan flew over from the United States in an attempt to enhance personal relationships (Meenaghan, 1983). The following examples illustrate the potential pay-off from improved bonding with key customers:

- The lavish entertainment facilities provided for Nabisco as title sponsor of the French Open tennis tournament enabled the company successfully to court a major French grocery chain that had previously rejected its products (Lowenstein & Lancaster, 1986).
- Computerland sponsors a Corporate Sports Battle. As a result of their hospitality program associated with the event, salesmen "get in the door a lot quicker with many potential customers."
- GTE, which started sports sponsorship in 1985 with the Indianapolis 500 auto race and subsequently became involved with over 60 events, including 5 professional golf tournaments, stated that its main goal was to court customers: "We use these events to entertain key customers. At the events we throw parties specifically for our sales reps to take their accounts to ... Snagging one $150 million customer is enough to pay for an event many times over.... Our events have brought about many positive changes in major customers relationships" (Penzer, 1990, p. 52).

In addition to fostering closer links with customers, hospitality opportunities can be used to perform the same function with other important publics. For example, Mazda Motors of America invested $3 million in sponsoring the Ladies Professional Golf Association Championship at Bethesda, Maryland. The area has a high percentage of professional women who constitute a big part of Mazda's market. However, there was another important target group. By holding the event in the Washington area, Mazda was in position to entertain and lobby politicians with its pro-am event that preceded the championship (Potter, 1993).

Frequently, distributors and retailers will also be targeted and a company's benefits may be structured so these groups are involved in the sponsorship with tie-ins and guest hospitality rewards:

- GTE used its Sun Coast Classic golf tournament as an incentive to increase the number of potential customers entering its retail phone-marts. The company offered dealers who bought 50 of certain pieces, two free tickets to the event. At the same time pre-tournament advertising and in-store appearances by several golf professionals were used to help the dealers increase their sales 20% during the week-long event (Penzer, 1990).

Similarly, hospitality may be used as a reward for the performance of sales staff or for increased productivity by the work force in general. Its potential for positively impacting employee morale was expressed by a Target executive:

I learned from our sponsorship of the Los Angeles Dodgers that if you give employees T-shirts and tickets to a ball game, they'll follow you anywhere. In Minneapolis we took the same approach, enabling dozens of Target employees to enjoy free or reduced-price basketball games (Eaton, 1991).

Risks Associated with Business Sponsorship

Sponsors enter partnerships with sports organizations to secure benefits, but there are risks associated with such investments beyond a company not receiving the benefits it anticipated. In some situations, the sponsorship could worsen a company's existing image and reputation. These types of risks can be classified into three categories: risk of poor presentation of an event, risk of poor performance at an event, and risk of disreputable behavior at an event.

An example of the risk associated with poor presentation of an event was given by the public relations manager of Labatt Brewery, Canada's biggest sponsor of sports events:

The brewery sponsored an ice skating event and paid for advertisements that stated a number of well-known Canadian skaters would appear. Many of the skaters never showed. Not only was the event unsuccessful, the brewery bore the brunt of some hostile consumer reaction. In these instances the backlash was against the major corporation sponsoring the event, not the promoter that nobody ever heard about ("Brewery, " 1986, p. 7).

Risk of poor performance is inherent in sponsorships that focus on teams or individuals within a sports event, rather than the overall event itself, because a central tenet of sports is that there are winners and losers. If a product is associated with a loser, it may convey connotations of failure and inferiority to a target market:

- A race car or racehorse which continues to finish "down the field" hardly projects a winning image. Rotary watches decided to opt out of motor car sponsorship after its car failed to get off the grid, a fact which did little to promote the jet set image of its product. (Meenaghan, 1983, p. 41)

- Chrysler's attempt to link its name with the Scottish World Cup team in the 1978 Soccer World Cup in Argentina went badly wrong. Not only did the team produce poor results on the field, but the disappointment was further compounded by newspaper stories of drunkenness and drug taking (Gratton & Taylor 1985, p. 224).

The risk of tainting an existing image by associating a company with a sporting event at which there may be disruptive behavior by either participants or spectators was exemplified by the project manager of Kraft's dairy group. He stated that Kraft elected to sponsor the U.S. Ski Team because "the possibility of scandal made pro sports out of the question" (Special Events Report, 1986b). If players at an event use foul language, fight on the field, abuse officials, are caught taking drugs or whatever; or if spectators engaged in violence, which has frequently occurred among soccer crowds in Europe, then sponsorship may damage a product's image.

The Media's Key Role in Enhancing Sponsors' Benefits

One of the central issues in negotiations between a sponsor and a sports manager is likely to be the probable extent of the event's media coverage. Based on its survey of 3,148 major sponsorship opportunities, the International Events Group (1992b) reported that 56% of all events had media sponsors. Of these radio was the most common, but 38% of events had arrangements with all three major media: newspapers, radio, and television.

If a sponsor is seeking increased awareness or image-enhancement benefits, then a key to receiving them is the extent of visibility and the quality of that visibility in terms of its compatibility with the intended projected product image, which can be achieved with the target audience. It is likely that a sponsor will require a projection of the extent of media coverage before committing to an investment. In addition to extending the audience, coverage by the media has a second important dimension in that it takes the form of news, which engenders greater credibility than exposure gained through advertising. Sport is a particularly valuable sponsorship vehicle because it is especially newsworthy. One comment made after an athlete adorned with a sponsor's name appeared on the cover of *Sports Illustrated* was that you could buy the back cover but you could not buy the front cover (Stotler, 1989).

There are two types of media exposure that sport sponsors may seek. First, there may be trade-outs, whereby the media provide promotional air time or space in exchange for recognition as the "presenting sponsor." Ideally, these partnerships would be negotiated with a television station, radio station, newspaper and outdoor billboard company. The benefits associated with this title may include rights to transmit the event, event tickets, or event merchandise, which the media sponsor can give away as prizes to its audience.

Alternatively, media exposure may be of an editorial nature. Many sponsors think of the media only as conduits to a wider target audience. However, in an editorial context there is no exchange of benefits, and the media are interested in satisfying their audiences, not sponsors. Sponsor visibility may be important to the sponsor, but it is not important to the media. To achieve exposure, the sponsor and sports manager have to start from a position of satisfying the media's needs by providing interesting and informative stories.

The media are frequently reluctant to accept and acknowledge the role of sponsors at a sports event. Many newspapers and television stations believe that to credit sponsors of sporting events in editorial coverage could potentially harm their advertising revenue, because companies are spending their communications money on the sponsorship rather than on advertising. A CBS executive noted, " 'When you are in the business of selling air time, you don't want to give away air time' " (cited in Lowenstein & Lancaster, 1986, p. 33). This explains why one company received so little television news coverage in its sponsorship of a major marathon:

> In more than three hours of coverage, our logo never appeared recognizably, even though it was on runners' bibs, start and finish line banners, and signs along the route. In fact, although pre-race interviews were conducted beneath the starting banner, shots were kept tight to frame our logo out of the picture. (cited in Eaton, 1991, p. 4).

Increasingly restrictive policies by television companies toward exposure of sponsors' names were instrumental in Seiko Time Corporation's terminating several of its sponsorship commitments (Niesyn, 1988). For over a decade, the large Seiko clock in right-center field was a fixture at Yankee Stadium. The clock often was seen on television. However, the stations stopped putting their cameras on the official timer name; thus, exposure was limited only to people who attended the games. Similarly, Seiko stopped sponsoring the New York Marathon after 4 years because it received less and less exposure each year from the ABC transmission.

The reluctance of media to recognize sponsors is exemplified by the ongoing debate over incorporating a sponsor's name in the title of a sports event or facility. In recent years, there has been increased interest by sponsors in having their name attached to sports facilities. The airlines have been particularly prominent in this movement. Examples include The United Center, which replaced Chicago Stadium as home of the Bulls and the Blackhawks; the USAir Arena, in which the Washington Bullets and Capitals play and which, before U.S.Air's investment of one million dollars per year, was called the Capital Center; the Delta Center in Salt Lake City, home of the Utah Jazz; and Phoenix's America West Arena, home of the Suns. The rationale for their investment was articulated by a Delta spokesman, " 'Every time the Jazz play at the Delta Center, it is exposure for us' " (cited in O'Brien, 1993, p. 10).

However, the media may not cooperate in providing the kind of exposure that sponsors anticipated. If the sponsor's name is attached to an existing well-known event or facility, it will be particularly difficult to persuade the media to include that name in their coverage. Thus, as part of The Great Western Bank's sponsorship of the Los Angeles Lakers basketball team, the playing arena was renamed The Great Western Forum. However, the media decided they were not in the business of giving free publicity to commercial interests and continued to call it "The Forum" (Downey, 1989).

Similarly, many media left "Sunkist" off the Fiesta Bowl, "Mobil" off the Cotton Bowl, and "John Hancock" off the Sun Bowl. Sponsors responded in different ways. The John Hancock Sun Bowl became the John Hancock Bowl, and the word "Sun" was omitted from the official title. Sunkist resolved the problem with NBC who televised the Fiesta Bowl game by agreeing to purchase 25% of the advertising time available on the game's telecast. In return, the Sunkist name was used on all on-air promotions for the game and in graphics and billboards during the game (Special Events Report, 1986b). The Sunkist solution recognizes that sport is a very important dimension of most newspapers and many television stations, and because sport needs sponsors the media have to be careful to balance their approach to providing sponsors with appropriate credits (Sleight, 1989). The intricacies and mutual benefits of these types of partnerships are illustrated in the following case study which describes the evolution of relationships between the Sun Bowl in El Paso, the John Hancock Company, and the CBS television network.

ANATOMY OF A SPONSOR-MEDIA RELATIONSHIP
A CASE STUDY

The Sun Bowl in El Paso, Texas, founded in 1935, is the oldest independent college bowl in the country. It had become the culminating event in a festival that starts in October and ends in January, and includes golf tournaments, parades, and endless parties. When TV rights began to dry up in the mid-1980s, the Sun Bowl was one of the victims, as CBS cut back on paying for sports events that had only marginal value. CBS had televised the Sun Bowl for 18 years, but saw the TV rating drop considerably between 1983 and 1985 because of competition from other, better-known bowl games, and from the NFL playoffs. The Sun Bowl was not alone in facing the threat of extinction. In 1985, ABC dropped the Gator Bowl and the $800,000 rights fee that went with it.

For approximately 2,000 volunteers in El Paso who worked on the 3-month community event, the imminent death of the Sun Bowl was a matter of civic bereavement. For El Paso's municipal and business leaders who ran the Sun Bowl and its attendant festival, the sight of the big, good-hearted insurance company from the East coming to their rescue must have been reminiscent of a scene in the last reel of an old-fachioned western movie.

Beginning in 1986, Hancock paid $500,000 a year for 3 years' rights to the El Paso event, with a 2-year option to renew. In return, the company received a variety of merchandising benefits in El Paso, including free game tickets, parties, and considerable on-site exposure for the Hancock logo. More important, Hancock gained exclusive entry into the small but influential southwestern TV market in which there are no major league franchises in any sport and where the Sun Bowl is the major sports activity. While CBS agreed to continue televising the game since Hancock was now paying most of the rights fee, the use of Hancock's logo on the field became a matter of serious contention.

The contract between Hancock and the network allowed the company to paint its famous script logo on the artificial surface of the Sun Bowl. The logo extends twenty yards at midfield between the two 40-yard lines, and is in a pivotal location that makes it visible for about half the game.

There were several other important matters to be negotiated before the 3-way deal was consummated. One involved the change in the official name of the event to The John Hancock Sun Bowl. Before consenting to the name change, CBS required that Hancock purchase 25% of the commercial advertising time. In return, CBS agreed to grant Hancock exclusive advertiser status in the financial service company category. CBS also guaranteed a 10 rating and at least a minimum amount of on-air promotion for the game.

The final negotiating hurdle to cross was the actual scheduling of the game. With major bowls dominating New Year's Day, most of the other secondary post-season college games were forced to pick alternate dates. One or two chose a weekend day before Christmas and New Year's, while others felt they would benefit by playing the game during the holiday break. Stung by poor late December ratings, Sun Bowl officials and CBS agreed to televise the El Paso game on Christmas Day. But when? CBS traditionally televised an NBA game starting at noon on Christmas Day, so the network suggested that the Sun Bowl now precede the basketball game. The suggestion received a cool reception from Sun Bowl and Hancock officials who loathed the idea of a noon-time start (Eastern time), which would reach West Coast viewers at 9:00 a.m. More that that, Hancock and bowl leadership courted the church-going audience and felt uncomfortable with the idea of their football game beginning at the same time as noon Mass. Football, television, and the Lord make strange bedfellows. After serious negotiations, CBS agreed to continue starting the professional basketball game at noon, followed by the Sun Bowl. This arrangement pleased Hancock management and its ad agency because more people watch TV later in the day.

While TV advertising has been a major part of John Hancock's marketing strategy, the company has thrived on the public relations values that it has gained from carefully selecting sports events and paying for exclusivity. The staid insurance company needs no further testimony to the value of sports marketing than the comment made by one of its agents in the southwest who said, "I cannot imagine anyone in El Paso not buying a John Hancock insurance policy or related financial service after what you've done for this city."

Note: From Sports for Sale: Television Money and the Fans by David A. Klatell and Norman Marcus, 1988, New York, NY: Oxford University Press, pp. 202-204.

In the case of a new facility or event that is not well known and established, there is more likelihood that the sponsor's name will be incorporated:

- When the NBA Minnesota Timberwolves were building a new arena one block from the headquarters of Target Corporation, the company negotiated its name being attached to the arena, so it became officially known as the Target Center. Because Minneapolis already had a Met Center, the media could not drop Target from the name without confusing the two. The Target Center is named in the local media almost every day and national sports coverage means that it is periodically transmitted all over the country (Eaton, 1989).

Companies try to maximize their exposure by locating signs and logos where they anticipate they will receive most camera visibility. It has been estimated that in televised baseball games, the centerfield camera aimed at home plate captures 75% of a game's action (Levin, 1993). In 1993 the American League allowed signage behind home plate, which, potentially, could substantially increase sponsor visibility. Similarly, Ricoh sponsored marathons and tried to increase its visibility through careful signage location:

- To maximize media coverage, the company identified where television crews and professional photographers were likely to be pointing their lenses. Ricoh signage and employees wearing Ricoh jackets, T-shirts, and hats, were strategically located at those places (Gannon, 1987).

However, these kinds of "best guess" strategies for obtaining serendipitous media exposure increasingly are being replaced by carefully negotiated agreements between sports events, media and sponsors. These often specify in the contract the number of times a company is mentioned on the air and when its sign is to be shown on camera.

Some companies have extended their audience by recording sports events and using the videotapes in promotional films, sales videos, corporate documentaries, in-store promotions, video news releases and photo displays which may reach millions of additional people:

- The Kemper Group has been documenting its participation with the Professional Golf Association for more than 20 years. The company videotapes each year's tournament and keeps the event before the public long after the last hole has been played. "Rather than have that awareness be one event on a year-long schedule of happenings, we do half-hour highlights of both the Men's and Women's events," said an executive. "We can then maintain that awareness through the course of the year." In 1988, television's use of these tapes meant they reached a viewership of 32 million people ("Sponsors Stretch," 1990).

- Timberland, a company known for its rugged outdoor clothing and boots, turned the powerful images of the Iditarod--a 2-week sled dog race through the Alaskan wilderness--into a VCR. The VCR promoted the company's new boot used by the sled drivers or "mushers." "It's a very effective selling tool," noted an executive, "The visual images are very powerful. It works for us all year round. Using video footage of the Iditarod, Timberland has also produced an eight minute sales video, banquet videos, point-of-sale displays, posters, and still shot publicity photographs" ("Sponsors Stretch," 1990).

Sponsorship and Unrelated Business Income

In 1991, the Internal Revenue Service (IRS) ruled that under some circumstances sponsorship revenues received by major nonprofit sporting organizations constituted payments for advertising rather than philanthropic contributions. Such revenues, the IRS suggested, should be subject to the unrelated business income tax (UBIT), because in the IRS' view, the sponsoring companies' funds are being used for commercial purposes and are not directly related to the prime function of the nonprofit organization.

The UBIT was levied at 34%, and among the initial test cases the IRS subjected to these rulings was The Mobil Cotton Bowl. The IRS ruled that the Bowl would have to pay the 34% tax on the $1.3 million that Mobil contributed to it, because the sponsorship contract was so specific in delineating the substantial *quid pro quo* that Mobil received in return for its sponsorship investment. The total pay-out to schools playing in Bowls in the 1991 football season was $64 million (Lipman, 1991). If the new IRS UBIT regulations were implemented, a substantial proportion of this amount would go to the U.S. government and less to the participating schools unless sponsoring corporations could be persuaded to increase their sponsorship investment commensurately.

The negative impact of these proposed regulations on nonprofit sports organizations aroused vigorous opposition. As a result, the IRS substantially liberalized its stance and issued revised regulations that generally exempted income from sponsorship arrangements from UBIT. These specified that sponsorship income is not treated as advertising income (which is subject to UBIT) if nonprofit organizations avoid language comparing a sponsor's project with another, do not provide qualitative information about a product, and do not urge attendees to buy the product. The regulations define advertising as the promotion of the sponsor's company, service, facility or products. In contrast, acknowledgments, which are not subject to UBIT, are simply the recognition of sponsorship payment. Acceptable acknowledgments include sponsor logos and slogans that do not contain comparative or qualitative descriptions of the sponsor's product, service, or facilities; sponsor locations and telephone numbers; value-neutral descriptions, including displays or visual depictions of a sponsor's project line or services; and sponsor brand or trade names and service listings.

This means that the IRS now allows common sponsor benefits to be classified as acknowledgments provided "the effect is identification of the sponsor rather than promotion of the sponsor's project." This includes product sampling and display, category exclusivity, title, pro-am spots, special previews, tickets, signage, and sponsor logo in advertisements. Even sponsorship arrangements "contingent upon the game being broadcast on television and radio" and contracts that stipulate that "television cameras will focus on the corporation's name and logo" are considered acknowledgment (International Events Group, 1993a). UBIT would apply when a nonprofit organization offers "a call to action; an endorsement; or an inducement to buy" or when sponsorship fees are contingent upon "the number of people attending the event or the television ratings."

SUMMARY

The distinctive features that differentiate sponsorship from philanthropy are that the former is a business relationship, and it is seen by companies as a means by which they can secure a commercial advantage. Sponsorship has grown exponentially in the past decade, so that by 1992 it was estimated that 4,500 companies spent $3.3 billion on event sponsorship. It now extends far beyond professional sports and the Olympic Games to embrace collegiate and high school sporting activities.

Sponsorship growth has been stimulated by nine major factors: (a) the advertising clutter resulting from a proliferation of television channels caused companies to seek an alternative communication medium; (b) the cost of television advertising escalated, while the audience fragmented and widespread use of the zapper emerged; (c) the increased number of channels created a need for more programming, and sport is relatively inexpensive to produce; (d) tobacco and liquor companies were banned from television advertising; (e) commercialization of sport has been increasingly accepted by organizing bodies; (f) sponsorships associated with the 1984 Los Angeles Olympic Games enjoyed high-profile success; (g) market segmentation has emerged as a guiding marketing principle; (h) the need to enhance relations with distributors developed because fewer but larger companies exercise increasingly more control in distribution channels; and (i) the increasing tendency of public agencies to charge for additional costs they incur as a result of an event increases the sport organization's costs of staging it.

Sponsorship offers a fifth communication vehicle that complements personal selling, advertising, publicity, and incentives, rather than supplanting any of them. It has two special strengths. First, it contributes to establishing a position in consumers' minds that differentiates one product from another, through its role in image enhancement. Second, it facilitates opportunities for a company to establish a more intimate relationship with its target audience than is feasible with the other communication vehicles.

Three types of sponsorship benefits may be solicited by sport managers: financial, media, and in-kind. The in-kind benefits may be in the form of product support, personnel support, communication resources and expertise, or the "institutional clout" associated with a sponsor's reputation. Sponsorship investment by companies may require a sports organization to accept some costs. Two are likely to be controversial. First, in return for their support sponsors may insist on changing the sporting event. Second, existing clienteles may perceive that the ancillary commercial needs of a sponsor become more important than the intrinsic merit of the sporting event itself.

A large number of relatively narrowly focussed benefits may be sought by businesses from sponsorship, but those directed at their customers can be classified into four broad categories: increased awareness, enhanced image, product trial or sales opportunities, and hospitality opportunities. These benefits are linked to the five stages of the customers' product adoption process: awareness, interest, evaluation, decision, and confirmation. A company's challenge is to design sponsorship benefits that will move customers from their present stage in the adoption process on to the next stage toward committed loyalty.

If products already have high levels of awareness, as most major sponsors' products do, then this benefit will not be sought because sponsorship could only marginally increase awareness. Image enhancement is more commonly sought. Sponsorship is unlikely to be effective in changing image because once people develop a set of beliefs and impressions about a product, it is difficult to change them. Thus, emphasis tends to be on reinforcing existing product image and giving existing purchasers good feelings about purchasing the product.

Sponsorship offers a vehicle for product trial. This is particularly valuable because until individuals try a product they are unlikely to purchase it, especially if it is a relatively expensive product. Sometimes product trial means demonstrating the excellence of a product's technology, rather than inducing potential customers to test it personally. An increase in sales may be the benefit sought by sponsors who sell product at the sporting event.

A sponsor's objective in creating hospitality opportunities is not likely to be to conduct business; rather, the intent is likely to be to use a relaxed informal atmosphere to create a personal interactive chemistry that will be conducive to doing business later. Hospitality can be used to foster closer links not only with customers but also with other important publics, such as distributors and retailers.

Companies seek benefits from their sponsorship, but they also incur some risks which could worsen their existing image and reputation. These are risk of poor presentation of an event, risk of poor performance by the sponsored organization, and risk of disreputable behavior by those attending or participating.

It is likely that a sponsor will require a projection of media coverage, which will extend the benefits sought beyond those in attendance at an event. In addition to extending the audience, coverage by the media has a second important dimension in that it takes the form of news, which engenders greater credibility than exposure gained through advertising. Media exposure may be obtained either through trade-outs or through editorial coverage. Media are reluctant to acknowledge the role of sponsors in editorial coverage, because companies are spending their communications money on sponsoring the event rather than on advertising their products in the media. This reluctance has led to the emergence of carefully negotiated agreements between sports events, media, and sponsors, which specify in a contract the number of times a company is mentioned on the air and when its sign is to be shown on camera. This type of contract has to be designed carefully if a nonprofit organization, such as a college or university, is involved, to ensure it does not contravene regulations that would require the organization to pay the unrelated business income tax. Audience extension may also be obtained by companies' using video tapes and photo displays of the sports event in their places of business.

Questions for Study and Discussion

1. What are some of the potential risks or costs incurred by sport organizations when entering into sponsorship agreements?
2. Explain how a sport organization can design a sponsorship program that will move potential customers from product adoption toward committed loyalty.
3. In cases where potential customer awareness of a sponsor's product is low, how would you design a sponsorship to expand product visibility?
4. Provide examples of situations where sport sponsorships can be used to induce direct purchase decisions.
5. Under current IRS rules what specific requirements must be met by nonprofit sports organizations to avoid paying unrelated business income taxes (UBIT) on sponsorship services?

REFERENCES

Abratt, R. & Grobler, P. S. (1989). The evolution of sports sponsorships *International Journal of Advertising, 8*, 351-362.

Armstrong, C. (1988, May) Sports sponsorship: A case-study approach to measuring its effectiveness. *European Research*, pp. 97-102.

Bentick, B. L. (1986). The role of the Grand Prix in promoting South Australian entrepreneurship; exports and the terms of trade. In J.P.A. Burns, J. H. Hatch and T.J. Mules (Eds.), *The Adelaide Grand Prix: The impact of a special event* (pp. 169-185). Adelaide: The Centre for South Australian Economic Studies.

Berry, L. L. & Parasuraman, A. (1991). *Marketing services: Competing through quality.* New York: The Free Press.

Bleakley, F. (1991, May 24). For Manny Hanny sponsoring races is good business. *Wall Street Journal*, p. A7B.

Brewery forms event production. (1986, June 2). *Special Events Report*, p. 7.

Brooks, C. (1990, October). Sponsorship: Strictly business *Athletic Business*, pp. 59-62.

Centerfold: Evaluating sponsorships. (1986, December 15). *Special Events Report*, p. 5.

The changing role of hospitality sponsorship. (1990, July 30). *Special Events Report*, pp. 4-5.

Cherpit, S. (1992, December 21). The bottom line on sponsorship. *Sponsorship* , pp. 4-5.

Cicora, K. (1991, December). Sponsoring special events. *Parks and Recreation*, pp. 27-29 and 74.

Cohen, A. (1993, April). Our unrelenting thirst for baseball. *Athletic Business*, p. 16.

Copeland, R. P. (1991). *Sport sponsorship in Canada: A study of exchange between corporate sponsors and sport groups.* MA thesis, University of Waterloo, Waterloo, Ontario, Canada.

Cunningham, P., Taylor, S. & Reeder, C. (1992). *Event marketing: The evolution of sponsorship from philantropy to strategic promotion.* Unpublished paper, School of Business, Queen's University, Kingston, Ontario, Canada.

Diggelmann, R. (1992, December 21). The bottom line on sponsorhip. *Sponsorship Report*, pp. 4-5.

Downey, M. (1989 June 21). Event names no longer are givens. *Los Angeles Times*, p.III1.

Eaton, R. (1991, September 9). Inside Target Stores' Sponsorship philosophy *Special Events Report*, pp. 4-5.

Gannon, J. (1987, February 16). Why Ricoh prefers cosponsorship. *Special Events Report*, p. 1.

Gratton, C. & Taylor, P. (1985). *Sport and recreation: An economic analysis.* London: F.N. Spon.

Gross, A. B., Traylor, M. B., & Shuman, P. J. (1987). *Corporate sponsorship of art and sports events in North America.* Paper presented at the ESOMAR Congress., The Hague, Holland.

Head, V. (1981). *Sponsorship: The newest marketing skill.* Maidenhead, Berkshire, England: Woodhead-Faulkner.

Hiestand, M. (1993, June 16). Sponsorship:The name of the game. *USA Today*, pp. 1c-2c.

International Advertising Association. (1992a, September). *Sponsorship: Its role and effects.* New York: The Global Media Commission of the International Advertising Association.

International Events Group. (1992a, August 24). Twin Laboratories pumps up sponsorship for sports drinks, *Sponsorship Report*, p. 6.

International Events Group. (1992b, November 6). Quantifying sponsorship: The state of more than 3000 properties, *Sponsorship Report*, pp. 4-5.

International Events Group. (1993a, January 25). Assertions, *Sponsorship Report*, p. 2.

International Events Group. (1993b, March 8). Reebok drops out of high school, *Sponsorship Report*, p. 3,6.

International Events Group. (1994, May 18). Assertions, *Sponsorship Report*, p. 2.

Irwin, D. (1993, May). In search of sponsors, *Athletic Management*, pp. 11-16.

James, P. (1986). The ideology of winning. In G. Lawrence and D. Rowe (Eds.), *Essays in the sociology of Australian sport* (pp. 138-149). Sydney, Australia: Hale and Iremonger.

Johnson, W. O. (1993, February 22). The clock is ticking, *Sports Illustrated*, pp. 164-172.

Kaufman, I. (1988, November 7). And now, even the NFL. *Sports Inc.*, pp. 42-43.

Kinder, D. (1989, May 15). Pass the gravy, please. *Sports Illustrated* p. 96.

Kotler, P. & Andreasen, A. (1991). *Strategic marketing for non-profit organizations,*

(4th ed). Englewood Cliffs, New Jersey:Prentice Hall.

Lamb, C. W., Hair, J. F. & McDaniel, C. (1992). *Principles of marketing.* Cincinnati, OH: South-Western.

Lavelle, B. (1991, July 11). How Bell Cellular boosted its return from events. *Special Events Report*, pp. 4-5.

Lawrence, G. (1986). In the race for profit: Commercialism and the Los Angeles Olympics. In G. Lawrence and D. Rowe (Eds.), *Essays in the sociology of Australian sport*, (pp. 204-214). Sydney, Australia: Hale and Iremonger.

Levin, G. (1993, April). Baseball's opening pitch: Winning over new fans. *Advertising Age*, p. 1.

Lipman, J. (1991, December 5). IRS ruling threatens firms' sponsorships. *Wall Street Journal*, p. 8.

Long, C. (1993, September 19). Sporting link wins marketing results. *The Sunday Times*, p. S13.

Lowenstein R. & Lancaster, H. (1986, June 25). Nation's businesses are scrambling to sponsor the nation's pastimes. *Wall Street Journal*, p. 33.

Maxie, D. (1989, April 19). Sports at Tech going commercial. *Atlanta Journal*, p. B1.

McCabe, L. J. (1989). Intergrating sponsorship into the advertising and marketing mix. *Special Events Report* 8(7) April 17: 4-5.

McCarthy, M. J. (1991). Keeping careful score on sports tie-ins. *Wall Street Journal*, April 24, Section B, p 1, col. 3.

Meenaghan, J. A. (1983). Commerical sponsorship. *European Journal of Marketing*, *17*(7), pp. 5-73.

Mihoces, G. (1993, June 16). Tents are center for corporate hobnobbing. *USA Today*, p. 9c.

Moritz, J. (1980, November). Sports marketing: Grass roots action. *Marketing Communications*, pp. 19-21.

Morse, J. (1989, July 24). Sponsorship from a small businesses perspective...or why a regional ice cream company has high event content. *Special Events Report*, pp. 4-5.

Niesyn, B. (1988, April 25). Why a sponsor drops out. *Sports, Inc.*, pp. 34-35.

O'Brien, R. (1993, July 26). Scorecard: Air Ball. *Sports Illustrated*, pp. 10-11.

Penzer, E. (1990, May). And now a word from our sponsor. *Incentive*, pp. 49-56.

Perelli, S. & Levin, P. (1988, November 21). Getting results from sponsorships. *Special Events Report*, pp. 4-5.

Potter, J. (1993, June 16). Automakers target buyers with golf. *USA Today*, p. 9c.

Reid, I. S., & Crompton, J. L. (1993). A taxonomy of leisure purchase decision paradigms based on level of involvement. *Journal of Leisure Research, 25*(2), pp. 182-202.

Reinert, B. (1989, September). Business plays key role in high school sports. *Boston Globe*, p. NH20.

Ruffenach, G. (1992, June 4). Olympic backers will pay Atlanta plenty for exclusivity and ambush protection. *Wall Street Journal*, p. 1.

Schlossberg, H. (1992, May 11). Olympic sponsorship a big deal, despite budget size. *Marketing News,* p. 14.

Sleight, S. (1989). *Sponsorship: What it is and how to* use it. Maidenhead, Berkshire, England:McGraw Hill.

Spectrum: California Agreements. *Athletic Business.* (1989, May). pp. 8,10.

Sponsors stretch the impact of special events with video. *Public Relations Journal* (1990, May), pp. 12-13.

Stotlar, D. (1989). *Successful sport marketing and sponsorship plans.* Dubuque, IA: Wm. C. Brown.

Target sponsors Wolves' den. (1990, August 27). *Special Events Report,* p. 3.

The changing role of hospitality in sponsorship. (1990, July 30). *Special Events Report,* pp. 4-5.

Wilson, N. (1988). *The sports business.* London:Piatkus.

SPONSORSHIP OF SPORT BY TOBACCO AND ALCOHOL COMPANIES

Learning Objectives

After completing this chapter, the reader should be able to:

1. **discuss the extent to which tobacco and alcohol companies are major investors in sport sponsorship and those factors which have sustained their continued investment in sport.**
2. **identify and discuss three central issues in the controversy over tobacco industry sponsorship of sporting events.**
3. **understand the ethical dilemma sport managers face in determining whether or not to solicit or accept sponsorship from alcohol beverage companies.**

CHAPTER 10

SPONSORSHIP OF SPORT BY TOBACCO AND ALCOHOL COMPANIES

The major sponsors of sport are alcohol and tobacco companies. This chapter reviews the issues associated with these relationships. To many people it appears incongruous that sport, which exemplifies a healthy, fit lifestyle, should be used as a promotional vehicle for products that appear to be the antithesis of this. In short, these linkages which are consummated for financial purposes, seem to defeat the broader *raison d'être* for sport. Although this conceptual anomaly is widely recognized, the incongruence of these linkages has aroused surprisingly little public controversy. They appear to have become such an ingrained ubiquitous part of the sports world that most people are indifferent to them. There are two major reasons for this.

First, many managers believe their sports would be less financially viable without sponsorship from beer and tobacco companies. These companies are inundated with requests for sponsorship funds. For example, an official in the event division of RJR Nabisco stated that he received approximately 20 requests a week for RJR Nabisco to sponsor sports events (Wichmann & Martin, 1991). The financial viability argument is exemplified by the Virginia Slims sponsorship that brought women's professional tennis to the forefront and is discussed later in this chapter.

If sponsorship by these companies was withdrawn, what would be the result? Sports managers frequently conclude that loss of those revenues would mean either that events would be eliminated or that ticket prices would be commensurately increased. The former outcome is likely to occur in some contexts, but an economist is likely to argue that the latter outcome is improbable. Both of these outcomes assume that costs would remain fixed if sponsorship revenues declined, but in many instances it is likely that efforts would be made to reduce costs. It is naive to believe that ticket prices would be increased. Most sports managers are charged with setting ticket prices at a level that will garner maximum revenues for their organization; consequently, the current price of tickets is likely to be the highest price the market will bear. If patrons could pay more, then sports organizations would charge more now. Thus, ticket prices could not be increased if sponsorship were withdrawn. The only way to retain viability or profit margin would be to reduce costs, which would involve reducing players' salaries, prize money, administrative overhead, etc.

In the case of those organizations whose events are dependent upon tobacco or alcohol sponsorship for survival, their support for a disassociation of sport from these products is likely to be dependent on the availability of a replacement source of funding. In Australia, where a ban on tobacco sponsorship was instigated with effect from July 1993, compensatory funding was provided by the state governments of Victoria, South Australia, Western Australia, and the Australian Capital Territory by imposing a 5% tax on the wholesale price of tobacco. This is used to fund state health foundations, which provide funding to sports and cultural organizations that might otherwise have depended on tobacco companies for support. A similar approach was adopted by New Zealand. However, given the absence of a tradition of government financing of sports in the United States, such a proposal appears to have little possibility of passage in this country (Blum, 1991).

A second major reason why linkages with these products have not been a highly visible controversial issue is that the media, which are usually in the vanguard of creating or at least sustaining public controversies, fail to chastise, investigate, or even publicize this issue, because it is not in their vested self-interest to do so. Expenditures for cigarette advertising in the United States tripled between 1968 and 1988 to reach $3.3 billion (Blum, 1991), and the nation's print media are the major beneficiaries of this. The story of how tobacco advertisements were banned from television is salutary.

In 1967 a recent law school graduate sent a three page letter to the Federal Communications Commission arguing that because cigarette advertisements were a controversial public issue, application of the Fairness Doctrine should require networks to balance these advertisements by broadcasting antismoking messages. To most people's surprise, the Commission agreed, and the networks were required to grant antismoking groups one free message for every three or four tobacco advertisements that were aired. DeParle (1989) vividly described the result:

Anti-smoking groups took to the air with an inordinate amount of creativity. Though television viewers were still being blitzed with ads that showed happy smokers in vigorous poses, now they received other visions too: a Marlboro-like man, bursting boldly through the saloon doors, only to collapse in a fit of coughs; a wrinkled hag on a respirator, cigarette in hand, asking, "Aren't I sexy?" Though still outnumbered, these hacking, wincing images of death began to register: cigarette consumption declined in each of the next four years. The cigarette companies weren't just losing the battle; through the Fairness Doctrine they were subsidizing the other side's artillery. In 1970, they went to Congress to say they wanted out. (p. 40)

Although Congress eventually acceded to their request, legislators first had to endure a sustained, vigorous lobbying effort by the television industry, which opposed the ban on television advertising. In 1970 the broadcasting companies received $250 million in tobacco advertising revenues. The companies did win a slight concession in that the ban did not commence until midnight on January 1, 1971. This was after the bowl games in which the tobacco companies advertised heavily were over. After

Congress legislated its ban, the broadcasters went to court and claimed the ban on cigarette advertising on television was an unconstitutional infringement of free speech, a violation of the First Amendment. The courts ruled that unlike the print media, the airwaves are public property, and thus what is broadcast is subject to regulation in the public interest.

The self-interest in their own financial health, which was exhibited by the media in the television ban battle, has caused them to avoid giving high visibility to the contentious issue of sponsorship by tobacco and beer companies. No other category of magazine-- fashion, politics, general-interest, or whatever--relies more heavily on tobacco advertisements than do sports magazines. On average, tobacco provided 11.3% of their income in 1986. In 1985 and in 1988 *Sports Illustrated* received $30 million and $35 million, respectively, in revenue from tobacco advertisements (White, 1988). A senior editor at *Sports Illustrated* observed, "Based on common sense, magazines do not like to upset their advertisers by publishing stories that are negative on an advertised product" (De Parle 1989, p. 44). This statement is supported by several reports that have provided strong evidence that magazines that accept tobacco advertising are unlikely to publish antismoking articles (Whelan, 1984; Whelan et al., 1981).

The impact of this vested-interest relationship was articulated by the director of the Massachusetts Department of Public Health, who in a letter to *Sports Illustrated*, wrote:

> From 1982 to mid-1986, *Sports Illustrated* ran 15 health stories of which five were on cocaine abuse, four on sports injuries, and two each on steroid use, heart disease and physical fitness. In the 15, tobacco was mentioned in only two. . . . In the story on physical fitness and adolescent health (1/7/83) lack of exercise and poor diet were cited more than 150 times as causes of cancer or heart disease, but tobacco was mentioned only 4 times. The story incorrectly stated that coronary bypass surgery is the main reason for the recent decline in deaths from heart attacks. According to the American Heart Association, the principal reason is the sharp decline in smoking by adult males. (White, 1988, p. 138).

The director's suggestion that the magazine publish a "front page picture" of Babe Ruth along with an explanation that the great baseball player's fatal oral cancer had been caused by his tobacco chewing was not well taken by the magazine.

Many media outlets are now owned by conglomerate corporations; thus, the self-interest may extend beyond a single outlet:

> Denunciations of RJR in *The Washington Post* could mean fewer ads for Camels, Oreos, and Smirnoff in *Newsweek*, just as an attack on Virginia Slims in *The New York Times* could lead to the end of the $900,000 of tobacco ads that appeared last year in its wholly-owned *Tennis* magazine. Obviously, both the *Post* and *Times* have had unkind words for tobacco; but neither can claim to have provided the kind of unforgiving coverage that tobacco has earned with a product that *every two years* kills more Americans than have died in all the wars of this century. (De Parle, 1989, p. 46)

If a magazine attacked tobacco and alcohol sponsorship in an article, affected companies could retaliate by withdrawing their advertising from that publication and others owned by the same publishing corporation. Indeed when *Newsweek* ran a story on "the uncivil war over smoking" in June 1983, all tobacco advertisers withdrew from the magazine (Chapman, 1986). In the broadcast media, examples of interrelationships inhibiting coverage of this issue cited by De Parle (1989) included the CEO of the CBS network, who also served as chairman of the board of Loews which owned Lorillard Tobacco, makers of Kents, Newports, and Trues; and ESPN, which was 20% owned by RJR Nabisco.

THE TOBACCO SPONSORSHIP CONTROVERSY

The first example of successful sponsorship of sport by tobacco companies appears to have occurred in baseball almost a century ago, when a substantial number of Bull Durham chewing tobacco signs were placed on the outfield fences of southern baseball stadiums. Because relief pitchers warmed up nearby, the term "bullpen" was coined (Muscatine, 1991). However, in more recent times, the impetus that stimulated tobacco companies to emerge as major sponsors of sports events was the closure of television to the industry's products in 1971. This ban encouraged the companies to turn to sponsorship as a new medium through which they could promote their products. Thus, for example, in 1971 the Virginia Slims ladies' tennis circuit and Winston Cup motor-racing sponsorships were launched, whereas Philip Morris' 15-year sponsorship of the Marlboro Cup horse race was launched dramatically in 1973 with a stellar winning performance by the legendary horse Secretariat.

Although the magnitude of tobacco sponsorship remains substantially lower than the investment made by beer companies, it is extensive, amounting to an estimated $125 million in the United States in 1990. The $50-billion tobacco industry is dominated by six major multinational conglomerates. Together, these six companies account for 40% of world cigarette production and almost 85% of the tobacco leaf sold on the world market. They are Philip Morris Co., RJR Nabisco Holdings Corp., American Brands Inc., B.A.T. Industries PLC (parent of Brown and Williamson), Loews Corp. (parent of Lorillard), and Brook Group Ltd. (parent of Liggett Group). These cigarette companies had advertisements in 22 of the 24 Major League ballparks in the United States in the late 1980s, typically in places that enhance broadcast coverage (DeParle, 1989). Skoal has its pinch hitter of the year in Major League Baseball. In soccer, Camel was one of four major sponsors of the 1986 World Cup in Mexico City. As part of the sponsorship agreement, 4 seven-meter Camel signs were posted next to the field where they were visible to the 650-million television audience who viewed the final alone. RJR Nabisco has been the chief sponsor of NASCAR's $18-million, 29-race Winston Cup Series and has stated that it sponsors approximately 2,500 sports events each year (Muscatine, 1991). Other examples include the Vantage Golf Scoreboard and the Vantage Cup Senior golf tour, Salem Pro-Sail races in yachting, Lucky Strike bowling and Lucky Strike darts tournaments, the Winston Rodeo, and the nationally televised Marlboro Cup horse race.

Perhaps the most visible long-term example of using sponsorship to promote a cigarette brand has been the Philip Morris company's use of tennis tournament sponsorship to promote Virginia Slims (see following case). Throughout the 1970s and 1980s, Virginia Slims was the umbrella sponsor for the women's tennis tour. Subsequently, the cigarette company had title sponsorship at individual tournaments and compiled the primary ranking system. The high level of exposure, awareness, and strength of association Virginia Slims has achieved clearly demonstrates that sponsorship can be a very effective use of promotion funds, especially when it is sustained over a long time.

VIRGINIA SLIMS: BENEFITS AND CRITICISMS
CASE STUDY

In 1971 Philip Morris brought out its first cigarette for women, called Virginia Slims. At the same time, Joseph Cullman III, who was a lifelong tennis fan and chairman of the board of Philip Morris, was approached by his friend Gladys Heldman and asked to support the fledgling women's tennis tour. He initially contributed $2,500, but it emerged as a fortuitous opportunity to combine a historic breakthrough for women with promotion of the new women's cigarette. From these small beginnings, players on the Women's Tennis Tour now compete for more than $20 million in prize money. Martina Navratilova's career prize money earnings exceeded $14 million; Chris Evert reached almost $9 million; and Pam Shriver $4 million.

Cullman's personal and financial support for women's tennis—particularly after the women were expelled from the United States Tennis Association for forming their own tour—led to extraordinary player loyalty toward his corporation. Nearly all the top women tennis players of the past 20 years—including Billie Jean King, Chris Evert, Martina Navratilova, and Pam Shriver—have supported maintaining a relationship with Virginia Slims even when other corporations, such as Proctor & Gamble, have offered more lucrative sponsorships.

As Cullman explained it, "With growing anti-cigarette publicity, a number of players are under pressure to reduce the dependence on Virginia Slims. But then there is great loyalty because we helped make the women's tour."

Virginia Slims underwrote the women's tour for over 15 years in return for worldwide publicity, access to audiences whose demographics matched the consumers of Virginia Slims, and opportunities for retail spin-offs. However, in response to criticism, the Women's International Professional Tennis Council, which oversees the tour and sanctions tournaments opted not to renew the Virginia Slims contract when it expired in 1989. Philip Morris lobbied to retain the sponsorship by switching it to General Foods Corporation which is one of the company's nontobacco subsidiaries. General Foods signed a 5-year contract paying an annual $16 million for umbrella sponsorship of the tour beginning in 1990. Its Post Cereals brand had overall sponsorship for tournaments in North

America and its Cafe Hag brand sponsored the tour in the rest of the world. Cafe Hag is a health coffee so it was a good fit with the tour. Virginia Slims continued to play a major role in title sponsorship of individual tournaments and kept its name on the season-concluding Virginia Slims Championships.

Tennis players are the epitome of physical fitness and vitality, and to use them to legitimize smoking has led to some scathing criticism of the tennis authorities for their continued linkage with Virginia Slims. One critic used top player Hana Mandlikova, who was featured in one of the annual press guides for the circuit, to illustrate his criticisms:

> Those of us less physically gifted than Hana Mandlikova can't help but envy the strength in her legs, power in her arms, and stamina in her lungs as she pauses, racket poised, before exploding into her backhand. It's precisely the rareness of these qualities that brings us to admire her so, and to pause a moment when looking at her picture. Because as Hana Mandlikova intently awaits a return, she does so in front of a big sign that says "Virginia Slims" – a product not known for promoting the powers of heart and lung that lie at the center of her trade. In fact, throughout the guide—not to mention the nation's sports pages and television broadcasts--we find these stars showcasing their enviable talents in front of cigarette ads. The bold corporate logo of the Virginia Slims series emphasizes the bond: a woman, sassy and sleek, holds a racket in one hand and a cigarette in the other.
>
> This is odd. Tennis champions, after all, are models of health, particularly the health of heart and lungs, where endurance is essential. And cigarette smoking, as the Surgeon General recently reminded, "is the chief avoidable cause of death in our society"—death, more precisely, from heart and lung disease.

Pam Shriver has said, "Virginia Slims doesn't mean cigarettes to me. To me it is people, it's a relationship, it's tennis. You don't see anyone wearing a Virginia Slim's patch on their shirt, and we would never be asked. Philip Morris is very sensitive to us and tries to make us comfortable...I don't feel bad at all about looking somebody in the eye and saying, `Virginia Slims is our sponsor,' because they're a great sponsor. Too bad they're a cigarette."

Shriver's comments mirrored those by Billie Jean King, who was the major driving force behind the successful launching of the women's tennis circuit. In 1983 King commented, "Personally I hate cigarette smoking. I hate cigarettes. Ninety-five percent of the girls do."

Critics respond to these types of comments by saying that this private view does not excuse the prominent role of tennis players in the very successful promotion of this brand of cigarettes over the past two decades. They suggest this type of response means: Let someone else get lung cancer, it won't be me; and

I'll get rich and famous in the process. These types of responses illustrate one of the main advantages of sports sponsorship to the tobacco companies which is that it tends to build a constituency of thankful and financially dependent recipients who can be relied upon to support the industry.

Note: This case was derived from information provided by Jason DeParle, "Warning Sports Starts May be Hazardous to Your Health", Alison Muscatine, "Where There's Smoke There's Ire: Tobacco Sponsorship Sparks Debate," and Elizabeth Comte, "Women's Tennis Replaces Slims."

Central Factors in the Controversy

The controversy over permitting tobacco companies to link with sports events by sponsoring them, revolves around three central issues. First, the linkage obscures the connection between cigarettes and chewing tobacco, and disease. There is no doubt that tobacco products are physiologically damaging even when used as they are supposed to be used. In 1993, the U.S. Centers for Disease Control linked 434,000 deaths a year in the United States to smoking (Freedman & Cohen, 1993), which constitutes about one-sixth of deaths from all causes. This makes the association of tobacco products with sport objectionable to many.

In 1954, a scientist at Memorial Sloan/Kettering Cancer Center painted tobacco fats on the backs of mice and produced tumors. This was the first scientific indicator that there might be a relationship between cancer and tobacco. The general public's awareness of the dangers of tobacco products was roused in January 1964 when U.S. Surgeon General Luther Terry issued his famous report linking smoking with lung cancer (White, 1988). This report was a review and summary of evidence that had been accumulated by scientists since the beginning of the previous decade. It led to action in 1965 when the U.S. Congress required cigarette packages to carry the warning "Caution: Cigarette Smoking May Be Hazardous To Your Health." As evidence documenting the severity of these hazards accumulated, the warning requirements were extended to advertisements and their tone became unequivocal. The four current warnings were mandated by the *Comprehensive Smoking Education Act in 1984,* and they state: "SURGEON GENERAL'S WARNING: Smoking Causes Lung Cancer, Heart Disease, Emphysema, and May Complicate Pregnancy", "SURGEON GENERAL'S WARNING: Quitting Smoking Now Greatly Reduces Serious Risks to Your Health"; "SURGEON GENERAL'S WARNING: Smoking by Pregnant Women May Result in Fetal Injury, Premature Birth, and Low Birth Weight;" "SURGEON GENERAL'S WARNING: Cigarette Smoke Contains Carbon Monoxide." This Act was followed in 1986 by the *Comprehensive Smokeless Tobacco Health Education Act* which required a similar set of warnings for smokeless tobacco products: "WARNING: This product may cause mouth cancer"; "WARNING: This product may cause gum disease and tooth loss"; "WARNING: This product is not a safe alternative to cigarettes". The surgeon general has declared smoking "the single largest preventable cause of death and disability," citing "overwhelming evidence from no less than 50,000 studies" (Freedman & Cohen, 1993, p. 1). White (1988) has observed that the substantial influence of the tobacco industry has ensured "two words do not appear on cigarette packs and advertising warning labels. They are: *death* and *addiction*" (p.20).

The success of tobacco companies in using sport to obscure the substantial hazards of their products is illustrated by DeParle (1989): "Quick speak the words `Virginia Slims' and what do you see? A) Chris Evert or B) the cancer ward? If you answered A)–and most people do–then Philip Morris has you right where it wants you" (p. 36). There is a link between the word "slim" and the activity of tennis as a means of becoming slim. Tennis champions are in peak physical condition, and because endurance is important, their hearts and lungs are particularly strong and healthy. The obvious implications of the linkage are that sport and smoking are both acceptable activities, and that smoking is acceptable, not harmful, and even desirable for women.

When Louis Sullivan was Secretary of Health and Human Services in the Bush Administration he stated, "'When the tobacco industry sponsors an event in order to push their deadly product, they are trading on the health, the prestige and the image of the athlete to barter a product that will kill the user'" (cited in Cimons, 1990, p. A23). DeParle (1989) observes,

> When the pitchmen of Philip Morris say, `You've come a long way baby', they could very well be congratulating themselves; their success in co-opting the nation's health elite to promote a product that leads to an array of fatal diseases is extraordinary (p. 35).

Most importantly, these associations with sport appear to have conferred on the tobacco products an unfortunate aura of respectability.

A second central issue in the tobacco sponsorship controversy is the belief that the sport linkage enables tobacco companies to penetrate the youth market. It was pointed out by Louis Sullivan that 80% of smokers start when they are teenagers. Thus, "tobacco companies are faced with a business problem. Either they get children to start smoking or they go out of business" (Muscatine, 1991, p. 3). Because tobacco kills 434,000 people each year and other smokers die from other causes or quit, replenishing the pool of customers at a rate of almost 1,200 per day has to be a primary goal of the industry. The failure of a generation of young people to start smoking would devastate it.

The impact of sponsorship on children was demonstrated by Ledwith (1984), who surveyed 880 children in Great Britain and reported that their recognition of cigarette brands varied according to which brands had recently sponsored televised sporting events. Similarly, the sports minister in Australia was convinced to support that country's ban on tobacco sponsorship by a study which found that different brands were most popular with children between 12 and 14 in each of three Australian states surveyed. In each case, the children preferred the brand that sponsored their state's major-league football competition (Pritchard, 1992).

In the United Kingdom, where cigarette advertising has been banned on television for more than a quarter of a century, 64% of children aged between 9 and 15 claim to have seen cigarette advertising on television. "The reason is that there is an average of one hour's television coverage each day of sports directly associated with a major tobacco brand" (Raphael, 1993, p. BF 4).

Tobacco companies deny that they target children with their promotion, but a document subpoenaed by the US Federal Trade Commission suggests the denial is merely a public relations stance (Chapman 1986). It reports advice the industry received from its research agencies about the approach it should take with children:

> Thus, an attempt to reach young smokers, starters, should be based...on the following major parameters:
>
> • Present the cigarette as one of a few initiations into the adult world.
>
> • Present the cigarette as part of the illicit pleasure category of products and activities.
>
> • In your ads create a situation taken from the day-to-day life of the young smoker but in an elegant manner have this situation touch on the basic symbols of the growing-up, maturity process.
>
> • To the best of your ability (considering some legal restraints) relate the cigarette to 'pot', wine, beer, sex, etc.
>
> • DON'T communicate health or health-related points.

The popularity among adolescents and children of automobile, motorcycle, and "monster truck" racing is likely to be a factor in the tobacco companies' prolific sponsorship of motor sports. RJR Nabisco is the leading sponsor of automobile and motorcycle racing in the United States. The company has sponsored entire categories of racing, including the Winston Cup Auto Racing Circuit of 29 televised stock-car races, Winston Drag Racing, Camel G. T. Series, Camel Mud and Monster Series, and Camel Motorcross. Similarly, Philip Morris through its Marlboro brand sponsors nationally televised races: the Marlboro Grand Prix, Marlboro 500, Marlboro Challenge, and Laguna Sea Marlboro Motorcycle Grand Prix (Blum, 1991).

In addition to impacting young people through media exposure, the tobacco companies reach them through third-party related product sales and their own newsletters. Thus, some adolescents wear racing clothes adorned with the logo types of tobacco and alcohol companies that they have seen on their favored drivers. Toy makers, such as Mattel, have manufactured toy racing cars with Marlboro and Camel decals that are sold at toy and hobby shops. Other toy cars with the names of smokeless tobacco brands, such as Chattanooga Chow, Copenhagen and Skoal have been manufactured by the Ertl Company. It has also been noted:

> The newsletter of the Inside Winston Cup Racing Sports Club includes a page of racing-related puzzles and games for children entitled "Kids' Korner." The winning entry of *National Dragster* magazine's 1989 drawing contest for children 10 to 16 years of age was a sketch of a Skoal drag-racing car. At the race tracks, children sport caps, t-shirts, patches, pins and pajamas with cigarette logotypes that can be purchased or won as prizes. (Blum, 1991, p. 916)

The industry's advertising reaches children because it appears in publications with large teenage readerships. For example, one-third of the readers of *Sports Illustrated* are boys under 18 years of age (Davis, 1987). Many teenagers perceive sports and sports' players to be glamorous. They readily identify with and imitate their athletic heroes, who exemplify success, accomplishment, high status, and high income. Sullivan comments, "It is inescapable that [tobacco's sports promotion efforts] would have an influence on the behavior of young people, because they have not yet reached the age of maturity to make their own independent decisions" (cited in Wichmann & Martin 1991, p. 128).

A third central issue in the controversy over tobacco companies' sponsoring sport is the contention that such sponsorship circumvents the ban on cigarette advertising and promotion in broadcast media. Critics argue that the inclusion of brand names and logos in broadcasts of events is a blatant breach of the spirit of the legislation against cigarette advertising. Indeed sports sponsorship offers one feature not available to tobacco companies in their advertising. That is, it enables cigarette brand names to be shown or mentioned on television and radio without being accompanied by the Surgeon General's health warnings that are required on print advertisements. It is significant that a primary criterion used by sponsors to measure effectiveness of their investment is the amount of media exposure received and its equivalent value in advertising time.

Although there are few studies that attempt to assess the impact of sponsorship on tobacco consumption, Ledwith (1984) provided empirical evidence that promotional activities have effects similar to traditional advertising. He concluded:

It is contended that the case rests that sports sponsorship on BBC TV has been shown to act as cigarette advertising to children. There would thus appear to be good grounds for calling for the cessation of tobacco sports sponsorship on T.V. so as to prevent further circumvention of the law banning the TV advertising of cigarettes. (p. 88)

In March 1985, the Federal High Court of Australia recognized that sponsorship could be in violation of the advertising ban that prevailed in that country. In ruling on coverage afforded Winfield cigarettes during the 1982 Rugby League Grand Final, judges determined that advertising matter was neither indirect nor incidental to the broadcast, but was in fact deliberate. The sponsorship contracts contained an escape clause for tobacco companies if the government or any other authority restricted or banned the type of advertising exposure they sought. Hence, the judges ruled that "the sponsorship arrangement was intended as an advertising opportunity rather than an act of sporting philanthropy" (Hindson, 1990). A similar ruling in the United States in 1991 by the Federal Trade Commission is discussed later in this chapter.

Tobacco Industry Rebuttals

The tobacco industry rebuts objections to its sport sponsorship activities primarily on the grounds (a) that the industry is exercising its freedom of speech and (b) that its activities do not lead to increases in smoking. The industry argues that it would be an infringement of First Amendment rights to freedom of speech if companies were not permitted to use sponsorship to promote their products, since they are legally available for sale. However, Thomas (1990) explained that the Supreme Court makes a distinction between commercial and political speech and "there is no absolute right to advertise a product that has been shown to pose a health hazard to the public" (p. F3). Because courts have upheld the rights of legislatures to ban the advertising of legal but potentially dangerous goods and services, Action on Smoking and Health - USA (1989) suggested "There would appear to be strong legal authority to ban the advertising of tobacco products including cigarettes, the most dangerous of all consumer products" (cited in Hindson, 1990, p. 2).

The publicly articulated goal of companies' sponsorship activities is not to increase number of smokers or the intensity with which each of them smokes. A spokesman for the Tobacco Institute, a Washington, DC- based trade association, explained their intent is to "reinforce brand loyalty or try to switch brand loyalty. The latter is extremely difficult, which is why a relatively large amount of money is spent every year on advertising and promotion" (cited in Wichmann & Martin, 1991, p. 126).

Opponents express skepticism of this limited goal because fewer than 5% of smokers switch brands each year (Garrett, 1991): "The number of people who switch brands is so infinitesimally small that to suggest they spend about $3 billion a year to accomplish it insults one's intelligence." (cited in Wichmann & Martin, 1991, p. 127). However, the industry received some support from a Quebec Superior Court Justice, who in 1991 overturned Canada's *Tobacco Products Control Act* which severely limited tobacco advertising and promotion, by accepting the argument that tobacco advertising was aimed at getting smokers to switch brands, rather than getting nonsmokers to start (Wichmann & Martin, 1991, p. 127). This action was appealed, and a final decision from higher courts is awaited. Opponents of cigarette advertising and sponsorship believe these activities may perpetuate or increase cigarette consumption by recruiting new smokers, inducing former smokers to relapse, making it more difficult for smokers to quit, and increasing the level of smokers' consumption by acting as an external cue to smoke (Davis, 1987).

Finally, the industry argues that abandoning tobacco-sponsored sports activities would have no effect on smoking. As evidence, they often cite Italy, where cigarette consumption per head has increased by 30% since advertising was banned in 1962 (Garrett, 1991). However, tobacco critics point out that during this period in which cigarette sales grew by a third, their price in real terms fell by more than 50%. Many agree with the industry view suggesting that the impact, especially on youth, of promotion is negligible compared to the influence of the three P's: parents, peers and price. DeParle (1989) sarcastically derides this viewpoint. "As if peer pressure were something that filtered down through the ozone layer and had nothing to do with race cars and tennis stars" (p. 41). Cigarettes taste horrible to people who have never smoked and White (1986) noted, "It takes a certain amount of perseverance to learn to smoke, so young people have to be motivated by peer pressure which is generated, at least in part, by alluring advertising [for promotion]" (p. 118).

The Movement to Ban Tobacco Sponsorship

New Zealand's Toxic Substances Board (1989) reviewed data from 37 countries and reported that those with the greatest degree of governmental restrictions of tobacco promotion had the greatest degree of annual average fall in tobacco consumption. Findings such as these have led to worldwide momentum building against cigarette advertising and promotion. In 1981, 57 countries had legislation to control smoking; 45 of these legislative actions included controls on advertising. By mid-1986, 10 more countries had introduced legislation and 3 had imposed more stringent restrictions (Raemer, 1986). When advertising is removed as an option, the companies invest more substantially in sponsorships because sponsorships offer an alternative means of promoting their products. This has caused some countries, including Norway, Sweden, Iceland, France, Canada, and Australia, to pass legislation limiting or prohibiting tobacco company sponsorship.

In France, this legislation led to cancellation of the 1992 French Grand Prix Formula One auto race and the 1993 French Motorcycle Grand Prix, because organizers could not guarantee that cars and equipment bearing cigarette logos would not be seized by the courts. An account in the *IEG Sponsorship Report* newsletter highlights the political cynicism which underlies legislative decisions made on tobacco sponsorship:

> The powerful anti-tobacco lobby in France got a $9-million fine levied on the Williams-Renault car racing team for "allowing" the Camel logo to appear on French television screens during race broadcasts from Japan and Australia!
>
> The court applied the 1976 Veil Act, an earlier attack on tobacco sponsors. An amendment excluded Philip Morris and Gitanes, the state-owned French cigarettes, but not Camel, because the brand was not active in French motorsports at the time.
>
> While France is lobbying the European Parliament to outlaw all smoking promotion, which would run Formula 1 racing off the continent, Germany and Britain--where more than 50,000 people work in motor racing--are vigorously opposing the effort. For their part, tobacco sponsors wouldn't mind if the races were moved: the EC is considered a "mature market" while the Far East, South America and Eastern Europe are full of potential (Ukman, 1993, p. 2).

Canada's *Tobacco Products Control Act* took effect on January 1, 1989. It banned all print and broadcast advertising of tobacco products, ordered the phase-out of all existing billboard and in-store tobacco advertising, and required stronger health warnings on tobacco packaging. Sponsorship survived the Canadian ban because sports and arts organizations argued that there were few alternative sponsors available (Freeman, 1989). However, under a compromise, tobacco companies were barred from using brand names in sponsorships, but they were permitted to use corporate names. Imperial Tobacco promptly circumvented the intent of this legislation by incorporating subsidiaries named after its three major brands: du Maurier Ltd., Players Ltd., and Matinee Ltd. Thus, the du Maurier Classic golf tournament became the du Maurier

Ltd. Classic. Other companies followed their lead. The rules bar Imperial from linking these sponsorships directly to tobacco products; therefore, all signs have to be corporate rather than brand oriented. This means, for example, the companies can use the same colors as their brand logos, but not the same typeface or emblems.

In Australia, broadcast and print tobacco advertisements were banned in 1976 and 1989, respectively. The industry compensated by making higher investments in sponsorships. However, in 1990 the Australian Supreme Court ruled that telecasts of tobacco-sponsored sporting events were indeed cigarette promotions and were illegal. The government reinforced this ruling by making tobacco company sponsorship of sports and the arts illegal with effect from July 1993, although existing contracts were permitted to be honored. A loophole was inserted by legislators who were concerned about adverse economic impact of the legislation. It allowed exemptions for a small number of international events, such as the Adelaide Grand Prix, but only if organizers could prove to the government that Australia would cease to host an important event if the ban were not lifted (Pritchard, 1992).

One critic of tobacco sponsorship, inspired by the ruling of the Australian Supreme Court, has suggested that U.S. law could be similarly interpreted and that if this were done such sponsorship would end:

> The Public Health Cigarette Smoking Act of 1969, which prohibits the promotion of cigarette brands on television, calls for enforcement of the law by the Attorney General of the United States and a $10,000 fine for each violation of the law. Were the law to be applied to the telecast of the Marlboro Grand Prix, complete with the levying of a fine of $59,330,000 (based on the 5933 Marlboro logotypes televised during the 1989 race and carefully counted by one of the author's colleagues), neither media corporations nor tobacco companies could afford to continue televising tobacco-sponsored sporting events. The ruling by the Australian Supreme Court in 1990 that such sports telecasts are indeed cigarette promotions strengthens the case for enforcement of the American law. (Blum, 1991, p. 216).

In the United States, the Federal Trade Commission provided a ruling in 1991 in *Federal Trade Commission v. Pinkerton Tobacco Company*, which appears likely to limit future tobacco sponsorship. Pinkerton Tobacco was using sporting events to advertise its Red Man brand of smokeless tobacco in an attempt to bypass the 1986 television advertising ban on smokeless products. The Commission's ruling in this case prohibited the use of a brand name of a smokeless tobacco product as the name of a sponsored event if "the logo, selling message, color, or design feature of the product or its packaging" was used. Pinkerton was also denied the use of these advertising features "on signage in the area on which cameras routinely focus, on signage on competing vehicles or other equipment on which cameras routinely focus... [or] on clothing of event officials, commentators, competitors or participants." The implications of this ruling may be substantial (Stotlar, 1992):

> Television, sponsors, and event owners have become a triumvirate in sport. The event owner depends on the sponsor for an operating budget, yet the sponsor is

willing to provide the needed assets only if television coverage can be guaranteed. Television, on the other hand, is more than happy to pay a rights fee to the owner, if the sponsors will promise to purchase advertising during the event. So goes life in the house of cards. If the sponsor does not receive enough clear, in focus camera time or sponsor mentions from the coverage, it will withdraw from or not renew the sponsorship agreement. If the sponsors withdraw, the owner or organizer must so reduce the scale of advertising and appearance fees that many top performers may not select the event; as a result, attendance may dwindle. As a result, television broadcasting companies, without guaranteed advertisers, with fewer stars and a small audience, could not justify television coverage, let alone a rights fee. (p 16)

Several bills have been proposed in the U. S. Congress that would further limit tobacco company advertising and sponsorship, but none have yet been passed. Initial momentum came from the House of Delegates of the American Medical Association calling for a complete ban on cigarette promotion in December 1985 and committing the AMA to work for such a ban (White, 1988). This action had a great impact not only because the AMA is a formidable lobbying force in Washington, but also because it had never been a leader in the antismoking movement. Hindson (1990) offers a review of the banning legislation that has been proposed in the last decade.

Congressman Mike Synar introduced legislation in 1986 that proposed banning all tobacco product advertising and promotion. After two days of hearings before the Subcommittee on Health and the Environment of the Committee on Energy and Commerce, no further action was taken during the 99th Congress. At the beginning of the 100th Congress, Synar again introduced an advertising and promotion ban (H.R. 1272). Hearings were held on this and a similar proposed ban introduced by Representative Bob Whitaker (H.R. 1532) before the Subcommittee on Transportation, Tourism, and Hazardous Materials, but no further action was taken before the 100th Congress adjourned.

In the 101st Congress, Synar again introduced a bill to restrict advertising and promotion of tobacco products (H.R. 1493). Part of the preamble of this proposed Act stated that "Through advertisements during and sponsorship of sporting events, tobacco has become strongly associated with sport and has become deceptively portrayed as an integral part of sports and the healthy lifestyle associated with rigorous sporting activity" (Children's Health Protection Act of 1989, p. 4).

The Act called for the following limitation on advertising:

No tobacco product advertisements shall be located in or on a sports stadium or other sports facility or any other facility where sporting activity is regularly performed, on cars, boats, or other sporting equipment used in or associated with any sporting event (Children's Health Protection Act of 1989, pp. 6-7),

and on promotion:

It shall be unlawful to...sponsor or cause to be sponsored any athletic...or other event in the name of a registered brand name, logo, or symbol of a tobacco product or in a manner so that a registered brand name, logo, or symbol of a tobacco product is publicly identified as a sponsor of or in any way associated with such an event, except if the registered brand name is also the name of the corporation which manufactures the tobacco product and both the registered brand and the corporation were in existence prior to January 1, 1986. (Children's Health Protection Act of 1989, p. 7)

Also to:

pay or cause to be paid to have the registered brand name, logo, or symbol of any tobacco product to appear...on any vehicle, boat, or other equipment used in sports, except if the registered brand name is also the name of the corporation which manufactures the tobacco product and both the registered brand and the corporation were in existence prior to January 1, 1986. (Children's Health Protection Act of 1989, p. 8)

Congressman Thomas Luken introduced the Protect our Children from Cigarettes Act of 1989 (H.R. 1250), which would have prohibited promotion of tobacco products in sports stadiums and other sports facilities. Promotion included sponsorship of events under the registered brand name of the tobacco product, unless the brand name was the name of a corporation in existence on August 1, 1988. Also prohibited would have been

displaying the registered brand name or logo of a tobacco product on cars, boats, animals, or other sporting equipment or on nontobacco products or services which are sold unless the brand name is the name of a corporation in existence on August 1, 1988 (Protect our Children from Cigarettes Act of 1989, pp. 8-9).

Although these bills were not passed, they are indicative of the kind of law which seems likely to be passed in the future, given the public momentum which has gathered in the United States against tobacco products over the past two decades.

Another legislative option that may emerge in the United States is rescinding of a clause inserted into the 1965 law requiring cigarette warnings, which forbade the states to regulate cigarette promotion. This takes all power away from the states to ban cigarette promotion. If it was repealed, the cigarette industry would have to deal with the actions of the 50 state legislatures.

In addition to the threat of legislative limitations, the tobacco industry is constantly confronted with personal damage suits alleging product liability. To this point, the industry has never paid out any money in product liability claims, but a June 1992 meeting of the U.S. Supreme Court makes it more likely they will in the future (Freedman & Cohen, 1993). The ruling said that although cigarette warning labels preclude smokers from bringing "failure to warn" cases, plaintiffs may file suits alleging that cigarette companies intentionally hid or misrepresented tobacco's health hazards. Given that the industry's efforts to distort the health hazards have been termed by a respected business publication, "the longest running misinformation campaign in U.S. business history" (Freedman & Cohen 1993, p. A1), it seems likely that such suits will ultimately be successful.

It is ironic that if all forms of tobacco promotion were banned, the profits of the tobacco companies in the short term would increase substantially because their costs would be reduced. It would be extremely difficult to introduce a new brand or for an existing brand to take away market share from another existing brand. Hence, the current brands would retain their market share for the foreseeable future.

Meanwhile in the absence of federal legislation, some sports organizations have enacted their own limitations and bans on tobacco sponsorships. The International Olympic Committee has a rule prohibiting the use of a national Olympic Committee's Olympic emblem for advertising alcoholic beverages and tobacco (Hindson, 1990). This stipulation, taken with the requirement that "use of the emblem must contribute to the development of the Olympic Movement and shall not detract from its dignity," implies that association of these two product categories would impinge on the dignity of the Olympic Movement. The 51 national governing sports bodies that are members of the United States Olympic Committee were surveyed and asked to list any products, services, or companies from which they would not accept sponsorship (Hindson 1990). Of the 45 who responded, 31 (69%) listed tobacco and 20 alcoholic beverages. No other products were listed by more than 6 organizations.

In a survey of 42 cities, 11 (27%) responded that they prohibited tobacco companies from sponsoring their events, compared to 3 (6%) that prohibited beer and wine, and 9 (21%) that prohibited hard liquor ("The Politics," 1988). In a more comprehensive 1991 survey of "properties" (i.e., organizations or events seeking sponsorship), conducted by the International Events Group (1992), they reported:

> Though it is a buyer's market, the number of properties with restrictive sales policies continues to rise. Percentage of properties with sponsor restrictions were:
>
> | 1990 | 10 percent |
> | 1991 | 26 percent |
> | 1993 | 30 percent |
>
> Tobacco is the most commonly restricted sponsor category; among the properties with restrictions, 86 percent now ban tobacco, up from 62 percent in 1991. Fifty-one percent of properties with restrictions do not accept spirits companies, while 37 percent eschew beer/wine sponsors.
>
> Those banning spirits or beer/wine almost always shun tobacco as well, 90 percent and 87 percent, respectively, while only 37 percent of properties restricting tobacco also avoid alcohol. (p. 4)

Momentum appears to be growing to prohibit tobacco companies' sponsorship of ski events. On Aspen's ski-slopes it was banned because it was not "consistent with a healthy family sport like skiing" ("Business Bulletin," 1990, p. A1). Similarly, the Jackson Hole Ski Corporation decided to stop the sponsorship of races at its resort by tobacco and alcohol companies This meant ending its association with the Marlboro Ski Challenge, the country's biggest amateur race program; refusing liquor company race sponsorships such as the Smirnoff Ski Trials and the Absolut Vodka Challenge; and terminating its Miller Lite NASTAR course association. Their spokesman noted, "The Ski Corporation doesn't want to give the impression that tobacco and skiing are compatible."

The NAIA and nearly 30% of the conferences in the NCAA have banned the use of smokeless tobacco by student athletes. The NCAA prohibits its use, and tobacco and alcohol advertising, during all postseason events. Major League Baseball has banned smokeless tobacco in many minor league affiliates, affecting more than two-thirds of the nation's minor league ball players (Herzog, 1992). Major league players were not affected by the ban because they are unionized, whereas minor league players are not, so any such policy would have to be negotiated with the Major League Players Association. The Oakland A's have prohibited smoking at their stadium and banned tobacco advertising in the game program. Eight other major league baseball teams have outlawed tobacco signs. Others may wish to do so, but some clubs do not own the billboards in their stadiums whereas others are required to honor long term contracts.

Since 1981, the National Hockey League has banned tobacco signs from the boards that surround its ice rinks. In Minneapolis, tobacco advertisements and consumption have been banned at The Target Center, home of the Minnesota Timberwolves, and the Metrodome, home of the Minnesota Twins and Minnesota Vikings (Wichmann & Martin, 1991).

THE ALCOHOL SPONSORSHIP CONTROVERSY

The connection between sports teams and alcohol has a long history. For example, Sugar (1978) traces the lineage of this linkage in professional baseball to its formative years:

Baseball started out as a natural extension of the brewery business. The original foundations of the hundred year-old game are as firm as the foundations of the local brewery, most of baseball's early investors being saloon owners and liquor interests. The very first "major" league--the National Association of Professional Baseball Players--was founded in a saloon.

Beer was so much a part of the very fabric of baseball that a device known as a German Disturber was part of most games during the 1880s. This was a keg of beer with a dipper attached, located at third base. Any player reaching third was entitled to quench his thirst with a dipperful of beer.

Through the late 1870s, 1880s and early 1890s, teams in St. Louis, Baltimore, Brooklyn, Cincinnati, New York and Louisville were owned by brewers, saloon keepers or distillers. (p. 3)

Today, the dominant sponsors of sport in the United States are the breweries, especially Anheuser-Busch which owns the St. Louis Cardinals; Miller; Coors, which is a major sponsor of the Colorado Rockies; and in Canada this position is occupied by Labatt Brewing Company, which owns the Toronto Blue Jays. Although sponsorship of sport is an important component of the alcohol industry's promotional mix, it is not as crucial as it is to the tobacco industry because only liquor products, not beer, are banned from television in the United States.

Anheuser-Busch purchased the St. Louis Cardinals baseball team in 1953, but its broader involvement in sports sponsorship did not emerge until the mid 1970s. Its involvement was a competitive reaction to the success that Miller experienced when that company initiated close association with professional sports in 1970, after being taken over by the Philip Morris Company. Philip Morris produced tobacco products, and it brought a new level of marketing sophistication to the beer industry. A vice-president of Miller Brewing noted "'Even our most heated competitors would agree that we were responsible for the marketing revolution in the beer business. We introduced them to segmented markets, target marketing, and image-oriented selling... . The beer people hadn't a clue about this sort of thing until Philip Morris bought Miller'" (cited in Johnson, 1988, p. 74). Their expertise resulted in quantum increases in the sales of Miller beers, especially the Miller Lite brand, which was launched in 1974. In 1970 Miller was seventh largest in the brewery industry, but by 1977 Miller had vaulted to second place, and much of this success the company attributed to sports sponsorship.

Although Anheuser-Busch was the largest brewery in the United States in the 1970s, it was described as "a $700 million company that was run like a corner grocery store" (Johnson, 1988, p. 75), and its marketing was outdated. In 1976 Miller's success caused Anheuser-Busch belatedly to recognize, and begin to consummate, the ties between sport and beer. Its size enabled the company to quickly catch up with Miller, and today it is the major investor in sports sponsorship. The magnitude of the company's investment was reported by Gloede (1990). In 1989 Anheuser-Busch sponsored 23 of the 24 domestic Major League Baseball teams, 18 of the 28 National Football League teams, 22 of the 27 National Basketball Association franchises, 13 of the 14 domestic National Hockey League teams, and 9 teams in the Major Indoor Soccer League. It also had sponsorship arrangements with more than 300 college teams and managed or promoted approximately 1,000 secondary or tertiary sporting events ranging from the Bud Iron Man Triathlon to hydroplane races. In the 10-year period after 1976, the Anheuser-Busch share of the national beer market went from 22% to 40%. This increase was attributed largely to the company's concentration on sports (Johnson, 1988).

A further indication of the powerful influence of Anheuser-Busch came during the 1993 expansion decisions made by the National Football League. Five cities competed for a team. One franchise was quickly awarded to the Charlotte Panthers. On the merits of the evidence presented, there appeared to be a consensus among objective observers that the other franchise should go to Baltimore and that the worst case was made by St. Louis (Reilly, 1993). However, one commentator incorrectly forecast that the owners would ignore the objective evidence and vote for St. Louis because of the city's strong ties with Anheuser-Busch.

St. Louis will get the franchise because the NFL is proud to be Buds with Budweiser, the St. Louis-based beer Godzilla that is the league's biggest advertiser. If Budweiser were headquartered in Pinkwater, Idaho, the NFL would be telling us how delighted it is finally to be tapping into the all-important Pinkwater market. So much for the review process (Reilly, 1993, p. 106). (In fact they voted for Jacksonville).

The substantial investment by beer companies in sports sponsorship has been explained in these terms: "Beer drinkers and sports fans are one and the same--indivisible, inseparable, identical! No one drinks more beer than a sports fan, and no one likes sports better than a beer drinker" (Johnson, 1988, p. 74). The ages of maximum beer consumption and maximum sports involvement are the same, both for men and for women. The peak beer-consuming years are from 18 to 29, which are the peak years for sports' participants and spectators. Males in the 18 to 34 age group constitute only 20% of the beer-drinking population, but they consume 70% of all beer. These heavy users are the most critical market segment for beer companies, and it is easiest to communicate with them through sports-associated events. Sugar (1978) suggested that breweries have sought tie-ins with sport because this offers them a "macho"vehicle that appeals to their core young adult male target audience.

Central Factor in the Controversy

As the magnitude of sports sponsorship by breweries has increased, it has been accompanied by a commensurate increase in criticism from those concerned about alcohol abuse. There has been heightened awareness in recent years that alcohol is a drug with the potential to become addictive. The concern is that there are about 13 million alcoholics in the United States and beer companies promote that it is natural for this intoxicating drug to be consumed while watching or after participating in a pleasant sporting activity. Sponsorship and advertising by beer companies promote the image that beer is not very different from soft drinks, and its negative consequences, such as traffic deaths, domestic violence, physical deterioration, and pregnancy risks, are ignored. It has been noted that "beer comes to share the luster of healthy athleticism" and that "it's really paradoxic that alcohol and all it stands for should be associated with excellent athletic performance. You cannot have one and the other at the same time. If you're going to perform as a top-grade athlete, you have to cut out alcohol" (Johnson, 1988, p. 78).

The close relationship between beer and sport has caused some "to wonder just what kind of cultural hypocrisy is going on when Americans relentlessly insist on immersing sport--our most wholesome, most admired, even (sometimes) most heroic institution--in a sea of intoxicating drink" (Johnson, 1988, p. 70). It is interesting to note that *Sports Illustrated*, the magazine that published the article from which this quote is taken, received $6.3 million in revenues from beer advertisements in 1988, the year that this article was written (DeParle, 1989)!

In response to these social concerns, liquor advertising is not allowed on television in the United States, regulatory agencies control the advertising of alcohol directly and indirectly to children, and alcohol cannot be promoted as a problem solver (Smart, 1988). Although liquor suppliers are part of the alcohol sponsorship controversy, beer companies are the focus of the debate because the magnitude of their investment substantially exceeds that of liquor producers. Beer sponsorship is further constrained by the Federal Alcohol Administration Act, which prohibits exclusive on-site sales; consequently, such exclusivity cannot be a condition of sponsorship. All sports events must allow a free market, permitting any brewer, regardless of size, to sell product.

In 1989, the NCAA executive director announced that the organization was considering banning beer advertising at its basketball tournament because such advertising appeared to be inconsistent with the NCAA's position opposing drug use. The result was a maelstrom of opposition led by the breweries, their advertising agencies, the television networks, and even officials within college athletics. The athletic directors believed that if a ban were enacted at the tournament, then they would be pressurized by their institutions to ban sponsorship and advertising by beer companies. Two of their leading spokesmen reacted by stating: " 'I think that philosophically, no one disagrees with this. But most of us are significantly dependent on such support for coaches' shows, local television game broadcasts and the sponsorships of campus activities" and "It is not like we're handing out beer at the doors. I would have trouble telling my sponsors, for example, that I'm going to cover up their signs in my arena because I've got the NCAA tournament coming in. If they're paying millions and millions of dollars to have billboards up in my facility, I can't see that they should have to cover them up' " (cited in Krupa, 1989, p. 49).

In some other countries, for example Austria, laws have been passed that prohibit all public references to alcoholic beverages at sporting events. Thus, the director of the Austrian ski federation states, " 'Sports and alcohol should never be placed together' " (cited in Johnson, 1988, p. 78). In the United States, several universities in recent years have moved to ban beer companies and their distributors from sponsoring events on campus. Some California cities, for example, Huntington Beach and Seal Beach, have banned sponsorship and advertising by beer companies on their beaches. This has effectively stopped sponsorship of professional surfing, body boarding, water-skiing, and volleyball in those areas, because beer companies are the primary sponsors of these activities. A Seal Beach official noted, "'Some people express concern over the mixed message our city might be sending its youth, supporting drug awareness programs and at the same time hosting events sponsored by a beer company. But a lot of our business people support these events'" (cited in Brown, 1991, p. 26).

The localized bans on sponsorship and advertising are a major concern to both breweries and the sports organizations that benefit from sponsorship revenues, because they perceive bans could gather momentum. Indeed, a *Business Week* poll in 1985 reported that 57% of Americans supported banning beer and wine advertisements from the airwaves (Welling, 1985). They fear that actions further constraining or prohibiting tobacco sponsorship by companies could be a catalyst towards eliminating or restricting the involvement of beer companies.

If beer sponsorship and advertising are banned from sport, then large amounts of money will disappear. Beer companies have a much larger investment in professional sports than do tobacco companies. With a tobacco ban, it would probably be lower level events that would suffer. A ban on beer sponsorship would have a much more dramatic effect. The President of the Seattle SuperSonics articulated the dilemma:

> It is a sensitive issue because you need the money, but you don't want to be seen
> as promoting the idea that people come to our games, get drunk and drive
> home. We'd be foolish to say we don't want a beer sponsor on moral grounds,

but at the same time that doesn't mean we encourage 21 year olds to down a case (cited in Johnson, 1988, p. 78).

In response to their social critics, the beer companies assert that their sponsorship and advertising activities have no effect beyond brand shifting among current drinkers. Further, they point out that when used in moderation, beer has not been shown to be a danger to health. Thus, George Sheehan (1989), who as well as being a medical doctor served as the philosophic guru of runners, summarized the evidence:

> There are numbers that suggest good things about alcohol. The happy, healthy, productive, long-lived people studied by sociologists in a famous Alameda County, California, project turned out to be moderate drinkers. They averaged a drink or two a day. And subsequent studies have confirmed the protection alcohol gives against coronary disease. A landmark study at the Kaiser Permanente in Los Angeles found a *50 percent decrease* in coronary disease admissions for those who took two drinks a day. Researchers have gone so far as to suggest alcohol *deficiency* is a risk factor. (p. 93)

There is no empirical evidence available on the effect of sponsorship by beer companies on consumption of their product. The difficulties associated with measuring sponsorship impacts are discussed in Chapter 12. These difficulties, the relative recency of the sponsorship boom, and the paucity of researchers working in the sponsorship field combine to explain why there are no such studies. However, limited findings have been reported on the impact of advertising on beer consumption. It seems likely that these may offer some insight into the likely impact of sponsorship.

The number of studies on this issue is small because of the difficulty of finding jurisdictions where an advertising ban has been complete, rather than partial, and uncontaminated from media influences in neighboring areas where there was no ban. A situation in which these problems did not arise occurred in Norway and Finland, which prohibited all alcohol advertising in 1975 and 1977, respectively. Neither of these two countries is subjected to much foreign media influence. An examination of per capita consumption figures for 1974-84 showed no obvious postban effect (Smart, 1988).

Another study compared alcohol consumption in 1972-81 in a group of countries where alcohol advertising was banned with consumption in a group in which it was unrestricted. Countries with no advertising did not have lower rates of consumption and the authors concluded that, "consumption must be affected by factors that are far more important than advertising" (Simpson, Beirness, Mayhew & Donelson, 1985, p. 64). It has been found that such factors as price, overall availability, and social influences are likely to be more potent influences on level of consumption than is advertising (Bruun et al., 1975; Ornstein & Hanssens, 1985).

The most comprehensive study of how exposure to advertising relates to the consumption of alcoholic beverages was undertaken by Atkin, Hocking & Block (1984). They reported, "The evidence indicates that advertising stimulates consumption levels, which in turn leads to heavy drinking and to drinking in dangerous situations." Another conclusion they offered was that "this evidence appears to indicate that mass media advertising for alcohol plays a significant role in shaping young people's attitudes and behaviors regarding excessive or hazardous drinking" (p. 324). However, this study has been criticized by several observers for both methodological deficiencies and interpretations of the data (Smart, 1988).

Based on his comprehensive review of the literature, Smart included the following comments in his conclusions about the impact of alcohol advertising on consumption:

- Advertising bans appear to have little impact on overall sales of alcohol, although a total ban has been very difficult to achieve, and few studies have been done.

- Numerous econometric studies indicate that alcohol advertising expenditures have no effect on total alcohol sales or beverage classes.

- A single set of exposure studies (Atkin et al., 1984) indicates that those exposed to larger amounts of alcohol advertising are more likely to drink. However, methodological problems with these studies prevent acceptance of their conclusions. Other exposure studies indicate that the effect of advertising is very small compared to several other variables.

- Current research suggests that advertising is, at best, a weak variable affecting alcohol consumption. Effective alcohol control might be better achieved by controlling prices and availability.

CONCLUDING COMMENTS

Increasing concern with controlling the cost of health care, and widespread recognition of the substantial proportion of those costs that can be attributable to tobacco, leads to a large number of bills being introduced in each Congressional session that would further restrict tobacco promotion activities. For example in the 101st Congress, bills were proposed to implement "tombstone" advertising, which would prohibit print media from using models, scenes, or slogans (H.R. 1250, H.R. 1493, H.R. 3943); to ban placement of tobacco products in films (H.R. 1250, H.R. 1493); to restrict the distribution of free cigarette samples (H.R. 1493, H.R. 1494, S.769), to restrict the sale of cigarettes through vending machines (H.R. 665, H.R. 1250); to label cigarettes as addictive (H.R. 1171, S.777); to disclose cigarette additives (H.R. 3943); and to eliminate tobacco advertising as a tax deduction (H.R. 304, H.R. 412, H.R. 1544, S. 776) (Mazis, Debra, Ringold, Perry & Denman, 1992).

There appears to be a sense of inevitability about further legislative curbs being imposed on tobacco advertising. Given the precedent emerging in a host of other industrial countries, these additional curbs are likely to embrace sponsorship limitations. If the vested interests of media, which receive advertising revenues; politicians, who receive substantial campaign contributions; and sponsor beneficiaries are able to stall legislation, then a restriction may come through market forces, either from the success of a personal damage suit alleging product liability or from public pressure. A number of examples are cited in the chapter that demonstrate the increasing willingness of organizations and events to reject tobacco sponsorship, because it offends the sensibilities of their clienteles.

Two factors make the decision confronting sport managers as to whether or not they should solicit or accept sponsorship from beer companies much more difficult than that associated with tobacco companies. First, the magnitude of sponsorship dollars that would be given up is substantially larger. Second, unlike tobacco, the problem is not the consumption of beer, rather it is the abuse of beer. In contrast to tobacco, beer when imbibed in moderation has not been shown to be harmful. Further, the existing evidence suggests sports sponsorship is not likely to induce consumption increases.

These two factors make it tempting for sport managers to rationalize that there does not appear to be a strong enough case to ban beer companies from sponsorship opportunities. Certainly, the case for a ban ostensibly appears to be much less compelling than the case that can be made to ban sponsorship by tobacco companies. However, the alcohol dilemma is compounded by the widespread abuse of alcohol and the consequences of that abuse. A reviewer of a paper written by one of the authors on this issue articulated the conundrum in the following terms:

> There is the contradiction of physical fitness being closely tied to drug uses. The advertising is aimed at youth and minorities. And, alcohol is a huge social problem in the U.S. (125,000 deaths yearly; indirect deaths from fires, traffic accidents, and drowning; $150 billion lost to job absenteeism, lost production, medical expenses, and work-related accidents; and the unmeasurable negative costs such as spouse and child abuse, desertion, emotional problems, and fetal alcohol syndrome). Should sport be at all connected with a drug that is responsible for such problems?

Clearly, there are contradictions with sport being associated with tobacco or alcohol products. Many sport managers are confronted with a dilemma: balancing a moral, ethical obligation to discourage tobacco use and alcohol abuse with the reality of surrendering substantial economic resources. The authors hope that the issues raised in this chapter assist sport managers in making informed ethical decisions.

SUMMARY

Tobacco and alcohol companies are the major investors in sport sponsorship. Despite the conceptual incongruity and hypocrisy of associating these two products with the healthy, fit lifestyle exemplified by sport, there has been relatively little controversy aroused by the relationship in the United States. This is because sport managers fear their organizations would suffer financially if sponsorship were withdrawn, whereas the media fear similar financial losses would accrue to them if they publicly criticized the relationships.

Investment by tobacco companies in sport sponsorship in the United States is estimated at $125 million. They derive three major benefits from this association. First, it confers upon them a positive image and an aura of respectability, which obscures their role in causing an array of fatal diseases. Second, it enables them to penetrate the youth market. Third, sponsorship of sport offers a means by which the tobacco companies can circumvent the ban on cigarette advertising and promotion in broadcast media.

The tobacco industry rebuts objections to its sport sponsorship activities on three grounds. First, it would be an infringement of First Amendment rights to freedom of speech if companies were not permitted to use sponsorship to promote their products, because they are legally available for sale. Second, their goal is not to increase number of smokers or the intensity with which each of them smokes, but rather to reinforce or to try to switch brand loyalty. Third, the industry argues that abandoning tobacco-sponsored sport activities would have no effect on youth smoking.

Worldwide momentum has been building against cigarette advertising and promotion. In some countries (e.g., France and Canada) sponsorship featuring tobacco brands is banned by legislation, whereas in others (e.g., Australia and New Zealand) replacement funds have been established by governmental entities to voluntarily encourage organizations currently receiving money from tobacco companies to replace it. Each session, bills are introduced in the U. S. Congress that would limit tobacco sponsorship, but none have passed.

The tobacco industry is constantly confronted with personal damage suits alleging product liability, but to this point the industry has never paid out any money in product liability claims. Although attacks on tobacco promotion in the legislative and legal arenas have been unsuccessful, an increasing number of sports organizations and events have voluntarily enacted their own bans and limitations on tobacco sponsorship.

The breweries have a long history of associating with sport because the ages of maximum beer consumption and maximum sports involvement are the same for both men and for women. However, as the magnitude of sports sponsorship by breweries has increased, it has been accompanied by a commensurate increase in criticism from those concerned about alcohol abuse. Beer companies have a much larger investment in sports than do tobacco companies, and the impact of a ban on the former would thus be much greater. Public sentiment to inhibit beer company sponsorship has been less strident than feelings towards tobacco sponsorship. This is probably because unlike tobacco, which causes disease and illness even if it is used as intended, the problem with beer is not its consumption *per se* but abuse of the level at which it can safely be consumed.

Questions for Study and Discussion

1. Explain why the media have not made much of an issue of the sport industry's heavy reliance on alcohol and tobacco company sponsorship.
2. Discuss the actions taken by countries around the world to ban tobacco sponsorship of sporting events. How so these various restrictions compare to the current status of tobacco products promotion in the U. S.?
3. Summarize the available research on how exposure to advertising effects the consumption of alcoholic beverages. Based on your interpretation, what position should sport managers take on accepting sponsorship from beer companies?

REFERENCES

Atkin, C., Hocking, J. & Block, M. (1984). Teenage drinking: Does advertising make a difference? *Journal of Communication, 34*(2), 157-167.

Blum, A. (1991). The Marlboro Grand Prix: Circumvention of the television ban on tobacco advertising. *The New England Journal of Medicine, 324*(13), 913-917.

Brown, K. (1991, May 20). Beer-ad ban darkens beach: California move threatens professional surfing, *Marketing (McLean Hunter)*, p. 26.

Bruun, K., Edwards, G., Lumino, M., Makela, K., Pan, L., Popham, R. E., Room, R., Schmidt, W., Skog, Jr., Sulkunen, P. & Osterberg, E. (1975). *Alcohol control policies in public health perspective*, Vol. 25, Helsinki: Finnish Foundation for Alcohol Studies (Distributed by Rutgers Center of Alcohol Studies, New Brunswick, NJ).

Business bulletin: Smokeless slopes. (1985, April 5). *Wall Street Journal*, p. A1.

Chapman, S. (1986). Advertising and smoking: A review of the evidence. In British Medical Association. *Smoking out the barons: The campaign against the tobacco industry.* New York: John Wiley.

Cimons, M. (1990, February 24). Tobacco firms' sports ties assailed. *Los Angeles Times.*, p. A23.

Comte, E. (1988, October 3). Women's tennis replaces Slims. *Sports inc.*, p. 1.

Davis, R. M. (1987, March 19). Current trends in cigarette advertising and marketing. *The New England Journal of Medicine*, pp. 725-732.

DeParle, J. (1989, September). Warning: sports stars may be hazardous to your health. *The Washington Monthly*, pp. 34-48.

Freedman, A. M. & Cohen, L. (1993, February 11). Smoke and mirrors: how cigarette makers keep health question "open" year after year. *Wall Street Journal*, p. A10.

Freeman, A. (1989, May 2). Tobacco firms in Canada grapple with ban on ads. *Wall Street Journal*, pp. B1.

Garrett, A. (1991, June 15). *Now even the admen want to give up smoking. The Independent,* p. M15.

Gloede, B. (1990, August 6). Endangered sponsorship: smoke could mean fire of controversy is brewing. *Sporting News*, p. 44.

Herzog, B. (1992). Just a pinch? *Safety and Training Baseball/Softball Supplement* pp. 51-58.

Hindson, L. J. (1990). *A clean bill of health for sport sponsorship? Survey of United States Olympic Committee member organizations.* Doctoral Dissertation, University of Iowa, August.

International Events Group (1992, November 16). Quantifying sponsorship: The state of more than 3,000 properties. *IEG Sponsorhip Report*, pp. 4-5.

Johnson, W.O. (1988, August 8). Sports and suds. *Sports Illustrated*, pp. 68-82.

Krupa, G. (1989, January 9). Beer ban criticized from within NCAA. *Sports Inc.*, p. 49.

Ledwith, F. (1984). Does tobacco sports sponsorship on television act as advertising to children? *Health Education Journal, 43*(4), 85-88.

Mazis, M.B., Debra, J., Ringold, E., & Denman, D. W. (1992). Perceived age and attractiveness of models in cigarette advertisements. *Journal of Marketing, 56*, 22-27.

Muscatine, A. (1991, April 24). Where there's smoke there's ire: Tobacco sponsorship sparks debate. *Washington Post,* p. F3.

Ornstein, S. I. & Hanssens, D. M. (1985). Alcohol control laws and consumption of distilled spirits and beer. *Journal of Consumer Research, 12*, 200-213.

Pritchard, C. (1992, May 18). Tobacco sponsorship must end next year. *Marketing (Maclean Hunter)*, p. 18.

Raemer, R. (1986). *Recent developments in legislation to combat the world smoking epidemic.* Geneva: World Health Organization.

Raphael, A. (1993, April 11). Advertising ban only way to beat tobacco barons. *The Observer,* p. BF4.

Reilly, R. (1993, November 15). Send in the clowns. *Sports Illustrated,* p. 106.

Sheehan, G. (1989). *Personal Best.* Emmaus, PA: Rodale Press.

Simpson, H.M., Beirness, D. J., Mayhew, D. & Donelson, A. E.(1985). *Alcohol specific controls: implications for road safety.* Ottawa, Ontario: Traffic Injury Research Foundation of Canada.

Smart, R. G. (1988). Does alcohol advertising affect overall consumption? A review of empirical studies, *Journal of Studies on Alcohol, 49*(4), 314-323.

Stotlar, D. (1992). Sport sponsorship and tobacco: Implications and impact of Federal Trade Commission v. Pinkerton Tobacco Company. *Sport Marketing Quarterly, 1*(1), 13-17.

Stout, H. (1988, June 12). Cigarettes: Still big business. *The New York Times,* p. F4.

Sugar, B. (1978). *Hit the sign and win a free suit of clothes from Harry Finklestein.* Chicago: Contemporary Books.

The politics of events. (1988, August). *Special Events Report,* p. 1.

Thomas, C. (1990, March 1). Perilous persuaders..tenacious zealots. *The Washington Times,* p. F3.

Tobacco ban smokes French race. (1992, December 11). *Houston Chronicle,* p. 10B.

Ukman, L. (1993, January 11). Assertions. *IEG Sponsorship Report, 12*(1), p. 2.

Welling, B. (1985, March 11). What if the airwaves can't hold their beer. *Business Week,* p. 112.

Whelan, E. M. (1981, March). Analysis of coverage of tobacco hazards in women's magazines. *Journal of Public Health Policy,* pp. 28-35.

Whelan, E.M. (1984, November 1). When Newsweek and Time filtered cigarette copy. *The Wall Street Journal,* p. A4.

White, L. C. (1988). *Merchants of death: The American tobacco industry.* New York: Beck Tree Books, William Morrow.

Wichmann, S. A. & Martin, D.R. (1991, November). Sports and tobacco. *The Physician and Sports Medicine, 19*(11), pp. 5-131.

CHAPTER 11

IMPLEMENTATION OF SPONSORSHIP PARTNERSHIPS

Learning Objectives

After completing this chapter, the reader should be able to:

1. discuss five major concerns businesses are likely to have when considering sport sponsorships
2. explain how sponsorships can be integrated with other communication vehicles: personal selling, advertising, publicity, and incentives.
3. describe the eight screening criteria most likely to be used by businesses when evaluating sport sponsorship opportunities, including:
   a. customer audience
   b. exposure potential
   c. distribution channel support
   d. competitive advantage
   e. level of resource investment required
   f. sport organization's reputation
   g. event characteristics
   h. entertainment and hospitality opportunities
4. discuss the four elements essential to effectively communicating a sponsorship proposal.

CHAPTER 11

IMPLEMENTATION OF SPONSORSHIP PARTNERSHIPS

Sport managers are most likely to succeed in soliciting sponsorship partners if a marketing approach is adopted, which means that they look at their sponsorship opportunities through the eyes of the businesses from which sport managers seek to attract investment. This approach is illustrated by the well-known marketing aphorism, "To sell Jack Jones what Jack Jones buys, you have to see Jack Jones through Jack Jones's eyes." The extent to which sport managers are able to see their opportunities through the eyes of potential sponsors, and tailor a proposal to meet the needs of businesses, is likely to determine their success. For this reason, the first half of this chapter focusses on understanding business organizations' approaches to sponsorship. The second half discusses how to solicit sponsorships.

UNDERSTANDING A BUSINESS ORGANIZATION'S APPROACH TO ENTERING A SPONSORSHIP PARTNERSHIP

This first half of the chapter discusses five major concerns businesses are likely to have when considering sport sponsorships. In chapter 9, benefits that may be sought from sponsorships by business organizations were discussed. Their first concern is likely to be to frame the benefits sought in terms of specific communication objectives. Their second concern will be the time period required to achieve the specified objectives. Sponsorship is likely to be effective only if it is integrated with other communication vehicles; therefore, a third concern is its potential for providing a "hook", or unifying theme, upon which other vehicles can be focussed to communicate the desired message. Sponsorship ambushing occurs when a company that is not an official sponsor promotes around a sports event to give the false impression that it is a sponsor. The extent to which an opportunity can offer protection from ambushing is a fourth concern. The final section describes the kinds of approaches companies use for screening proposals.

Sponsorship Objectives

Many times sponsors' objectives indicate only what the sponsor would like an investment to accomplish in general terms. For example, consider the following statement by a Kodak executive:

Kodak's event marketing objectives for film products include encouraging people to buy more film, to purchase more than one roll at a time, to try different speeds of film, to get excited about taking pictures and to have the film processed by a Kodak Colorwatch dealer (Barr, 1988, p. 4).

The problem with these objectives is that they fail to meet the key criteria for effective objectives, which are that they should be specific, measurable and prioritized. *Specific* means that they should delineate target markets, quantity of impact, and timing. Sleight (1989) notes, "There is no such thing as a generally effective sponsorship in an abstract sense" (226). The types of benefits a sponsorship could offer may be discussed in general terms, but those sought should then be specified in measurable terms.

Measurable objectives achieve two things. First, they facilitate evaluation and accountability, because only if objectives are measurable can the outcome from a sponsorship be evaluated. Second, they serve to crystalize executive thinking, since managers are forced to consider the limitations of sport sponsorship and examine carefully whether or not it is the best vehicle to achieve the specified objective.

Most sport sponsors have an intuitive feeling for what their investment might deliver. Unfortunately, relatively few express their expectations in measurable terms. However, their numbers are increasing as the demands for accountability heighten. There is a big difference between "the objective of our sports sponsorship is to increase consumer awareness of Product X," and "the objective is to increase awareness of Product X by 10% among professional working females aged between 25 and 40 in the Atlanta metropolitan area in the next 3 months."

Sponsorship goals have to fit within the broader goals of a company's overall communications strategy. At Cadillac, for example, a particular sport sponsorship investment's objectives must specifically contribute to one of two broad goals:

Two goals dominate our marketing strategy at Cadillac. A specific sport sponsorship investment's objectives must specifically contribute to one of these broad goals. One is to impact our narrow and demographically specific target market with direct product exposure that will result in immediate sales. The second goal, though more abstract, is equally important--to reinforce and enhance Cadillac's image among the general public--to use our name as a metaphor for excellence: "The Cadillac of its class." (Perelli & Levin, 1988, p. 4).

Dixon (1985) has developed a series of questions that constitute a type of audit. Answers to them offer a basis for formulating a set of measurable objectives for a sponsorship investment:

- How are we trying to influence--raise brand awareness, build trial, enhance corporate image etc.?
- Whom are we trying to influence--what is/are the specific target audiences we are trying to influence?
- What is the nature and size of the event--how and where can the target audience be reached?
- What is the brand-usage level, corporate image, brand awareness, etc. prior to the event--what is the level at which we are starting?
- What levels of effect, increase, change, etc. are desired/necessary in order to proceed with sponsorship or consider the event to be successful?
- What are specific ways in which the event would be promoted? How extensive would this promotion be, and how will prospects be reached?
- What would be done to merchandize the brand following the event and over what period of time?

Length of Commitment

There is a consensus that for sponsorship to be effective there should be a relatively long- term commitment. Three to five years is often advanced as the optimum time period (Meenaghan, 1983). Armstrong (1988) and Copeland(1991) empirically confirmed this timeframe. Copeland (1991) reported that 46% of the 71 major Canadian companies in his sample who sponsored sports events typically committed for between 3 and 5 years, whereas 86% indicated commitments of between 1 and 5 years. Short-term commitments do not provide adequate time to exploit a sponsorship. It usually takes longer to establish a linkage between the sports event and a sponsor's product in the target market's mind, and this linkage is key to achieving the awareness and image benefits being sought. A one-off sponsorship may generate some short-term awareness, but there is unlikely to be any positive image benefit. Further, once the event is over, awareness is likely to dissipate quickly. Sleight(1989) suggests to companies that the following sequence is likely to occur:

> The first year will be spent learning about the event or activity, making contacts (and probably quite a few mistakes) and finding your way in this new area. The second will start to show the potential you are hoping for, while the third should, if you have done your work correctly, see the benefits accrue, the audience accept your presence and motives, and the media to be comfortable with linking you with the activity. (p. 124)

Long-term commitments of more than 5 years are also problematic for three main reasons. First, market conditions may change over this period, making the sponsorship less effective. Second, a company's management may change, leading to different directions in its communications strategy. The London Marathon sponsorship by Mars was an illustration of this. The Mars candy bar was promoted on its energy-giving properties. Linking it with a high profile high-energy event like the Marathon appeared to be a natural marriage. However, Mars dropped the title sponsorship because "the new brand manager wanted to wipe the slate clean so he could write his own programs. (This by the way is a dumb but not uncommon reason for sponsor hopping)." (Assertions," 1988, p. 2). Another observer of this shift commented, "Even more astounding, the company were heard to complain about the time it will take to break the link between the company and the event that has so effectively been formed in the public's mind!" (Sleight, 1989, p. 116).

A third reason why investment may not be warranted beyond 5 years is that after this lengthy period of sponsorship there may be a reduction in impact or a disassociation of sponsors from the sponsored activity. For example, Gillette, which sponsored various sports for many years, found from its research that consumers were more likely to associate Gillette with sport than with safety razors. They also found that public consciousness of the company's sponsorship was not cumulative year after year. Repeated sponsorship of the same event seemed eventually to prove unproductive in reaching new consumers, as awareness levels reached a plateau and then stayed there, or even fell away (Gratton & Taylor, 1985).

Integrating Sponsorship with Other Communication Vehicles

There are two attributes of sponsorship that suggest it is likely to be most effective if it is integrated with other communication vehicles, rather than used in isolation. First, increased awareness and enhanced image benefits of sports sponsorship accrue by providing implicit messages generated by the linkage between a company and the sporting event. Unlike advertising or sales promotions, sponsorship does not offer direct messages indicating why a product should be purchased. If the target audience is aware of the name, but has no idea what the product is or does, then awareness and image benefits are not delivered: "There is absolutely no point in using sponsorship to create name awareness and to develop an image based on association with an event if supporting explicit information is not available to the audience of the sponsorship" (Sleight, 1989, p. 43). If the other communications vehicles are not used in conjunction with a sponsorship, the effort may end up like that used to promote name awareness of the brandy Metaxa: "Major television exposure gained from a linkage with international soccer tournaments left millions of people around the world aware of the name but totally unaware of what it meant!" (Sleight, 1989, p. 3).

A second attribute of sponsorship is that it provides a theme that can be incorporated into the message of the other communication vehicles: personal selling, advertising, publicity and incentives. It provides a "hook"-- a focus or unifying theme--to which the other communication vehicles can relate. The importance of this was emphasized by Klein (1988), who noted that the Sunday newspaper may contain 50 advertising inserts; the average household watches more than an hour of commercials during prime time every day; and the average consumer receives approximately three pieces of unsolicited mail a day. Given the extent of this clutter Klein concluded:

> That's why theme marketing events which can synergistically unite all aspects
> of the communications mix, make sense to Maxwell House. They create a
> point of difference for our brands and let us build our franchise with both the

grocery trade and the consumer, without incurring exorbitant advertising expenses. (p. 4)

Sponsored activities may subsequently be used as part of a company's mainstream advertising. This should be planned in advance, rather than "ad hoced" afterwards so that photographs or video footage can be purposefully taken for subsequent integration into the advertising.

The Xerox Marathon case is an excellent example of integrating sponsorship with other communication vehicles, using a common theme--the ability to run indefinitely. An advertising campaign in both print and television media was directly linked with the sponsorship. Publicity was forthcoming from the substantial coverage the events received both on television and in other media. This was reinforced by the formation of Team Xerox, comprising top-class marathon runners who competed in the races. The sales force were provided with a platform from which to engage in personal selling, because invitation for a team entry was by invitation only, and that invitation had to come from a Xerox representative. Thus, the sales force in each district office invited their top 100 customers, interacted with them in a social and sporting environment at the event, and subsequently presented them with results and photographs.

THE XEROX MARATHON CAMPAIGN: AN EXAMPLE OF INTEGRATING OTHER COMMUNICATIONS VEHICLES WITH SPONSORSHIP

CASE STUDY

This campaign was created to support the launch of a new line of photocopiers designed to re-establish Xerox's position in the Copier market. The marketing strategy was for the new product line to be introduced internationally with a common theme and the decision was to use sponsorship to link in with the product advertising campaign. The company and its agencies undertook extensive research to determine the attributes purchasers of copiers wanted in the product. This research showed that the machine did not break down--it should have the ability to run indefinitely.

Because of the international introduction the company had to develop a common marketing strategy with a universal message. Once again research was used to determine that the name 'Marathon' produced the same perceptions in all markets, perceptions of endurance and strength. The advertising campaign used to launch the product used the marathon runner theme in print and television advertising in the US, Europe and Latin America.

The objectives for Xerox's use of sponsorship were to get increased exposure for the new product launch on an international basis, to attract media attention, to provide a means to inform the salesforce, and to attract existing and new customers. Alongside these objectives was the determination to integrate the Xerox advertising campaign with the sponsorship of events. Every element used in the advertising was incorporated into the sponsorship and associated promotions.

Fortunately for Xerox a major boom in running coincided with the launch of the new product line, so the company, since it was prepared to react quickly, became a major sponsor of international marathon events under the Marathon label. Also, the company discovered that the demographics of marathon participants were the same as the Xerox target audience so they were easily able to target the business audience they were looking for. Most of the marathon events Xerox sponsored achieved television coverage, and where this occurred the company placed television product advertising within the coverage. Among the events the company sponsored was the Rotterdam Marathon which brought together for the first time the two best marathon runners of the day and achieved significant television exposure. Xerox also sponsored the New York City Marathon along with many regional events that were tied in to local Xerox offices and their customers. The company sponsored the World Cross-Country Championship, held for the first time in the United States, as well as the US Men's Olympic Marathon Trials and the Los Angeles Olympic Games. All of these events achieved significant television exposure that included corporate branding.

At all these events the company and its agencies worked hard to get the Xerox name across to both on-site and television viewers. Xerox branding was placed on every conceivable object that would be viewed on-site and by the television cameras. Finish line tape, blankets to wrap competitors in as they finished, runners' bibs, signage and banners all had Xerox identification.

With event sponsorship in place the company created their own team. Team Xerox comprised a team of top-class marathon runners who competed in most of the events the company sponsored, outfitted, of course, in a Team Xerox uniform. Finally the company organized a promotion called the Xerox Corporate Marathon Relay aimed at bringing together the company's salesforce and their customers.

These events were unique in that entry was by invitation only and that invitation for a team entry had to come from a Xerox representative. Invited corporate teams comprised ten runners, at least two of whom had to be women, and each team member had to run just over two and a half miles. The top three teams won an award and the winning team received a trip to the Xerox National Championship held in a different location each year.

This newly-created sponsorship provided the Xerox salesforce with the golden opportunity to go directly to its customers and invite them to enter the company's event. All invitational packages were sent to the Xerox district offices and the salesforce then took on the job of inviting their top 100 customers.

At the event the salesteam were able to meet once again with the customers or potential customers and mix with them in a social and sporting environment. After the race the salesteam would return with results and photographs for all the teams. At just one of their events Xerox had the opportunity of bringing together over 1500 customers—the sort of opportunity that most companies would dearly love to have. In 1984 the winning team in each of the Corporate Relay events was given a trip to the Xerox Relay Championship held just three days before the Olympic Trials. The winning team was also given a trip to the Olym-

pic Games at Xerox's expense. According to Xerox these promotions had very beneficial results. Not only did extensive publicity impinge directly on their target audience but the promotions aimed at the corporate clients reached that audience and impacted on the company's salesforce who were very enthusiastic about the campaign. In addition to the tremendous amount of goodwill the promotion generated among existing and potential clients, the company also sold 400,000 Marathon copiers in the first 21 months of the campaign—an effect that is directly measurable on the bottom line and amounts to a very successful new product launch.

Note: From *Sponsorship: What It Is and How to Use It* (pp. 102-104) by S. Sleight, 1989. McGraw-Hill.

The following three vignettes illustrate some of the different ways in which sponsorship can be integrated with other communication vehicles. Cadillac integrated nationwide television and dealer tie-ins, whereas Keystone Beer used point-of-sales advertising and a sweepstakes competition. The Benjamin Moore vignette offers examples of opportunities for building promotions or incentives around a sponsorship. These opportunities can generally be classified into three categories: (a) competitions based on the product, with prizes associated with the sponsorship, for example, tickets to the event or dinner with a sports celebrity; (b) customers receiving incentives associated with the sponsorship when the product is purchased; and (c) coupons that may be redeemable against entry to the event or qualify users for drawings with prizes associated with it.

- Cadillac sponsored the American Grandprix Association show-jumping events because it delivered a high income clientele and was a prestigious series. The company had title sponsorship of the 10 national events. Five of these were covered on ESPN, and were accompanied by a full-package media buy, which gave Cadillac a commanding television presence. On-site product displays, ID and hospitality tents broadened the company's exposure to those in attendance.

   Dealer involvement was another key element. Dealers furnished cars and sales personnel for on-site displays and were encouraged to participate in charity tie-ins leading up to the finals. This put Cadillac dealers before prospects and prominent members of the community. The promotional reach of the sponsorship was also extended through a direct-marketing follow-up program. Event attendees received a letter offering an overnight test-drive at their local dealer (Perelli & Levin, 1988).

- Coors promoted its new Keystone Beer by being major sponsor of a team on the NASCAR Winston Cup circuit. Primary reason for the sponsorship was to give the company leverage with retailers in the South. The first phase of promotion revolved around its new 12 packs. Secondary packaging advertised the sponsorship, and cans carried the Winston Cup schedule. The 12-packs arrived on Daytona Beach shelves a few weeks before the Daytona 500 race and then expanded out to the rest of the region. Retailers received special 12-pack displays. This was accompanied by a sweepstakes competition that was promoted through point-of-purchase materials. (International Events Group, 1992a).

- Benjamin Moore & Co. manufacture paints and stains. The company sponsored the New York Yankees baseball team as part of a strategy for regaining market share from private label brands sold by discount home improvement stores. The sponsorship was exploited by using consumers and trade hooks, as well as print, radio and television exposure.

    A month-long retail promotion offered paint purchasers a discount on an old-fashioned Yankees' cap. The company also conducted in-store drawings for tickets to Yankee games. These incentives were promoted by 30-second spots during radio game broadcasts. To encourage trade involvement, Moore hosted Yankee-run baseball clinics at the stadium for participating retailers. Moore's package included signage at Yankee Stadium and a promotional night at which it distributed logoed painter's caps. Company ID appeared on pocket schedules and score cards, and during an in-stadium video that highlighted great Yankee plays. Moore also gained exposure through advertisements in *Yankee Magazine* (International Events Group, 1992b).

A study done by NutraSweet evaluating effectiveness of the company's sponsorship found it was important for the on-site sponsorship presence to incorporate an interactive experience to maximize its impact on attendees. This case is discussed later in chapter 12. Another study reported that a sponsoring company selling frozen yogurt met its on-site sales goals, but its unaided recall score was lower than those of other sponsoring companies. The suggested reason for this was that the company did not have an interactive presence; consequently, attendees perceived it to be a vendor rather than a sponsor (Johnson, 1992). These studies suggest that if a sales promotion effort involves people actively doing something, such as signing up for information at a product display or entering a sweepstakes, then the sponsorship is likely to make a stronger impact on them.

A commonly used strategy for obtaining integrated advertising support is for a sponsor to give cosponsoring media, event tickets, event merchandise, sponsor's products or the opportunity to meet a celebrity in exchange for media time. This type of arrangement is particularly prevalent with radio stations, and the ratio of air time value to merchandise value with radio station trade-outs usually approximates 5 to 1 ("Assertions," 1988).

Some imaginative companies have taken the concept of cosponsorship and expanded it into cross-promotion with other companies. These arrangements are often difficult to negotiate, but if the sponsors are compatible and are in noncompeting businesses, additional opportunities can be created, especially in the area of sales promotions. If sponsors cooperate in a cross-promotion, the integration is likely to extend impact of their sponsorship because it exposes each partner to the others' established clienteles and offers each of the clienteles added value. Two examples of effective cross-promotion are provided in the following vignettes.

NATURITE AND SEVEN-UP CROSS-PROMOTION AT THE LOS ANGELES MARATHON

Naturite and the Seven-Up/RC Bottling Companies of Southern California implemented a successful cross-promotion at the 1988 Los Angeles marathon race. Naturite gave Seven-Up 200,000 marathon-themed bottle collars, some with vitamin samples, and Naturite inserted Seven-Up coupons in its packages.

"This was the most successful of our marathon promotions," said the director of marketing for vitamin-maker Naturite Inc. "Our objective with any event is to provide retailers with a promotional opportunity and to have them put money into reaching the consumer. Selling vitamins to retailers doesn't have the intensity of selling soft drinks, so our Seven-Up tie-in gives us access to a well established sales force that is in the stores practically seven days a week."

As an example of the power of the cross-promotion, the marketing director pointed to a Thrifty Drug and Discount Stores full-page advertisement in the Sunday *Los Angeles Times* promoting Naturite and Seven-Up.

"The bottom line is how much new business we generate. Naturite is now in three chains and several independent stores that we had never been in before. We also are a solid part of the promotional plans of our existing customers, many of whom called me to make sure we'd repeat the promotion," the marketing director said.

Note: Adapted from "Using Events for Cross-Promotions," December 12, 1988, *IEG Sponsorship Report*, p. 5.

CROSS-PROMOTION ON THE CART CIRCUIT

The opportunity for joint promotions was one of the main reasons Mobil Oil Corp. agreed to cosponsor the Domino's Pizza Team Shierson, said Mobil's retail lubricants promotions manager. "We knew we'd be getting involved with other companies that had strong marketing and distribution systems, and targets and strategies similar to ours."

Mobil's objective was realized at the 1988 NISSAN INDY CHALLENGE, when Mobil teamed up with Domino's Pizza, Inc., Coca-Cola Co., and Ralston-Purina Co. on the largest cross-promotion the CART circuit had ever seen: a $1.5-million coupon offer.

During the month leading up to the Nissan race in Miami, the four team sponsors distributed Hot Ticket booklets with product discount or rebate offers from each sponsor. The booklet also included ticket discounts from race organizers and an entry form for a Nissan pace car. Nissan Motor Corp. U.S.A., which provided the car but did not put up cash for its participation, distributed 25,000 booklets through its nine Miami dealers.

Domino's distributed 550,000 booklets, attaching one to each pizza sold. Mobil Mart stores distributed another 75,000 through locations in Dade and Broward counties. Ralston-Purina put 100,000 booklets into boxes of Honey Graham Chex, while Coke placed some of the coupons on 300,000 can and bottle ringers it supplied to Mobil Marts.

Domino's, Mobil and Nissan tagged Miami TV ads with the Hot Ticket offer and Ralston ran newspaper ads supporting the promotion.

"When you look at the total impact of the different distribution channels, these types of promotions become irresistible," said Dan Criscenti, Domino's manager of racing programs. "And sponsorship provides a unique focal point."

Note: from "Using Events for Cross Promotions," December 12, 1988, *IEG Sponsorship Report*, p. 4.

Integration has cost implications. The *direct* sponsorship investment represents only part of a company's total investment. The associated *indirect* costs incurred in using other communication vehicles in concert to optimize a sponsorship's impact may include those associated with a company's own media promotion highlighting tie-ins, advertising related to the event (e.g., air time or program inserts), merchandising, hospitality, video coverage, and dealer or customer tie-ins.

The indirect costs are likely to be at least equal to those of the direct investment and often range up to three times direct costs. For example, a senior executive of American Express observed that sponsors rarely spend enough money promoting their activities. He stated that American Express normally spends $3 on promotion for every $1 spent on the sponsorship (Graham, 1988). A list of items that should be included to identify total costs associated with a sponsorship is given in Table 11-1. Sleight (1989) advises companies, "A promotional spend less than an equal amount to the sponsorship fee suggests that you are not spending enough to secure the proper level of benefits for *you*--as opposed to the event" (p. 119). Many sports managers seeking sponsorship fail to consider these indirect costs and try to convince potential buyers of the sponsorship's value based only on the direct cost.

To reduce sponsorship costs some companies have focused on investments that have the potential for being at least partially self-liquidating. For example, Target paid $250,000 increasing to $400,000 over a 5-year period, for title of the arena where the Minnesota Timberwolves play, but the company could liquidate the majority of its sponsorship costs by utilizing vendor relationships:

- As part of its package, Target received rights to a number of promotional opportunities at the new 18,500-seat arena. By including brands like Coca-Cola and Kodak in these promotions, and perhaps linking their participation to increased shelf space or displays in Target stores, Target could tap into hundreds of thousands of manufacturer's promotional dollars. For example, Target promoted a Timberwolves Birthday Party Club, which let two children host parties for their friends at each game. The retailer could sell cosponsor-

Table 11-1	
Items Contributing to the	
Total Cost of a Sponsorship Fee	
ITEM	$ COST
Sponsorship fee	
Advertising costs:	
Print	
Radio	
Point-of-purchase	
TV	
Printed materials	
Signage/Banners	
Staffing/Van	
Apparel	
Hardware/Airtime costs	
PR opportunities	
Ticket purchases	
Other	
Total cost	

Note: From Bell Cellular Inc. cited in *IEG Sponsorship Report* (1991). July 1, p. 5.

ship of this event to another company, such as a toymaker, and use the fee to offset its title sponsorship costs ("Target Sponsors," 1990).

In addition to cooperative tie-ins with product manufacturers or distributors, self-liquidation may be achieved through direct merchandising and sale of television rights fees:

- Volvo sponsored an NFL exhibition game between the Minnesota Vikings and the Chicago Bears in Sweden. The company gave a financial guarantee of $2.5 million ensuring that both teams would earn at least as much as if they played on their home fields. However, staging the game only cost Volvo $300,000. The majority of their investment was recovered by sale of the European television rights and direct gate receipts. The game was broadcast live in the U.S. and the company's distinctive blue and white banners adorned the stadium. The company's high exposure cost less than one minute of Super Bowl air time (Lohr, 1988).

Sponsorship Ambushing

Ambush marketing occurs when a company that is not an official sponsor promotes around a sports event to give the false impression that it is a sponsor. It has been defined as "a planned effort (campaign) by an organization to associate themselves indirectly with an event in order to gain at least some of the recognition and benefits that are associated with being an official sponsor" (Sandler & Shani, 1989, p. 11).

There are two key points in this definition that should be emphasized. First, ambush marketing is a well-planned effort, not a one-shot commercial or *ad hoc* decision. It may be costly to get consumers to perceive the ambushing company as being a sponsor, involving prime-time advertising and expensive tie-in promotions. Thus, the popular perception that ambushing may capture the benefits of a sponsor at a fraction of the official sponsor's costs often is fallacious. Second, the main objective is not exposure *per se* because this could be achieved by regular advertising independent of the sports event. Rather the intent is "to create miscomprehension in the consumer's mind about who the sponsor is and therefore gain the benefits associated with being a sponsor or weaken the impact of a main competitor being the exclusive sponsor of an event" (Sandler & Shani, 1989, p. 11).

Potential ambushers are the sponsor's competitors. This approach has been termed "parasitic marketing" because ambushers are "taking something that doesn't belong to them and diminishing something they don't own" (Ruffenach, 1992, p. B1). The president of the Greater St. Petersburg Grand Prix noted, "Lots of companies, many of whom are major sporting event sponsors hire people to hang unauthorized banners at event sites. At our event these people come out at 4 a.m. and think no one will know. However, we place a seal on all official sponsor signage so volunteers can recognize and tear down unauthorized banners" ("Managing and Leveraging," 1990). An early example of ambushing took place at the 1984 Winter Olympic Games in Sarajevo:

- Domino's Pizza was not an official Olympic sponsor. However, in the local language Dominos Pizza translated into a lewd, bawdy saying. For this reason, many local people sought out Domino's signs and took great delight in holding them up alongside the bobsled run. Thus, Dominos gained exposure in every ABC bobsled broadcast and appeared to be a sponsor of the Games, all for very little cost (Urbanski, 1992).

There are two popular forms of ambushing. First a company's sponsorship may be ambushed by a major competitor paying for advertisements within a television program covering the event. This allows the ambushing company to be associated with the event without paying fees for the right to be an "official sponsor":

- Wendys used this strategy to ambush McDonald's in the 1988 Winter Olympics. While McDonald's paid a substantial amount of money for the right to be an official sponsor of the Olympics. Wendy's associated itself with the Games for a fraction of the cost by featuring ski-racing posters announcing, "We'll Be There!"; by printing Olympic stories on its tray liners; and by advertising during the Olympic broadcast, which earned them the right to become "A proud sponsor of ABC's broadcast of the 1988 Winter Olympics" (Sandler

& Shani, 1989).

- Visa paid $20 million to become the official Olympic credit card for the 1992 Olympic Games. During the Games, American Express sought to ambush their rivals by repeatedly running two television commercials that were set in Barcelona and that used language evocative of the Summer Games. One concluded, "And remember to visit Spain, you don't need a visa," whereas the other stated, "Obviously, we're here for more than just the fun and games" (Elliott, 1992). Although the word "Olympics" was not used in any American Express advertising, the International Olympic Committee threatened to sue American Express for "ambush marketing" and being "regularly involved in trying to create the impression that it is [an Olympic] sponsor" (McKelvey, 1993). No suit was filed in response to American Express' U.S. advertising campaign. However, in an advertisement in its own publication *Expressions*, circulated to 400,000 cardmembers in Europe, the company's European division carelessly used the Olympic rings. The French Olympic Organizing committee filed suit in the Court of the First Instance in Paris, which resulted in a fine of $26,000 against American Express (Levin, 1992).

If a company is sponsoring an event, it will want to keep competitors from participating as vendors or from advertising in media associated with the event, because these are potential sources of ambush. A key to avoiding being ambushed is careful contract negotiation, especially with media partners. A sports organization could prohibit its broadcast partner from "subletting" its event trademark rights to unauthorized companies through the use of composite logos and titles that convey to the public an "official" association between the non-sponsor and the event. For example, they should not permit a company to be the "Proud Sponsor of the 1996 Olympic Games *telecast*" (McKelvey, 1993). An example of this strategy occurred in 1992 when NBC paired its logo with the Olympic rings and used it on advertisements that "thanked" and promoted a variety of network advertisers, many of whom were not Olympic sponsors. This access to the corporate logo was intended to provide advertisers with "value added" assistance and was available to corporations seeking to ambush their competitors that had purchased official sponsorship rights.

A second popular form of ambushing occurs when companies negotiate directly with individual teams, athletes, or players' unions (McKelvey, 1993). For example, Pepsi-Cola entered an endorsement arrangement with Bo Jackson, who was playing for the Kansas City Royals baseball team. This weakened the impact of Coca-Cola's official sponsorship agreements with both the Royals and Major League Baseball. Similarly, after the 1991 World Series, Minneapolis-based General Mills negotiated individual endorsement contracts with two Twins players and featured them on a World Series "commemorative box" in direct competition with an officially licensed commemorative box issued by Kellogg's, which was the official cereal company of Major League Baseball.

The first legal challenge to an ambush marketing campaign was the case of *NHL v. Pepsi-Cola Canada* in June 1992. The case related to Pepsi-Cola Canada's ambushing of the National Hockey league and Coca-Cola, the league's official soft drink sponsor. The case has been described and its implications analyzed by McKelvey (1992, 1993). A review is given in the following example. The outcome clearly indicates that the law favors ambush marketers.

NHL V. PEPSI-COLA CANADA: OVERVIEW OF A SPORTS AMBUSHING CASE

CASE STUDY

In the spring of 1990, Pepsi-Cola Canada conducted a widely publicized consumer contest called the "Diet Pepsi $4,000,000 Pro Hockey Playoff Pool," whereby fans matching information under bottle caps with actual NHL Playoff results became eligible for prizes. The NHL (probably under pressure from Coca-Cola) filed a lawsuit, alleging that Pepsi-Cola Canada, which had no rights to NHL trademarks, had engaged in misappropriation and unfair competition by using marks "confusingly similar" to those owned by the NHL, had infringed on the NHL's trademarks, and had unlawfully interfered with the NHL's business associations.

The Supreme Court of British Columbia ruled against the NHL. The Court found that Pepsi-Cola Canada had used three techniques which effectively defended them from this charge. First, they generically referred to the promotion as the "Pro Playoff Hockey Pool" instead of the NHL Playoff Pool. Second, in all their promotion material relating to the contest they included a disclaimer that the contest "is neither associated with nor sponsored by the National Hockey League." Third, under the bottle caps and scratch cards were city names of NHL playoff participants, not the full trade marketed team names.

Pepsi's commercial spots advertised the promotion during NHL broadcasts, and they featured former NHL coach Don Cherry, a regular on the television program *Hockey Night in Canada*. The NHL argued that the defendant's advertising by using a personality clearly identified with the NHL games and by causing the commercials to appear during and in conjunction with the broadcasting of NHL playoff games was "clearly designed to tie into and trade upon the goodwill and regulation of the NHL and to thereby misrepresent or create confusion with the public as to Pepsi-Cola Canada's relationship with the NHL." This argument was rejected by the Court who indicated that by purchasing advertising within the playoff broadcasts, Pepsi had a legitimate connection with the games.

Note: from "NHL v Pepsi-Cola Canada, Uh-Huh! Legal Parameters of Sports Ambush Marketing," by S. McKelvey, Fall, 1992, *The Entertainment and Sports Lawyer*, p. 14.

There are some situations in which it is not possible to defend against ambushing. A prime context is one in which the sponsor and/or sports organization is unable to control access to an event, for example, a marathon race using public thoroughfares. Another nondefendable competition strategy is to create a counter attraction to adversely affect the sponsor's impact:

- Anheuser-Busch was prohibited from bringing its Clydesdales into a Miller sponsored rodeo. Thus, Anheuser-Busch siphoned people and media attention away by scheduling the horses' visit to the city on the same day as the rodeo ("Managing and Leveraging," 1990).

Published empirical evidence assessing results of ambushing is limited to a study reported by Sandler and Shani (1989). They evaluated the relative effectiveness of official sponsorship and ambushers at the 1988 Winter Olympics by assessing recall and recognition of the companies involved in seven product categories. When the data were aggregated across categories, official sponsors were able to achieve significantly higher levels of awareness than ambushers. However, in only four of the seven categories were official sponsors identified more than ambushers. In two of the three other cases, official sponsors were not major advertisers on the Olympic telecast and in the third case the ambushers engaged in extraordinarily heavy advertising. These results appeared to reinforce the importance of supporting official sponsor status with strong advertising.

Reactions to ambush marketing reflect perspectives of the parties involved (McKelvey, 1992). Many will argue that ambush marketing is a healthy business practice consistent with the U.S. tradition of encouraging competition in the market place. However, sports organizations are likely to see it as unfairly undermining the significant time, effort and expense they invest in developing meaningful sponsorship programs. Similar negative reactions will probably be forthcoming from sponsors who see the return on their investments diminished, and fans who may be misled into purchasing a product or entering a sweepstakes based on the belief that one company rather than another is in fact, the official sponsor.

Approaches for Screening Proposals

The number of sports sponsorship opportunities offered to companies known to use this communication medium can be overwhelming. For example, it has been reported that Philips in 1984 received 10,000 written enquiries for sponsorship (Kohl & Otker, 1985) and that in 1987 Anheuser-Busch received approximately 200 sponsorship proposals a day (International Advertising Association, 1988; Stotlar, 1989). As sponsorship has grown, companies have developed approaches for sifting through the multiple opportunities they are offered to identify those that will yield highest return on their investment. The criteria and screening sought and tools they use are intended to ensure the benefits specified in a company's sponsorship objectives are delivered.

The screening criteria likely to be most pertinent to businesses engaged in sponsorship can be summarized under eight headings from which the mnemonic acronym CEDAR SEE is derived: customer audience, exposure potential, distribution channel audience, advantage over competitors, resource investment level required, sport organization's reputation, event's characteristics, and entertainment and hospitality opportunities. A set of screening criteria that operationalize these eight major concerns is shown in Figure 11-1. They are derived from a synthesis of screening criteria that have been reported by a variety of authors (Ensor, 1987; Frankel, 1988; Furst & Furst, 1991; Perelli & Lewin, 1988; Riffner & Thompson, 1987; Sleight, 1989; Tortorici, 1987; Ukman, 1984).

A company is unlikely to consider all of the criteria listed in Figure 11-1 in its screening process. To do so would create an unwieldy and unmanageable system that would defeat the objective of clarifying the process. Further, a common set is unlikely to be appropriate for all companies because the benefits sought from sponsorship are different. Rather, each company is likely to select from this comprehensive list the 12 to 15 criteria that are deemed to be most salient to meeting its objectives.

Many companies screen sponsorship proposals by using a quantitative procedure. Thus, each sponsorship opportunity may be evaluated against each of the selected criteria on a rating scale with, for example, a 1 through 10 scoring system. If different levels of importance are ascribed to the selected screening criteria, then the criteria should be weighted. The total figure gained by adding up the score for each criterion multiplied by its weighting gives a final score for each proposal being assessed. If the cost of the project is then divided by the total score, this gives a relative cost figure that can be used to compare projects. The approach can be improved over time by comparing predictions given by the system to actual experience with events. The relative importance of the criteria may be adjusted by modifying their weighting in order to refine the system.

An example of an evaluation process that used weighted criteria is shown in Table 11-2. This company's screening criteria focussed on three areas: sales opportunities, which were weighted 50%; advertising equivalency, which constituted 30%; and corporate image building, which made up the remaining 20% (Lavelle, 1991). These types of quantitative approaches impose discipline. They enable the potential contribution of a sponsorship to be measured against marketing objectives and facilitate comparison between sponsorship opportunities. They also make it possible to give specific feedback to sports organizations whose proposals are rejected, by reporting to them the particular aspects of their proposals that must be improved before sponsorship would become appealing to the company.

SOLICITING SPONSORSHIPS FROM BUSINESS ORGANIZATIONS

The efficiency and effectiveness of efforts to solicit corporate sponsorship are likely to be a function of (a) the philosophy that underlies a sport organization's approach and (b) the extent to which the approach is systematically organized. A marketing approach to solicitation involves carefully targeting specific companies or types of companies, identifying their motivations for investing, and designing marketing programs that will bring about mutually satisfying exchanges over an extended period of time. Sports managers who accept this philosophy and use it to guide their actions are likely to view themselves as brokers who are concerned with furthering the welfare of the potential sponsor companies by encouraging them to "buy into" the organization's services. They seek situations in which both the business and agency win.

Figure 11-1
Screening Criteria Used by Business Organizations
to Determine Which Sport Sponsorship
Opportunities Will be Supported

---

1. CUSTOMER AUDIENCE
- Is the demographic, attitude, and lifestyle profile of the target audience congruent with the product's target market?
- What is the on-site audience?
- Is sponsorship of this sports event the best way to communicate about the product to this target audience?

2. EXPOSURE REACH
- What is the inherent news value of the event?
- What extended print and broadcast coverage of the sponsorship is likely?
- Will the extended coverage be local, regional, or national? Is the geographical scope of this media audience consistent with the product's sales area?
- Can the event be tied into other media advertising?
- Can the sponsorship be used to create consumer and trade promotions?
- Will concession areas at the event cooperate in selling the company's product and brand-logoed items?
- What opportunity does the event offer for a sustained presence? That is, what is its future growth potential? How long is the sponsorship usable before and after the event?
- Are banners and signage included in the sponsorship? How many? What size? Where placed? Will they be visible during telecasts?
- Will the product's name or logo be identified on promotional materials for the activity?
    - Event posters? How many?
    - Press releases?   How many?
    - On tickets or ticket order forms? How many?
    - Point-of-purchase displays? Where?
    - Television advertisements? How many spots? Which stations?
    - Radio advertisements? How many? Which stations?
    - Print advertisements? How many? Which publications?
- Where will the product name appear in the event program? On the front or back cover? How many and size of program advertisements? Number of programs to be printed?
- Will the product's name be mentioned on the Public Address system? How many times?
- Can the sponsor have display booths? Where will they be located? Will they be visible during telecasts?

Figure 11-1 cont'd.

3. DISTRIBUTION CHANNEL SUPPORT
- Are the sponsorship's advantages apparent to wholesalers, retailers or franchisees? Will they participate in promotions associated with the sponsorship?

4. COMPETITIVE ADVANTAGE
- Is the event unique or distinctive?
- Has the event previously had sponsors? If so, how successful has it been in delivering desired benefits to them? Is it strongly associated with other sponsors? Will "clutter" be a problem?
- Does the event need co-sponsors? Are other sponsors of the event compatible with the company's product? Does the company want to be associated with them? Will the product stand out and be recognized among them?
- If there is co-sponsorship, will the product have category and advertising exclusivity?
- Will competitors have access to signage, hospitality, or event advertising? Will competition be allowed to sell its product on site?
- If the company does not sponsor the event, is it likely that a competitor will? Is that of concern to the company?

5. LEVEL OF RESOURCE INVESTMENT REQUIRED
- How much is the total sponsorship cost, including such items as related promotional investments, staff time and administrative and implementation effort, and in-kind resources as well as the sponsorship fee?
- Will it be unwieldy and difficult to manage the sponsorship investment?
- What are the levels of barter, in-kind, and cash investments?
- Does the sports organization guarantee a minimum level of benefits to the company?

6. SPORT ORGANIZATION'S REPUTATION
- Does the sports organization have a proven track record in staging this or comparable events? Does it have the expertise to help the product achieve its sponsorship goals?
- Does the organization have a reputation and image with which the company desires to be associated?
- Does it have a history of honoring its obligations?
- Has the company worked with this sports organization before? Was it a positive experience?
- Does the sports organization have undisputed authority and control over the activities it sanctions?
- How close to its initial projections has been the sport organization's previous performances in delivering benefits to sponsors?
- How responsive is the organization's staff to sponsors' requests? Are they readily accessible?
- Is there insurance and what are the company's potential liabilities?

Figure 11-1 cont'd.

7. EVENT CHARACTERISTICS
- What is the perceived stature of the event? Is it the best of its kind? Is it prestigious? Will involvement with it enhance the product's image?
- Does it have a "clean" image? Is there any probability it will be controversial?
- Does it have continuity or is it a one-off?

8. ENTERTAINMENT OR HOSPITALITY OPPORTUNITIES
- Are there opportunities for direct sales of product and related merchandise, or for inducing product trial?
- Will celebrities be available to serve as spokespeople for the product? Will they make personal appearances on its behalf at the event, in other markets, or in the media? At what cost?
- Are tickets to the event included in the sponsorship? How many? Which games? Where are the seats located?
- Will there be access to VIP hospitality areas for the company's guests? How many will be authorized? Will athletes appear?
- Will there be clinics, parties, or playing opportunities at which the company's guests will be able to interact with the athletes?

The marketing approach requires a sports organization to identify what companies are likely to want in return for investing their resources. This information forms the basis for developing a presentation for each prospect. Too often, sports organizations spend too much time thinking about their own needs and not enough time considering what their prospect, the potential investor, wants.

Primary reasons for sponsors' rejecting what appear to be good investment opportunities relate to budget cycles and amount of lead-time. Budgets are planning documents that operationalize what a company is committed to doing for the next 3, 6, or 12 months, depending on the length of budget cycle used. If a sponsorship is not included as part of that plan, then it is unlikely that either money or manpower will be available to support it. Thus, it is critical for sports organizations to be familiar with their target companies' budget cycles and to bring a sponsorship opportunity to their attention in advance of the budget's being formulated so it has a chance of being included.

Other possible constraints reinforce the need for a long lead-time. After there is agreement in principle, detailed contract negotiations will take time. A company is likely to support the sponsorship investment with related promotions and advertising that must be included in the budget. Implementing an integrative approach will require company resources (e.g., personnel, funds), which have to be planned and allotted so they are available at the time they are needed. Sleight (1989) notes, "Advertising is one of the major determinants of lead-time due to the time required to prepare and place advertising in the media. For these reasons, it is unlikely that companies

Table 11-2
An Example of Weighted Criteria Used to Evaluate Sponsorship Proposals

Sales Criteria	Weight
Sales opportunity	50
Creation of data base	20
Demographic criteria met	20
Opportunities for cross promotions with cosponsors	10
Major account/dealer tie-in	20
Promotional subtotal (50%)	**120**
Advertising Criteria	
Media exposure	30
Banners, signage, program opportunities	20
PR value	20
Advertising subtotal (30%)	**70**
Corporate Image-Building	
Consistent with core values	20
Enhancement of corporate credibility	10
Company product/services featured	10
Company VIPs profiled	10
Image-building subtotal (20%)	**50**
Total Points	**240**

Note: From Bell Cellular Inc. cited in *IEG Sponsorship Report* (1991). July 1, p. 5.

will consider sponsorship proposals which cannot be included as part of their regular budgetary planning process" (p. 123).

It has been noted that "every company is a potential sponsor for *some* event but not every company is a potential sponsor for *every* event" (Decker, 1991, p. 46). The initial discussion in this second half of the chapter focusses on what constitutes a good fit between a company and a sports event, because considerable effort is wasted if companies are approached that do not offer a good match. This is followed by suggestions of how to identify and nurture a set of companies whose images and target markets are compatible to that of the sports event.

Before approaching targeted companies, a proposal has to be developed. Hence, the third and fourth sections discuss preparing proposals and pricing the benefit packages included in them. Communicating the proposal involves finding out who in a company should be contacted, delivering the presentation, handling objections to points included in it, and closing, during which a sponsorship commitment is sought. The chapter concludes with a discussion of the contract and ways of fostering a close joint working relationship between a sports organization and its sponsors.

Matching a Sports Event with Sponsors

This section discusses two key conditions that characterize a good fit between a sports event and its sponsor. First, the desired image of the company and the image of the sports event must match. The second condition, which is discussed later in this section, is that the target market of the company and the target market of the sports event must match. Sponsorship activities transmit implicit rather than explicit messages; thus, image association is of central importance. By linking their product with a sports event through sponsorship, a business hopes to "borrow" the image of the sports event and use it to enhance the product's image with its target audience.

Strength of image linkages between a product and a sports event can be conceptualized along a continuum (Figure 11-2). If there is no obvious link between a company and the sports event it is sponsoring in the target audience's mind, then it is unlikely the company will receive commensurate return on its investment. For example, Southland Corporation, the former owner of 4,000 7-Eleven convenience stores, sponsored cycling. However, there was no obvious link between the stores and cycling. "They never figured out a way to use it to get people in the stores" (Lowenstein & Lancaster 1986, p. 33). The lack of a natural link between sponsor and the event means a target audience is likely to subconsciously filter out the relationship as being irrelevant.

Figure 11-2
Continuum of Linkage Strengths Between
a Product and a Sports Event

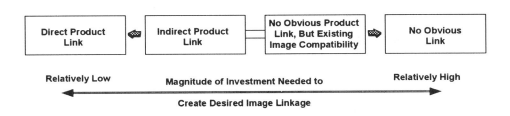

There are examples of successes where there is no obvious linkage. Cigarette brands that have forged strong image links with particular sports fall into this category. The magnitude of investment in direct and indirect expenditures needed to achieve such successes is likely to be relatively high (Figure 11-2). However, the benefits accruing to sponsors in image terms also are likely to be relatively high, because more added value will have been "borrowed" from the sport by the product.

In some cases, there may be no obvious product link, but there may be existing image compatibility. Thus, Alka-Seltzer Plus sponsored the U.S. Ski Team because: "The team has the same needs as the product's customers. Neither can let a cold stop them" ("Alka-Seltzer Plus," 1987, p. 6). Similarly, Proctor & Gamble's Old Spice line of men's toiletries sponsored stops on the Pro Beach Volleyball Tour because "Beach Volleyball builds on Old Spice's longstanding sea imagery. Plus the sport is synonymous with young men and that is our target." (International Events Group, 1992c, p. 3)

It has been suggested that this type of image matching may be facilitated by sports managers' listing a set of descriptors which best describe their event, then seeking products whose existing or defined image fits with those descriptors (Goslin, 1992) Typical words may include

accuracy	health	masculinity
strength	aggression	uniqueness
perseverance	thirst	reliability
speed	femininity	softness
risk	excellence	creativity
danger	co-operation	versatility
problem solving		

For image transfer from sports event to a product to be effective, a target audience must perceive there to be a natural and "comfortable" relationship between them. Indirect product link (Figure 11-2) means there is a logical link between using a product when spectating or participating, but that the product is not essential for those activities to take place. The most pervasive sport sponsors of this type are the beverage and food suppliers, but as the following two cases illustrate, the potential is much broader than that:

- Subaru was the dominant sponsor of American skiing. The company's initial sponsorship coincided with its introduction of the first 4-wheel drive passenger car into the United States in 1975. It was recognized that the car would appeal to skiers and mountain residents. Sponsorship of skiing was a natural fit. After the first year of ski-team sponsorship Subaru sold twice as many cars in the United State as it had originally projected (Raabe, 1989).

- Canon USA committed to a 3-year, seven-figure sponsorship to be official camcorder of Little League Baseball. The sponsorship was the result of a survey that revealed primary buyers of camcorders were parents of 6 to 12 year-olds, who earned average and above-average incomes. A central theme of the promotional campaign Canon used to support the sponsorship was that parents tape their children in action as a way to "preserve vivid memories" and "enhance your child's enjoyment of the game by serving as an instructional tool for hitting, fielding, base running, etc." (Little League, 1990, p. 7).

Shoe, clothing, and equipment products are the most visible sponsors classified as having direct product links with sport (Figure 11-2) because their products are essential for participating or spectating. At the high school level, Meagher (1992) identifies the following categories of potential sponsors who are likely to be perceived as having logical ties with sports and so could readily enhance their image by associating with appropriate events:

1. Those who design and construct sport venues--architects, engineers, contractors and sub-contractors.
2. Those who manufacture uniforms and protective equipment--from sweaters to face masks, shoulder pads to boxing gloves, track spikes to baseball gloves.
3. Those who develop, fabricate and install sport lighting systems, indoors and out.
4. Those who make and market sports medical supplies--tape, wraps, ice packs, taping tables, whirlpools and so on.
5. Those who manufacture and install sport surfaces--gym floors, tracks, aerobic floors, weight room floors and rinks.
6. Those who develop and install equipment for heating, ventilating, dehumidifying, air conditioning and acoustically treating sport venues.
7. Those who benefit from sport schedules--hotels, motels, restaurants, bus lines and travel agencies.
8. Those who design and print tickets, programs and other visual materials.
9. Those who manufacture and install the seats to accommodate spectators.
10. Those who make, distribute and service the implements of sports--the balls, sticks, bats, pucks, and nets.
11. Those who make and sell T-shirts, sweatshirts and souvenir items that bear sport team names or logos.

After image compatibility has been explored, the second key condition that characterizes a good fit is that the target market of the company and target market of the sports event must match. It is important to be able to say to a company, "Your clients are our clients." The most common type of match is on the basis of sociodemographics, especially income:

- Rolls-Royce moved its sponsorship from polo to sporting clays because polo became overcrowded with other sponsors and was "no longer just a Rolls-Royce sport." An executive noted, "People who shoot $20,000 shotguns tend to be people who buy Rolls-Royce automobiles." Further, a sporting clays event, whose attendance can be kept to 50 people or fewer, offers a "more exclusive setting" than a polo match, which can attract 5,000 or more spectators. At the events, car models were displayed and participants offered test drives ("Rolls-Royce Revamps," 1989).

- Similarly, Rolex used polo to reach its target market in France, but in the United States market the company sponsored show-jumping for exactly the same purpose, because the 3-5 million horse owners in the United States had an average income of $60,000, with 54% having houses worth $297,000 on average and an average of 2-3 cars. As the Rolex director of special events said, "We're looking for people who are able to spend $8,500 on a watch" (International Advertising Association, 1988).

- Acura, the luxury imported automobile, invested in a presenting status sponsorship at the Virginia Slims Tennis Championships in New York. An executive commented, "It's really very simple. Tennis matches our demographics and psychographics. And the media that goes with the package hits our users and intenders."

  Average buyers of the line's Integra model earn $60,000-plus per year and skew slightly male; Legend buyers skew further male, make $125,000; and Vigor buyers fall inbetween. Attenders of the event are 52% male with a median income of $49,000, and 15% make more than $100,000 (International Events Group, 1992).

An alternative approach to sociodemographics for matching the markets targeted by a sports organization and a business is compatibility of their lifestyles:

- Silhouette Vodka sponsored skiing and sailing following the findings of a study showing that those who participated in these activities exhibited relatively high vodka consumption. An effective sponsorship could be translated into these sports for several reasons. First, people consumed the product either immediately before, sometimes during, or after the event without violating any athletic rules. Second, there were alcohol retail outlets, such as ski lodges and yacht clubs, which provided steady on-site sampling opportunities. Third, the sports were perceived as upscale image building and lifestyle oriented (Dixon, 1987).

- An executive responsible for Toyota's luxury car model, Lexus, explained why Toyota competed so strongly with Cadillac for title sponsorship of the Senior PGA Tour Series, when the car was first launched: "We did a lot of research on what our potential customers do in their leisure time. They go to art, they go to theaters, they play golf. We want Lexus to be there as part of their environment" (cited in Serafin, 1989, p. 16).

- Kinder-Care Learning Centers operate 1,200 centers in North America. The company became official childcare provider of the Ladies Professional Golf Association Tour. Many of the less successful players on the tour could not afford to bring their own nannies. Tour moms agreed to mention Kinder-Care when being interviewed about their children. A Kinder-Care official noted, "The LPGA has a strong reputation with all women, so the testimonial of the players is invaluable." Kinder-Care vans picked up players' children from about 30 events, took them to the local Kinder-Care centers, then returned them when their mothers finished ("Kinder-Care, " 1988).

The emphasis placed on compatibility of target audiences makes it imperative for sport managers to initiate research which delineates the audience profile of their event. Thus, the main reason Bausch & Lomb's Contact Lens Division became a sponsor of the NBA was that research identified sports usage as the primary motivation for contact lens purchases. A detailed example of the benefits of this approach that accrued to Bassing America Corporation is given in the following case study. Sponsors are unlikely to invest if these types of research data are not available.

HOW BASSING AMERICA IDENTIFIED POTENTIAL SPONSORS FOR ITS AMATEUR FISHING TOURNAMENTS*

CASE STUDY

Drawing from its 55,000 members, Bassing conducts an annual survey at its spring events. In 1989, 75% of participants in its amateur fishing tournaments completed the four-page survey that included questions about product usage. Bassing used the results to target new sponsors.

In the 1989 survey, Bassing discovered, for example, that 67% drank liquor, and 61% cited bourbon as their liquor of choice. After analyzing brand preference and researching the industry, Bassing targeted two bourbons for proposals. Neither brand was a category leader; they were brands that Bassing felt could gain market share by sponsoring their events.

Within a few weeks, favorable responses were received from both. Bassing met with one and held the other on the sidelines. After two successful meetings, they were thrown a curve. The company's management wanted to use the tournaments to promote its rye brand instead. Bassing reminded the company that the research showed only 8% of their liquor drinking members chose rye, but the company was determined. Bassing declined the offer and broke off talks because they believed the sponsorship was doomed to fail. They contacted the other bourbon brand, George Dickel Tennessee Sippin' Whiskey, and signed a contract and promotional package at the first meeting.

Another question on the survey that helped Bassing obtain a sponsor was, "Do you eat while fishing?" It was followed by "If yes, what?" Seventy-eight percent of respondents said they ate while fishing, and 38% wrote in "Vienna sausage." Bassing researched Vienna sausage makers and found only one brand had ample distribution within their tournament territory. They made a presentation to that brand, Amour Star Canned Meats, but were turned down because they missed the company's budget cycle. The following year an agreement was signed.

This type of survey can be conducted by all sports organizations. They could conduct on-site interviews themselves or hire a research firm. After two or three surveys, a definite mainstream customer lifestyle is likely to emerge. The organization is then in a strong position to systematically approach a prospective sponsor with a niche or target for its product or service.

Note: Adapted from "Evaluation: Measuring Return in Investment" by J. H. Brett, April 16, 1990, *IEG Sponsorship Report*, pp. 3-6.

Developing a Set of Potential Company Sponsors

The geographic scope of an event's audience, including any media audience, will dictate whether the search for sponsors should be limited to regional companies and regional offices of larger companies or whether a national or international set of companies is likely to be more appropriate. This decision guides the types of reference sources that will be used to develop an initial list of potential sponsors whose images and target markets are compatible to those of the sports event. Such reference sources exist at all levels, and a key to success lies in developing a thorough, detailed and systematic approach to identifying and pursuing prospective companies.

To test the efficacy of the initial set of prospect companies, one experienced manager advises (Charney, 1993): "Put yourself in the shoes of the CEO or marketing director of the prospective sponsor, and if you can't see why she/he would become excited about being a partner in your event, don't waste your time, or theirs." If "the shoe doesn't fit" the sports organization might succeed in attracting a sponsor the first year, but the sponsor is then likely to withdraw with some level of bad feeling, and the organization has to replicate the effort to attract another company in the subsequent year.

After an initial list has been assembled, a profile of each company on the list should be developed. The information should be entered into a system that facilitates easy access and retrieval. A typical system, which was developed by an organization in the Kansas City area, is described in Figure 11-3. Each potential sponsor is issued an account code of 0 through 6 using the following classification:

> 0 -- <100 employees
> 1 -- 101-250 employees
> 2 -- 251-500 employees
> 3 -- 501-1000 employees
> 4 -- National Headquarters (regardless of size)
> 5 -- >1000 employees
> 6 -- Civic, social, and service organizations

Each record contains the account number, the company name, address, phone number, contact person and title, type of company, product or service provided, advertising budget, cycle, advertising media and space to record any sponsorship investment that a company has made.

The budget cycle for each company's promotion budget is identified. Each week the computer prints out a list of corporations whose advertising budget cycle is due to begin in eight weeks' time. This 8-week lead period gives staff the time to reestablish contact with the corporation's decision makers and to prepare a sponsorship proposal for possible inclusion in their next year's advertising budget.

A second file, FOLLOW-UP, maintained a record of all contacts made with prospective sponsors or contributors by phone, mail, or in person. Each record contains the company name, the person contacted, and the project with which the contact was concerned. Files are provided for the dates and explanations of four contacts, their decisions to accept or decline a proposition, and comments they make about the asso-

Figure 11-3
A Sample Sponsorship Tracking System

Account Type:	4
Prospect Corp:	Jones Manufacturing
Mailing Address:	P.O. Box 1000
Mailing City:	Kansas City
Mailing State	MO
Mailing Zip:	64141
Location:	31st & Southwest Trafficway
Location City:	Kansas City
Location State:	MO
Location Zip:	64141
Telephone:	(816) 968-1234
I Contact/Title:	Frank Jones - Chief Executive Officer
II Contact/Title:	Bill East - President
Type of Company:	HEADQUARTERS building systems manufacturing
# of Employees:	500
Product/Service:	Engineering, manufacturing, marketing of building systems for nonresidential construction and grain-storage bins and farm buildings. Underfloor electrical distribution systems, agricultural products and energy-management systems.
Budget Month:	October
Adv. Budget:	$3,000,000
Adv. Media:	Newspapers, consumer magazines, business publications, direct mail to consumers and business establishments, network and spot radio.
Investment A:	
Date A:	00/00/00
Project A:	
Investment B:	
Date B:	00/00/00
Project B:	
Investment C:	
Date C:	00/00/00
Project C:	
Reason Declined:	

ciation that might be helpful at a later date (See Figure 11-4). In this file staff also keep a log of the companies to which a sponsor or contributor proposal was sent, the date it was mailed, and all follow-up contacts concerning that project. This type of system is valuable in preventing duplication; companies are not invited by different people from the sports organization to sponsor different events without internal coordination of these requests.

Once a company has committed to a sponsorship, it may be possible to invite it to involve other companies, which may belong to the same corporate family or with whom they frequently do business (Jones, 1993, p. 4):

> Offer existing sponsors a commission if they bring another sponsor to the table. We just signed Pepsi to the Goodwill Games for several million dollars. If Pepsi brings in Frito-Lay, it gets $500,000 back; if Pepsi brings in Pizza Hut, Taco Bell, or KFC, it gets another $500,000. There's a million-dollar incentive to help us within the company's system. Leverage your sponsor's buying power. We signed Digital Communication Associates as

Figure 11-4
A Sample Follow-Up File

Company:	Jones Manufacturing
Contact:	Bill East
Project:	Sponsorship of temporary building for hospitality purposes at LPGA Gold Tournament
Date:	07/09/94
Explain:	Mailed 1992 and 1993 details for tournament Mailed plans and schematics
Date:	07/17/94
Explain:	Received letter asking to set up time for a presentation. Set meeting for August 1, 1994, 9:00 am
Date:	08/01/94
Explain:	Meeting with Mr. East and Mr. Jones. Explained the project and the concepts. They will be in touch with us after they make a decision
Date:	09/01/94
Explain:	Mr. Smith phoned. Jones Manufacturing accepted our proposal.
Conclusion:	Will construct structure on site
Comment:	

title sponsor of a new triathlon in Atlanta. The next day I went into the company's purchasing office and said, "Who can we get money out of? To whom can you say, `Hey, we're doing business with you, support our event?'"

Preparation of Proposals

Company managers are unlikely to review anything more extensive than one or two pages initially. They are likely to scan rather than read the material; thus, the first two paragraphs are particularly critical. Hence, the first approach should be limited either to one or two pages, or should comprise a full proposal with a brief executive overview at the front. If after receiving the one or two-page proposal interest is forthcoming, then the rest of the material and perhaps a short video can be used to supply more details. Alternatively, if a company is interested, it may respond by sending the sports organization a standard questionnaire to complete, which it uses to evaluate the investment's potential against the company's objectives and other sponsorship opportunities available to it.

The event or organization's design theme should be used in the proposal presentation since "The more you can create an 'identity' for the event in the eyes of potential sponsors, the more they are likely to perceive you as a serious possibility now or in the future" (Sleight, 1989, p. 270). Video is effective, but it takes time. In case prospects do not have time to review the whole video, they should be cued as to the most critical 2 or 3 minutes of it.

A complete proposal should incorporate the elements shown in Table 11-3. Essentially, these elements reflect the screening criteria likely to be used by companies which were identified in Figure 11-1. The proposal specifies benefits which can be made available to the sponsor and a list of those most frequently offered is given in Table 11-4.

The sports organization will be requested by experienced sponsors to provide a detailed budget of the event's costs. This will allow investors to understand the role of their investment in the context of the total budget and to reassure them that the event is adequately funded. Sponsors may also be able to identify various elements for which they can assist in reducing costs. For example, companies can often obtain better prices on printing, advertising, or other items than can sports organizations.

At the end of the short proposal indicate an intention to call in a week to ten days to see if the company is interested, and if so to arrange a meeting. This prevents the problem of companies' taking weeks to respond and means that if the response is negative the organization can focus its efforts on more likely prospects.

Developing and Pricing Sponsorship Benefit Packages

There are a variety of different ways and levels at which corporate sponsors can become associated with a sports event. Thus, it is normal practice to create different levels of benefit packages so that a wide range of investment opportunities can be

Table 11-3
Elements to Include in a Proposal

1. PROFILE OF THE SPORTS ORGANIZATION
- Brief description of the activity or event
- Brief history
- Mission goals and objectives of the sports organization

2. DESCRIPTION OF THE EVENT
- Date, day, time, location
- Past attendance figures and target audience description
- Content, theme
- Organization's capabilities and experience in presenting the event

3. COMPATIBILITY WITH POTENTIAL SPONSOR'S IMAGE AND TAR-GET MARKET
- How is the event compatible with the sponsor's image?
- Why would the sponsor be willing to associate with the event?

4. SPONSORSHIP BENEFITS
- Clearly outline all sponsor opportunities and benefits. Try to provide information on exactly what the sponsor could derive from the partnership; for example,
  · public awareness of this similar sponsorship reached x percent, compared to only y percent for z.
  · it would have a television audience of x million viewers of which about y percent are in your target market
  · in terms of interest, x ranks above every other sport in the country among your target markets
  · each year, thousands of people come to the team's games and we had x hundred column inches in the local paper, whose circulation is x thousand
  · list the opportunities for exposure of the sponsor's involvement.

5. MEDIA AND PROMOTION PLAN
- State proposed (or approved) media coverage.
- Explain how the event will be promoted.

6. SPONSORSHIP INVESTMENT
- The range of opportunities for investment and their magnitude

7. IMPACT MEASUREMENT
- How the sponsor's benefits will be measured and evaluated

8. ADDENDA SUPPORT MATERIALS
- Newspaper clippings, photos, letters from satisfied sponsors at previous events
- Past event programs or brochures
- Video material

Table 11-4
Possible Sponsor Benefits

1. SPONSOR'S NAME EXPOSURE:
-   Inclusion in the event or team title
-   Banners and signage
-   Competitors' clothing
-   Advertisements in program, yearbook, press guide, score cards
-   Scoreboard and P.A. exposure
-   Product display areas, branded merchandise, and give-aways
-   Logo on award trophies and certificates
-   Press release and broadcast promotion exposure
-   Expected media attendance, budget for promotions and advertising
-   Involvement of personnel as Master of Ceremonies, officials, or presenters of awards
-   Production of sponsor boards recording highlights with color photos for display in the sponsor's place of business
-   The right to record the event for the company's own purposes and have unlimited right to use those recordings to extend its involvement with the event

2. HOSPITALITY:
-   Availability of free tickets
-   Facilities for hospitality
-   Availability of celebrities for sponsor promotion
-   Parking passes
-   Product sampling opportunities; couponing
-   Cosponsorship benefits

offered. The number of levels is likely to vary with size of the event, but the standard structure that has emerged in the sports event area in recent years consists of four categories of sponsorship: title sponsorship, presenting sponsorship, official sponsorship, and official supplier status. Each higher level of sponsorship should build on the benefits package offered at the previous level. Brooks (1990) notes:

> There is no established list of rights for each of the categories. In fact, these sponsorship categories have no legal meaning other than what is agreed upon when the sponsorship package is designed. There is, however, a general pattern that distinguishes the four sponsorship categories from each other. (p. 59)

Title sponsorship means that the sponsor's name becomes integrated into the event title or team name. This is the highest form of association with an event and offers a sponsor maximum leverage for "borrowing" the image of the sports event to improve its product's (or corporate) image. The major risk is that if unexpected costs occur, then the title sponsor may have to increase its financial commitment rather than risk being closely linked to an inferior event. The title sponsor is likely to insist on the right to veto unsuitable cosponsors.

Presenting sponsors of a sports event generally pay about one-fourth of what the title sponsor pays (International Events Group, 1992d). They are given exclusive rights to associate with an event within a product category. Because this association is not available to competitive products, it can be exploited as a positioning factor in the product's marketing strategy.

Official sponsors typically are charged about 10% of the title fee. Their benefit package is substantially smaller than that of presentation sponsors. It is unlikely they will be permitted to invest if presenting sponsors in the same product category have committed to the event. This low level offers smaller companies an opportunity to associate with relatively little financial risk, but given the commensurately small benefit package they are likely to have to work very hard to obtain their promotional objectives.

Official suppliers are not directly linked to the sports event itself. Rather they offer their goods or services to the sports organization staging it or to the participants or spectators who are part of it. Typical of such sponsors would be food and beverage suppliers, credit card companies, and equipment suppliers.

A variation of this four category model was used by the P.G.A. Tour (International Event Group, cited in USA Today, 1993):

> The average professional golf tournament receives $1.9 million -- about 75% of its revenues -- via corporate sponsorships. Among the typical categories of corporate involvement available for a PGA Tournament were:
>
> *Title sponsor*: Corporate name used in tournament title, with other benefits, including hospitality tent, on-site signs, 300-500 event tickets, 48 entries in the professional-amateur tournament. Cost: $750,000, plus a guarantee to buy $1 million in network TV advertising time.
>
> *Presenting sponsor*: Comparable benefits to title sponsorship, but corporate name won't be in event title. Cost: $300,000, plus a $500,000 requirement to buy network TV advertising.
>
> *Associate sponsor*: As many as seven sponsors at this level, which includes signs and/or on-site entertainment. Cost: $30,000-$35,000.
>
> *Smaller sponsorships*: Costs: $16,500 for four participants spots in pro-am; $4,000-$16,000 for hospitality tent; $3,000-$10,000 for signs.

An excellent example of packaging sponsorship levels is provided by the organizers of the 1994 World Cup Soccer Tournament. The three-tier sponsorship arrangement they created is described in the following vignette. Table 11-5 (p.328) illustrates how the World Cup organizers provided exclusive benefits by category or product area to each of its ten first-tier official sponsors.

SPONSORSHIP PACKAGES AT THE 1994
WORLD CUP SOCCER TOURNAMENT

The World Cup Soccer Tournament was played for the first time in its 64 year history—(it is held every four years) in the United States in 1994. A world wide television audience of 3 billion different people was expected to visit the games held between June 17 and July 17, increasing to a cumulative 32 billion viewing audience during the month period with 1.1 billion watching the final game alone. A three-tier sponsorship package was developed, although the third tier was divided into three levels.

Official Sponsor was the first tier which was sold for an average of $15 million. It included worldwide rights to all works related to the World Cup, category exclusivity and two to four sign boards per venue. The ten official sponsor opportunities were sold to Canon, Coca Cola, Fuji, Gillette, JVC, Mars, MasterCard, McDonald's, Philips, and General Motors. The categories reserved for Fuji, Mars, Gillette, JVC and McDonald's are listed in the accompanying table to illustrate the level of detail involved in documenting what constitutes category exclusivity.

Official Marketing Partners paid $7 million and received worldwide rights to all marks, category exclusivity and one signboard per venue. These were purchased by American Airlines, Sprint Communication, Adidas, Upper Deck, ITT Sheraton, Anheuser Busch and Electronic Data Systems.

The third-tier consisted of three levels:

(i) *Official Product/Service Company* which was the only third-tier level that offered unrestricted logo use. These opportunities were priced from $1 million to $2.5 million, depending on the product category, number of brands involved, and whether the purchaser wanted U.S. or worldwide rights.

(ii) *Equipment Suppliers* were given worldwide or U.S. rights to World Cup in print only, were not permitted use of the term "official" in their designation, and were not promised category exclusivity. These were sold for between $300,000 and $1 million, plus the in-kind provision of needed equipment.

(iii) *Regional Supporters* were granted exclusivity and marketing rights to one of the Cup's nine venues and its surrounding ADI. Sponsors were required to purchase all the games played at a particular site (which ranged between four and eight) at a cost of $40,000 per game.

SOURCE: Materials provided by World Cup USA 1994 Inc. and a report in *IEG Sponsorship Reports* 12(6) March 22, 1993:pp.1-3.

An alternative taxonomy to the four sponsorship categories model described earlier is to use Gold, Silver, and Bronze designations. At the 1991 International Special Olympics there were five sponsorship levels ranging from $50,000 to $1 million (Kuzma, Shanklin, & McCally, 1992): Premier Sponsors, $1 million and above; Gold Sponsors, $500,000; Silver Sponsors, $250,000; Bronze Sponsors, $100,000; Patron Sponsors, $50,000. Each sponsorship level had a package of premiums and benefits commensurate with the sponsorship contribution. The event was able to attract 10 Premier Sponsors, 7 Gold Sponsors, 16 Silver Sponsors, 21 Bronze Sponsors, and 17 Patron Sponsors.

Table 11-5
CATEGORIES RESERVED BY OFFICIAL SPONSORS

FUJI
*Film-Disc & Instant
*Photographic paper
*8mm,16mm,35mm motion picture film
*Graphic arts film (PS plate)
*X-ray film
*Microfilm
*Computer floppy disk
*Projecting equipment for above mentioned
*Processing equipment for above mentioned
*Albums,bags,for above mentioned
*Paper envelopes, packing materials for above mentioned

MARS
*Candy & Confections
*Block chocolate,cocoa
*Chocolate covered snack bars,bisquits,mints
*Chocolate covered granola snacks,hard candies
*Potato chips
*Tortilla chips
*Corn Chips
*Nuts
*Pretzels
*Popcorn
*Puffs,curls,balls

GILLETTE
*Shaving systems
*Razor Blades
*Shaving devices,wet/dry
*Shaving creams gels
*Shaving foams, soap
*Aftershave lotions
*Aftershave colognes
*Aftershave powders
*Deodorants/anti-perspiration
*Writing instruments
*Correction fluids
*Pens & Pencils
*Ball-point pens
*Porous-point pens
*Rolling ballpens
*Broadtip markers
*Oral Care products
*Toothbrushes
*Toothpastes
*Mouthwashes

JVC
*Receivers
*Amplifiers
*Tuners
*Turntables
*Speakers
*Graphic Equalizers
*3-in-1 hi-fy systems
*Hi-fy stereo systems
*Radio cassette recorders/players
*Cassette decks
*Headphones
*Phonograph cartridges
*Audio Accessories
*Microphones
*Speaker units
*Phonograph motors
*Magnetic heads
*KARAOKE
*CD Players
*Blank audio tapes
*Digital audio tape recorders/players
*Blank digital audio tapes
*Video Category
*TV receivers
*Cassette recorders/players
*Video tape recorders/cameras
*CCTV systems
*16mm telecine projectors
*Video disc recorders/players
*Video accessories/blank tapes
*Electronic organs/acoustic pianos
*Furniture (non-exclusive)

McDONALD'S
*Hamburger
*Cheeseburger
*Filet of Fish
*¼ lb Cheeseburger
*Big Mac
*McChicken Sandwich
*McNuggets-6 pieces
*McNuggets-9 pieces
*McNuggets-20 pieces
*McDLT
*Small Fries
*Medium Fries
*Large Fries
*Egg McMuffin
*Handheld sandwiches
*Big Breakfast
*Hotcakes & Sausage
*Hash Browns
*Sausage McMuffin w/Egg
*Garden Salad
*Chef's Salad
*Side Salad
*Chunky Chicken Salad
*Happy Meal/Hamburger
*Happy Meal/Cheeseburger
*Happy Meal 4/6 piece McNuggets
*Pizzas
*Cooked Bone-in Chicken
*Prepared Fajitas,Burritos
*Prepared Spaghett/Hot Dogs
*Any national restaurant chain
*Any quick service restaurant
*Any quick service
*café restaurant
*Sit-down coffee shops
*Lunch centers
*Small café/cafeteria
*Any convenience food store
*Any family restaurant

For sport managers seeking smaller levels of sponsorship, it may be more useful to use a benefits model with two categories, which offers title and strategic sponsorship opportunities (Milgram, 1993):

• Title sponsorship may offer three options:

• Day at the Arena e.g. Ford Truck day, which gives concentrated exposure. Sponsors often incorporate sampling or offer discounted admission with proof-of-purchase on their day.

• Facility sponsorship, which provides a permanent anchor location from which a company can run promotions throughout the event or season. Sponsors may also be included in the promotion of events scheduled at the facilities they title.

• Event sponsorship, which lets a company be associated with an event taking place in the arena e.g. a half-time promotion.

• Strategic sponsorships are for companies interested in single benefits, such as product sampling and premium sales, rather than the whole package.

The different benefits associated with each sponsorship level should be specified in detail. For example, when United Airlines agreed to pay $17.5 million over 20 years for the title to Chicago's new basketball and hockey stadium, they received a number of additional benefits. In the new United Center, their logo appears on the arena playing floor, concourses, marquee and ceiling banners, as well as on courtside signage, ushers' jackets and concession cups and napkins. United also have two automatic airline ticketing machines at the venue. The company received one of the arena's 216 skyboxes which sell for $75,000 annually. All boxes have an aviation motif and a direct line to a United reservations desk. Their arrangement also includes official airline status with the venue's co-owners, the NBA's Bulls and NHL's Blackhawks (International Events Group, 1992g).

The use of different sponsorship levels allows sponsors who may not be able to afford the investment if only one level were offered, to choose a lower level of sponsorship. If this is not done a sports manager may offer only a $100,000 proposal when the company has only $40,000 to invest. Thus, the opportunity to secure $40,000 of support is lost. One experienced sports marketer noted (Dixon, 1987):

I like to set price ranges: "Our packages start at $25,000 and go up to $500,000." This forces interaction between myself and the potential sponsor. I do not know how much money he has and he really does not know how much I can deliver and what the value is. But we sit down and work out a package. (p. 5)

The importance of this kind of flexible interaction is increasingly being recognized. It enables sport managers to get a better understanding of the needs and sponsorship potential of the targeted company and enables managers to work with a company to customize a package. Cherpit (1992, p. 5) noted, "We have no standard event packages, say at the $25,000 level or $50,000 level. To have companies buy in without any modification to their needs won't work." Similarly, Castillo (1992, p. 5) observed, "Sponsors are saying, `Create something that's mine.' When we tailor a package to their needs, there's no wasted money."

However levels of sponsorship are defined, a single price should be attached to each package of components that is developed. If components of packages are individually priced, then a sponsor is likely to look for items to cut. If sponsors want to negotiate certain elements to reduce the price, then they will raise the issue. The sports manager should not invite this action by individually pricing components in the initial proposal. It has been suggested that signage is often the most overpriced element of a sponsorship package (Jones, 1993, p. 4):

> For example, in the soft drink category, Coke and Pepsi are almost universally known, so signage is worth little to those brands. Conversely, a sign for PowerAde, a new challenger to Gatorade, is more valuable. The pricing of most properties does not reflect this reality.

Many companies prefer to offer in-kind services rather than cash as their sponsorship investment. For example, a Coca-Cola spokesman suggested (International Events Group, 1993, p. 6):

> When you think of Coca-Cola don't only think of cash. Think of us as a TV network in terms of the millions of impressions we can offer you as rightsholders in a very relevant way. We reach millions of consumers daily through product advertising, truck-pack ad panels, in-store displays and so on, which we can convert to support our relationship with a property.

In order to ascertain the level of benefits a sponsor should receive in exchange for these services, a valuation of them has to be made. This is likely to be challenging. For example, if a company provides computing systems software and advice or courier service, how is the real value of these services determined? Some guidance was offered by the International Events Group (1992f):

> Treat in-kind deals the same as cash deals if they are substitutes for line items in your budget. For example, if you have no need for a car, do not let an auto company offset its cash payment by throwing in a car. However, if you require air travel, treat the airline as a cash sponsor. Clarify how you will calculate the value of its payment. For example, is it based on the value of the lowest discounted air fare or the retail rate? (p. 5)

An additional concern related to accepting in-kind products is the potential for theft or loss. One experienced sports manager commented, "I would be very cautious to accept in-kind products unless they are consumable. Things disappear even when you have trustworthy people working for you. The worst thing you could do is burn bridges of a sponsor. It may be wise to spend money and rent the good" (McCally, 1990).

The bulk of a sponsorship fee, at least 65%, should be paid when contracts are signed, because costs associated with obligations to the sponsor, such as exposure in collateral materials, are likely to be incurred for a period of time before the event takes place.

It was noted earlier in this chapter that 3 to 5 years was a preferred length of commitment for sponsoring businesses. A sports organization should offer discounts for multiyear commitments, because they save time, labor, and the legal fees that an equivalent number of one-year contracts would require.

Communicating the Proposal

There are four elements to consider in communicating the proposal. First is the preparation effort when a sports organization determines who in the targeted company should be approached with the sponsorship proposal and then seeks information about these contact people that will aid communication with them. The presentation element itself incorporates two other considerations: handling negative reactions and closing.

Preparation. After a list of the most probable sponsors has been derived, the next stage is to prepare an approach tailored to each of these prospects. The preparation commitment is time consuming, but it is essential. Success in soliciting support is more likely to result from good preparation than from good presentation techniques. Key questions in the preparation phase are "Who in the company should be contacted?" and "What is their role?"

In companies that are extensively involved in sponsorship, it is likely to be the responsibility of a specialist executive or of a sponsorship department. In other companies, however, sponsorship decisions may be made by the chief executive if the business is relatively small .

In large companies with multiple brands, if product rather than corporate sponsorship is being solicited, then brand managers rather than senior corporate officials are likely to be the relevant contacts. Finally, sales managers of regional offices should not be overlooked because an increasing number of companies are decentralizing marketing functions and funds.

The worst sort of approach is to send a proposal to "The Vice-President of Marketing" or "The Chief Executive Officer." The proposal should be addressed personally to the contact person. The relevant individual can be tracked by phoning the company's public relations or press office, the company's receptionist, or the secretary or assistant of the vice-president of marketing.

Proposals should be directed at the highest level to which the sports organization can gain access because it has been observed that "top level managers are paid to say yes, while middle-managers are paid to say no." Too often there is a mistaken tendency to contact employees at a lower level because sports managers feel less intimidated and more comfortable with them, and hope that the request will filter up to the key decision makers. Despite all that has been said about companies' objectively evaluating proposals, there are still instances when if all else is approximately equal, the egos and personal interests of senior executives or marketing directors may be a consideration in the decision. Indeed, it has been argued that "the chairman's choice" may contribute to a sponsorship's success for two reasons: (a) if the senior executive has ego-involvement in the sponsorship there is likely to be added incentive to make it succeed, and (b) it ensures commitment from the highest levels in the company (Meenaghan, 1983).

Once the contact person has been identified, that individual's role in the decision-making process has to be ascertained. There are likely to be several corporate actors who play a role in the decision process, and they fall into three categories: gatekeepers, influencers, and decision makers. However, one person may fill more than one of the roles.

It is most probable that the contact person in a large company will be a *gatekeeper*. This person may simply receive the sponsorship proposal and forward it to others who make the decisions. Alternatively, the gatekeeper may be assigned the role of a "first screener" who eliminates some proposals and forwards a selective list to the decision makers. The manner in which a gatekeeper passes along a request may be critical. If he or she is not personally supportive, the information may be relayed less favorably and with fairly evident disapproval. Thus, the gatekeeper is a key person in determining the success of a request and must be "won over." Sports managers should try to persuade gatekeepers to permit them to present their case directly to the decision makers. This will ensure that the proposal is presented in its best light and that there is an opportunity to answer any questions or objections the decision makers may have.

An *influencer* is a person whose views or advice help shape the attitudes of decision makers and who thus exerts some influence on the final decisions. The third type of actor is the *decision maker* who decides whether or not to support the proposal. In this preparation stage it is important to identify who will have final decision authority.

For these reasons, it is useful to ask who will be representing the company at the meeting, their position, status, and role in the decision process. This will influence who attends from the sports organization. One sports manager experienced in sponsorship solicitations suggests always taking one more person to the meeting than the sponsor will have there. He believes that "one additional nodding head is always an advantage in any sales situation."

An important adage in soliciting sponsorships is that people invest in people first and organizations second. This is true of corporate executives. "It is not what you know, but who you know" is a valid aphorism in soliciting sponsorship. Sports managers are not only selling sponsorship investments, but they are also selling relationships. Success is likely to be as attributable to positive personal chemistry as to the worthiness of the investment. The optimum scenario for a sports manager is to have a well-known track record of successful sponsorship partnerships and a network that enables him or her to personally call the decision maker in a targeted company, brief the individual on the proposal, and then follow up with a comprehensive document.

The importance of personal chemistry makes it imperative that a sports organization search for linkages between its personnel and the gatekeepers, influencers, and decision makers in a targeted company. The key questions are "Who in the organization knows any of the key corporate actors" and "Whom can we enlist as an ally?" The best types of linkages are personal acquaintances, but if these links are weak, then it becomes important to seek referrals. Are there any mutual contacts who could introduce organization personnel to key company officials?

The organization's task is to learn as much as possible about the individuals who are gatekeepers, influencers, and decision makers and to match their backgrounds with senior personnel from the organization who have similar backgrounds. A substantial body of empirical research demonstrates that positive interaction between the potential contributor and agency representatives is greatly facilitated if their backgrounds, personalities, interests, and lifestyles are compatible. The greater the perceived similarities, the stronger the mutual attraction or affinity between them is likely to be. This matching process necessitates finding out background information relating to interests, hobbies, families, goals, etc. The contact person's secretary or receptionist may be willing to give this type of information.

Presentation. An effective presentation explains all aspects of the organization's proposition as it relates to the benefits sought by the prospective sponsor. The first minute of a presentation can be the most critical part of it even though it represents only a minuscule percentage of the total presentation time. There is only one opportunity to make a first impression, and this often will determine receptivity in the mind of the potential sponsor to the central substance of the presentation.

While there are many ways of making a presentation, the best approach is interaction, with the prospects being active participants in the communication. This approach begins by exploring the client's needs: "What benefits do you want to see from a sponsorship in which you invest?" and "What criteria are most important in your evaluation of sponsorship proposals?" The primary task of the sports manager during this stage is to listen and to suppress premature tendencies to talk about what his or her organization has to offer. During the listening phase, the sports manager should be considering the **f**eatures, **a**dvantages and **b**enefits (FAB's) of the organization's event which are relevant to the potential sponsor's needs.

After the potential sponsors have explained their needs, the sports manager is in a position to organize and tailor the presentation to show how the event is able to meet them. The presentation should be careful not to promise more than can be delivered. In the interests of developing a long-term, ongoing relationship with a sponsor, it is always better to underpromise and then deliver more. Indeed, if it becomes apparent after listening to the company's expectations that the event cannot deliver them, then in the interest of a long-term relationship the organization should articulate that view and gracefully withdraw.

Using the FAB approach, the sports manager begins by explaining to the prospective sponsor the organization's credentials and the outstanding and unique features of the event. The advantages portion of the presentation addresses ways in which this opportunity is superior to other investment options available to the company. The benefits section translates features and advantages into benefits and addresses the central question of how the event can help the sponsors achieve their objectives. For example, if the sponsor's primary aim is to increase sales in a market the event can reach, then the presentation will concentrate on packaging trade incentives that can be presented to dealers, retailers, franchises or wholesalers to encourage them to sell more products (Sleight, 1989). Alternatively, if awareness is the major objective, then the presentation will identify ways the event could extend the product's audience reach, gain more publicity, or link with a media co-sponsor. The benefit packages the sports manager had in mind will probably need to be customized and amended to get the best fit with a company's objectives.

It may be beneficial to demonstrate how the sports organization would work with the company's advertising agency, because the company may rely on their advice.

Such agencies are frequently not supportive of sponsorship investments because they take dollars from the advertising budget, and agencies work on a fixed percentage commission of that budget. Thus, if the agency can see a useful role for advertising as part of the sponsorship program, the proposal is more likely to gain its support.

By the end of the presentation, company executives must feel comfortable with the sports manager's attitude toward the proposed arrangement and toward them as partners. They must feel the organization is willing and able to fulfill its commitments and that it has an understanding of the sponsor's commercial needs.

Handling Negative Reactions. If the presentation is to yield the anticipated result, it is necessary to elicit any objections that the potential sponsors may have. Negative reactions should not be dreaded; they should be welcomed. They provide valuable feedback and are the prospect's way of communicating how to make the presentation successful. Answering objections removes barriers, and the objections provide clues as to the best approach to take for the remainder of the presentation.

Quiet prospects who hold questions and reservations in their minds and give few clues about their inward resistances are likely to be least influenced by the presentation. If no objections are raised, then it suggests either that the company was prepared to respond positively at the start or that the prospect was not sufficiently interested to raise an objection.

Over a period of time, sports managers are likely to hear all of the various negative reactions that can be raised and will not be surprised by them. They should "keep track of flack," that is, document the objections received and determine the best way to handle them.

Closing. At the closing stage the sports manager typically summarizes the major benefits on which there has been agreement, addresses anticipated objections or reservations concerning the sponsorship, and requests that the prospect take specific affirmative action. Many people find that closing is the most difficult part of a presentation. They feel guilty or lack the self-confidence to ask for a commitment, or they have not thought through ahead of time how they will orchestrate the closing to obtain a commitment from the company.

There are many approaches to closing that could be used. Three of the most common are illustrated below.

- Obtain agreement on a major benefit and then build upon it: "If I understand you correctly, Mr. Smith, you are most interested in increased visibility from your investments." "Yes." "An investment of $50,000 would enable us to. . ."
- Ask an open question and pause: "Mr. Smith, you've seen the benefits this investment could provide. What are your reactions?" or "How should we now move ahead?"
- Use the "based-on" technique that refers to a major point which was previously agreed and builds upon it: "Based on your desire for maximum visibility, I'd like to suggest an investment of $50,000, which would give you high visibility with the new target you are trying to reach."

Often a company may not be prepared to invest in a project at the level the organization seeks when the question is asked at closing. However, there may be a willingness to invest at a lower level. Thus, it is desirable for the organization to have more than one investment level in mind, so that if the main investment opportunity is rejected other options can be presented.

At the end of the meeting, the sports manager should have a clear idea of what happens next. The company representatives should be asked if they require any further information from the organization, or whether the sports manager should prepare a more comprehensive proposal for presentation to a committee or board. Finally, there should be clarification of who will contact whom and when.

Handling Rejections

Sponsorship may be conceptualized as a product that a sport organization is selling. From this perspective, it is reasonable to anticipate that development of a sponsorship program may follow a typical product life cycle curve, progressing from introduction through take-off and maturation to saturation. The introduction stage may last two or three years before the sponsorship product gathers momentum and enters the take-off stage. During this period a sports organization may experience a large number of rejections to its sponsorship proposals.

The success or failure of an initial personal communication interaction with a prospect should not be viewed in the immediate context of whether or not sponsorship support was forthcoming. Rather, the contact should be regarded as the beginning of a long-term relationship. A period of time may be needed to consolidate the personal relationships which have been established before sponsorship support emerges. Early efforts may yield relatively little but they are made in the anticipation of increased return in the future as the personal relationship and confidence in the sport organization is nurtured.

When a targeted sponsor rejects a sponsorship proposal there should always be an effort to find out why. This involves asking questions like, was the package wrong? Did we fail to deliver enough benefits? Was the return on the sponsor's projected investment inadequate? Did we ask for too much of an investment." Did we misread the sponsor's target market? Did we send the wrong person? Was the presentation ineffective?

It is essential to follow-up. The objective is not to challenge the decision, but rather to ascertain why the proposal was not accepted and if the company would be interested in working with the sport organization in the future. When proposals are turned down it is often not because a business cannot benefit from them, but rather because their timing is not right for the company. Polite persistence pays off. Thus, immediately after an unsuccessful effort, a thank you letter should be sent letting a prospect know that the time spent visiting with the organization's representatives was appreciated. Contact should be maintained with the targeted company on the assumption that it may be a prime prospect for sponsorship support in the future.

The Contract

The notion of an exchange relationship is the conceptual underpinning of all marketing transactions. However, in the context of sponsorship, a fluent exchange is especially challenging to transact because it involves a business relationship between, at best, organizations with vastly different aims and, at worst, a commercial company and an amateur organization with different needs and expectations (Sleight, 1989). The two parties often operate in totally different environments, do not understand each other's businesses, have dissimilar reasons for their involvement, and seek different ends from the arrangement. In addition, the sponsorship medium is inherently complicated because it embraces so many different issues (Table 11-6).

For these reasons, once general agreement has been reached with a sponsor, some form of written document should be developed to insure that both sides' interests are protected. Initially, this should be drafted without input from lawyers by representatives from both sides, in order that issues be freely discussed. When a draft has been completed, then legal advisers may be used to ensure the intent is accurately expressed.

Sponsorship agreements may be documented by a confirming letter, a letter of agreement, or a formal contract (Martin, 1993). The magnitude of resources being exchanged and the expectations of the sponsor will guide the appropriate format. A confirming letter is not a contract *per se* since it is not signed by both parties. The letter agreement is a contract signed by both parties, but is less formal, less expensive, and often less intimidating than a standard contract. The formal contract is no more enforceable than a letter agreement, but it does commit the parties to giving greater attention to the details involved.

The central purposes of the written agreement are to (Martin, 1993)

- Denote the rights of the sponsor (acquiring).
- Denote the rights of the promoter (retaining).
- Delineate exclusivity.
- Protect the parties from unwanted liability.
- Protect the parties' reputations and trademarks, logos, symbols.
- Protect the parties' respective proprietary and other interests in the event (to avoid sponsor theft of the event and/or to preserve the sponsor's long term benefit).

Sleight (1989) has observed that

Misunderstandings usually arise when the parties to the agreement have different views as to who will do what to exploit the sponsorship. The way to avoid this is to go through every possible element of the project beforehand and to agree the areas of responsibility. These details should be included in the contract so that in the event of any disagreements the original arrangement can be referred to. (p. 192)

A comprehensive list of the types of issues to be covered in contract agreement discussions has been developed by Brooks (1990) and is reproduced in Table 11-6. However, given the element of unpredictability associated with sporting events (e.g. weather, injury, etc.) and the large number of facets involved in a sponsorship partner-

Table 11-6
Issues to Address in a Sponsorship Agreement

- Official status:
  What is the sponsorship category? Are there veto rights with this category? That is, does a sponsor in this category have a say in who else can be a sponsor?
- Sponsorship fee:
  What is the fee? How and when is the fee to be paid? Is the fee refundable for any reason?
- Title rights:
  Will the sponsor's name appear in the title? How will trophies be named? Who will present the trophy or prizes?
- Television exposure:
  Who owns and controls TV rights? Does the sponsor have rights of first refusal on television advertising spots? Is there a ratings guarantee? Will there be a rebate if ratings fall below this guarantee? Can the sponsor use TV video footage in its regular advertising? Does the sponsor need to obtain permission prior to using video clips for commercial reasons? Who is responsible for negotiating television time? Is a portion of the sponsorship fee credited to the TV coverage?
- Public relations and media exposure:
  Will key athletes mention the sponsor's name when being interviewed by the media? Will the sponsor's name be included in media releases? Who is responsible for media releases? Can the sponsor develop its own media marketing campaign?
- Logo use:
  Under what conditions can the sponsor use the organization's logos or trademarks? If special logos are developed, who owns them? Can the sponsor use the logo to promote its own image and products? Does the sponsor have merchandising rights? That is, can it make and sell souvenir items?
- Signage:
  How many banners, athlete patches, placards, arena boards or flags can the sponsor use? What size? Where can banners be placed and what can appear on them? Who is responsible for making and paying for the signage? Who is responsible for placing the signage on-site?
- Advertising rights:
  In what manner can the sponsor use the organization or event for advertising purposes? Will the sponsor's name be on stationery or in the program? Where will it be placed? Can the sponsor use photographs related to the sponsorship for product promotion and advertising? Who is responsible for individual consent to the use of the photographs in advertising? What limitations are placed on the use of photographs?

Table 11-6 cont'd.

- Athlete use:
  Will athletes make personal appearances on behalf of the sponsor? Will key athletes or coaches attend pre- or postcompetition parties? Will athletes wear the sponsor's name during competition?
- Hospitality rights:
  Does the sponsor have the right to a hospitality tent? Does the sponsor receive free tickets for tie-in contests, for gifts to key clients, or for other use?
- Point of sale promotion:
  Can the sponsor's products be sold on-site? What type: cigarettes, alcohol? Can the sponsor run on-site or off-site promotions associated with the sponsorship? Can the sponsor team with other companies to form cooperative promotions?
- Direct mail lists:
  Will mailing lists of ticket holders or athletes be made available to the sponsor? What form of promotions can the sponsor undertake with these mailing lists?
- Product sampling:
  Will a place be made available for product display and sampling? What type of products can be made available for sampling? Will you accept cigarettes and beer?
- Legal liabilities:
  Who is responsible for injuries to spectators, participants or officials? What if it rains or there are TV problems? Who pays existing expenses?
- Future options:
  How many years does the sponsorship last? Does the sponsor have renewal options? How many years does the option last? How are sponsorship fee increases to be determined next year? After that?

Note: From "Sponsorship by Design" by C. Brooks, December 1990, *Athletic Business*, pp. 61-62. Reprinted with permission.

---

ship, both parties should recognize the need for some degree of flexibility in interpreting their contracted agreement.

Working Together to Make It Happen

When a partnership agreement is reached, this should not be regarded as the terminal consummation of a relationship. From a sponsor's perspective, it may only be a trial offer from which the business will withdraw if returns are not satisfactory. The sports organization also should view it from this perspective and recognize that the agreement offer is a tentative initial step. Sometimes all efforts are directed to securing a sponsorship, and little thought is given to servicing it. A long-term association and commitment will evolve only if a sponsor's objectives are met.

Sponsors add another dimension of responsibility for the sports organization. It is required to make additional efforts to coordinate the sponsors' desires, and they become a second "audience" that must be satisfied. A key to a successful ongoing resource support effort is not the securing of new supporters; rather it is the retention of previous investors. There is an old marketing adage that says, "Your best customers are your best prospects." If investors are pleased with the results accruing from their support expenditure, then they are likely to be receptive to future support requests. They are also likely to be valuable sources of testimonials and referrals. It is much less costly in time and effort to sustain an existing sponsorship arrangement than it is to find a new partner. This means the short-term perspective that "we need the checks from sponsors so we can go about our business" (Charney, 1993, p.55) is likely to be very costly in the long term.

There should be a plan and timetable agreed upon with each sponsor for implementing all the promotional activities expected by each partner. These activities should be carefully coordinated with the partners' independent promotional investments that they use to support and extend impact of their sponsorship. Coordinating interactions with the media is particularly important to ensure sponsors and sports event are communicating consistent and complementary messages at complementary times. If a sports organization does not have the level of expertise in media relationships that is available to its major sponsor, then it should consider inviting the sponsor to coordinate this function.

A key to nurturing a close working relationship and building goodwill is constant communication between the parties and a total commitment to meeting the sponsor's needs. The sport organization should assign to each sponsor a staff member to be contact liaison, who serves as a conduit through which all communications pass. This individual should be positioned as an advocate within the organization charged with seeking to further the sponsor's goals.

If multiple sponsors are involved, regularly scheduled meetings that all attend will facilitate interchange of promotional ideas and make sponsors feel part of the event. Sleight (1989) observes:

> Many organizers are nervous about bringing sponsors together and avoid it at all costs, but this route is fraught with dangers. Far better to get everybody to state their objectives in advance and to work together to satisfy them. Since the aims for each sponsor should be different there need be no conflict between them and there are many cross-sponsorship promotions that can be done when all parties cooperate. (p. 279)

The organizers of the Olympic Festival in Minneapolis called their sponsors a Patron Advisory Group and used this regular meetings approach to good effect (cited in McCally, 1990).

> The Patron Advisory meetings were really a selling point for some smaller companies who wanted to get next to the big guys. Company representatives

really looked forward to networking among themselves, to be able to create new business. We used the meetings to invite potential sponsors and show them how many sponsors were already on board and to show that this was a real live event. Also, it was a chance to tell all the sponsors the same thing at the same time. It gave them the perception that every one was getting equal treatment and were on an equal level.

The advisory meetings were also a way for the partners to gain publicity and to show off to each other. Many of the meetings were held at the corporate headquarters of the respective hosts. "3M gave out its corporate pin and Post-it Notes that announced its association with the Festival during one of the first meetings. That set the stage for the other sponsors. Some got really carried away and took it to the extremes. Dayton's/Target held an elaborate ceremony in the Metrodome where they set-up Greek architecture and had chariots riding around. It was great fun," a spokesperson exclaimed.

The more that executives and employees of a sponsoring business can be involved and feel ownership in planning and implementing the sports event, the more likely it is that a long- term commitment will evolve. As part of this process, key decision makers should be given access to celebrity sports people, behind-the-scenes areas where ordinary spectators are not permitted, and excellent seats from which to view the event.

Post-Event Follow-Up

The way in which the follow-up is handled will influence the likelihood of receiving future support from investing companies. The intent in the follow-up stage is to enhance relationships that have been established. The follow-up should consist of three actions. First, an evaluation of the extent to which a sponsor's objectives were achieved should be done in association *with* the sponsors, rather than *for* them, to be sure the post-event assessment meets their needs. This issue of assessing the impact of a sponsorship constitutes the theme of chapter 12. The second follow-up component consists of a portfolio that includes photographs, stories, copies of all promotional material mentioning the sponsor, and a short video showing highlights of the sports event and the company's role in it. Finally, discussions should be initiated about future investments in the event. These will be guided by the timespan and arrangements for renewing or cancelling that were included in the contract. The discussions should be held soon after the event; thus, maximum time is available to make changes for the next event or to find another sponsor if necessary.

SUMMARY

The first half of this chapter was concerned with understanding a business organization's approach to entering a sponsorship partnership, and it discussed five major issues businesses are likely to address when considering sports sponsorships. First, it is desirable that a business formulate a set of specific, measurable, prioritized objectives for its sponsorship investment. This will assist both partners in crystallizing thinking about how the sponsorship opportunity can be best exploited and in evaluating the level of success the investment delivered.

A second issue is the length of commitment, and there is a consensus that 3 to 5 years is an optimum period for many sponsorships. A third concern is how sponsorship will be integrated with a company's other communication vehicles. Sponsorship can only offer implicit messages and cannot indicate why a product should be purchased. Other vehicles have to be coordinated with it to provide explicit support information. Sponsorship offers a "hook" or a unifying theme that can be incorporated into the messages of the other communication vehicles to provide a coherent promotional focus. Integration has cost implications. The indirect costs associated with using other promotional vehicles in concert to optimize a sponsorship's impact are likely to be at least equal to those of the direct investment and often range up to three times the direct costs. Sport managers may fail to consider these indirect costs and try to convince companies of a sponsorship's potential return on investment based only on the direct cost. To reduce costs, some companies have focused on sponsorship investments that have the potential for being at least partially self-liquidating.

As recognition of the effectiveness of sponsorship has grown, companies have developed criteria and screening procedures for sifting through the multiple opportunities they are offered. This selection process is a fifth concern of businesses, and they tend to focus on eight factors in their evaluation: customer audience, exposure potential, distribution channel audience, advantage over competitors, resource investment level required, sport organization's reputation, event's characteristics, and entertainment and hospitality opportunities.

The second half of the chapter addressed how to solicit sponsorships from business organizations. The marketing approach requires that proposals focus on the potential for delivering what a targeted company is likely to want in return for investing its resources. Sport managers should perceive themselves as brokers who are concerned with furthering the welfare of potential sponsor companies by offering opportunities in which both the business and organization win.

There are two key conditions that characterize a good fit between a sports event and its sponsor. First, the desired image of the company and the image of the sports event must match. Sponsorship activities transmit implicit rather than explicit messages; therefore, image association is of central importance as a business hopes to "borrow" the image of the sports event and use it to enhance its product's image with its target audience. The second characteristic of a good fit is that the target market of the company must match that of the sports event in their sociodemographic or lifestyle profiles. With these two guidelines, a list of potential sponsors and a profile of each company on the list will be developed and entered into an information retrieval program.

A short one- or two-page proposal should be sent to the targeted companies, with a follow-up call occurring a week or 10 days later. Opportunities should be packaged to offer different levels of benefit packages so that a wide range of investment amounts can be accommodated. The most frequently used benefit structure at major sports events consists of four categories: title sponsorship, presenting sponsorship, official sponsorship, and official supplier status.

There are four elements to consider in communicating a proposal. First is preparation, which involves identifying who in the targeted company should be approached with the proposal and seeking out information about him or her. This information includes determining the role, that is, whether the contact person is a gatekeeper, influencer, or decision maker; whether the individual is acquainted with anyone in the sports organization; and background material on the person's interests, family, lifestyle, etc. which will help facilitate positive personal interaction between the individual and the sports organization's representatives. The second element is the presentation, and this should be interactive. The sport manager listens to the potential sponsor's benefit needs and then explains the features, advantages, and benefits the event is able to offer that address those needs. Third, negative reactions to the proposal should be solicited; thus, there is an opportunity to address and reverse them. The final element of the presentation is closing, which is when the potential sponsors are asked to commit to an investment.

When a sponsorship proposal is rejected, reasons for the negative outcome should be identified. If these can be rectified in the future, then the initial rejection may constitute only the beginning of a long-term relationship. When a proposal is accepted, a written contractual document should be developed to ensure that both sides' interests are protected. To nurture a long-term relationship the sport organization has to view the sponsor as a partner and work to help the company realize its objectives. This may be achieved by nominating a staff person to be a liaison with the company and to be its advocate within the sport organization. If multiple sponsors are involved, facilitating interaction and networking among them may be productive. Follow-up actions after the event is completed involve helping the key decision makers in the company evaluate the extent to which their objectives were met and initiating discussions about future investments in the event.

Questions for Study and Discussion

1. Provide examples of how sponsorships can be integrated with each of the other four communication vehicles: personal selling, advertising, publicity, and incentives.
2. Define the term "ambush marketing" and provide a recent example of ambushing related to a sporting event. What are two actions event managers can take to defend against ambushing?
3. Assume you have been hired to solicit corporate sponsorships for a celebrity golf tournament on behalf of your city's local American Heart Association. Using a marketing approach, describe how you would proceed in recruiting event sponsors. How far in advance of the tournament would you seek sponsors, and why? What essential issues would you address in targeting potential sponsors? What different types or categories of sponsorship would you propose?

REFERENCES

Alka-Seltzer backs U.S. ski team. (1987, April 20). *Special Events Report*, p. 6.

Armstrong, C. (1988, May). Sports sponsorship: A case-study approach to measuring its effectiveness. *European Research*, pp. 97-102.

Assertions. (1988, September 12). *Special Events Report*, p. 2.

Barr, J. (1988, May 2). Boosting sales through sponsorship. *Special Events Report*, pp. 4-5.

Brooks, C. (1990, December). Sponsorship by design. *Athletic Business*, pp. 58-62.

Castillo, P. (1992) The bottom line on sponsorship. *Sponsorship Report 11*(24) December 21:4-5.

Charney, B. (1993). Sponsor renewal: How to keep them coming back. *IFA's official guide to sponsorship* (pp. 53-60). Port Angeles, WA: International Festivals Association.

Cherpit, S. (1992) The bottom line on sponsorship. *Sponsorship Report 11*(24) December 21:4-5.

Copeland, R. P. (1991). *Sport sponsorship in Canada: A study of exchange between corporate sponsors and sport groups.* Unpublished master's thesis, University of Waterloo, Waterloo, Canada.

Decker, J. (1991, December). Seven steps to sponsorship. *Parks and Recreation*, pp. 44-48.

Dixon, D. R. (1985, September). Research in sports marketing. *Marketing Communications*, pp. 79-82.

Dixon, D. R. (1987, April 20). How to package, price and sell your event to sponsors. *Special Events Report*, pp. 4-5.

Elliott, S. (1992, July 15). Jousting by mass marketers is the newest Olympic sport. *New York Times*, p. D1.

Ensor, R. J. (1987, September). The corporate view of sports sponsorship. *Athletic Business*, pp. 40-43.

Frankel, B. (1988, December 5). Event marketing: Panacea or problems? *Marketing News*, p. 12.

Furst, D. & Furst, A. (1991, May 20). A method for scrutinizing sponsorship opportunities. *Special Events Report*, pp. 4-5.

Goslin, A. (1992, April/May). Preparing sponsorship proposals for recreation events. *Trends (SAART)*, p. 1.

Graham, J. (1988, July 31). Warner Canto: AmEx exec. on prowl for special events. *Advertising Age*. p. 13.

Gratton, C. & Taylor, P. (1985). *Sport and recreation: An economic analysis.* London: FN Spon.

International Advertising Association. (1988). *Sponsorship: Its role and effects.* New York: The Global Media Commission of the International Advertising Association.

International Events Group. (1992a, April 6). Coors shifts Keystone ties into high gear. *Sponsorship Report*, p. 6.

International Events Group. (1992b, April 20). Benjamin Moore covers Yankees' Bases. *Sponsorship Report*, p. 6.

International Events Group. (1992c, September 7). Old Spice digs beach volleyball. *Sponsorship Report*, p. 3.

International Events Group. (1992d, September 7). Pricing: How to determine what your property is worth to sponsors. *Sponsorship Report*, pp. 4-5.

International Events Group. (1992e, November 2). Acura loves women's tennis ties. *Sponsorship Report*, p. 6.

International Events Group. (1992f, November 21). Bausch & Lomb to contact men, teens through NBA. *Sponsorship Report*, p. 2.

International Events Group. (1992g, September 7). United Airlines lands title to Chicago Stadium. *Sponsorship Report 11*(17) pp. 4-5.

Johnson, R. (1992, January 20). How the Chicago mayor's Office of Special Events uses surveys in its sponsorship program. *IEG Sponsorship Report*, pp. 4-5.

Jones, R (1993, April 26). Selling more sponsorship. *Sponsorsip Report 12*(8) p.4.

Kinder-Care watches kids while mom play. (1988, February 22). *Special Events Report*, pp. 7-8.

Klein, J. (1988, June 13). Using events to increase sales at General Foods and Maxwell House. *Special Events Report*, pp. 4-5.

Kohl, F. & Otker, T. (1985, November). *Sponsorship -- some practical experiences in Philips' consumer electronics.* Paper presented at the below-the-line and sponsoring ESOMAR Seminar, Milan: ESOMAR.

Kuzma, J. R., Shanklin, W. L. & McCally, J. F. (1992, April). *An overview of the issues affecting the sponsorship decision and satisfaction for major sponsors of the 1991 International Special Olympics.* Paper presented at the International Conference on Sports Business, Columbia, SC.

Lavelle, B. (1991, July 1). How Bell Cellular boosted its return from events. *Special Events Report*, pp. 4-5.

Levin, G. (1992, February 10). AmEx's Olympics ambush may goad IOC into action. *Advertising Age*, p. 2.

Little League catches big sponsor in Canon. (1990, October 8). *Special Events Report*, p. 7.

Lohr, S. L. (1988, September 5). Volvo broadens a sports marketing strategy. *New York Times*, p. A 30.

Lowenstein, R. & Lancaster, H. (1986, June 25). Nation's businesses are scrambling to sponsor the nation's pastimes. *Wall Street Journal*, p. 33.

Managing and Leveraging: Ambush marketing and other guerilla tactics. (1990, April 16). *Special Events Report*, pp. 1-3.

Martin, E. L. (1993). How to prepare a sponsorship contract. In *IFA's official guide to sponsorship* (pp. 39-44). Port Angeles, WA: International Festivals Association.

McCally, J. F. (1990). *Corporate sponsorship and the U.S. Olympic Festival '90: A mutually beneficial marketing arrangement.* Unpublished manuscript, Mankato State University, Department of Marketing.

McKelvey, S. (1992, Fall). NHL v Pepsi-Cola Canada, Uh-Huh! Legal parameters of sports ambush marketing. *The Entertainment and Sports Lawyer*, pp. 5-17.

McKelvey, S. (1993, March). Corporate bushwhackers. *Athletic Business*, p. 14.

Meagher, J. W. (1992, May). And now a word from our sponsor. *Athletic Business*, p. 14.

Meenaghan, J. A. (1983). Commercial sponsorship. *European Journal of Marketing*, *17*(7), 5-73.

Perelli, S. & Levin, P. (1988, November 21). Getting results from sponsorship. *Special Events Report*, pp. 4-5.

Raabe, S. (1989, February 10). Sponsorship of ski events buys Subaru mountains of publicity. *Denver Post*, p. C1.

Riffner, D. & Thompson, F. G. (1987, June). Special event programming -- relative value assessment. *Special Events Report*, pp. 4-5.

Rolls-Royce revamps sponsorship chucks polo for sporting clays. (1989, June 12). *Special Events Report*, pp. 6-7.

Ruffenach, G. (1992, June 4). Sport: Olympic backers will pay Atlanta plenty for exclusivity and ambush protection. *Wall Street Journal*, p. B1.

Sandler, D. M. & Shani, D. (1989, August/September). Olympic sponsorship vs. ambush marketing: Who gets the gold. *Journal of Advertising Research*, pp. 9-14.

Serafin, R. (1989, August 21). Caddy goes for golf: Luxury cars vie for sponsorship. *Advertising Age*, p. 16.

Sleight, S. (1989). *Sponsorship: What it is and how to use it.* Maidenhead, Berkshire, England: McGraw Hill.

Stotlar, D. K. (1989). *Successful marketing and sponsorship plans.* Dubuque, IAa: Wm. C. Brown.

Target sponsors Wolves' den. (1990, August 27). *Special Events Report*, p. 3.

Tortorici, T. (1987, April 6). Coca-Cola. *Special Events Report*, pp. 1-3.

Urbanski, A. (1992, November 9). Fast Track: Strategies for Business Success. What's a sponsorship worth? *Newsweek* [Suppl.].

Ukman, L. (1984, November). Sports Is It! *Marketing Communications*, pp. 23-26.

CHAPTER 12

METHODS OF
MEASURING THE IMPACT
OF SPONSORSHIP

Learning Objectives

After completing this chapter, the reader should be able to:

1. understand the importance of establishing measurable objectives prior to the occurrence of a sponsored event.

2. discuss various types of media coverage measures and their conceptual and pragmatic limitations.

3. design a study which measures changes in target market awareness of a company or product attributable to a sponsorship activity.

4. discuss the conditions under which a sponsorships' impact on future and direct sales can be measured.

CHAPTER 12

METHODS OF MEASURING THE IMPACT OF SPONSORSHIP

In the past, many companies' measures of sponsorship effectiveness have been cursory and simplistic. However, as both the dollar value of sponsorship investments and their proportion of companies' marketing budgets have grown, the demands for valid evidence demonstrating the effectiveness of sponsorship have increased commensurately. The pressures were illustrated by General Motors' Director of Consumer Influence Operations, who stated: " 'If cuts in our ad budgets are made, the first thing to go is events sponsorship, because nobody knows for sure what they are getting' " (cited in Penzer, 1990, p. 162). This statement suggests it is particularly important for sponsors to be able to quantify and justify their investment, if it is perceived to be an alternative to advertising.

From the perspective of a sports organization trying to sell a sponsorship, it is important that measurement audits are included in the sponsorship package that is presented. These are likely to be especially credible if they are done by an external consulting organization, like that described later in this chapter in the Joyce Julius and Associates case study, rather than done internally. This demand for impartial evaluation of sponsorship effectiveness has created a niche for companies that specialize in doing these assessments.

The type of measurement used to evaluate sponsorship should be governed by its objectives. If these are clearly specified, then the best measure to assess the extent to which they are met can be selected. This emphasizes the importance of establishing objectives in terms that can be measured before the sponsored event occurs, not after it is over. Even if this is done, however, there are several factors which make it challenging to assess the impact of sponsorship investments. These include (Meenaghan, 1983)

1. *The simultaneous use of other communications mix variables.* Since sponsorship is usually used in conjunction with other components of promotion, it is difficult to isolate its unique impact. Even if other promotional tools are not being used simultaneously, there is likely to be some carry-over effect from previous marketing communications' efforts that make it difficult to isolate the impact of sponsorship.

2. *Uncontrollable environmental factors.* Changes in sales levels may be attributable to environmental changes rather than the sponsorship. For example,

an increase or reduction in the intensity of competitive effort, or varying levels of discretionary income as a result of changes in economic conditions.

3. *The pursuit of multiple objectives.* Sponsors often seek multiple benefits from their investment, which means that a variety of measurement methods may be required to assess effectiveness of the sponsorship.

LINKING SPONSORSHIP TO THE COMMUNICATIONS PROCESS

The process through which companies seek to communicate a message to individuals in their target market through sponsorship is shown in Figure 12-1. The sponsor codes messages into a transmittable form (or arranges and locates those messages so the media will incidentally transmit them). The form may include written captions, company or brand name, logo, or oral material. The coded message is transmitted by print media, broadcast media, or personal contact. For communication to occur, the message has to be received, interpreted, and absorbed by individuals in the target market. The ultimate goal of a total communications strategy is to generate sales, and a company's expectation is that its sponsorship investment ultimately will contribute to that end.

An intervening variable shown in the model is noise. Noise consists of other stimuli or communications that compete for the intended receiver's attention. A message from a sponsoring organization to its target market is subject to the influence of extraneous noise and distracting stimuli that interfere with communication of the message. This noise may distort or distract attention from the transmission or reception of the message at any stage in the process. It may prevent the message from being received by members of the target market, or it may lead to their interpreting it differently from the way the sponsor intended. In the context of sponsorship where the message is incidental to the main event, there is likely to be substantial noise that may cause the message to appear inconsequential and to be ignored.

Figure 12-1 shows the stages in the communication process at which the effectiveness of sponsorship can be measured. The further through the process an evaluation takes place, the stronger is the evidence of a sponsorship's contribution to increasing sales. Most frequently, sponsorship objectives relate to creating a climate conducive to the development of sales in the future rather than to stimulating immediate sales. For this reason, most evaluations are undertaken earlier in the communications process (Figure 12-1). If sales are not measured, then the next most convincing measures for demonstrating economic return from a sponsorship (i.e., the probability that a desired increase in level of sales will result) are those that are completed at the reception stage of the process, because this is only one step removed from the sales purchase action.

Individuals pass through a series of stages from first becoming aware of a product or company to finally making a purchase decision. These stages are generally known in the marketing field as the product adoption process. The three stages in this process that precede purchase action, and that are encapsulated in the reception stage of the

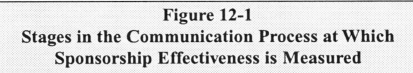

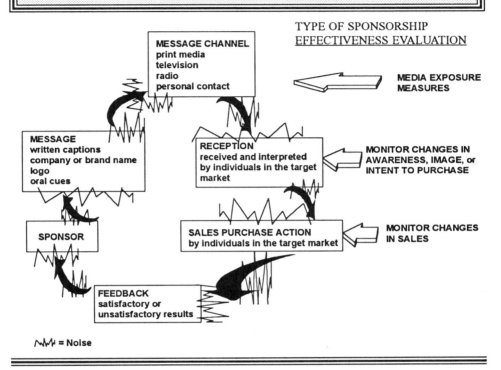

Figure 12-1
Stages in the Communication Process at Which
Sponsorship Effectiveness is Measured

communication process (Figure 12-1), are awareness, interest, and intent-to-purchase. The product adoption process emphasizes that a decision to participate is usually the culmination of a process that may have started long before the actual purchase takes place. Thus, sponsorship of a sports event is likely to ultimately affect sales if it succeeds in moving individuals from their present stage in the adoption process on to the next stage towards making a purchase decision.

MEASURING MESSAGE EXPOSURE

The most frequently used type of sponsorship effectiveness measure is taken at the message channel stage (Figure 12-1). This approach assesses the extent and value of media coverage the product or company receives. It usually involves quantifying
- duration of television coverage, including both oral and visual mentions;
- duration of radio mentions;
- extent of press coverage as measured in single column inches.

Thus, for example, in one year Volvo, the Swedish car maker, measured that its pro tennis sponsorship generated 2.02 billion impressions, or 5.5 million a day. That is, if a sports photograph appeared with a Volvo banner in a newspaper with a circulation of one million, that would equal one million impressions. Similar calculations are done for television broadcasts and magazine and news articles where the corporate name appears (Lohr, 1988).

Typically, these media mentions are tracked, and each is assigned a dollar value based on the paid advertising rate. For example, Volvo calculated that in 1990, it received $7 in value for every $1 spent on its sponsorship of tennis. This resulted from 2.26 billion impressions, including television, print, radio, event attendance, and promotions. These impressions were calculated to translate to $32.8 million in equivalent value and Volvo spent less than $5 million on its sponsorship (Schlossberg, 1991). The first case describes how these data are collected and distributed by a consulting company that specializes in measuring the value of sponsorships. The second case describes how these media coverage data were used by John Hancock Financial Services to evaluate effectiveness of their sponsorship of the John Hancock Bowl.

HOW PROFESSIONAL SPONSORSHIP MEASURERS WORK: JOYCE JULIUS AND ASSOCIATES INC.

CASE STUDY

Bob Cotman was senior vice-president of Domino's Pizza, and his wife Joyce Julius Cotman was the marketing director. In the early 1980s they were having problems justifying Domino's sponsorship of an Indy racing car to franchisees. In their search for more concrete data, they found a $40-a-year newsletter called *The Sponsors Report.* It was published by an individual in Chicago who sat in his basement with a television and a stopwatch and calculated sponsorship values on Indy car broadcasts.

Sensing that marketing departments at other companies were also in dire need of such numbers, the Cotmans left Domino's and established Joyce Julius and Associates in Ann Arbor, Michigan. They purchased *The Sponsors Report* and invested $700,000 in installing a comprehensive tracking service which monitored a wide range of sports. They publish a series of standard reports, for example, a 21-issue review of all Indy car events, which costs subscribers $1,290, and a 31-issue of golf sponsorship retailing at $1,225.

They undertake any kind of custom report that clients require, including measuring television-equivalent values of event site promotion, radio mentions, and newspaper coverage. These customized assignments can cost as much as $15,000. Eight of the top ten *Fortune 500* companies and 15 of the top 25 advertisers use Joyce Julius' services.

They have 25 people who watch video tapes of every event their clients want monitored. Every time any corporate logo appears on a sign, a baseball cap, a TV graphic—whatever—a Joyce Julius operator enters the number of seconds it appears into a computer. They also tabulate oral mentions. The total exposure time is tallied for each sponsor and then multiplied by the nondiscounted cost per a 30-second television spot for the individual broadcast being monitored. They call this the National Television Impression Value, or NTIV.

The influence of this type of measurement data was illustrated by the key role it played in defending Bausch & Lomb's $15-million investment as a sponsor in the 1992 Winter Olympics. While watching the Olympics, company officials were outraged that other manufacturers of ski goggles, like Cebe and Bolle, were getting more on-screen exposure than was their company's Ray-Ban brand. There was a rule that logos of nonsponsors could not exceed 3/8" in height on any equipment, but the United States Olympic Committee did not seem to be enforcing it.

Bausch & Lomb had Joyce Julius monitor every second of the Winter Games and, on the strength of their report, won what amounted to make-goods from the USOC for the Summer Games, plus a commitment on their part to police attempts at ambush marketing.

Note: Adapted from "What's a Sponsorship Worth? Fast Track: Strategies for Business Success," by A. Urbanski, *Newsweek*, Nov. 9, 1992. [supple.].

THE JOHN HANCOCK BOWL: MEASURING ADVERTISING EXPOSURE*

CASE STUDY

John Hancock Financial Services sponsor the John Hancock Bowl held in El Paso, Texas, on New Year's Eve. For the 1990 Bowl, the company calculated that it received $5.1 million worth of advertising exposure in return for the $1.6 million it invested in sponsoring the bowl. A Hancock senior executive commented, "The bowl is an extraordinary efficient media buy. It would cost us a great deal more money to help influence sales by normal advertising."

Hancock scoured magazines and newspapers across the country, counting the number of stories about its bowl and measuring numbers of column inches, circulation and advertising rates. It determined its television exposure value from factors such as the precise number of times announcers mentioned John Hancock and the number of times the name was on screen in pre-game promotions and during the broadcast.

The company collected a seven-foot stack of newspaper clippings on the bowl game. Together with a handful of television segments, there were 7,829 stories with a total value of $1,080,995 in advertising equivalency. This refers to what Hancock would have paid to buy the same amount of commercial time on television or advertising space in the papers.

The Hancock staff review each clip and place an advertising value on it based on each publication's circulation and advertising rate. For example, a four-column, four-inch story on the John Hancock Bowl in the *Detroit News* is valued at $3,312; a two-inch item in *Time* magazine, $6,800; and a three-column, seven-inch-deep article in the *Laramie* (Wyoming) *Boomerang*, $145.

However, the bulk of the advertising value came from CBS's broadcast of the game. Combined with repeated references to the John Hancock Bowl, the John Hancock logo appeared at midfield, on uniforms, sidelines and scoreboards, for a total of about 60 minutes on the 4-hour broadcast. The company equated this to the equivalent of $3.12 million of advertising exposure.

John Hancock Financial Services calculated the following costs and benefits of sponsoring the 1990 John Hancock Bowl:

COSTS	$
Sponsorship fee	$1,000,000
Television rights fee, including 10-15 minutes of commercial time during the broadcast	500,000
Contribution to various charities, scholarships and a game banquet in El Paso, Texas	100,000
TOTAL	$1,600,000

BENEFITS: Exposure measured in advertising value, based on the amount of coverage and what Hancock would have had to pay for the same amount of advertising space in print or commercial time on television:

CBS game broadcast	$3,120,000
Newspaper, television reports	1,080,995
CBS pre-game promotions	900,000
Total	$5,100,995

Note: Adapted from "Keeping Careful Score on Sports Tie-Ins,"by M. J. McCarthy, *Wall Street Journal*, April 24, 1991, p. B1. Reprinted with permission.

If media coverage is used as a measure of sponsorship effectiveness, the exposures should be weighted to reflect the relative attractiveness of different types of media coverage and quality of the coverage, which is likely to vary widely across companies. This means that the appropriate portion of advertising equivalency costs to use as a measure of value of media exposure will also vary. To some companies a sponsorship mention may be worth only 10% of equivalent advertising time in a particular medium, whereas to others it may be worth 100%. Because tobacco companies, for example, are unable to advertise on television, sponsorship mentions in that medium are likely to be valued more highly by those companies than similar exposures achieved by a soft drink supplier. If a company or product has very high unaided recall before a sponsorship, then the value of media exposure is likely to be relatively small. For example, Coca-Cola has an unaided recall of around 95%; thus, media coverage is not likely to be as important to that product as it would be to a new soft drink trying to build awareness.

Quality of media coverage is likely to vary from the highly favorable to the somewhat less favorable. Furthermore, the location and nature of coverage obtained even within a single medium will influence its impact. For example, a favorable editorial mention may be considered to be of greater value than mentions in the sports column. Some companies assign different values to different publications by using weightings. Thus, Cartier International assigned points to its print exposure by type of publication--upscale readership carried more weight than wide circulation--and by type of mention--the company's name in a headline or photograph rated higher than in text ("Centerford," 1990).

A final type of quality measure that is used seeks to reflect the extent of clutter encountered by a sponsorship. This measure expresses media coverage achieved by the sponsor as a percentage of total coverage of that activity and/or as a percentage of total mentions attained by all sponsors of that activity. If this percentage is reasonably high, then it is deemed more likely to emerge from the clutter of other sponsors and make an impact.

Measures of media coverage frequently inflate its real value. This inflation occurs in three ways. First, article length is measured and equated with advertising space, even through the sponsor's name may be mentioned only a couple of times in the article. Second, typically, the maximum rate card value is assumed when quantifying the cost of equivalent advertising space, and few companies in fact pay these full rates (Sleight, 1989).

The third and most fundamental source of inflation is the assumption that 2 seconds here and 4 seconds there of background signage or logo, when summated, equate to a television spot that gives an advertiser 30 straight seconds of time in which to sell. Thus, an editorial in *Sponsorship Report* commented on the procedures used by John Hancock, "Ad equivalencies are *bunk.* If Hancock management thinks 30 seconds of ID has the same value as a 30 second ad spot, that's its problem" (International Events Group 1992, p. 2). A defender of these procedures responds: " 'Is it better to interrupt a broadcast with your message? Is it better to upset viewers? Of course you usually won't upset them because they are probably in the kitchen or the bathroom.' " (cited in Urbanski, 1992). This type of defense is not convincing. Sponsorship lacks the direct impact possibilities normally associated with direct advertising. This is widely recognized and explains why the "rule-of-thumb" adopted by sponsors who do use media-coverage measures as their primary evaluation tool is that total exposure received should be worth at least three to four times the cost of their sponsorship.

In addition to the pragmatic limitations of the media exposure approach discussed in the previous paragraphs, there is a fundamental conceptual flaw in considering it as a proxy measure of a sponsorship's impact on awareness. Measurements of media exposure are taken at the message-channel point in the communications process (Figure 12-1). That is, they purport to assess the extent of media output of the company's message that has occurred. Media output, however, does not equate to awareness in the target market, which occurs at the subsequent reception stage:

> While you can certainly get a guide to the visibility of your sponsorship and the potential for awareness among your target audience, you certainly cannot tell by measuring media mentions how many of your *target audience saw and regis-*

tered the mentions, nor how the viewers' attitudes to you or your product has been influenced by the sponsorship. (Sleight, 1989, p. 227)

For awareness to occur, members of the target market have to interpret the message and then absorb it. There is a substantial probability that this will not occur because individuals are exposed to many more communications than they can possibly accept or decode. If a name, picture, cue, logo, banner, or whatever does not appeal, or if there seems to be no good reason why it should be noted, then an individual is unlikely to open his or her senses to it; consequently, it will not be received. Hence, communication is not a one-way process from the sponsor organization to its target market, which use of the media-exposure measure implies. Rather, it is a two-way process that is dependent upon the intended recipients' being sufficiently interested to interpret and absorb the communication.

In addition to broadcast and print media, many sports events offer hospitality benefits and benefits to an on-site audience that also have economic values. To formulate a more comprehensive equivalency value of name exposure, these additional benefits can be captured by assigning a dollar value to each of them. Examples are given in Figure 12-2. The cumulative dollar value of the benefits is then divided into the total sponsorship cost to determine the value received, expressed as a percentage of the overall value (Ensor, 1987). This kind of system may be useful in a variety of sport sponsorship contexts and gives insight to those soliciting sponsorships as to how their proposals may be evaluated.

Figure 12-2
Assigning Dollar Values to Sponsorship Benefits

SPONSORSHIP BENEFIT	DOLLAR VALUE
Stadium/arena banners	$500 per banner per game
Hospitality for wholesalers/relatives	$50 per person
PA/message board announcement	$50 per announcement
Parking passes	$5 per pass per game
Sponsor ID in press guide	$2,500 for one page, full color
Pocket schedules	10¢ each
Brand music during the game	$50 each time

Note: Adapted from "The Corporate View of Sports Sponsorship" by R. J. Ensor, September 1987, *Athletic Business*, p. 43.

Some sponsors admit to the inadequacy of the media exposure method they use. For example, the Special Events Director of Gallaher, a large tobacco company in the United Kingdom, commenting on the investment in sport sponsorship made to promote the company's Benson & Hedges brand observed, "'At the end of a year I can give a figure for the number of hours and minutes Benson & Hedges has appeared on T.V. at its events. It doesn't prove anybody has bought one more cigarette'" (cited Wilson, 1988, p. 162).

MEASURING IMPACT ON AWARENESS

USING SPONSORSHIP TO RAISE AWARENESS LEVELS OF CORNHILL INSURANCE COMPANY

CASE STUDY

Cornhill Insurance Company is located in the United Kingdom and in 1977 was ranked 12th in size among UK insurance companies. In that year, research showed that unprompted spontaneous awareness of Cornhill among U.K. residents was less than 2%. The company believed the reason for this was that insurance was sold via third-party brokers, agents, or salesmen and hence the company was relatively distanced from its consumers. Most of the company's promotional activities at that time were directed at insurance brokers rather than consumers in order to influence brokers to place business with their company. Therefore, consumers lacked any direct association with the company. In addition, insurance is not a "glamor" product. It is purchased out of a reluctantly perceived necessity rather than desire.

Another influence on Cornhill's management at that time was the bad publicity generated by the collapse of a number of insurance companies. This led Cornhill to conclude that the public would be increasingly reluctant to purchase insurance from an unknown company.

At the same time as Cornhill was identifying their awareness problems, the international cricket world was being shaken by Kerry Packer and his World Series Cricket. International cricket matches for over a century had been organized by the governing bodies of cricket in each country. However, Kerry Packer, an Australian entrepreneur, announced plans to sign the best players from each country to lucrative contracts and to promote his own series of matches independent of the governing bodies. The Test and County Cricket Board (TCCB), which is the governing body in England, was desperate to find a sponsor who would match the salaries offered by Packer so that TCCB could retain control of these players and of international games.

Cricket is a central feature of English life, and this battle for the players was a major news story in all the national media. Seeing an opportunity, Cornhill made contact with the TCCB and a £1 million sponsorship fee, over the next 5 years, was agreed. The international matches were to be called The Cornhill Test

Matches. (A test match is the name given to official international cricket matches. Each match usually lasts for 5 days from 11 a.m. to 6:30 p.m. each day and is televised live nationally from beginning to end. There are usually five such test matches in a summer cricket season.) At that time, this was one of the largest sponsorship commitments ever made to sport in the United Kingdom. Its announcement created a tremendous amount of national interest. It was made while an international match was being played, and on that day the game was stopped because of rain. This meant the media gave added attention to the sponsorship because there was no news to report from the cricket game!

Cornhill analyzed the benefits from its sponsorship in 1981. During 140 hours of television coverage the company received 7,459 banner ratings on screen and 234 oral mentions. In addition, there were 1,784 references on radio, 659 in the national press, and 2,448 in the provincial press. The 250 tickets that Cornhill received for each Test Match were also a valuable aid in improving relations with brokers and customers.

Cornhill launched a program to measure the effectiveness of sponsorship which involved undertaking a research study every 6 months. Any increases in awareness could be attributed to the sponsorship because that, and its associated advertising, were the only promotional activities undertaken by the company. Unprompted awareness can be measured by asking respondents to mention any insurance company that comes to mind. The results of four 6-monthly research studies indicated that unprompted awareness increased from 2% to 8% to 13% to 16%. Interestingly, these studies showed that level of awareness fell quite substantially in the periods between series of international matches, suggesting that awareness created by sponsorship is not long-lasting and needs constant reinforcement.

Cornhill's brokers told them that policies were much easier to sell as a result of the greater awareness of the company's name. Cornhill estimated that its investment of £2 million (£1 million in event cost and £1 million backup cost) over the 5-year period returned £10 million in increased annual premium income. Cornhill's sponsorship was especially successful because it was perceived as coming to the aid of a national institution and was a very topical news event.

Note: Information for this case was obtained from material in Sleight, S. (1989). *Sponsorship: What It Is and How to Use It*; Meenaghan, J. A. (1983). "Commercial Sponsorship," *European Journal of Marketing*; Hulks, B., "Should the Effectiveness of Sponsorship be Assessed and How?" *Admap*; Dinmore, F., "Cricket Sponsorship," *The Business Graduate*; and the Central Council of Physical Recreation's Committee of Enquiry into Sports Sponsorship, The Howell Report.

The positive impact of sponsorship in creating awareness is described in the preceding Cornhill Insurance case. Although the case illustrates an application of awareness research, it is likely to be atypical for two reasons. First, Cornhill did not engage in any form of communication except sponsorship and its associated advertising, and second, the company had a very low awareness level at the beginning of the sponsorship. These factors made it relatively easy to measure increases in awareness attributable to the sponsorship. However, for products that do not exhibit these characteristics a more complex research design should be used. Such a design is likely to incorporate a control group that is not exposed to the sponsorship which can be measured and used to discount the effects of other simultaneous communication efforts in which a company may be investing, and a three-part survey conducted before, during, and after the event. This approach will enable changes in awareness and/or image in the target audience to be measured:

- A packaged-goods company sponsored NASCAR to "accelerate consumer acceptance" of a product it recently had introduced in the Southeast. Its impact was monitored by a series of surveys throughout the season. In the early stages of the NASCAR season, unaided awareness of the brand was approximately equal among fans and nonfans. At the end of the season, unaided awareness had doubled among fans, but was relatively unchanged among nonfans. In addition, fan trial of the brand in the last three months of the season was markedly higher than nonfan trial (Crimmins. 1993).

Research results reported in the NutraSweet case, which is presented in the follwoing case study, emphasize the importance of getting visitors involved in tie-in activities associated with the sponsorship, rather than relying only on name exposure to maximize increases in awareness levels. The evaluation procedure used by NutraSweet compares levels of awareness between two samples: One participated in the tie-in; the other did not. This conclusion was consistent with that reported by Johnson (1993):

We also learn from tracking sponsor awareness levels that those sponsors which actively engage the consumer on-site at the events with raffles, sweepstakes, sampling, or redemption programs stand a greater chance of being remembered as a sponsor once the event is over. (p. 8)

AWARENESS RESEARCH AT NUTRASWEET
CASE STUDY

NutraSweet sponsored state games in Massachusetts, Illinois, Florida, New York, Indiana, Texas, and North Carolina. The company matched each sponsorship dollar with a minimum of one dollar in promotional spending. A research firm was commissioned to evaluate the effectiveness of their sponsorships.

The sponsorship goals for NutraSweet were to establish a link between the sweetener and good health (the sweetener is positioned as a nutrient) and to promote awareness and favorable opinions of NutraSweet on a grassroots level. The research was designed to measure consumers' reactions to the brand's participation in the state's games. Specifically, the research was designed to measure

- Awareness of NutraSweet sponsorship and what the sponsorship said about NutraSweet.

·   Reaction to NutraSweet Place among visitors.

NutraSweet tested two groups of people at the games: people who had been exposed to NutraSweet's activities center and people who attended the games but did not stop by NutraSweet Place (an activities center). Names for the first group were collected at NutraSweet Place by means of entry blanks for a prize drawing. The second group of names was collected in the field from attendees who passed an initial screening question, again by means of an entry blank for a prize drawing.

Telephone interviews then were conducted in the 2 weeks following the games with open-ended questions designed to elicit recall and reaction to sponsors in general, followed by questions specific to NutraSweet's on-site activities. On a combined aided and unaided basis, virtually all survey respondents were aware that NutraSweet had sponsored the games. Visitors to NutraSweet Place were significantly more aware of NutraSweet's sponsorship due to their exposure to the center's activities. On an unaided basis, 86% of people who attended the activities center recalled the sponsorship, versus 50% of nonvisitors to the center.

Attendees' attitudes were more favorable toward NutraSweet after attending the states' games, and a significantly larger percentage of visitors to NutraSweet Place felt more favorable toward the company than did nonvisitors. No one felt less favorable.

Of the sponsors included in the study, NutraSweet received the highest overall rating—"excellent/very good." Again, visitors to NutraSweet Place rated the company higher than did nonvisitors. Eight out of 10 visitors rated NutraSweet excellent or very good, versus 7 out of 10 nonvisitors.

Nearly all respondents—98%—considered NutraSweet to be an appropriate sponsor of the state games, specifically because of its health and fitness positioning. Of the visitors to NutraSweet Place, nearly 60% learned something about the product. About two-thirds of the visitors took product samples, brochures, and/or coupons with them and, among those, about 75% reported having read the material.

In summary, research indicated that NutraSweet's active presence and promotional activities on-site, that is the extensive support activities for the sponsorship, made a significant difference in how well the brand attained its goals of increased awareness and favorable image. From the research, it was determined that sponsorship opportunities must offer NutraSweet

·   An exclusive or dominant sponsorship identity in all media and promotion.
·   The ability to play an active role on-site.
·   Sales promotion opportunities for NutraSweet customers in the food and beverage industry.
·   VIP entertainment in conjunction with the event.

Note: Adapted from "Evaluating Sponsorship: Beyond the Numbers at NutraSweet" by S. Baldwin, March 12, 1987, *Special Events Report.*

NutraSweet used a similar research design approach of comparing results between control and treatment groups to assess the extent of linkage perceived by their target market with their figure-skating sponsorship:

- NutraSweet was sole corporate sponsor of the United States Figure Skating Association. Executives believed that sponsoring such events as the World Professional Figure Skating Championship, the Challenge of Champions, and national Ice Skating Month, gave NutraSweet an "uncluttered environment, television exposure, promotion extensions and positive public relations." To assess the strength of the linkage, the company commissioned a study of sales and attitudes about its association with the sport in four television markets that carried the world championships. In two of the four markets, NutraSweet commercials were deliberately blocked out, but reviewers recalled seeing NutraSweet advertisements anyway. The company considered this to be indicative of the positive image emitted from association with figure skating (Schlossberg, 1990).

A long-term approach to measuring changes in awareness would focus on the degree of association of the company or product with the sponsored activity (Meenaghan, 1991). It involves determining the extent to which respondents correctly identify sponsors with sponsored activities, and monitoring trends in the association over time. Table 12-1 shows results of level of awareness and degree of association reported in a study of motor sports sponsorship. The findings show a substantial increase over time in level of association and correct association of all the major motor racing sponsors

Table 12-1
Motor Racing Sponsorship Awareness

	% Mentioning each sponsor			
	1974	1977	1980	1988
Texaco	18	45	47	60
John Player	22	43	44	66
Marlboro	6	25	42	55
Rothmans	11	13	13	50
None/Don't Know	35	20	19	N/A

Note: From "The Role of Sponsorship in the Marketing Communication Mix" by J. A. Meenaghan, 1991, *International Journal of Advertising. 10*, 45. Reprinted with permission.

MEASURING IMPACT ON IMAGE

Image enhancement or positive attitude change towards a product or company is a stage closer to the desired sales outcome than awareness (Figure 12-1). The distinction between these two stages was illustrated by Waite (1979) cited in Meenaghan (1991):

- A manufacturer and distributor of alcohol sponsored a horse racing classic for fifteen years in a bid to achieve a greater awareness of the company's leading brand among cognac drinkers who were followers of this sporting activity. With media coverage exposure showing an annual increase, the company assumed that the brand was achieving significant awareness amongst its target markets [a questionable assumption!]. They commissioned a market research study to identify extent of positive attitude change. The findings showed that attitudes to the brand were no more positive among those cognac drinkers who could identify the brand's association with the sponsorship, than among those respondents who were unaware of the brand sponsorship. These findings suggested to the company that the sponsorship investment (which was over $500,000) had no impact on level of positive attitude to the brand, and thus the company considered withdrawing from it.

The data in Table 12-2 emphasize the importance of measuring changes in image attributable to sponsorship some time after an event has finished, rather than on the site. These data were collected by one of the authors in an attempt to measure the impact of sponsorship on image. Six major sponsors of the event (shown in bold type) were each paired with a nonsponsoring company in the same industry. One additional pair of companies, both of which delivered phone services, was included to serve as controls, even though neither of them was a sponsor.

A probability sample of respondents was presented with the pairs of companies as they entered the site and asked to "express how you feel about them" on a 7-point scale ranging from *very poor* (1) to *very good* (7). In a follow-up mail survey that the same respondents completed 1 to 5 weeks after the event, they were asked the same question. The results are reported in the "Before" and "After" columns of Table 12-2.

It was anticipated that sponsoring companies' scores would be higher after the event as a result of their investment. The results show that in 13 of the 14 cases, image score declined in the follow-up survey. This suggests that awareness surveys conducted at, or immediately after, an event are likely to yield optimistic results. This may be attributable to the excitement and positive experience being enjoyed at that time by attendees, extending to their perceptions of the products' images. However, at a subsequent time when the immediacy of an event's excitement has passed, excitement about the sponsoring products may also dissipate.

Table 12-2
Results of an Attempt to Measure Changes in
Image Resulting From Sponsorship

NAME OF COMPANY	BEFORE	AFTER	DIFFERENCE SCORE
Pepsi-Cola	4.69	4.47	-.22
Coca-Cola	5.54	5.66	+.12
Miller Beer	4.58	4.15	-.43
Budweiser Beer	4.24	3.82	-.42
Lone Star Factory Outlet	4.29	4.03	-.26
Mall of the Mainland	4.31	3.66	-.65
Continental Airlines	4.67	4.51	-.16
Delta Airlines	4.74	4.45	-.29
Randall's Food Markets	5.52	5.16	-.36
Kroger Food Stores	5.02	4.95	-.07
Kodak Photographic Products	5.80	5.70	-.10
Fuji Photo Film, U.S.A.	4.81	4.36	-.45
AT&T Phone Services	5.54	5.35	-.19
MCI Phone Services	4.29	3.88	-.41

MEASURING IMPACT ON INTENT-TO-PURCHASE

The product adoption process suggests that potential purchasers move from awareness to interest to intent-to-purchase before investing in a sales action (Figure 12-1). Hence, intent-to-purchase studies are perhaps the most useful indicators of the impact of sponsorship on future sales. Bassing America is a membership organization of 55,000 fishermen. A key to their success in attracting and retaining sponsors is the research that Bassing does each year into their members' purchases and intentions-to-purchase:

- Bassing tries to find out what members own by brand, what they have purchased by brand, their intent to purchase by brand and when they anticipate buying. The information is compared to prior years' results, going back three or four years to determine if sponsors' products are being supported. Findings are especially helpful when contract renewals are near. The results show sponsors how involvement with Bassing has increased their sales. For example, in 1986, 15 percent of members owned a Ranger boat and another 21% said they intended to purchase one. By 1989, 27% owned and 43% intended to buy a Ranger boat (*"Evaluation,"* 1990).

A qualitative approach to assessing sponsorship's impact on intent-to-purchase was adopted by Xerox Corporation. After they entertained clients at professional golf tournaments that they sponsored, managers completed reports, 3, 6 and 9 months after the event, estimating what impact the occasion had on client orders (McCarthy, 1991).

MEASURING IMPACT ON SALES

A sponsorship's direct impact on sales is measurable only when one of three conditions exists. First, sponsorship is the sole method used to promote a company, particularly if the company had low visibility before the program started. The Cornhill Insurance case, which was discussed earlier in this chapter, is an example of this. Second, sales changes may be measured if short-term or localized sponsorships are used because this makes it easier to undertake comparisons with control areas or periods of time in which they were not used:

- Wrangler conducts market research to determine the incremental sales volume generated by a sponsorship. It measures pre-and post-buying habits of attendees of Wrangler-sponsored events. Once this number is determined, the profit margin is multiplied by the total additional sales due to the sponsorship. The cost of each sponsorship program--for example, sponsorship fees, media buys, point-of-sales materials and all promotional support--is subtracted to determine the net profit contribution for each sponsorship (Ulkman, 1984).
- An executive of R.J. Reynolds, referring to his company's sponsorship of the NASCAR Winston Cup Series, stated "We're in the cigarette business. We're *not* in the sports business. We use sports as an avenue for advertising our products.... We can go into an area where we're marketing an event, measure sales during the event and measure sales after the event and see an increase in sales." (cited in DeParle 1989, p. 38).

The third, and most common, condition in which direct impact on sales can be measured is the one in which there are tie-in promotions with the event:

- Burroughs Wellcome Company experimented with a women's tennis sponsorship to market a new sunscreen lotion. By distributing coupons at the venue, then tracking how many were redeemed, the company found that the tennis events effectively reached the target audience of upscale women 30 and older. In the following year, based on those results, the company expanded its sponsorship to 12 major tournaments.
- McDonalds in their 1984 Olympic Games sponsorship set targets of 5% for extra store sales and 8% for extra store transactions. They utilized the distribution of more than 300 million Olympic-theme game cards to boost interest and they increased percentages to 5.8% and 11.2%, respectively (International Advertising Association, 1988).
- Bell Cellular Inc. spent $500,000 (Canadian) on sponsorships a year and a similar amount promoting those ties. They cosponsored such events as

the Cadillac Golf Classic. To prompt attendees to subscribe on-site, Bell Cellular offered coupons worth $C110 off the first year's bill. With couponing the company could tell exactly how many activations each event generated. For instance, in 1990, they signed up 1,675 new subscribers accounting for nearly $C1 million (Lavelle, 1991).

Most evaluations do not attempt to measure the direct impact of a sponsorship on sales. This is because either one of the three above conditions is not met and thus impact on sales is not measurable, or the sponsorship objective was not to directly generate extra sales.

CONCLUDING COMMENTS

Copeland (1991) surveyed 65 major Canadian companies engaged in sports sponsorship and reported that the methods most frequently used to measure its impact were awareness and media exposure (61%), sales (41%), dealer/trade feedback (26%) and attendance (15%). Although image was frequently cited by the companies as a benefit sought from sport sponsorship, only 10% of Copeland's companies evaluated image change. Similarly, in a survey of 450 active sponsors in the United States., 73% reported that they calculated results in terms of advertising equivalences (Ogden, 1993). Crimmins (1993) noted

Sponsors are measuring the wrong things. We measure what's easy--visibility--rather than what is critical--impact. The fact that people have seen our logo doesn't count for much. Does anybody remember seeing it? Does anybody mentally link my brand to the property I've paid to identify with? Is the extra cost I've paid to be seen in this particular environment worth any more than being seen on the side of a building somewhere? Does anyone know that I am bringing this event? Does anyone care? (p. 1)

Crimmins went on to point out that these questions can be answered only by measuring impact, which he defined as the ability to positively influence consumer attitudes toward a brand in order to increase brand choice.

Despite the substantial limitations associated with using media exposure and advertising equivalency visibility measures to evaluate the impact of sponsorship, these measures continue to be widely used for three practical reasons. First, they are easy for management to understand. Second, these types of data are relatively easy to collect. Third, they offer quantifiable statistics that give the appearance that sponsorship decisions are being based on supportive data and thus offer peace of mind to those responsible for making those decisions. Sports managers who want to include a measure of the potential of their event in sponsorship proposal packages also can relatively easily adopt this measure. Indeed, media exposure is the only evaluative measure they can undertake without intruding into the business of the event's sponsors. Other measures requiring, for example, pre and posttests of awareness levels of a sponsor's product or sales performance, are likely to be outside the organizer's realm of access.

Companies with ongoing monitoring and evaluation procedures are able to use these measures to gauge where a sponsorship is in its life cycle (Samson, 1989). Is it at the introductory, maturation, or decline stage? Does it deserve more support, or is it time to look for alternatives? The evaluation may suggest that an event is declining in popularity, but still enabling the sponsorship objectives to be met. Alternatively, it may reveal that the potential benefits from the sponsorship have peaked and incremental spending is counterproductive:

- Canon made a commitment of $5 million to sponsor the major professional soccer league in England. In a 3-year period, awareness of Canon went from below 20% to more than 80%. The company decided reaching the last 15% or 20% would not be cost effective; consequently, it withdrew from its soccer sponsorship. However, Canon did this in a very positive way. It invited all the journalists who covered the original announcement 3 years earlier to a press conference and explained how successful the sponsorship had been. Coverage of its withdrawal was very upbeat and the league was able to find a new sponsor without any problem ("Centerford," 1986).

Evaluation answers the question "Where is the sponsoring company now in relation to where it said it wanted to be in its objectives?" Its primary purpose is to discover and act on, if necessary, deviations from the desired outcome from a sponsorship. It identifies sponsorships that are not meeting their objectives. In these cases there needs to be a reappraisal of what the sponsor did and what could be done to improve the results. Thus, evaluation guides actions and reduces influence of the emotional dimension of decision making.

SUMMARY

The effectiveness of sponsorship can be measured at various stages in the communication process, but the further through the process an evaluation takes place, the stronger is the evidence of a sponsorship's contribution to increasing sales. The most frequently used measure is to assess the extent and value of media coverage the product or company receives. Some evaluations of this type may incorporate weightings that reflect the relative importance a company attaches to different types and quality levels of media coverage or assessments of sponsorship clutter with which their message has to compete. There is a tendency for these equivalency measures to inflate the real value of the media coverage. In addition, this approach is conceptually flawed because it measures only the extent of media output and offers no insight as to whether or not consumers received, interpreted, or absorbed the message. Communication is a two-way process that is dependent upon the intended recipient's absorbing the communication, and media output measures fail to consider this.

Measuring changes in consumers' level of awareness attributable to sponsorship involves comparing responses of those exposed to the sponsorship with those of a control group whose members were not exposed to it. Image enhancement or positive attitude is a stage closer to the desired sales outcome than is awareness in the product adoption process. However, perhaps the most useful indication of the impact on future sales are intent-to-purchase studies because they are the stage in the process immediately preceding a purchase action.

A sponsorship's direct impact on sales is measurable only when one of three conditions exist: (a) sponsorship is the sole method used to promote a product; (b) the sponsorship is short-term or localized so that comparisons can be made with control areas or periods of time when it was not used; and (c) when there are tie-in promotions associated with the sponsorship.

Questions for Study and Discussion

1. The Cornhill Insurance Company case provides an example of one company's effort to evaluate the effectiveness of its sponsorship investment. Critically evaluate the approach Cornhill used to measure increases in awareness attributable to the sponsorship. What are the strengths and deficiencies of the method employed? What recommendations would you make for enhancing the evaluation procedure used by the company?
2. In what three ways can measures of media coverage frequency inflate real levels of awareness?
3. Explain why most evaluations do not attempt to measure the direct impact of sponsorship events on the sale of sponsor products.

REFERENCES

Baldwin, S. (1987, March 12). Evaluating sponsorships: Behind the numbers at NutraSweet. *Special Events Report*, pp. 4-5.

Centerfold: Evaluating sponsorships. (1986, December 15). *Special Events Report*, p. 5.

Centerfold: A guide to sponsorship evaluation. (1990, September 24). *Special Events Report*, pp. 4-5.

Copeland, R. P. (1991). *Sport sponsorship in Canada: A study of exchange between corporate sponsors and sport groups*. Unpublished master's thesis, University of Waterloo, Waterloo, Ontario, Canada.

DeParle, J. (1989, September). Warning: Sports stars may be hazardous to your health. *The Washington Monthly*, pp. 34-48.

Dinmore, F. (1980, Autumn). Cricket sponsorship. *The Business Graduate*.

Ensor, R. J. (1987, September). The corporate view of sports sponsorship. *Athletic Business*, pp. 40-43.

Evaluation: Measuring return on investment. (1990, September 7). *Special Event Report*, pp. 3, 6-7.

Hulks, B. (1980, December). Should effectiveness of sponsorship be assessed and how? *Admap*, pp. 623-627.

International Advertising Association. (1988). *Sponsorship: Its role and effects*. New York: The Global Media Commission of the International Advertising Association.

International Events Group (1992, May 18). Editorial associations. *Sponsorship Report*, p. 2.

Johnson. R. (1993). How to use market research effectively. In *IFA's Official Guide to Sponsorship* (pp. 5-10). Port Angeles, WA: International Festivals Association.

Lavelle, B. (1991, July 1). How Bell Cellular boosted its return from events. *Special Events Report*, pp. 4-5.

Lohr, S. L. (1988, September 5). Volvo broadens a sports marketing strategy. *New York Times*, pp. A30.

McCarthy, M. J. (1991, April 24). Keeping careful score on sports tie-ins. *Wall Street Journal*, p. B1.

Meenaghan, J. A. (1991). The role of sponsorship in the marketing communications mix. *International Journal of Advertising 10*, 35-37.

Ogden, G. (1993). Sponsorship analysis. In *IFA's Official Guide to Sponsorship* (pp. 61-78). Port Angeles, WA: International Festivals Association.

Penzer, E. (1990, October). How do sponsors gauge the payoffs from event marketing? *Incentive*, pp. 162-164.

Samson, R. (1989, May 1). Using evaluation to determine what's working and what's not. *Special Events Report*, p. 5.

Schlossberg, H. (1990, April 2). Sports marketing. *Marketing News*, p. 6.

Schlossberg, H. (1991, July 1). Volvo proves marketing through sport pays. *Marketing News*, p. 19.

Sleight, S. (1989). Sponsorship: *What is it and how to use it*. Maidenhead, Berkshire, England: McGraw Hill.

Ukman, L. (1984, November). Sports is it! *Marketing Communications*, pp. 23-26.

Urbanski, A. (1992, November 9). Fast track: Strategies for business success. What's a sponsorship worth? Supplement in *Newsweek*.

Wilson, N. (1988). *The sports business*. London: Piatkus.

CHAPTER 13

FUND RAISING

Learning Objectives

After completing this chapter, the reader should be able to:

1. understand fund raising as a "purposive set of activities" for the express purpose of soliciting donations to enhance the organization's ability to sustain and/or expand sport services.
2. discuss several models for effectively organizing athletic support groups (ASGs).
3. describe a number of safeguards sport managers can institute to bring booster or ASGs under effective organizational or institutional control.
4. articulate pertinent fund raising nomenclature including: endowments, gifts-in-kind, and bequests and trusts.
5. describe in appropriate detail a systematic program for acquiring major donations from individuals and corporations.
6. discuss the application of cause-related marketing to sport events and organizations.

CHAPTER 13

FUND RAISING

Fund raising in the context of this book is defined as the purposive process of soliciting and accepting monetary gifts, in-kind services, personnel or materials to supplement a sport organization's existing resources (Kelly, 1991). Although sports organizations have had a long tradition of conducting fund-raising events such as annual auctions and "Sports Days," only recently have some segments of the industry established formal, ongoing fund-raising programs, often headed by professional managers. Within the last decade, collegiate athletic departments have made the most substantial commitment to fund raising among sport organizations, followed by a number of organizations from the private, nonprofit sector such as the American Amateur Union (AAU) and the Little League Foundation. Although many high school athletic programs are involved in fund raising, principally through the formation of athletic support groups (ASGs) or booster clubs, often their efforts are more ad hoc, lacking systematic planning and structure. The intent of this chapter is to view fund raising--much the same as sponsorship--as *a purposive set of activities* for the express purpose of soliciting donations to enhance an organization's ability to sustain and/or enhance sport services.

Fund raising and sponsorship are viewed as different but related activities that are intended to acquire additional resources for the organization. Sponsorships, as discussed in chapters 9-12, focus exclusively on a two-way exchange between a sports organization and a *business* from which the company expects tangible *commercial* benefits in the form of increased visibility and sales and an enhanced image in the marketplace. In return, companies as sponsors underwrite all or a portion of the expenses associated with staging a particular special event or sports program.

Fund raising tends to focus more on obtaining donations from *individuals*. Close to 90% of all charitable giving in the United States is made by individual donors, with corporations contributing less than 10% (Kelly, 1991; Williams, 1991). This general profile appears to apply to college athletics. For example, in 1992 the Ohio State University Athletic Department estimated that 70% of the $6 million received in charitable donations came from individual donors and 30% from corporations. The benefits sought by donors differ substantially from those sought by corporate sponsors. Private giving is more often characterized as a voluntary, one-way transfer of income or goods to an organization (Johnson, 1973). The motives underlying donations are more altruistic than commercial. Donors are likely to contribute because of their emotional attachment to a sports organization, whereas corporations are likely to enter a sponsorship based on return on investment considerations. Although altruism plays a larger role in fund raising, it does not diminish the fact that for many, self-interest plays a role in motivating charitable contributions to athletic programs. As will be shown later in the chapter, the most effective fund-raising programs recognize that both psychic rewards such as ego enhancement, and tangible rewards, such as preferred seating privileges, are integral components of donor solicitation.

Finally, it is important to recognize that donations potentially provide managers with much greater flexibility and independence in the way in which they can be utilized. Whereas sponsorships are sport or event-specific, charitable contributions can be unrestricted, allowing a sports organization the freedom to use the gift in any way it sees fit. Increasingly, athletic departments are providing incentives to donors to make unconditional or unrestricted donations to their programs (Bradley, 1993).

This chapter initially provides a review of the nature and scope of fund raising in organized sport with a particular emphasis on its practice in intercollegiate athletics. The focus on college sports reflects the fact that within the sports industry, collegiate athletic departments have devoted the most attention and organizational resources to fund raising, and as a result, more examples are available for analysis and discussion. In almost every case, the organizational models and fund raising practices adopted by college athletic departments can be transferred to other types of amateur or nonprofit sport organizations.

The formation and operation of athletic support groups or booster clubs, the sport industry's most commonly utilized approach to fund raising, are discussed. Several successful models of ASGs are presented to illustrate the various ways in which sport organizations can effectively organize and conduct fund-raising activities. Finally, recent and proposed changes in income tax benefits related to charitable donations and their implications for sport organizations are discussed.

The chapter concludes with a section on cause-related marketing, which describes a strategy used by corporations to tie their charitable donations directly to the sale of their products. Thus, every time somebody uses its products, the company makes a cash contribution to the sport organization. This approach first emerged in the 1980s and has become an important promotional strategy for many corporations. To date, relatively few sport organizations have developed ties of this nature, but it is an approach with considerable fund raising potential which is likely to be adopted more frequently by sport organizations in the future.

Fund Raising and Intercollegiate Athletics

As hard-pressed college athletic programs have struggled with cuts in tax support, mandated growth in womens' sports, and escalating costs, they have become increasingly active in raising money from external support groups. As Sperber (1990) points out, "One of the fastest growing areas of athletic department revenues is supporters' donations" (p. 70). In the most recent survey reporting the financial status of college athletics conducted by the NCAA, contributions from boosters and alumni accounted for 15% of the annual revenues of Division IA programs, an average of $1.55 million per program (Raiborn, 1990). The importance of this source of revenue has increased appreciably over the past 25 years. When the NCAA conducted its first financial assessment in 1965, funds raised from alumni and boosters accounted for only an average of 5% of an athletic department's budget. The real growth and potential for fund raising, however, is most apparent when the most successful collegiate sport fund-raising programs are considered. For example, in 1993 the Fresno State University Athletic Department received slightly over *one-third* or $4 million of its annual operating revenues from solicited monetary donations.

Nowhere is the crucial importance of supportive contributions more evident than for private institutions at the Division II level. According to the 1990 NCAA study, almost half (46%) of all revenues received by these moderately sized athletic programs came from monetary donations from alumni and athletic support groups. A 1991 survey of the fund-raising practices of Division II athletic departments provided the first comprehensive view of the extent to which smaller intercollegiate athletic programs have engaged in fund raising. Fifty-eight percent (110) of the 191 colleges and universities in the Division II classification completed the survey which asked athletic departments to respond to questions "about the structure and strategies of their fundraising programs." (Marciani, 1991, p. 49) A summary of the key findings are provided in Table 13-1.

As the importance of fund raising has become more apparent, a growing number of athletic departments have established formal fund-raising programs. It is common to find, particularly within the largest athletic programs, an Associate or Assistant Athletic Director designated as the Director of Athletic Development or Fund Raising. Typically, this staff member's responsibilities include developing a fund-raising program, cultivating potential donors and serving as the liaison to the department's athletic support group. It is interesting to note that most athletic departments have adopted the term *development* rather than fund raising to describe these activities. This practice is common among fund-raising practitioners, particularly those at colleges and universities, who want to avoid the connotations associated with fund raising (Carbone, 1987). As Payton (1987) noted, "There is often a stigma attached to asking for money. . . (an) unwillingness to 'lower oneself' to the ordinate role petitioner" (pp. 41-42). The emerging prominence of fund raising as an integral part of athletic department operations encouraged the National Association of College Athletic Directors (NACDA) in 1993 to establish a branch affiliate organization called the National Association of Athletic Development Directors (NAADD) to support the specialized needs of athletic fund raisers.

Most athletic development officers devote their energies toward soliciting two primary types of gifts: (a) annual and (b) major. *Annual* gifts are generally donations solicited yearly from a broad base of donors including alumni and boosters. Usually, they are smaller, lower level gifts, typically ranging from $100 to $10,000. Annual gifts are normally used to defray current operating expenses, such as the cost of grants-in-aid, travel, and recruitment. *Major* gifts are generated from a small, selective group

Table 13-1
Profile of Athletic Fund Raising
at NCAA Division II Schools

Title of Person in Charge
of Fund Raising

Athletic Director	36%
Assoc. Ath. Dir. Fund raising	27%
Dir. of Athletic Development	13%
Handled Outside Ath. Dept.	12%
Officer in Univ. Develop.	7%
Exec. Booster Club	5%

Level of Giving Required for Highest
Booster Club Membership Category

Less than $1,000	30%
$1,000 to $1,999	31%
$2,000 to $4,999	19%
$5,000 to $8,000	15%
More than $8,000	5%

How Fund Raising
Revenue Was Spent

Athletic Scholarships	76%
Equipment Purchase	54%
Recruitment	46%
Team Travel	36%
Capital Improvements	27%
Coaching Salaries/Benefits	13%

Structure for Athletic
Fund Raising Organization

In-house, Athletic-Dept. controlled	68%
Private, incorporated foundation	32%

Minimum Giving Requirement
for Membership in Booster Club

Less than $25	24%
$25 to $49	50%
$50 to $99	13%
$100 or more	13%

Amount of Annual Fund
Raising Revenue

Over $500,000	3%
$400,000-499,999	2%
$300,000-399,999	7%
$200,000-299,999	13%
$100,000-199,999	23%
$100,000 or Less	52%

of donors. Generally they are one-time donations of significant monetary value often directed at capital projects, such as a new arena. Another type of major gift that is growing in popularity is endowments (i.e., gifts that are invested to generate income, which is available for spending in perpetuity). Also included in the major gift category are *planned* or *deferred* donations. These gifts are not outright gifts in that their benefits are deferred through legal instruments like wills and insurance policies until the death of the donor. The donor makes the financial commitment during his or her lifetime, but the benefits do not accrue to the athletic program until some future time, often after the donor's death. Examples of both endowments and deferred gifts are provided later in the chapter.

ANNUAL DONOR PROGRAMS

The following section examines several approaches currently being utilized by athletic departments to acquire both annual and major gifts. With few exceptions, the formation of athletic support groups is the principal mechanism through which athletic departments solicit annual contributions. Alternative models for maintaining booster support organizations are discussed in detail. The section concludes with the presentation of a systematic program for acquiring major donations from individuals and corporations.

Athletic Support Groups

The centerpiece for most annual donor programs is the athletic support group or booster club. The fund-raising capabilities of these organizations are immense. Table 13-2 provides a summary of the size and monetary impact of some of the most successful ASGs in the United States.

Interestingly, at the collegiate level, alumni are often not the principal source of support for athletics. Sperber (1990) reported that "rarely do more than one to two percent of them [alumni] contribute to their alma mater's sports teams" (p. 71). Research has shown that alumni are much more inclined to direct their donations toward

Table 13-2
Examples of the Fund Raising Capacity of Some of the Most Successful Athletic Support Groups

Name of Organization (Institutional Affiliate)	Number of Members	Total Donations ('93)
IPTAY (Clemson)	20,000	$5.94 million
I-Club (Iowa)	13,000	$4.65 million
Bulldog Foundation (Fresno State)	4,000	$3.95 million
Buckeye Club (Ohio State)	1,600	$3.30 million

educational programs which enhance the academic reputation of their schools (Frey, 1982). As a consequence, in most cases a majority of those who belong to ASGs and contribute the lion's share of financial support to athletic departments are business owners and individual fans who were never students of the university. Of the 13,000 members who belong to the I-Club, the primary booster club at the University of Iowa, approximately 8,000 are not graduates of the institution (*I-Club*, 1990).

Alumni do play a significant role in ASGs because former students are obvious targets for any broad-based annual donor campaign. However, evidence suggests that efforts to attract alumni are likely to be most successful if they link support for athletics to academic achievement. The Buckeye Club at The Ohio State University, which has had a great deal of success in generating alumni support, emphasizes this approach in all of its booster club recruitment literature. The following excerpt from the Buckeye Club brochure provides a good example of how academic achievement is integrated into solicitation efforts.

> The most important benefit you receive as a result of membership is the personal satisfaction that comes from participation in the program. Imagine the pride involved in knowing your gift made an academic career possible for a gifted young athlete.

Businessmen "boosting" athletic programs have long been a tradition in college athletics (Boorstin, 1965). According to Frey (1985),

> It was good business to promote athletics, particularly a winning athletic program. Businessmen saw athletics as a stimulus to their profits, and because most athletic programs ran deficits, even in their early history, it was only natural that they 'boost' the activity with a financial subsidy" (p. 117).

These boosters, less concerned about the educational mission of the school, often view

> their five- and sometimes six-figure donations as 'investments' in their favorite programs. In their opinion, this money not only grants them certain perks--the best seats, special parking spaces, the ear of the AD and of the coaches--but also entitles them to a say on how the college sports franchise should be run. (Sperber, p.79).

Unfortunately, recent history is replete with many instances in which prominent boosters have used ASGs to further their own interests independent of any kind of athletic department authority or overall institutional control. Perhaps, the most notable example of the kind of power and autonomy exercised by a booster group was the 1982 hiring of Jackie Sherill as coach and athletic director at Texas A&M University by the Aggie Club. Led by H.R. "Bum" Bright, a prominent donor and club official, the Aggie Club signed Sherill, then head football coach at the University of Pittsburgh, to an unprecedented multiyear $1 million contract, "*without* the knowledge of the university president or incumbent football coach" (Sperber, p. 70).

The desire of some overzealous boosters to win at any cost at the expense of NCAA regulations has created serious problems for many universities and their athletic programs. Through 1989, nearly half the 2000 sanctions levied by the NCAA against member institutions involved violations committed by boosters. Recent events indicate that despite increased efforts by the NCAA to bring ASGs under greater institutional control, problems with boosters continue to plague athletic programs. In 1993, three major institutions were punished severely for unethical practices by boosters. Texas A&M, Washington and Syracuse Universities were penalized for not controlling supporters who were found to have made illegal gifts to athletes in the form of no-interest loans or wage payments for summer jobs that existed in name only.

Bringing Athletic Support Groups Under Institutional Control

It is evident from the preceding section that athletic administrators have had a great deal of difficulty in bringing booster clubs under internal control. Indeed, Sperber (1990) and others contend that in too many cases presidents and athletic directors have taken little or no action to control ASGs because their financial dependence on these groups is so great.

In the face of increased pressure for reform, in the early 1990s, the NCAA for the first time explicitly charged athletic directors with the responsibility for assuring that booster clubs and their members operated in compliance with NCAA rules and regulations. In a document titled *Principles of Institutional Control*, first issued in the spring of 1992, athletic programs were mandated to develop and maintain rules-education programs for all constituent groups including boosters. To assist athletic departments with the implementation of rules orientation programs the NCAA compliance staff established a Booster Education program. A "Resource File" containing basic information on compliance responsibilities is available on request from the NCAA.

The most explicit advice for managers attempting to control the activities of athletic fund raising organizations was provided by Bradley in his 1993 article in *Athletic Management*. Bradley, after careful analysis of booster club activities, recommended that athletic departments at both the collegiate and high school levels take the following steps to ensure greater control of ASGs.

1. The very first step in establishing control is for the athletic director to sit down with ASG's board or officers to establish a written constitution or charter and bylaws for the organization. The document should explicitly define the purpose and delimit the powers of the club, including two critical provisions:
   a. a statement which stipulates the club as a subordinate group ... "a support mechanism--nothing more" (p. 17)
   b. a requirement for "rolling board memberships" which limits board terms to no more than 3 years. "If some people are allowed to stay on the board for 10 to 15 years, they can get enough informal power so that they can run the board" (p. 17)
2. Imposition of financial control provisions which ensure that all monies raised by the ASG will be spent only with the approval of the athletic director. "Make sure all checks are processed and handled through the athletic department, not some renegade, off-campus organization" (p. 22)

3. Finally, and particularly in the case of collegiate athletic programs, it is essential that athletic directors establish a thorough rule-education program for *all* booster club members. The effort at educating boosters on their compliance responsibilities must be continuous. . . "You can't just put an article in the booster club letter once a year telling them to be good" (p. 19).

The relationship between the Fresno State University Athletic Department and its primary support group, the Bulldog Foundation, provides a good example of the adoption of many of Bradley's control safeguards. The Foundation is run by a Board of Trustees, with eight scheduled meetings a year. The ASGs charter requires that four members of the university athletic department sit on the Board. Internal financial control is assured by the requirement that a senior administrator in the athletic department cosign all foundation checks, thus complying with the institutional controls mandated by the NCAA.

Approaches to the Organization and Operation of ASGs

Athletic support groups are commonly organized as either *private foundations* or *athletic department-operated clubs*. Under the first arrangement, the support group incorporates as a nonprofit, tax exempt foundation independent of the university. Private foundations have been both a blessing and a curse to athletic programs. On the positive side, some of the most successful ASGs have operated as private, nonprofit fund raising organizations. For example, in 1993, Fresno State's Bulldog Foundation and Clemson's IPTAY Foundation raised $4 million and $6 million, respectively, in support of athletic programs at their affiliate universities. Unfortunately, on the negative side, too often the independent status of these external booster groups has allowed them to get out of control. Operating without any formal reporting responsibility to the university or athletic department to which they are nominally affiliated, many "work(ed) in a clandestine manner, violating rules. . .making end runs around the Athletic Director's attempts at exercising institutional control" (Bradley, 1993, p. 15). Although Bradley contends that many booster clubs "still remain out of control," the NCAA's recent efforts at demanding meaningful institutional oversight and accountability over ASG activities has substantially reduced the autonomy of private foundations and with it the potential, at least, for their committing serious rule violations.

The alternative form of booster club organization is for the athletic department to establish its own "in-house" ASG. Under this arrangement, the club "resides" within the department and is staffed by departmental personnel. This internal booster club model has worked well for many institutions, including Ohio State's Buckeye Club and Iowa's I-Club.

Regardless of organizational form, ASGs have tended to approach annual fund raising from two contrasting philosophical orientations. The first approach takes a more exclusive or narrow view towards club membership. Although any interested fan or booster may join, typically the minimum donation required for a membership starts at $500 a year. Membership incentives are tied to increased "perks" or benefits. As Figure 13-1 illustrates, the greater the donation, the greater the benefits. In the Buckeye Club example, individuals or corporations become "Full Members" only when they contribute at least $2,000. Not only do these members receive the full benefit package but their larger contribution substantially enhances the quality of the two season tickets they have the "opportunity to purchase."

The Buckeye Club is an example of the more concentrated approach to ASG membership. Typical of many department-sponsored clubs, their effort has been directed at attracting boosters who have the means to make large donations. For example, in their most recent campaign to recruit new members, athletic department staff who oversee the operation of the Buckeye Club directed a targeted mail campaign toward upper income households in central Ohio. Buckeye Club membership brochures were sent to 18,000 households in the region that had been prequalified as good booster club prospects on the basis of an annual household income of $60,000. In addition, Buckeye Club ads were placed in several "upscale" magazines throughout the state of Ohio. The 1993 campaign generated 150 new donor-members. This *concentrated* approach, in which "a relative few give a lot," has been a successful model for the Ohio State University Athletic Department. In 1993, over 50% of the Buckeye Club's 1,600 members contributed over $2,000. In fact, the per capita donation for each Buckeye Club member came to $2,187. The approximately $3.3 million raised through membership contributions funded all 365 scholarships granted by the Athletic Department and helped defray team travel costs and expenses related to the maintenance of sport facilities.

The second basic approach to annual fund raising is for the ASG to take a very broad view to club membership. Athletic support groups adopting this *grassroots* orientation focus on mass appeal. Rather than concentrating on a relatively small number of major donors, the emphasis is on generating broad-based involvement. Requirements for membership are very modest, often in the $25-$50 minimum range. The I-Club is a good example of an ASG that has relied on this high volume-minimum contribution approach. The minimum donation required for inclusion in the University of Iowa's 13,000-member ASG is $40. In 1993, I-Club members donated $4.65 million to the Athletic Department. Although the average contribution came to about $360, a substantial number (3,500) of the I-club members' donations were at the minimum level of between $40-$100. The Development Director for the University of Iowa Athletic Department recognized the trade-offs associated with maintaining a broad-based membership: "while we probably don't make much off of the minimum donor, we figure once we get them in the door, then we can work at upgrading them." A number of incentives are offered to induce larger donations. According to the Director, "While every gift entitles a seating privilege, the more you give, the higher the seating priority" (Jennings, 1994). Preferred seating and other incentives appear to provide impetus toward upgraded or increased giving. Almost 25% of the I-Club's members made contributions of $1,000 or more in 1993.

Figure 13-1
Buckeye Club
Benefits by Membership Level

Benefits of
Your Buckeye Club Membership

	Horseshoe Club Level $500-$999	Scarlet & Gray Club Level $1,000-$1,999	Buckeye Club Full Membership $2,000-Up
Membership Card	√	√	√
Automobile Decal	√	√	√
The Buckeye Club Reception	√	√	√
Media Guide (Football)	√	√	√
Team Schedules	√	√	√
Opportunity to Purchase *Two Season Football Tickets*	√	√	√
Membership in The Presidents Club			√
Ticket Priority-Away Games			√
Bowl Game Ticket Priorities			√
Preferred Parking-Football*			√
Tax Deduction**	√	√	√

*As available
**Contributions are tax deductible to the extent the contribution exceeds the value of any courtesies or benefits provided.

The Point System

Many athletic departments have established "point systems" as a way to more systematically assign football and basketball tickets to donors. Usually, these unpublished systems award points on the basis of the amount of annual giving, number of consecutive years of contributing, and number of consecutive years of purchasing season tickets. The more points accumulated by the donor, the more preferred the seating location. Generally, the greatest number of points is awarded for gifts of the greatest magnitude, with each of the other categories receiving equal weight.

The IPTAY Scholarship Foundation at Clemson University provides perhaps the best illustration of an ASG using the grassroots approach. IPTAY--originally I Pay Ten A Year, "inflation-adjusted" to Ten Times Ten--has achieved an enviable record as the Athletic Department's fund raising arm. The growth of IPTAY has been remarkable. Increases in membership as well as contributions have occurred in 28 of the last 29 years. The approximately $80 million raised by IPTAY since its inception in 1934 has furnished athletes at Clemson with a ($2.5 million) learning center, an indoor tennis center, an outdoor track, and even a 1,300-foot airstrip extension. In addition to completely underwriting the $3.5 million in current annual athletic scholarship costs, Clemson's ASG assists with a number of nonathletic programs. "IPTAY has endowed a $1.6 million academic scholarship fund and hands the University president $150,000 a year in discretionary money" (Weiberg, 1991, 5C).

Empirical evidence provides some insights into why the grassroots approach pays dividends. A number of social psychology studies have found that asking for a small donation leads to a greater likelihood of receiving a donation than initially requesting a large donation. In a series of imaginative experiments, Weyant and Smith (1987) found that asking for a generous contribution significantly decreased the percentage of people who donated and failed to increase the average size of contribution by those who gave. They concluded that overall, fundraising campaigns can raise more money by asking for less. The researchers account for the results on the basis of Cialdini and Schroeder's (1976) notion of "legitimizing small requests." This notion assumes that suggesting a small amount has a legitimizing effect. "Many people who might otherwise fail to donate will contribute provided that the modest sum they are willing to give seems appropriate. . .whereas suggesting a large donation tends to imply that modest sums are inappropriate" (Weyant & Smith, 1987, p. 399).

Team Concept of Fund Raising

A growing number of ASGs are utilizing a "team" approach to organizing their annual fund raising campaigns. Bradley (1993) attributes the origination of the idea to the Louisiana State University Athletic Department. Analogous to the athletic teams they support, under the team concept, boosters are placed on teams that compete against one another to see who can raise the most money. As Fresno State's Bulldog Foundation description (see Figure 13-2) indicates, in many cases an elaborate organizational structure is established, complete with league commissioners, team names, captains, league standings, and a sophisticated reward system.

The first year the Texas A&M-Kingsville athletic support group applied the concept, it increased its annual contribution to the athletic program tenfold, from $20,000 to $200,000. Ten, five-person teams "squared off" to compete for a number of incentive awards. According to the institution's Sport Information Director, "it gets pretty competitive. They have to switch the team members every few years to try to cool things down" (Bradley, 1993, p. 21).

MAJOR GIFTS PROGRAMS

No criterion exists for precisely defining what constitutes a major gift. It is generally described as a substantial, one-time contribution. A capital gift campaign organized by the University of Nevada, Las Vegas Athletic Department specifically stipulates "Major Gifts" as donations from $100,000 to $1 million (Clontz 1992). However, depending on circumstances, a major gift could be anywhere from $5,000 to $50 million or more (Williams 1991).

With major gifts, the emphasis is on targeting a limited number of prospects who have the potential of making significant contributions, rather than attracting many small gifts. In general, fund raisers have found that a very few donors account for the largest portion of funds raised. This consistent pattern has led to the adoption of a formal principle known as Rule of Thirds, which says you should expect one-third of your campaign goal from the top ten donors, the next third from the next 100 donors, and the remaining third from all others (Campbell, 1989, p. 26).

More recently, Kelly (1991), however, contended that the Rule of Thirds may be too broad, and that given the increased competition for philanthropic dollars, even fewer donors--from 1 to 10%--account for one-third to half of all dollars raised. It would appear the key to success in any effort to attract major gifts is establishing a well-organized system for identifying, cultivating, and soliciting the relatively few prospects who would be both capable and willing to make extraordinary contributions to the athletic department.

Major gifts may be either outright or planned donations. In the case of outright donations, the gift is made directly to the athletic department in the form of cash or gifts-in-kind (e.g., nonmonetary contributions). Planned gifts, such as bequests, trusts, or life insurance, are gifts whose benefits are deferred through legal instruments (wills or insurance policies) until the death of the donor. The National Society for Fund Raising Executives Institute (1986) defined a planned or deferred gift as "a commitment or gift established during the donor's lifetime, but whose principal benefits usually do not accrue to the charitable recipient until some future time, often after the donor's death." (p. 28)

Drawing from a classification scheme developed by Williams (1991), the specific forms of outright and planned gifts are described in the following section. Actual examples are included wherever possible to illustrate how athletic departments may utilize these major gift options.

Figure 13-2
Bulldog Foundation Team Concept

THE
BULLDOG
FOUNDATION
FRESNO STATE UNIVERSITY
P.O. Box 6057 · Fresno, CA 93703 · (209) 294-4140

FUND DRIVE

The Bulldog Foundation Fund Drive is held annually for six weeks from the middle of April to the end of May, although pledges are accepted any time during the fiscal year March 1 to February 28. During this concentrated time volunteers working under the "team concept" strive to renew the pledges of current members and solicit new pledge donors. In a spirit of competition the players solicit funds to be used for recruitment and scholarships by the Fresno State University Athletic Department.

THE TEAM CONCEPT

Based upon the National and American football leagues, 26 teams are established with 13 under each league and its commissioner. Team owners are assigned, usually from previous participation, who in turn select the volunteers who comprise their team "players." The teams are given the names of the pro football teams.

FUND DRIVE EVENTS

Events are held during the drive to further contact between teams and to promote enthusiasm toward continued success. At the end of the drive awards are given for outstanding achievement by team and individuals. The following sections hold explanations of Fund Drive events:

Team Owner Dinner
Orientation Sessions
Fund Drive Kickoff Dinner
Report Sessions
Awards Banquet

PREPARATION

Team Owners from the previous year are contacted and asked if they wish to again form a team for the Fund Drive. The Membership Vice-President serves as the Fund Drive Chairman and he selects the two league Commissioners with the assistance of the Executive Director. Team rosters (complete with name, address, business and home telephones) are

---

Figure 13-2 cont'd.

---

submitted to the BDF office and players are then entered into the computer by teams. Player numbers are assigned and a master roll is prepared. Letters of welcome are sent to each Team Owner and player outlining the upcoming events.

TEAM OWNER DINNER

The FSU coaches and Fund Drive team officials (Commissioners, Team Owners) meet for dinner to outline and kick off the upcoming drive. Invitations and arrangements for this dinner are made by the Athletic Director's office.

ORIENTATION SESSIONS

Two successive nights are designated for team player orientation. These sessions are held in a large meeting room at a centrally located hotel and they usually take place between 7:00 to 8:30 p.m. Team Owners and their players meet on the night of their choice for an outline of the Fund Drive, pertinent dates of events, report sessions, and annual update information relating to the BDF and the FSU athletic program. These Orientation Sessions have been deemed mandatory for the new "rookies" to the drive and optional for "veteran" players. Players are oriented in pledge levels, completing pledge cards, solicitation procedures and donor benefits. Orientation Sessions are helpful in assuring detailed explanation of the drive and related procedures to those players who have never before participated.

KICKOFF DINNER

The Kickoff Dinner usually held the third week of April is for the benefit of Team Officials, Team Owners, Players, FSU Coaches and FSU Administrators. Letters of invitation are mailed out well in advance with a request for R.S.V.P in order to have an accurate count for the caterer. There is no arranged seating at this informal function, but team members usually sit together. The BDF Executive Director serves as master of ceremonies.

The evening includes a complimentary dinner, review of Fund Drive procedures, emphasis of report session dates/time/place, introduction of the FSU head coaches, and a guest speaker if appropriate. Player information packets are distributed to Team Owners and consist of:

Fund Drive Team Goals	Membership Roster
Renewal Pledge Cards	New Donor Pledge Cards
Membership Brochures	Fund Drive Procedures
Map of Bulldog Stadium	Map of Selland Arena

REPORT SESSIONS

Report Sessions are organized for the purpose of turning in pledges and monies received by the team players during the Fund Drive. A banquet room is reserved at a hotel for five consecutive Thursdays beginning the last Thursday in April following the Kickoff Dinner.

<table>
<tr><td>Figure 13-2 cont'd.</td></tr>
</table>

Individual team player printouts are grouped by teams, and used to record incoming pledges: name, amount, etc. and money received each week. Ladies of the Women's Bulldog Foundation volunteer to record pledges on the tally sheet.

The fifth Report Session is used as a "clean-up" session to encourage all players to submit outstanding pledges, and also as a deadline for awards determination.

These weekly sessions allow the Executive Director to measure the actual incoming pledge amounts against the drive goal, and that information against the same period in previous years. He prepares a weekly newsletter providing progress updates.

AWARDS BANQUET

Following the Fund Drive a catered banquet is held to award those teams and players who assisted profitably in the drive. Those players who turned in a predetermined amount of pledges will be treated to a complimentary dinner at this banquet.

Awards are chosen according to pledge dollars raised. These awards are ordered by the players no later than the final Report Session. The BDF office staff places the orders with the specialty advertisers with an effort to have the awards available at the Awards Banquet. The awards are distributed by team.

OUTRIGHT GIFTS

Cash.
* According to Williams (1991), "a check is the best gift of all, because an organization can put it to use right away." (p. 16). For gifts of cash, a donor is entitled to an income tax deduction up to 50% of his/her adjusted gross income with a 5-year carry-over period for the excess.

Securities.
* The contribution is made in the form of a security transfer in which the donor turns over the appreciated value of a stock or bond certificate to the athletic department. Typically, the transfer takes place in one of three ways:

(1) The donor delivers stock certificates directly to the organization and endorses the necessary stock powers.

(2) The donor sends unendorsed stock certificates by registered mail and mails the executed stock powers under separate cover.

(3) The donor deposits the securities with a bank or broker, and the intermediary advises the organization of the gift. This is generally the most convenient way to handle the transaction.

The value of such gifts is determined by the market value of the security on the day in which it was donated. For gifts of long-term appreciated securities, the limit on tax deductions is 30% of the donor's adjusted gross income, and the donor will be able to avoid the capital gains tax that would have applied had he or she sold the securities.

Real Estate.
* The transfer of real property to the athletic department may be in the form of a simple outright gift or deferred in a number of ways (see below). A donor can transfer ownership of his or her personal residence to the athletic department or nonprofit sports organization and receive (a) recognition for a significant gift (b) a current income tax deduction for the property's discounted value and (c) continue to use the property as long as he or she lives.

It is advisable to order a "transactional environmental audit" before accepting gifts of *commercial* real estate. The audit would identify any hazardous waste problems created by the previous owners, thereby minimizing potential liability issues for the organization accepting the gift.

Gifts-in-Kind.
* Nonmonetary contributions are readily accepted by athletic departments. Often the aggregate benefits derived from such contributions over time elevate them to major gift status. For example, the University of Iowa Athletic Department benefits from an extensive courtesy car program that involves more than 60 car dealers who donate more than 70 cars to coaches and administrators. In addition, Townsend Engineering Company, owned by an Iowa alumnus, has presented the I-Club with the use of its company Learjet as a gift-in-kind. Coaches have been able to use the aircraft to make quick, long-distance recruiting trips across the country.
The value of a gift-in-kind contribution is treated as if the athletic department had purchased the good or service itself. An example would be an individual who donates weight-training equipment that has a retail value of $1,500 as a gift-in-kind. Although the equipment may not have cost the contributor $1,500, he/she is still credited with giving a $1,500 gift. Thus, all such gifts are recorded at their relative cash value.

Matching Gifts.
* A number of athletic departments actively encourage booster club members or prospective donors to take advantage of matching gift programs that may be offered by their current employers. Many companies offer incentives for employees to make contributions to charities and nonprofit organizations by offering to "match" employee donations on a 1 to 1, 2 to 1, or even 3 to 1 basis. Marathon Oil, for example, will *double* current employees' philan-

thropic contributions while matching on a dollar-for-dollar basis the monetary value of its retired employees' gifts. The I-Club publishes materials that encourage members "to contact their company's human resources or personnel office to find out if your employer will match your contribution to the Hawkeye Fund." Unfortunately, an increasing number of companies will no longer match employee contributions to intercollegiate athletic programs, particularly those in which employees receive direct benefits such as preferred seating privileges at football games. Many athletic departments and ASGs have attempted to overcome this objection by requesting that employee-donors stipulate to their employers that the matching gift be used exclusively in support of scholarships.

PLANNED GIFTS

Endowments

* The donor makes a sizable cash gift that is invested to generate income in perpetuity. In other words, only the interest income provided by the initial gift is used. The principal or original amount donated is left untouched in a perpetual interest-bearing account providing an enduring source of revenue for the athletic department.

* An innovative endowment-by-position program pioneered by the University of Southern California Athletic Department has proven to be extraordinarily successful (Davis, 1991). Since initiating the program in 1983, USC has endowed at least 30 positions on its football team, all 22 starting positions on offense and defense plus 3 kickers and a growing number of second-team positions. The minimum requirement for endowing each position is $250,000. The interest earned from the investment of each donation funds a full athletic scholarship for each position (tuition, books, room and board) -- about $23,000 per school year in 1993. In return for the endowment gift, each donor has his or her name "attached to the position. . .for life"(Davis, 1991, p. 5C). Don Winston, the associate athletic director who created the program, attributes its success to the way it "personalizes" the gift: "One donor told me that if I asked him to simply donate money for a scholarship, he wouldn't have done it. But attaching his donation to a specific position made a big difference to him" (cited in Davis, 1991, p. 5C). Despite the success of the USC program, Clemson University has opposed the position endowment concept on philosophical grounds. Their opposition is based on a concern that "buying" a position implies assumed ownership by the donor.

* A number of athletic departments at public institutions--where the cost of a full scholarship is considerably less (around $8,000 annually) than private universities--have established full endowments at minimum levels from

$100,000 to $150,000. The Ohio State University, which realized $300,000 from endowment earnings in 1993, established $100,000 as the basic requirement.

Although donors are encouraged to make the $100,000 contribution in one lump-sum payment, Ohio State, like many athletic departments, will allow contributors to fulfill their total endowment commitment over a 3- or 4-year period. Typically, the donor furnishes an initial payment of $15,000 to $25,000, and pledges to contribute the balance in equal annual installments over the next few years.

Real Estate

* A donor transfers the ownership of his or her personal residence to the sport organization. Recently, the Ohio State athletic department accepted the deed from a donor for a home appraised at $1 million. The net proceeds from the sale of the donated residence were to be applied toward the construction of a new baseball stadium.

* Other more creative uses of real estate cited by Kelly (1991, p. 16) include (a) *Gifts with retained life income* where the donor uses the value of his or her real estate to fund a unitrust (see Charitable Remainder Trusts) or (b) *live-at-home gifts*, where the donor transfers title to the sport organization but retains the right to reside on the property for life.

Life Insurance

* The donor designates the sport organization as the sole beneficiary of a whole-life insurance policy. Future premiums paid on the policy by the donor can be treated as a charitable gift and taken as a tax deduction.

* Many athletic support groups and athletic departments have become very cautious in accepting insurance gifts. All too often, individuals, after stipulating an athletic program as the beneficiary so that they could receive tickets and/or preferred seating benefits, either stopped making annual premium payments or stipulated another beneficiary. As a result, athletic support groups like the I Club have now established stringent guidelines for accepting life insurance policies. The University of Iowa athletic support group stipulates, for example, a minimum cash surrender value of $15,000. In addition, to receive I Club benefits, the donor must make an annual cash contribution in addition to making annual premium payments. Further, in the event the donor should fail to pay an annual premium, the I Club reserves the right to "cash out" the current surrender value of the policy.

Bequests and Trusts

* A donor either makes the sport organization or, in the case of an athletic department, its ASG, the beneficiary of his or her will or establishes a trust which pays a fixed percentage of the trust's assets each year (unitrust) or equal income payments annually (annuity trusts) to the sport organization. In the case of a charitable remainder trust, the donor places a sum of money or transfers securities or real estate into a trust account on behalf of the sport organization. Typically, while giving up control of the contributed funds, the donor retains a "life income" – a designated percentage or fixed payment from the trust annually – until deceased. Upon death, the remainder of the trust assets come to the sport organization. The Ohio State athletic department has coupled the charitable remainder trust mechanism with its efforts to endow positions on its sports teams. Donors are encouraged to commit a minimum of $250,000 to an irrevocable unitrust which pays them the interest earnings realized each year from the trust's assets. When the donor (or the beneficiaries) dies (die), the trust income reverts to the athletic department, specifically to endow a position in the name of the donor.

SYSTEMATIC APPROACH TO SOLICITING MAJOR GIFTS

The key to successfully acquiring major gifts is establishing a well-organized program for soliciting large donations. This section describes a systematic approach to obtaining significant contributions from individuals and corporations. The approach consists of five stages which have proven effective in generating support for sport and recreation organizations. They are: (a) prospecting and targeting, (b) preparation, (c) presentation, (d) closing, and (e) follow-up.

Prospecting and Targeting

These initial stages address the first part of a well-known sales aphorism, "Plan your work–and then work your plan." Often, too little thought is given to planning a major gifts program. Typically, sport organizations and athletic support groups, because of a lack of know-how or limited staff resources, tend to be reactive rather than proactive in their solicitation efforts. Some sport organizations have had the good fortune of occasionally receiving unsolicited gifts from generous supporters or alumni. However, those organizations that have had the most success carefully target prospective donors and then design a solicitation approach specifically tailored to each prospect's needs.

Two tasks are involved in the target identification stage. The first is to compile a comprehensive list of all those individuals and businesses that appear to be potential prospects, and the second is to priortize these prospective donors based on how likely they are to be responsive to requests for contributions.

When prospecting for major gift donors, the "Rule of Thirds" suggests the list will be short. That, in fact, the most generous donors will come from a relative handful of supporters. As discussed earlier in the chapter, the majority of people who contribute money to intercollegiate athletic programs are not alumni. Historically, those inclined to give the most generously are boosters who belong to the university's athletic support group. Denny Hoobler, Director of Development for The Ohio State University Athletic Department, finds that "most of my major donors come directly from either the Buckeye Club (the athletic department booster club) members who have been long-time supporters of Ohio State athletics, or through referrals they make to us. Often, they'll actually have folks call us who are looking for a way to get involved." The University of Nevada, Las Vegas, athletic department keeps an inventory of annual donors and targets them as prime prospects for major gifts. According to Laura Clontz (1992), Director of Development at UNLV, "Many universities have strong annual giving campaigns but never capitalize upon the success of that program by targeting top prospects for further attention, the kind that can lead to truly significant gifts" (p. 15).

Although existing supporters should be identified as first-line potential targets, selected alumni such as former letter-winning athletes and those who own successful businesses, should also be given careful consideration. At this point, coordination with the institution's alumni development office is essential. Competition between the athletic department and the university's general fund-raising department should be avoided at all costs. At the University of Iowa, to ensure that the athletic department's fund-raising efforts dovetail with the university's overall alumni development program, the development director for men's athletics is housed in the University of Iowa Foundation Alumni Center. Careful coordination and prescreening can reduce the list of eligible alumni to those referred by the university development office as the very best prospects for making sizable gifts to the athletic program.

Once the prospect list has been developed, the individual prospects should be assigned to one of three categories: "hot," "medium," and "cold". This rating should be based on two basic criteria: (a) their *ability* to give and (b) their *inclination* to support sport programs. The obvious intent is to identify those who are worth the most effort. An effective way to initiate a rating program of individual prospects is to seek "silent" peer-level ratings from a group of individuals who may be familiar with the prospects. The confidential process asks each individual rater to evaluate prospects as to their gift range by dollar amount and previous position to support athletics. Often, the athletic support group's Board of Directors or selected members can play a central role in this process.

Preparation

After a list of the most probable prospects has been derived, the next stage is to prepare an approach tailored to each of these prospects. The preparations commitment is time consuming but essential. Success at soliciting support is more likely to result from good presentation techniques. Three questions should be addressed in the preparation stage:

1. *What benefits does the donor hope to realize from providing the gift?* Here the intent is to try to discover as precisely as possible prospective donors' motivations for giving. Input from knowledgeable volunteers may prove valuable to answering this question. It is important to recognize that individuals are not inclined to give just because the sports program *needs* money. Major donors contribute because they are motivated to do something special, to make an impact. The opportunity to give something back to the athletic department by endowing the quarterback position in their name in perpetuity may be "that" special opportunity for certain individuals. In the case of potential business donors, the key question may be restated as "what's in it for them?" Altruism may be replaced with a more pragmatic realization that most businesses make contributions because they believe it is in their self-interest to do so. Similar to the benefits sought by corporations entering into sponsorship agreements, businesses may seek enhanced visibility, an improved community image, and/or reduced tax obligations by making a major contribution.

2. *Who should do the asking?* Research has shown that one key motivator is the person who asks (Williams 1991). People of influence who are connected with the sports program or athletic support group "can often be the best askers because prospects are impressed with being asked by them" (Williams, 1991, p. 14). The highly successful major gift campaign conducted by the University of Nevada, Las Vegas Athletic Department relied heavily on a gift committee comprising the "largest current contributors, corporate heads, wealthy people, influentials in the community. . . who had a genuine appreciation of the athletic department and who could articulate the department's needs to potential donors" (Clontz, 1992, p. 15). Each of the gift committee members was matched with an identified pool of "target" prospects to which they made the direct solicitation appeal on behalf of the UNLV athletic department.

3. *How should they ask?* The answer to this question depends largely on the nature of the relationship between the prospective donor and the asker. According to Williams (1991), "depending on how close the solicitor is to the prospect and how much is known about him, the first meeting may not be the right time to ask" (p. 38). If the prospect does not know much about the the sport organization for which the appeal is being made or appears unready to commit, the initial meeting may be best used for cultivation and fact-finding. It is hoped that, at the very least, by the end of the first visit, the asker will have answers to the following questions:

*How does the prospect feel about the sport organization and its needs?

*What size gift is likely?

*What giving method is most likely?
*What should happen next?

Presentation

Although the degree of formality used in the presentation at the initial meeting will depend again on a number of factors, such as how well the solicitor knows the prospect and the magnitude and complexity of the type of gift being sought, best results are often achieved by a carefully organized presentation. Although there are many ways of making a presentation, one effective approach is to organize the solicitation appeal around three elements: features, advantages, and benefits (FAB). The FAB approach begins by identifying the specific *features* of the major gift program (e. g., endowment-by-position, charitable remainder trust) that are relevant to what is known about the prospect's desires for making a major gift. The *advantages* portion of the presentation addresses ways in which the unique gift opportunity is superior to other charitable investment opportunities available to the potential contributor. The *benefits* portion transforms features and advantages into benefits and directly addresses the key question "What's in it for you. . .or your business?" (e. g., personal recognition, opportunity to give something back to your alma mater, increased visibility for the company).

Williams (1991) suggests keeping several factors in mind during the solicitation effort:

* The prospect is under no obligation to give.
* The prospect is probably a busy person, so don't drag out the conversation.
* Concede points if the prospect is argumentative. Never press your views over those of the prospect.
* Be prepared to help the donor decide on the size of the gift. Do so by noting the size of your gift and those of others, the average gift to date, and the period of time over which the pledge can be paid.
* Don't stress your organization's needs, but try to uncover the ways a gift can fill the prospect's personal needs. Determine which of the prospect's needs match the needs of your organization.

Closing

Many people find that closing is the most difficult part of the solicitation effort. They aren't sure how to ask or how much to ask for. Often, the best approach is to simply ask, "Would you consider a gift in the X dollar range?" On occasion, a prospect may not be prepared to invest in a project at the level the sport organization seeks when the question is asked at closing. However, there may be a willingness to invest either in a different project at that level, or in the same project at a lower level. Therefore, it is desirable for any organization to have more than one project and more than one investment level in mind. Then if the main investment opportunity is rejected, the solicitor can present other options.

If the donor is willing to make a commitment, Figure 13-3 provides an example of a written pledge form that in effect, confirms the contributor's intent to make a gift in a specific amount. Ideally, the solicitor can obtain the donor's signature on the form at the close of the meeting.

Follow-up

Regardless of the outcome of the initial meeting, the prospect should always be thanked in writing for the time he or she allowed the organization. If a commitment was made at the desired level, make sure that all appropriate parties (board chairperson, athletic director, etc.) acknowledge the contribution, and with the donor's consent, proper recognition should be extended (news release, press conference, etc.).

If a commitment was not secured at the first meeting, because the prospect either needed more information or raised certain objections, then a written response specifically tailored to the prospect's concerns should be sent. At this point, it is important to realize that early efforts may yield relatively little. A period of time may be needed for further education about the gift program and its potential benefits, and to build personal relationships before the resource support is given. The way the follow-up is handled determines the likelihood of eventually receiving some level of commitment. If the prospect needed more information, the solicitor should make sure it is sent in an appropriate format. If the prospect raised questions or concerns the solicitor could not deal with during the first meeting, then the sport organization should be sure that explanations are furnished promptly and/or by the appropriate people. A second meeting should be scheduled to further discuss the proposal.

According to Williams (1991), "Don't give up if the answer was 'no'" (p. 41). Polite persistence pays off. Thus, immediately after an unsuccessful effort, a thank-you letter should be sent to let prospects know that the time they spent visiting with the organizational representative was appreciated. The organization should keep in touch with these people and proceed on the assumption that they may be prime prospects for support at a future time.

ANATOMY OF A MAJOR GIFT PROGRAM: UNLV'S VISION PROJECT

The UNLV Vision Project, a 5-year, $25-million campaign, was instituted in 1989 to secure major gifts from individuals, businesses, organizations, and foundations within the Las Vegas community and beyond. By 1993, over $26 million had been raised, establishing the Vision Project as one of the most successful major gift programs ever conducted by an intercollegiate athletic program. The following describes how the campaign was organized and conducted (Clontz, 1992).

Figure 13-3
UNLV VISION PROJECT

John F. O'Reilly
Chairman, *UNLV VISION PROJECT*
Department of Intercollegiate Athletics
University of Nevada, Las Vegas
Thomas & Mack Center
4505 Maryland Parkway
Las Vegas, NV 89154

   Re: My/Our intent to make a gift to the *UNLV VISION PROJECT.*

Dear John:

   It is my/our intention to contribute to the *UNLV VISION PROJECT-* in cash, securities and/or marketable real or personal property- a total of $_____payable over the next _____ years. I/we plan to divide this gift into payments as follows:

AMOUNT TO BE PAID		DATE/s BY WHICH PAYMENT/s WILL BE MADE TO UNLV
_____	---	_____
_____	---	_____
_____	---	_____
_____	---	_____

☐   Please have the campaign office send me/us a statement thirty (30) days in advance of each due date.

☐   My/Our initial payment of $_____is enclosed.
  Please make check payable to: UNLV FOUNDATION - VISION PROJECT

The following is the manner in which my/our name is authorized to appear on any official/public *UNLV VISION PROJECT* recognitions:

   (Please type or print) _____
OR, list my/our gift: ___ In Memory Of; ___ In Honor Of the person identified above.

  ☐ Please do not list my name as I/we wish to remain anonymous.

I/We will make every effort to honor the scope and timing of this commitment, but reserve the right to modify the above mentioned in the event of unforeseen circumstances. (Optional: ☐ -In order to insure payment of my commitment to the UNLV VISION PROJECT, I will stipulate the terms and conditions of this gift in a codicil to my Will.)

        Sincerely,

Date:_____Signature:_____
Your Name (please type or print):_____
Mailing Address:_____
City/State:_____ Zip: _____ Daytime Phone: ____/_____

Note: Reprinted with permission of Netzel Associates, Inc.

Campaign Organization

To help design the campaign, the UNLV Athletic Department retained the services of Netzel Associates, Inc., a professional fund-raising consulting firm. In addition, the department secured counsel from charitable-giving specialists to clarify the tax consequences and benefits related to major gift options. A 32-member Executive Council, chaired by the CEO of a major corporation and staffed by three athletic department personnel, including the athletic director, the director of development, and the coordinator of the Vision Project, was established to oversee all matters pertaining to the planning and implementation of the Vision Project. Specific responsibilies of the Executive Council were as follows:

* Review and approve the general plan (including project elements, calendar, etc.)
* Finalize the UNLV Vision Project organizational structure and campaign goal of $25,000,000.
* Identify and list key leadership positions for the UNLV Vision Project Campaign (Campaign chairpersons).
* Assist with the identification of top-level prospects deemed essential to the success of the campaign.
* Meet monthly during the organizational phase of the campaign.

Campaign Purpose and Appeal

The three major objectives of the campaign were to: (a) endow all of the approximately 220 athletic scholarships granted by the athletic department, (b) build new sport facilities including a $1.5 million baseball stadium and a $2.0-million track complex, and (c) secure funds to immediately enhance current sports programs. While these concrete objectives served as the focal point for the solicitation effort, the general appeal to donors emphasized two fundamental themes: (a) enhancing the academic reputation of the university and (b) improving the quality of the educational experience for student athletes. Featured in all "collateral"(e. g., brochures, videos) produced for the campaign was the theme that "intercollegiate athletics is a vital contributor to the growth and development of UNLV. . .the athletic program generates enthusiasm, pride, and support for the mission of UNLV in a manner and scope that is difficult to achieve by any other means." In addition, prospects were encouraged to give because their gifts would "create the resources that would produce exceptional achievement. It will enhance the ability of the department to attract and graduate the nation's highest calibre student-athletes, improve the quality of the educational experience afforded student-athletes, and provide the opportunity for UNLV to serve as a national leader and exemplary model for intercollegiate athletics."

Campaign Structure

Three major gift categories were established by the Executive Council:
Founder's Gifts . . .$1 million plus
Major Gifts. . .$100,000 to $1 million
Special Gifts. . .$10,000 to $100,000

Once the gift categories were determined, volunteers were recruited to serve along with selected members of the Executive Council on committees that focused on each of the specific gift categories. A *Founder's Gift Committee*, comprising 6 to 8 highly regarded members of the Executive Council, was created to seek and secure, on a face-to-face basis, commitments of $1 million or more from a highly select group of prospective donors. Members of this committee were individuals who themselves had the capacity and inclination to make their own significant contribution to UNLV athletics. A *Major Gifts Committee* composed of 15 members of the Executive Council was established to cultivate and attract gifts in the range of $100,000 to $1 million. Finally, to solicit the potentially more numerous prospects targeted for outright gifts of under $100,000, a 19 member Special Gifts Committee was organized. The targeted number of gifts in each category and their overall contribution to the Vision Project's $25 million goal are shown in Table 13-3.

Conducting the Campaign

The identification and assignment of targeted prospects for each level of giving was coordinated by the Executive Council. Many of the prospects were initially suggested by committee members and/or identified through their history of annual giving. Once prospects were targeted for a certain gift category, cultivation activities ranged from sending birthday cards, newsletters, and invitations to arranging special events, campus/facility tours, and private dinners. Each prospect was assigned to a team of two or three committee members. Within each team, a "leader" was designated, who along with an athletic department staff member, was given primary responsibility for maintaining contact with the potential donor.

Throughout the campaign, it was imperative that staff keep committee members fully informed of the progress of the fundraising effort. Staff were directed to "pamper your committee members; allow them to enjoy the benefits of being on the 'inside' of athletic department events. Ensure that your committee members have personal contact with athletic department leaders. A very real incentive for the committee members' involvement may well be the special atmosphere of importance you create for them. (Clontz 1992, p. 15)

CAUSE-RELATED MARKETING

With the onset of the economic recession of the late 1980s and early 1990s, officers at may companies were under pressure from shareholders to reduce their company's

Table 13-3
Targeted Gift Categories for UNLV's VISION PROJECT

Number of Gifts	In the Range of	Will Produce	Cumulative Production	% of Goal
2 @	$2,500,000 and Above =	$5,000,000	$5,000,000	20%
6 @	1,000,000 - 2,499,999 =	6,000,000	11,000,000	44%
8 @	500,000 - 999,999 =	4,000,000	15,000,000	60%
18 @	250,000 - 499,999 =	4,500,000	19,500,000	78%
36 @	100,000 - 249,999 =	3,800,000	23,300,000	93%
100	Under $100,000 =	1,700,000	25,000,000	100%

level of donations. Shareholders were increasingly critical of company altruism and wanted evidence that donations resulted in increased market share and profits. In this environment, cause-related marketing flourished since it directly links a corporation's donations to the explicit objective of directly increasing sales of its product. Every time somebody uses its products, the company makes a cash contribution to a designated sports organization. The organization receives not only the cash contribution but also extensive publicity. The company's promotional effort typically includes an extensive advertising campaign that stresses the programs and virtues of the designated recipient of the donations.

American Express coined and copyrighted the phrase "cause-related marketing" and has been its most visible advocate. Others have used the terms "philanthropic marketing" and "affinity-group marketing" to describe the same phenomenon. Its success is based on an appeal to the pride, attachment, and loyalty that individuals feel towards the recipient organization. In the words of the American Express CEO, "cause-related marketing is our way of doing well by doing good." By tapping people's loyalty to their university or favorite nonprofit sports organization, corporations have an opportunity to encourage brand-switching and increase their market share. It gives people a reason to do business with one company rather than its competitors. The power of tying in with a cause was illustrated by Thrifty Car Rental.

In 1991 Thrifty Car Rental Company tested different sales incentives on older adults. When they offered a 10% discount only 11 percent of the older adults said it would be a major motivation for renting a Thrifty car. But when they offered to use a portion of the car charges to buy vans for senior citizens' centers, 40% said it would make them choose Thrifty ("Cause-Related," 1992, p. 2).

By offering to donate to a cause meaningful to the consumer if he or she makes a purchase, the perceived value of the product or service is increased at no additional cost to the consumer (Ross, Peterson & Stutts, 1992).

The approach first received national prominence when American Express linked with the organization responsible for restoration of the Statue of Liberty and Ellis Island in 1983. The company's chief executive officer has stated:

> At first, we didn't know whether we'd found a new way to help
> business or just an interesting formula for giving money away.
> It's both. The increase in business we've seen in our cause-related
> markets proves the concept is as successful as any marketing
> program we've ever tried. We're doing good deeds, and we're
> also pleased with the commercial results. (cited in Higgins, 1986)

When the campaign was initially conceived, the company projected an 18% increase in credit-card transactions during that period. In fact, card use jumped 78%, and applications increased by 45%. A telephone survey of cardholders commissioned by the company revealed that those questioned had a high awareness of the widely advertised promotion. A substantial number also said that they had indeed used their card more often to help this good cause.

Each cause-related marketing program initiated by American Express begins with the announcement that the company will donate a small sum to the "cause" every time one of its clients in the area:

—uses the American Express card (typically between 1 cent and 50 cents for each purchase).

—purchases a travel package of $500 dollars or more (excluding air fare) at an American Express vacation store (typically $5 for each package).

—applies for and receives a new American Express card (typically between $1-$2 for each approved application).

Thus the size of the donation to the selected cause depends on business done by the company in a specific geographic area during a set time period, usually 3 months.

Some advocates of cause-related marketing talk about the greater "bonding" with their brand that results when wholesalers, employees, and customers identify with the cause that is championed. Others have stated that retail chains are far more willing to adopt product promotions that are tied to a cause.

The surge of interest in cause-related marketing in the late 1980s reflects the continuous search by companies to find a means of differentiating and distinguishing their product or service from those of competitors. It has been argued that a good cause helps shape a service's personality: "It can make one box of suds seem much more appealing than the next." Further, this approach is far less expensive for major corporations than is a prime-time advertising campaign. However, the cause must fit a company's overall strategy, goals, product line, corporate mission, and its image with various target markets.

Denny's Inc. linked with the Michigan High School Athletic Association in a cause-related marketing program. The director of marketing for the restaurant chain stated, "We're trying to dispel the impression that Denny's is just another national chain; becoming involved in the community is part of the strategy" ("Denny's," 1990, p. 7):

* Denny's tied its athletic commitment to sales. Each time a restaurant customer presented a Training Table Membership Card, the company made a

donation to MHSAA. All 49 Denny's restaurants in Michigan carried the cards and the company mailed special versions to 24,000 coaches. The program was promoted by radio and television advertisements and in-store materials. Level of involvement was tracked by card usage. High redemption from a smaller pilot program in the preceding year was the key reason for Denny's expanded state-wide program.

Cause-related marketing opens a potentially new channel for monetary support for many sports organizations. Given the emotional attachment many feel toward a community's high school athletic team, varsity team sports, and the performance of national teams at the Olympic Games, it seems likely the cause-related partnerships will be increasingly used in the future.

SUMMARY

The intent of this chapter is to portray fund raising as a systematic, purposive set of activities for soliciting monies in support of sport organizations. Only within the last decade have a substantial number of collegiate athletic departments and selected amateur sport organizations like the Amateur Athletic Union made a significant and sustained commitment to fund raising. For a growing number of these organizations, monetary donations represent a significant portion of their annual revenues.

The first part of the chapter distinguished between two primary types of gifts: annual and major. Annual gifts are generally smaller denomination donations ($50 to $1,000) solicited on an ongoing or once-a-year basis. Athletic support groups or booster clubs are the primary organizational mechanisms through which annual gifts are solicited. Bringing these athletic department support groups under greater institutional control is a major concern of the NCAA. The two major approaches to organizing ASGs (either "in-house" or as independent foundations) and the two contrasting philosophies (grassroots versus concentrated) for soliciting annual gifts were discussed at length.

Major gifts are substantial (depending on the circumstances, the donation could be from $5,000 to $1 million) one-time contributions. Rather than attempting to attract numerous small gifts, the emphasis is on acquiring a limited number of significant contributions. Major gifts may be either outright or planned donations. Outright gifts that are made directly to the sports organization include cash, securities, real estate, gifts-in-kind and matching contributions. Planned gifts, such as bequests, trusts or life insurance, are gifts whose benefits are deferred through legal instruments until the death of the donor. A systematic plan for obtaining major gifts, modeled after the University of Las Vegas, Nevada Athletic Department's Vision Program, was described in detail. The approach consists of five interrelated stages including (a) prospecting and targeting, (b) preparation, (c) presentation, (d) closing and (e) follow-up.

The final section of the chapter described cause-related marketing, a strategy for linking a corporation's donation to a sport organization to increased sales of its product. Denny's relationship with the Michigan High School Athletic Association in which donations to MHSAA were tied to customer purchases of the restaurant chain's membership card is an excellent example of the concept. This form of "philanthropic marketing" has great potential for expanding the fund-raising prospects for sport organizations.

Questions for Study and Discussion

1. Explain the fundamental distinction between fund raising and sponsorship. What are the respective pros and cons of each of these activities?
2. Nearly half the serious sanctions levied by the NCAA against member institutions have been the result of violations by members of athletic support groups (ASGs). Describe three ways in which athetic directors can bring ASGs under more effective institutional control.
3. What are the two basic approaches for organizing ASGs? Generally speaking, which of these organizational alternatives do you prefer, and why?
4. Differentiate among the following major gift options: (a) endowment, (b) unitrust, (c) annuity trust, and (d) life insurance. Provide examples of each to illustrate how a sports organization may utilize these deferred gift options.

REFERENCES

Boorstin, D. (1965). *The Americans: The national experience.* New York: Random House.

Bradley, M. (1993, October/November). Controlling the fanfare. *Athletic Management,* pp. 15-21.

Campbell, D. A. (1989, June). Second to none: If you've asked the right giver for the right amount, your lead gift will lead the way. *CASE Currents,* pp. 22-26.

Carbone, R. (1987). *Fund raisers of academe* (Monograph No. 2). College Park, MD: University of Maryland, Clearinghouse for Research on Fund Raising.

Cause-Related reasoning, (1993, January). *American Demographics,* p. 2.

Clontz, L. (1992, June). How to maximize your fund-raising campaign. *Athletic Administration,* pp. 14-17.

Davis, M. (1991, October 15). Southern California innovation: Endowments by position. *USA Today,* p. 5C.

Denny's other sponsors true to their schools. (1990, February 12. *Special Events Report,* p. 7.

Frey, J. (1985). Boosterism, scarce resources, and institutional control: The future of American intercollegiate athletics. In D. Chu, J. Segrave and B. Becker (Eds.), *Sports and higher education* (pp.115-129). Champaign, IL: Human Kinetics Publishers, Inc.

Higgins, K. T. (1986, May 9). Cause-related marketing: Does it pass the bottom-line test? *Marketing News*, pp. 1,18.

I-Club : The University of Iowa--history, structure and purpose (1990). Iowa City, IA: The University of Iowa Foundation.

Johnson, D. (1973). The charity market: Theory, and practice. In A. Achian (Ed.) *The economics of charity: Essays on the comparative economics and ethics of giving and selling, with applications to blood* (pp. 63-68). London: The Institute of Economic Affairs.

Kelly, K. S. (1991). *Fund raising and public relations: A critical analysis.* Hillsdale, NJ: Lawrence Erlbaum Associates, Inc.

Marciani, L. (1991, May). Mining for division II gold. *Athletic Business*, pp. 49-52.

National Society for Fund Raising Executives (NSFRE) Institute (1986). Glossary of fund-raising terms. Alexandria, VA.

Payton, R. L. (1987). American values and private philanthropy: Philanthropic values; A philanthropic dialogue. In K. W. Thompson (Ed.), *Philanthropy: Private means, public ends* (pp. 3-46). Lanham, MD: University Press of America.

Raiborn, M. H. (1990). *Revenues and expenses of intercollegiate athletic programs: Analysis of financial trends and relationships 1985-1989.* Overland Park, KS: National Collegiate Athletic Association.

Ross, J. K., Peterson, L. T. & Mary Ann Stutts (1992). Consumer perceptions of organizations that use cause-related marketing. *Journal of the Academy of MarketingScience, 20*(1), 93-97.

Sperber, M. (1990). *College sports inc.: The athletic department vs the university.* New York: Henry Holt and Company.

Weiberg, S. (1991, October 15). Fund-raising arm keeps Clemson in the black. *USA Today*, p. 5C.

Weyant, J. & Smith, S. (1987). Getting more by asking for less: The effects of request size on donations of charity. *Journal of Applied Social Psychology, 17*(4), 392-400.

Williams, J. (1991). *Big gifts.* Rockville, MD: Fund Raising Institute.

Index